Cognitive Aspects of Human-Computer Interaction for GIS

Cognitive Aspects of Human-Computer Interaction for GIS

Special Issue Editor
Dieter Fritsch

MDPI • Basel • Beijing • Wuhan • Barcelona • Belgrade

Special Issue Editor
Dieter Fritsch
University of Stuttgart
Germany

Editorial Office
MDPI
St. Alban-Anlage 66
4052 Basel, Switzerland

This is a reprint of articles from the Special Issue published online in the open access journal *ISPRS International Journal of Geo-Information* (ISSN 2220-9964) from 2018 to 2019 (available at: https://www.mdpi.com/journal/ijgi/special_issues/Human-Computer_Interaction_GIS)

For citation purposes, cite each article independently as indicated on the article page online and as indicated below:

LastName, A.A.; LastName, B.B.; LastName, C.C. Article Title. *Journal Name* **Year**, *Article Number*, Page Range.

ISBN 978-3-03921-568-3 (Pbk)
ISBN 978-3-03921-569-0 (PDF)

© 2019 by the authors. Articles in this book are Open Access and distributed under the Creative Commons Attribution (CC BY) license, which allows users to download, copy and build upon published articles, as long as the author and publisher are properly credited, which ensures maximum dissemination and a wider impact of our publications.

The book as a whole is distributed by MDPI under the terms and conditions of the Creative Commons license CC BY-NC-ND.

Contents

About the Special Issue Editor vii

Preface to "Cognitive Aspects of Human-Computer Interaction for GIS" ix

Dieter Fritsch
Guest Editor's Editorial "Cognitive Aspects of Human-Computer Interaction for GIS"
Reprinted from: *ISPRS Int. J. Geo-Inf.* **2019**, *8*, 337, doi:10.3390/ijgi8080337 1

Chengshun Wang, Yufen Chen, Shulei Zheng and Hua Liao
Gender and Age Differences in Using Indoor Maps for Wayfinding in Real Environments
Reprinted from: *ISPRS Int. J. Geo-Inf.* **2019**, *8*, 11, doi:10.3390/ijgi8010011 10

Čeněk Šašinka, Zdeněk Stachoň, Michal Sedlák, Jiří Chmelík, Lukáš Herman, Petr Kubíček, Alžběta Šašinková, Milan Doležal, Hynek Tejkl, Tomáš Urbánek, Hana Svatoňová, Pavel Ugwitz and Vojtěch Juřík
Collaborative Immersive Virtual Environments for Education in Geography
Reprinted from: *ISPRS Int. J. Geo-Inf.* **2019**, *8*, 3, doi:10.3390/ijgi8010003 30

Lukáš Herman, Vojtěch Juřík, Zdeněk Stachoň, Daniel Vrbík, Jan Russnák and Tomáš Řezník
Evaluation of User Performance in Interactive and Static 3D Maps
Reprinted from: *ISPRS Int. J. Geo-Inf.* **2018**, *7*, 415, doi:10.3390/ijgi7110415 55

Andrew Plowright, Riccardo Tortini and Nicholas C. Coops
Determining Optimal Video Length for the Estimation of Building Height through Radial Displacement Measurement from Space
Reprinted from: *ISPRS Int. J. Geo-Inf.* **2018**, *7*, 380, doi:10.3390/ijgi7090380 80

Yebin Zou, Yijin Chen, Jing He, Gehu Pang and Kaixuan Zhang
4D Time Density of Trajectories: Discovering Spatiotemporal Patterns in Movement Data
Reprinted from: *ISPRS Int. J. Geo-Inf.* **2018**, *7*, 212, doi:10.3390/ijgi7060212 87

Ahmed Elashry, Abdulaziz Shehab, Alaa M. Riad and Ahmed Aboul-Fotouh
2DPR-Tree: Two-Dimensional Priority R-Tree Algorithm for Spatial Partitioning in SpatialHadoop
Reprinted from: *ISPRS Int. J. Geo-Inf.* **2018**, *7*, 179, doi:10.3390/ijgi7050179 106

Marjan Čeh, Milan Kilibarda, Anka Lisec and Branislav Bajat
Estimating the Performance of Random Forest versus Multiple Regression for Predicting Prices of the Apartments
Reprinted from: *ISPRS Int. J. Geo-Inf.* **2018**, *7*, 168, doi:10.3390/ijgi7050168 125

Mingguang Wu, Taisheng Chen, Kun Zhang, Zhimin Jing, Yangli Han, Menglin Chen, Hong Wang and Guonian Lv
An Efficient Visualization Method for Polygonal Data with Dynamic Simplification
Reprinted from: *ISPRS Int. J. Geo-Inf.* **2018**, *7*, 138, doi:10.3390/ijgi7040138 141

Kai Sun, Yunqiang Zhu and Jia Song
Progress and Challenges on Entity Alignment of Geographic Knowledge Bases
Reprinted from: *ISPRS Int. J. Geo-Inf.* **2019**, *8*, 77, doi:10.3390/ijgi8020077 159

About the Special Issue Editor

Dieter Fritsch, Research Professor and Professor Emeritus of the University of Stuttgart, Germany has served the Geospatial Community for more than 55 years. In addition to having served as Full Professor at the University of Stuttgart (1992–2016) and Director of the Institute for Photogrammetry, he has published in total more than 420 articles and papers, including 30 textbooks, dealing with laser scanning, photogrammetry, remote sensing, GIS, statistical inference, computer vision, and computer graphics. He also served as Vice President of Higher Education (1998–2000) and President (2000–2006) of the University of Stuttgart. He continues to be an active Research Professor and has supervised 40 PhD students in Stuttgart and co-supervised more than 50 PhD students nationally and internationally. He is a networker in Academia and the Geospatial Industry, has co-founded the German University in Cairo (GUC), and supports underrepresented countries with lectures and advice.

Preface to "Cognitive Aspects of Human-Computer Interaction for GIS"

Since the evolution of digital computing in the 1940s, human–computer interaction (HCI) has been an issue. From the very beginning, HCI has been treated as a task–artifact cycle, and as technology advances, the interface between the user and the data and information to be processed has become most critical for creating effective, efficient, and pleasant systems. The task–artifact cycle is described in more detail by the following: (1) Humans have needs and preferences, (2) technologies are created to suit these needs, and (3) as humans use these technologies, the needs and preferences change continuously. Comparing the use of geographic information science (GIS) hardware and software in the last three decades (1990 to 2020) shows us that it is now completely different: First, closed and monolithic systems were used running on mainframes, workstations, and desktop computers. Today, open architectures and cloud-based systems interconnecting desktop and mobile computing devices are used. Geospatial data and information are used daily by everyone. Mobile devices completely changed the social behavior of humans, and so did geographical data. The following question can be asked: How did people meet in town in 1990 and in 2019? The answer is simple: Today, mobile devices track visits, movements, and coordinate meetings with friends. Further, navigation on the mobile device has become very simple, and people rarely get lost.

The widespread use of emerging technologies for 3D modeling and 3D visualization, such as Augmented Reality, Virtual Reality, and 3D/4D app developments, offers GIS new interfaces for human–computer interactions. This also goes along with progress in big data analyses using machine learning and deep learning methods, but this is still in its infancy with regard to GIS data analysis. Most of the high-quality urban scenes, such as 3D vectorized buildings and city models, are output by interactive workflows, which should be replaced, step-by-step, by more automation in the near future. Therefore, this Special Issue will deliver the state-of-the-art in 3D modeling using interactive and semiautomated and fully-automated workflows, in particular when 3D urban scenes have to be interpreted and vectorized. Today, we may let tell 3D objects their own stories, in text and messages, audio, and video. This requires the definition of storyboards to present further geometries, images, and semantics. Therefore, an integration of semantic models/ontologies with geometric data and metadata is necessary—also in order to offer semantic details in coarse-to-fine modes, just to adapt them to the user level. A child in kindergarten may play with a 2D, 3D or 4D GIS app, purely for fun, and school pupils might use it to learn about their home town and its history, while students and adults might expect more complex and dense information. GIS is no longer the only bridge for disciplines in surveying—it has become one of many fascinating fields and technologies collaborating together. This means data collectors, data processors, and data presenters should collaborate closely; for example, we may link photogrammetry and computer vision with geoinformatics and building information modeling on the one hand, and with computer graphics and serious gaming on the other. The boundaries of the different fields intersect, and it is exciting to see the output of these intersections. Serious gaming offers platforms for advanced 3D modeling and rendering and therefore also plays an important role in cognitive aspects of human–computer interaction.

Dieter Fritsch
Special Issue Editor

Editorial

Guest Editor's Editorial "Cognitive Aspects of Human-Computer Interaction for GIS"

Dieter Fritsch

Institute for Photogrammetry & Institute of Distributed and Parallel Systems, University of Stuttgart, Stuttgart 70147, Germany; dieter.fritsch@ifp.uni-stuttgart.de

Received: 26 July 2019; Accepted: 29 July 2019; Published: 30 July 2019

The first Hypertext System and HCI

It was Vannevar Bush [1] in the 1930s, working at the MIT, who was heading in the direction of hypertext linking and a pre-prototype system of human-computer-interaction (HCI). While George Stibitz and Konrad Zuse were trying to develop the circuitry that would eventually lead to the invention of a digital computer, Bush was developing a machine he later called the differential analyzer. This was an analog computer using all ten digits of the decimal system rather than using the binary system of digital computers. Claude Shannon, a student of Bush, was at the same time working on his Boolean algebra and electrical circuitry theories, by which finally the differential analyzer became obsolete. Bush went on to invent the rapid selector, a microfilm storage and retrieval device, that he expanded, at least in theory leading to the memory expander, just called memex [2], see Figure 1a. Memex, a proto-hypertext system, has foreshadowed modern computer and hypertext linking that gives Bush his place as a pioneer of the Internet and HCI.

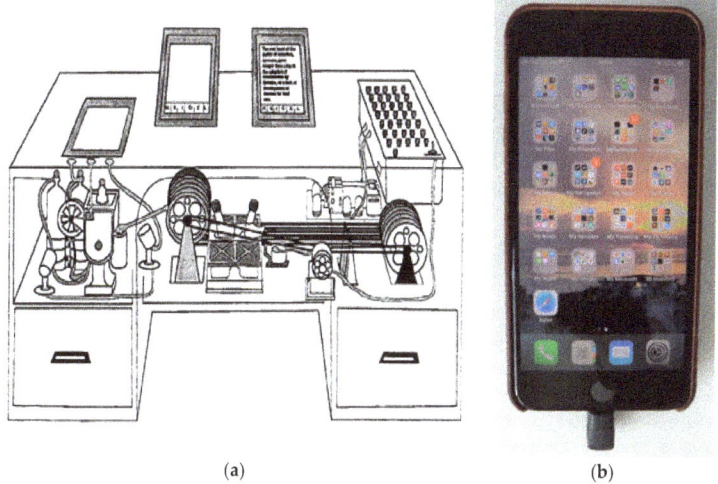

Figure 1. (a) The memory expander (memex) of V. Bush. (b) iPhone7 Plus with San Disk USB flash drive.

Bush described the device as electronically linked to a library and able to display books and films from that library, with the capability to automatically follow cross-references from one work to another. A large desk was hiding a combination of electromechanical controls and microfilm cameras and readers. Most of the microfilm library would have been contained in this desk, but the user could add or remove microfilm at will. Obviously, the technology of memex is often confused with that of hypertext. Although Bush's idea inspired the creation of hypertext, it is not considered to be hypertext. However, taking Bush's idea of linking the device to a library and use it to display text, photographs and films comes very close to today's performance of mobile devices and USB flash drives, see Figure 1b.

HCI and the NLS, ARPANET and Internet

The publication of V. Bush, "As We May Think" [3], has got the attention of another computer pioneer, Douglas Engelbart, who developed the basis for today's computer interfaces, already during the 1960s. He liked Bush's idea of a machine that would aid human cognition.

At that time, Engelbart founded the Augmentation Research Center (ARC), a development environment at the Stanford Research Institute (today SRI International, located in Menlo Park, near the Stanford University Campus) [4]. He and his colleagues, W.K. English and J.F. Rulifson, created the oN-Line System (NLS), the world's first hypertext implementation. NLS was an integrated environment for natural idea processing, at a time when most people (and even programmers) had no direct contact with a computer. This environment created already the mouse-pointing device for on-screen selection, a full windowing SW architecture, a one-hand chording device for keyboard entry, on-line help systems and the concept of consistency in user interfaces. Engelbart's work directly influenced the research and development at Xerox PARK, which in turn was the inspiration for Apple computers. NLS was able to do hypertext linking, tele-conferencing, word-processing, emails and could be individually configured and programmed by the user. In 1991, Engelbart and his colleagues got the prestigious ACM Software System Award for their work on NLS. The development of NLS was more or less finished in 1968. The Mother of All Demos demonstrated on December 9, 1968 its important features to a small crowd of specialists in San Francisco, via leased telephone lines which connected the ARC scientists to a huge screen at the meeting place.

Parallel to the developments of ARC at SRI another important innovation project was launched in the beginning of the 1960s—the Advanced Research Projects Agency Networks (ARPANET) [5]. It was the world's first operational packet switching network, and the predecessor of the Internet. The packet switching concept revolutionized the methods of data communication. Previously, data communication was performed by circuit switching, in which a dedicated circuit is tied up for the duration of a phone call and communication takes place with a single user only, on the other end of the circuit. With packet switching, each packet could be routed independently of other packets. The system was able to use one communication link to communicate with more than one machine by assembling the data into several packets.

Packet switching is therefore the basis for today's data transfer via the Internet, independent of its application which is quite diverse: Text messages, e-mails (with/without attachments), voice-over-IP (VoIP), MP3 audios (audio podcasts), MP4 videos, (video podcasts), video-on-demand (VoD), and IP Television (IPTV).

However, there was still a long way to go, from the first ideas of ARPANET to today's largest library in the world—the Internet with its millions of web servers [6]. The earliest ideas of a computer network intended to allow general communication between users of various computers were formulated 1962 by the psychologist J.C.R. Licklider [7]). His memos discussing "The Galactic Network" contained almost everything that the Internet is today. When he was appointed head at the US Department of Defense Advanced Research Projects Agency (DARPA), he was the one who convinced Ive Sutherland and Bob Taylor for the necessity of such a computer network. Licklider left DARPA before any actual work on his vision was performed.

The initial plans for the ARPANET began late spring and summer 1967, more than 50 years ago. It was Larry Roberts, a former associate of MIT Lincoln Laboratory, who got the responsibility at DARPA for realizing the ARPANET idea (late 1966). The company Bolt, Beranek and Newman (BBN) was awarded with a contract to implement initial ARPANET deployments on April 7, 1969. A first, the ARPANET link was established on January 14, 1969, between the Network Measurement Center of

UCLA and the D. Engelbart's ARC at SRI (where the NLS was already operating). BBN finished as contracted the entire 4-node network linking UC Los Angeles, UC Santa Barbara, SRI, and the University of Utah, by December 5, 1969. BBN followed the plan of Roberts closely—small computers known as interface message processors (IMPs) performed at each site store-and-forward packet switching functions. They were connected to each other using modems to leased lines, running at 50 Kbit/s. The host computers were connected to the IMP and ARPANET via custom bit-serial interfaces. The first email via ARPANET was sent in 1971. By 1973, 75% of ARPANET traffic was email. In the same year, the file transfer protocol (FTP) was defined and implemented to enable file transfer via ARPANET. Also, a voice traffic protocol was worked out in the 1970s, but conference calls did not work well with the ARPANET.

At the beginning, the ARPANET relied on the 1822 protocol, which served well within the IMP nodes. With the growth of the network and its increased usage, this protocol was replaced by the Network Control Program (NCP) to use a more advanced standard method to establish reliable flow-controlled and bidirectional communication links between different processes running on different hosts.

In 1983, TCP/IP protocols replaced NCP as the standard protocol of the ARPANET, and the ARPANET became just one component of the fledgling Internet. Further in 1983, the US military portion of ARPANET was broken off as a separate network, called MILNET. Obviously, there is a myth telling that " ... The ARPANET was designed to be a communication backbone that could survive a nuclear attack ... ", which definitely is not true. The ARPANET was shut down in 1990. Most university computers that were connected to it were moved to networks connected to the NSFNET, the Internet of today.

The Internet entered the public arena in 1994, when Tim Berners-Lee's World Wide Web became accessible through the commercial browser NETSCAPE. In the last 25 years, it has evolved to an indispensable tool transforming business and politics, spawning its own industry of search engines (e.g. Google, Yahoo, Bing, etc.), and contributing to new concepts in research, education and teaching.

HCI in general today

Since the evolution of digital computing in the 1940s, the human-computer-interaction (HCI) has been an issue. From the beginning, it was treated as a task-artifact-cycle and as technology advances, the interface between the user and the data and information to be processed has become most critical for creating effective, efficient and pleasant systems. According to [8], the task-artifact-cycle is described in more detail: (1) Humans have needs and preferences, (2) technologies are created to suit these needs, and (3) as humans use these technologies, the needs and preferences change continuously. Comparing the use of geographical information science (GIS) hardware and software in the last three decades (1990 to 2020) is completely different: First, closed and monolithical systems were used running on mainframes, workstations and desktop computers. Today, open architectures and cloud-based systems interconnecting desktop and mobile computing devices are used. Geospatial data and informations are used daily by everyone. Mobile devices changed completely the social behavior of humans and so did geographical data. The following question can be asked: How did people meet in town 1990 and 2019. The answer is simple: Nowadays, the mobile device tracks visits, movements and coordinates meetings with friends. Also, navigation on the mobile device has become very simple and people rarely get lost.

However, there are also conflicts to be resolved [9]. The user needs are sometimes conflicting needs and there are difficulties weighting them against each other, and moreover, many values are not explicitly communicated. Considering the weighting of values leads directly to the following questions: (1) Should all services be free-of-charge? (2) Should it be privacy-preserving? Then, there is the issue of the implicit values: (3) How to offer minimal efforts in getting started and using it? (4) What is the social status of a technology—the coolness factor? It seems today, that for most daily problems, people are using applications—in short "Apps"—running on smart phones and tablets, including also geospatial environments.

The HCI today is all about visible innovation. It is often not seen as a problem before there is a solution. If problems are identified, they are typically easy to understand by non-experts. Once a solution is there, people will generally not remember that there was a problem, and the good and in particular, great solutions often appear obvious—once they exist. Summarizing the problems, the challenges and solutions can be stated as follows: The step from problem to solution is, however, not trivial. However, this is often forgotten, once there is a solution.

According to the working definition of the ACM SIGCHI [10] the HCI is generally understood as "A discipline concerned with the design, evaluation and implementation of interactive computing systems for human use and with the study of major phenomena surrounding them". It needs the support of many disciplines (see Figure 2), like computer science to contribute with application design and engineering of human-computer interfaces; psychology contributing with the application of theories of cognitive processes and the empirical analysis of user behavior; sociology and anthropology considering interactions between technology, work and organization, and to design to create interactive products.

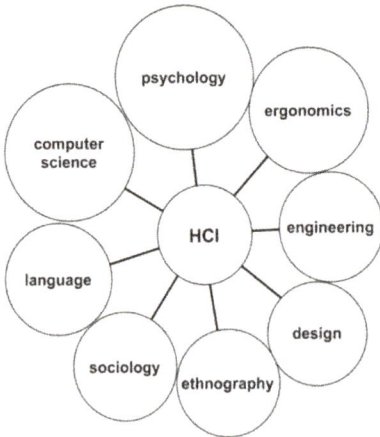

Figure 2. Human-computer-interaction depends on many disciplines.

HCI and GIS

The widespread use of emerging technologies for 3D modelling and 3D visualization, such as augmented reality, virtual reality and 3D/4D Apps developments offers to the geographical information science (GIS)—also called geoinformatics or geoinformation science —new interfaces for human-computer interactions. This goes also along with the progress in big data analyses using machine learning and deep learning methods, but this is still in its infancy stage with GIS data analysis. Most of the high quality urban scenes, such as 3D vectorized buildings and city models are outputs of interactive workflows which should be replaced step by step by more automation in the near future. Therefore, this issue will deliver some articles reviewing the state-of-the-art in 2D and 3D modeling by interactive and semi-automated and fully automated workflows, in particular when 3D urban scenes have to be interpreted and vectorized.

Today, 2D and 3D objects tell their own stories, in text and messages, audio, and video [11–13]. This requires the definition of storyboards to present further geometries, images, and semantics. Therefore, an integration of semantic models/ontologies with geometric data and metadata is necessary, and also to offer semantic details in coarse-to-fine modes, just to adapt it to the user level. A child in Kindergarten may play with a 2D, 3D and 4D GIS App purely for fun. The school pupil might use it to learn about their home town and its history, while students and adults might expect more complex and dense information.

GIS is no longer the only bridge for disciplines in surveying—it has become one of many fascinating fields and technologies collaborating together, as given in Figure 3. This means the data collectors, data processors and data presenters should collaborate closely, for example, to link photogrammetry and computer vision with geoinformatics and building information modeling on the one hand, and with computer graphics and serious gaming on the other hand. The boundaries of the different fields intersect and it is exciting to see the output of these intersections. Serious gaming offers platforms for advanced 3D modeling and rendering and therefore, plays also an important role in cognitive aspects of human-computer-interaction.

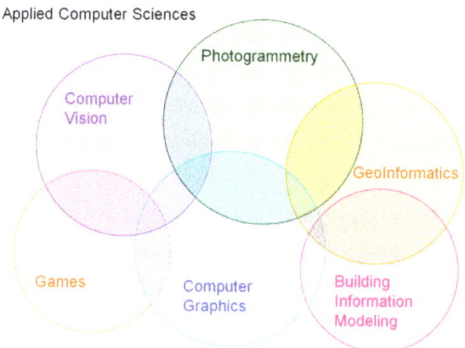

Figure 3. Collaboration of several scientific fields in 2D, 3D and 4D modeling and visualization.

Therefore, the issue of GIS human-computer-interaction just started and new developments, integrating mixed realities, 3D/4D App developments and progress in automated 3D urban scene modeling, machine learning and deep learning, visual analytics and many more are expected to further develop the general ideas and implementations of HCI.

The example taken from [13] illustrates the HCI and GIS experience by means of 3D and 4D Apps developments. Computer games have been used for real-time visualizations for the past three decades [14]. For the development of Apps, the software package, Unity, has been used. It is a cross-platform engine developed by Unity Technologies and accomplishes to develop video games for PCs, mobile devices and websites. With an emphasis on portability, the engine targets the following APIs: Direct3D on Windows and Xbox 360; OpenGL on Mac, Linux, and Windows; OpenGL ES on Android and iOS; proprietary APIs on video game consoles. Unity allows specification of texture compression and resolution settings for each platform that the game engine supports, and provides support for bump mapping, reflection mapping, parallax mapping, screen space ambient occlusion (SSAO), dynamic shadows using shadow maps, render-to-texture and full-screen post-processing effects. Unity's graphics engine's platform diversity can provide a shader with multiple variants and a declarative fallback specification, allowing Unity to detect the best variant for the current video hardware and, if none are compatible, to fall back to an alternative shader that may sacrifice features for performance.

In the European Union funded 4D-CH-World Project, the game engine Unity has been used to develop two applications:

(1) The application, Calw VR
(2) The application, Tracing Hermann Hesse in Calw.

The overall aims for the application development are given as follows: (1) Use operating systems Android, iOS and Windows; (2) provide real-time 3D environments using OpenGL ES 3.0; (3) the

GUI should offer autoscaling and orientation; (4) allow for additional steering using embedded accelerometers and gyroscopes; (5) all text, audio and video narration must be available for at least two languages (English, German); (6) allow for augmentation through target tracking; (7) triggering scenes by using GPS sensors; (8) provide an interactive map display with turn-by-turn directions, and (9) overlay original site artefacts with reconstructions.

Before designing and implementing an App, a storyboard has to be defined. Storyboards are graphic organizers in the form of illustrations or images displayed in sequence for the purpose of pre-visualizing a motion picture, animation, motion graphic or interactive media sequence. The storyboarding process, in the form it is known today, was developed at the Walt Disney Studio during the early 1930s, after several years of similar processes being in use at Walt Disney and other animation studios. Figure 4 displays an excerpt of the main menu of the storyboard for the Calw VR App.

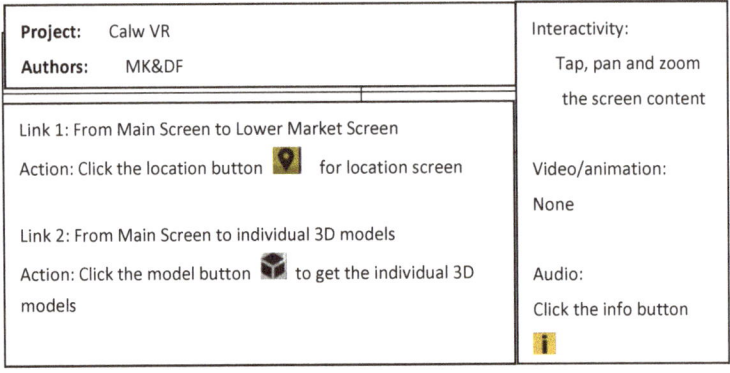

Figure 4. Excerpt of the storyboard's main menu of the Calw VR App.

Designing a storyboard for an App is a very time-consuming process, but very important, as it creates for the programmer an outline of which features and functions must be fulfilled.

Figure 5 presents the main screen of the Calw VR App and a closer view of the Calw lower market square with the town hall.

Figure 5. *Cont.*

Figure 5. Screen (above) and closer view to the town hall (below) of the App Calw VR.

HCI and GIS in this issue

As stated before, human-computer-interaction and geographic information science is an ongoing topic. Therefore, the authors are pleased to offer below nine articles dealing with different aspects and presenting advanced tools to access and interpret geospatial data.

The review article of K. Sun, Y. Zhu and J. Song [15] describes the "Progress and Challenges on Entity Alignment of Geographic Knowledge Bases (GKBs)". To overcome the heterogeneity of GKBs, an entity alignment provides an effective way to find correspondencies of entities by measuring the multidimensional similarity between the entities from different GKBs. After defining basic definitions and a general framework, the state-of-the-art algorithms are reviewed and applied. Obviously, there is a lack of methods to assess the qualities of the GKBs—the aligment process is likely to be improved by determining the best composition of heterogeneous features, optimizing alignment algorithms and incorporating background knowledge.

The article of C. Sasinka et al. [16] deep-dives into "Collaborative Immersive Virtual Environments for Education in Geography". A unique application for implementing a collaborative immersive virtual environment (CIVE) was developed by an interdisciplinary team as a software solution for educational purposes, with two scenarios for learning about hypsography, i.e., explanations of contour line principles. Both scenarios allow switching between a usual 2D contour map and a 3D model of the corresponding terrain to increase the intelligibility and clarity of the educational content. Gamification principles were also applied to both scenarios to augment user engagement during the completion of tasks.

C. Wang et al. [17] reflect "Gender and Age Differences in Using Indoor Maps for Wayfinding in Real Environments". This study intends to explore gender and age effects on the use of indoor maps for wayfinding in real environments. Eye-tracking and retrospective verbal protocol methods are used to conduct a wayfinding experiment in a newly opened building. The statistical data was collected and three findings were obtained. Example Finding 1: Males had no significant differences to females in indoor self-location, route reading, and route following. However, males paid less visual attention to the landmark and legends than females during route reading. For the other findings, please read the article.

The article of L. Herman et al. [18] outlines the "Evaluation of User Performance in Interactive and Static 3D Maps." The main objective is to identify differences between interactive and static 3D maps. They also explore the role of different tasks and inter-individual differences of map users. In the experimental study, effectiveness, efficiency, and subjective preferences are analyzed, when working with static and interactive 3D maps. The study includes 76 participants and uses a within-subjects design. The experimental testing is performed using an own testing tool 3DmoveR 2.0, which is based on a user logging method and open web technologies. Statistically significant differences between interactive and static 3D maps in effectiveness, efficiency, and subjective preferences are demonstrated.

A. Plowright, R. Tortini and N.C. Coops [19] communicate experiences in "Determining Optimal Video Length for the Estimation of Building Height trough Radial Displacement Measurement from Space". They present a methodology for estimating building heights in downtown Vancouver, British Columbia, Canada, using a high definition video (HDV) recorded from the International Space Station. An iterative routine based on multiresolution image segmentation is developed to track the radial displacement of building roofs over the course of the HDV, and to predict the building heights using an ordinary least-squares regression model. The linear relationship between the length of the tracking vector and the height of the buildings is excellent ($r^2 \leq 0.89$, RMSE ≤ 8.85 m, $p < 0.01$).

The article of Y. Zhou et al. [20] refers to "4D Time Density of Trajectories: Discovering Spatiotemporal Patterns in Movement Data". In cartography, a common way to visualize and explore trajectory data is to use the 3D cube (e.g., space-time cube), where trajectories are presented as a tilted 3D polyline. As larger movement datasets become available, this type of display can easily become confusing and illegible. In addition, movement datasets are often unprecedentedly massive, high-dimensional, and complex (e.g., implicit spatial and temporal relations and interactions), making it challenging to explore and analyze the spatiotemporal movement patterns in space. In this paper, the 4D time density as a visualization method for identifying and analyzing spatiotemporal movement patterns in large trajectory datasets is proposed.

M. Ceh et al. [21] deliver an article dealing with "Estimating the Performance of Random Forest versus Multiple Regression for Predicting Prices of the Apartments". The goal of this study is to analyze the predictive performance of the random forest machine learning technique in comparison to commonly used hedonic models based on multiple regression for the prediction of apartment prices. A data set that includes 7407 records of apartment transactions referring to real estate sales from 2008–2013 in the city of Ljubljana, the capital of Slovenia, is used in order to test and compare the predictive performances of both models. Apparent challenges faced during modelling include (1) the non-linear nature of the prediction assignment task; (2) input data being based on transactions occurring over a period of great price changes in Ljubljana whereby a 28% decline was noted in six consecutive testing years; (3) the complex urban form of the case study area.

The article of Ahmed Elashry et al. [22] describes "2DPR-Tree: Two-dimensional Priority R-Tree Algorithm for Spatial Partitioning in SpatialHadoop". Among spatial information applications, SpatialHadoop is one of the most important systems for researchers. Broad analyses prove that SpatialHadoop outperforms the traditional Hadoop in managing distinctive spatial information operations. This paper presents a two dimensional priority R-Tree (2DPR-Tree) as a new partitioning technique in SpatialHadoop. The 2DPR-Tree employs a top-down approach that effectively reduces the number of partitions accessed to answer the query, which in turn improves the query performance. The results are evaluated in different scenarios using synthetic and real datasets.

Finally M. Wu et al. [23] present an article about "An Efficient Visualization Method for Polygonal Data with Dynamic Simplification". The polygonal data often require rendering with symbolization and simplification in geovisualization. A common issue in existing methods is that simplification, symbolization and rendering are addressed separately, causing computational and data redundancies that reduce efficiency, especially when handling large complex polygonal data. Here, an efficient polygonal data visualization method by organizing the simplification, tessellation and rendering operations into a single mesh generalization process is presented. First, based on the sweep line method, a topology embedded trapezoidal mesh data structure is proposed to organize the tessellated polygons. Second, a horizontal and vertical generalization operation is applied to simplify the trapezoidal meshes.

References

1. Bush, V. Internet Notes 2007. Available online: http://www.kerryr.net/pioneers/bush.htm (accessed on 24 July 2019).
2. Memex. Internet Notes 2007. Available online: http://en.wikipedia.org/wiki/Memex (accessed on 24 July 2019).
3. Bush, V. As we may think. In *The American Monthly*; National Society of the Daughters of the American Revolution: Washington, DC, USA, 1945.
4. Engelbart, D. Internet Notes 2007. Available online: http://www.iath.virginia.edu/elab/hfl0035.html (accessed on 24 July 2019).
5. ARPANET. Internet Notes 2007. Available online: http://livinginternet.com/i/ii_arpanet.htm&http://en.wikipedia.org/wiki/ARPANET (accessed on 24 July 2019).
6. Salus, P.H. *Casting the Net: From ARPANET to Internet and Beyond*; Addison-Wesley: New York, NY, USA, 1995.
7. Licklider, J.C.R. Internet Notes 2019. Available online: https://en.wikipedia.org/wiki/J._C._R._Licklider (accessed on 24 July 2019).
8. Carroll, J.M. Human-Computer-Interaction—Brief Intro. In *The Encyclopedia of Human-Computer Interaction*, 2nd ed.; Soegaard, M., Dam, R.F., Eds.; The Interaction Design Foundation: Aarhus, Denmark, 2013; Available online: http://www.interaction-design.org/encyclopedia/human_computer_interaction-hci.html (accessed on 24 July 2019).
9. Bulling, A. Human-Computer-Interaction. In *Lecture Notes. Computer Science*; University of Stuttgart: Stuttgart, Germany, 2019.
10. ACM SIGCHI: Curricula for Human-Computer Interaction. Available online: http://www.acm.org/sigchi/cdg/ (accessed on 24 July 2019).
11. Fritsch, D. Podcasting Photogrammetry—A Contribution to Life-Long-Learning. In *Photogrammetric Week 07*; Fritsch, D., Ed.; Wichmann: Heidelberg, Germany, 2007; pp. 335–344.
12. Fritsch, D.; Klein, M. 3D Preservation of Buildings—Reconstructing the Past. In *Multimedia Tools and Applications (MTAP)*; Springer: Berlin/Heidelberg, Germany, 2018; Volume 77, pp. 9153–9170.
13. Fritsch, D.; Klein, M. Design of 3D and 4D Apps for Cultural Heritage Preservation. In *Digital Cultural Heritage*; Ioannides, M., Ed.; Lecture Notes Computer Science (LNCS); Springer: Cham, Switzerland, 2018; Volume 10605, pp. 211–226.
14. Harrison, L.T. *Introduction to 3D Game Engine Design Using DirectX and C#*; Apress: Berkeley, CA, USA, 2003.
15. Sun, K.; Zhu, Y.; Song, J. Progress and Challenges on Entity Alignment of Geographic Knowledge Bases. *ISPRS Int. J. Geo-Inf.* **2019**, *8*, 77. [CrossRef]
16. Sasinka, C.; Stachon, Z.; Sedlak, M.; Chemlik, J.; Herman, L.; Kubicek, P.; Sasinkova, A.; Dolezal, M.; Tejkl, H.; Urbanek, T.; et al. Collaborative Immersive Virtual Environments for Education in Geography. *ISPRS Int. J. Geo-Inf.* **2019**, *8*, 3. [CrossRef]
17. Wang, C.; Chen, Y.; Zheng, S.; Liao, H. Gender and Age Differences in Using Indoor Maps for Wayfinding in Real Environments. *ISPRS Int. J. Geo-Inf.* **2019**, *8*, 11. [CrossRef]
18. Herman, L.; Jurik, V.; Stachoni, Z.; Vrbik, D.; Russnak, J.; Reznik, T. Evaluation of User Performance in Interactive and Static 3D Maps. *ISPRS Int. J. Geo-Inf.* **2018**, *7*, 415. [CrossRef]
19. Plowright, A.; Tortini, R.; Coops, N.C. Determining Optimal Video Length for the Estimation of Building Height through Radial Displacement Measurement from Space. *ISPRS Int. J. Geo-Inf.* **2018**, *7*, 380. [CrossRef]
20. Zou, Y.; Chen, Y.; He, J.; Pang, G.; Zhang, K. 4D Time Density of Trajectories: Discovering Spatiotemporal Patterns in Movement Data. *ISPRS Int. J. Geo-Inf.* **2018**, *7*, 212. [CrossRef]
21. Ceh, M.; Kilibarda, M.; Lisec, A.; Bajat, B. Estimating the Performance of Random Forest versus Multiple Regression for Predicting Prices of the Apartments. *ISPRS Int. J. Geo-Inf.* **2018**, *7*, 168. [CrossRef]
22. Elashry, A.; Shehab, A.; Riad, A.M.; Abdoul-Fotouh, A. 2DPR-Tree: Two-dimensional Priority R-Tree Algorithm for Spatial Partitioning in SpatialHadoop. *ISPRS Int. J. Geo-Inf.* **2018**, *7*, 179. [CrossRef]
23. Wu, M.; Chen, T.; Zhang, K.; Jing, Z.; Han, Y.; Chen, M.; Wang, H.; Lv, G. An Efficient Visualization Method for Polygonal Data with Dynamic Simplification. *ISPRS Int. J. Geo-Inf.* **2018**, *7*, 138. [CrossRef]

© 2019 by the author. Licensee MDPI, Basel, Switzerland. This article is an open access article distributed under the terms and conditions of the Creative Commons Attribution (CC BY) license (http://creativecommons.org/licenses/by/4.0/).

Article

Gender and Age Differences in Using Indoor Maps for Wayfinding in Real Environments

Chengshun Wang [1], Yufen Chen [1,*], Shulei Zheng [1] and Hua Liao [2]

1 Zhengzhou Institute of Surveying and Mapping, Zhengzhou 450052, China; wcs2000-1@163.com (C.W.); z_score2@163.com (S.Z.)
2 Faculty of Geographical Science, Beijing Normal University, Beijing 100875, China; liaohua@mail.bnu.edu.cn (H.L.)
* Correspondence: cyfbeijing@163.com; Tel.: +86-371-8162-2294

Received: 25 September 2018; Accepted: 12 November 2018; Published: 27 December 2018

Abstract: Users more easily become lost in complex indoor environments than in outdoor environments. Users with diverse backgrounds encounter different self-location, route memorization, and route following problems during wayfinding. This study intends to explore gender and age effects on the use of indoor maps for wayfinding in real environments. We used eye-tracking and retrospective verbal protocol methods to conduct a wayfinding experiment in a newly opened building. Statistical data were collected and three findings were obtained. Finding 1: Males had no significant differences with females in indoor self-location, route reading, and route following. However, males paid less visual attention to the landmark and legend than females during route reading. Finding 2: Age-related differences were significant in indoor wayfinding. Younger adults generally outperformed elderly adults in wayfinding in real indoor environments. Finding 3: Gender and age interactive effects were significant in self-location and route memorization. The mean differences of visual attention on the self-location map reading and route memorization between males and females increased with age.

Keywords: indoor wayfinding; eye-tracking; gender effects; age effects; retrospective verbal protocol

1. Introduction

Wayfinding is defined as a purposive, directed, and motivated behavior to efficiently find one's way from an origin to a destination in a familiar or unfamiliar place using sensory cues (maps, signs, and verbal instructions) from the external environment [1,2]. Wayfinding (especially in unfamiliar environments) is a complex, challenging process that requires participants to be aware of their self-location and to orient themselves [3]. Cartographers have paid attention to the influence of map representations on visual attention and user performance in self-location and spatial orientation during wayfinding [4]. Researchers investigating human-centred navigation [5] have looked for ways to redesign cartographical representations to improve the efficiency and effectiveness of wayfinding for users with spatial cognitive difficulties. However, the focus of these studies was outdoor wayfinding [6,7] and an exploratory study on how users accomplish their wayfinding behaviors in indoor environments is a challenging endeavour.

Participants have been found to encounter more spatial cognitive difficulties such as problems acquiring spatial knowledge when reading multi-level indoor maps and getting lost or disoriented at complex turning positions (corners, elevators, and lifts) in indoor environments than in outdoor environments [8,9]. We argue that users still encounter these difficulties with the assistance of maps. Researchers have found that users with different backgrounds have different wayfinding problems because human factors (gender, age, spatial abilities, and expert knowledge) play an important role in the wayfinding process [10,11]. Although the influences of human factors have been extensively researched in outdoor wayfinding experiments, these factors have been ignored in indoor environments. Thus, it is necessary to identify users' individual indoor wayfinding patterns and redesign indoor maps to meet the needs of map users with different backgrounds.

In this article, we aim to investigate the effects of gender and age factors on indoor wayfinding behaviors. Specifically, we focus on the following three questions:

1. Are there differences between males and females in terms of visual attention and user performance in wayfinding in real indoor environments?
2. Are there differences between younger adults and older adults in terms of visual attention and user performance in wayfinding in real indoor environments?
3. Are there any cross effects of the gender and age factors on wayfinding in indoor real environments?

To solve these problems, we conducted an experiment in a newly opened shopping mall. Section 2 presents related work. In Section 3, we present details of a two-factorial (males/females and younger/elderly adults) wayfinding experiment in a real indoor environment. In Section 4, we describe how eye movements and retrospective verbalizations results were recorded to analyze the participants' visual attention and user performance in wayfinding. These quantitative and qualitative results are discussed in Section 5. In Section 6, we answer the above three questions based on participants' indoor wayfinding behaviors and extract some implications that might be helpful to improve indoor map representations for participants with indoor cognitive difficulties.

2. Related Work

2.1. Gender and Age Differences in Wayfinding

Wayfinding is a major area of spatial cognition research that consists of a series of cognitive processes [12]. These cognitive processes include reading a map, remembering the route, finding one's location, and maintaining one's orientation with external features or landmarks. Two behaviors (self-location and spatial orientation) are crucial processes during wayfinding [4]. Self-location refers to identifying one's position in spatial scenery and includes several sub-processes such as map orientation, feature matching, and configuration matching [6]. Spatial orientation is closely related to self-location and refers to determining the direction that one is facing when given an external instruction (cognitive or real maps) [13].

Over the years, both common belief and scientific literature have reported that the sexes differ in their ability to perform spatial and geographic tasks [14] especially in wayfinding or navigation [15]. These research achievements have essential implications for the design of maps and navigation systems. Although it is widely believed that gender differences exist in wayfinding, the research results have not been consistent across different experiments. For example, Tlauka, Brolese, Pomeroy, and Hobbs [16] found that men could more rapidly locate targets in the virtual environment. Andersen, Dahmani, and Konishi [17] reported that, in virtual navigation, gender differences occurred only in environments devoid of landmarks and disappeared in environments containing multiple landmarks However, Liao [4] found that men and women showed slightly significant differences in user performance and visual attention in 3D outdoor environments.

Researchers have also reported that there were age-related differences in wayfinding [18,19] and that such differences were not similar in different wayfinding experiments. Taillade, Sauzéon, and Dejos [20] found that elderly people encountered difficulties in finding landmarks and locating themselves in unfamiliar environments. The elderly participants demonstrated a poor ability to remember a planned route. Adamo, Briceño, and Sindone [21] reported that there were no significant age differences in distance reproduction wayfinding in a virtual environment. Taillade, N'Kaoua, and Sauzéon [22] observed age-related differences in navigation tasks in a real environment. In addition, some researchers have found cross effects of the gender and age factors on wayfinding. For example,

Brown and Khanan [23,24] showed that gender-related and aged-related factors could both influence participants' spatial cognitive abilities in laboratory tests or in a virtual environment.

In summary, scientists have shown that age and gender-related factors play important roles in wayfinding but those results differed across experimental settings. Researchers have mainly focused on age and gender-related differences in outdoor environments. It is unknown whether and how far the findings from outdoor environments can be applied to indoor environments. Furthermore, existing studies have employed virtual environments to investigate age and gender differences [25]. Whether these differences occur in a real indoor environment is still a mystery.

2.2. Wayfinding Research in Indoor Environments

It is not easy for participants to find their ways in a complex public building [26]. Thus, scientists have made great efforts to determine participants' indoor wayfinding difficulties. Li and Giudice [27] constructed a multi-level virtual building and found that participants encounter more location and spatial orientation problems without the assistance of map representations. Burigat, Chittaro, and Sioni [28] built a 3D virtual building model to focus on indoor wayfinding problems and found that participants more easily became lost at turning positions and that 3D maps were more helpful than 2D maps in helping people solve orientation problems. Trine and Thorsteinn [29] designed a wayfinding experiment in real-world environments and showed that the type of map appears to be an important determinant of indoor wayfinding performance and should be varied according to age and skill level. Similar results were also found in a real-world library environment [30]. These works showed that people rely on existing indoor navigational aids [31] and that an indoor map is an effective means of reducing the spatial cognition load during indoor wayfinding [32]. Researchers should adjust indoor maps to provide salient and relevant wayfinding information for users with different cognitive difficulties.

To capture indoor wayfinding behaviors efficiently and accurately, researchers have adopted various methods such as questionnaires [33], pose estimation [34], and real-time tracking methods [35] (GoPro, Google Glass, and Eye-tracking). Among these methods, eye-tracking methods have proved to be effective methods for geo-spatial cognition research [36]. Eye-tracking technology can directly capture users' gaze movements and assist researchers in analyzing spatial abilities in both quantitative and qualitative ways [36]. Therefore, there is an increasing interest in using eye tracking for spatial research in recent years. For instance, Liao and Dong [37] used a Tobii T60 eye tracker to detect the wayfinding difference between 3D and 2D map users in a lab environment. They also used eye trackers to analyze gender effects in outdoor wayfinding in the lab [4]. Kiefer [38] focused on utilizing mobile eye-tracking applications to reveal wayfinding difficulties in real-world urban environments. Brügger, Richter, and Fabrikant [39] utilized eye-trackers to investigate how navigation systems could guide users' attention to support spatial knowledge acquisition during real outdoor wayfinding.

Although eye-tracking technologies provide many benefits in wayfinding research, there are also accompanying difficulties that should not be ignored. Eye movement metrics might not be able to determine what strategy a participant is actually using to find his or her way. For instance, users who prefer a direction strategy for orientation will also observe store landmarks while walking along the wayfinding route [40]. Therefore, eye tracking is often combined with questionnaire, interview, and verbal protocol. The retrospective verbal protocol is a method users' verbalizations that their experimental process are collected after they perform a task [41] and this method can provide additional information in wayfinding research. Kinsley, Dan, and Spitler [35] combined GoPro and verbal protocol methods to analyze users' wayfinding and predict their internal decisions in a library. Liao and Dong [4] used eye-tracking and verbal protocol methods to capture spatial orientation performance. In summary, eye-tracking and verbal protocol methods can be helpful for researchers when investigating map users' indoor wayfinding difficulties.

3. Experiment

We designed and conducted a two-task wayfinding experiment. We specifically hypothesize that:

- Males and females have different visual attention regarding the indoor map and environment and males might perform better than females in indoor wayfinding.
- Younger and elderly adults have significant differences in visual attention and younger adults might have better indoor wayfinding performance than the elderly.
- Gender and age effects impact participants' wayfinding behavior.

3.1. Participants

It was important that participants should not have memory problems. We applied the Wechsler Adult Intelligence Scale (WAIS) [41] to test users' memory abilities. Participants who could repeat eight disordered numbers were selected to take part in the experiment. Twenty-two people took part in the experiment, but two of them did not pass the WAIS test. In the end, twenty people participated in the experiment voluntarily. All of them did not ask to read the routes map again during the route following/wayfinding.

The experiment was a two-factorial design: gender (male x female) x age (young x elderly). The participants were divided into an aged adult group and a younger adult group with 5 males and 5 females in each group.

The participants in the aged adult group were aged between 60 and 67 years old (mean age = 62.3, $SD = 2.50$). They held high school graduate (n = 8) or undergraduate (n = 2) degrees and all of them were retired and had no experience in the geo-related field but had used paper maps before. None of them were familiar with the study area.

The participants in the younger adult group were aged between 18 and 29 years old (mean age = 23.1, $SD = 3.92$), they held undergraduate (n = 7) or graduate (n = 3) degrees, and seven of them had experience in non-geo-related fields (three males and four females) while the others majored in geo-related fields. They had all used maps regularly and were not familiar with the study area.

All of the participants had normal or corrected-to-normal vision and could complete the experiment independently. Each participant was given ¥25 (*Yuan*) as a reward. The experiment was reviewed and approved by the local institutional review board (IRB). All of the participants provided their written informed consent to participate in the experiment.

3.2. Equipment

We selected the Tobii Pro Glasses 2 (Tobii AB, Sweden, www.tobii.com) mobile eye tracker with a wide angle HD scene camera (1920 x 1080) and an integrated microphone. The sampling rate of the eye tracker is 50 Hz. It only weights 45 grams, which allows participants to wear the eye-tracker in a flexible way. All participants' sampling rates were above 90%. Tobii Pro Glasses Analyzer software (Figure 1b) was used to manage and analyze eye movement data.

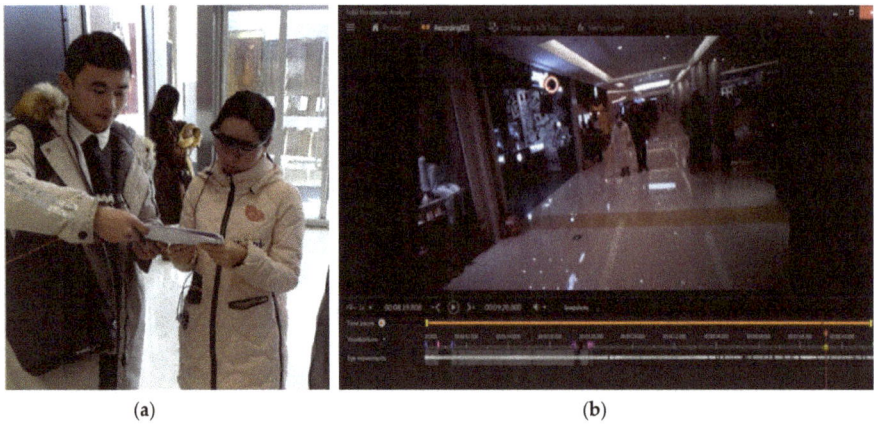

Figure 1. Equipment and analyzing application: (**a**) Participant wearing Tobii Glasses 2 in pre-test phase and (**b**) Tobii Pro Glasses Analyzer.

3.3. Materials

As shown in Figure 2, Baidu Indoor Maps (https://ditu.baidu.com/) were selected as the experimental materials. It has been widely used by the general public in China, which guarantee participants have a similar level of familiarity. Baidu Indoor Maps contain all of the detailed cartographic elements, which are essential for users to find task-relevant information.

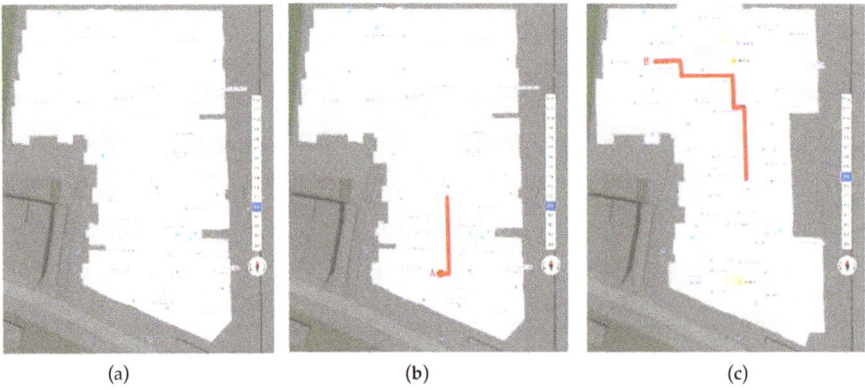

Figure 2. Indoor map for wayfinding: (**a**) Indoor map of the 1st floor for Task 1, Routes of 1st floor (**b**) and 4th floor (**c**) for Task 2 and Task 3.

For our real-world indoor experiment, it is important to guarantee that the participants have the same level of familiarity with the study area [42]. Thus, we selected the newly opened shopping mall, Dennis David Mall, as our study environment. Dennis David Mall, in downtown Zhengzhou, China, has a complex indoor environment that includes 11 floors and hundreds of stores.

We selected the Mall's first floor map for Task 1 (described below). Participants were required to point out their location on the map. We chose the 1st and 4th floor for Task 2 and Task 3. A route was highlighted on the map. It began from the starting point A, which is a service counter (first floor), and ended at the destination B known as Fairwhale (a famous shore at the fourth floor). Each map spanned a 450 x 370 m area in the Mall. These materials were presented on a pad during the experiment.

3.4. Procedure

The participants were first welcomed and asked to fill out a form with their background information (gender, age, education, and occupation) and a self-reporting assessment on the pad, which was used to assess the participants' familiarity with the experimental area (familiar or not familiar).

At the pre-test training session, the participants were instructed on how to wear Tobii Glasses 2 to read the indoor map and find the destination at DaShang Mall 100 meters from the experimental shopping mall. The 1-point calibration method was used to calibrate their eyes. Once the participants understood the experimental procedure, they were guided to the Dennis David Mall.

After the pre-test training session, the participants were guided to the experiment area. They were required to complete three tasks in sequence. Before each task, their eyes were checked and recalibrated if necessary. Each participant took approximately half an hour to complete the tasks. Instructions of the tasks are as follows. The participants were told that they would be timed but there was no time limit for all tasks.

Task 1: Self-location: Assume that you are shopping in the Dennis David Mall. Now you are standing somewhere in the Mall. Please read the map on the pad (Figure 1a) and compare it with the surrounding environment to determine where you are. You can turn around but you are not allowed to walk around. Please tell the experimenter where you are and how you can find your location on the map.

Task 2: Route memorization: Now, please read the next two maps on the pad (Figure 1b and 1c). The maps contain the first and fourth floor of the mall. You need to remember the route from A to B on the pad. This is the route you are about to navigate.

Task 3: Route following / Wayfinding: Now, you need to walk to the destination following the route you have just memorized. During walking, we will follow with you. If you make an error, we may ask you to stop until you find the destination. If you forget the route, we will provide the map to you. It is important that you do not talk with anyone except the experimenter. After finding the destination, we will replay the eye-tracking video for you and you should recall and speak aloud your thoughts about the wayfinding.

4. Analysis and Results

4.1. Task 1 (Self-location)

4.1.1. Visual Attention on Map Reading

Eye movement metrics were collected to examine how the participants read the indoor map for their self-location. It was labor-intensive to analyze video-based eye-movement data because we allowed the user to freely observe the indoor map and the environment. To facilitate this process, we used the 'automated mapping' function provided by the Tobii Analyzer to match video frames to the static map automatically.

In the self-location phase, each participant was required to stand at a starting position (red point in Figure 3), identify his or her location, and mark the point on the map. To analyze the differences in their self-location behavior, we selected the experimental location area as the area of interest (AOI). The AOI includes a service counter landmark. To account for the imprecision in eye movements, a buffer of 25 pixels (approximately 10 m) was created for aggregation of fixations in the AOI.

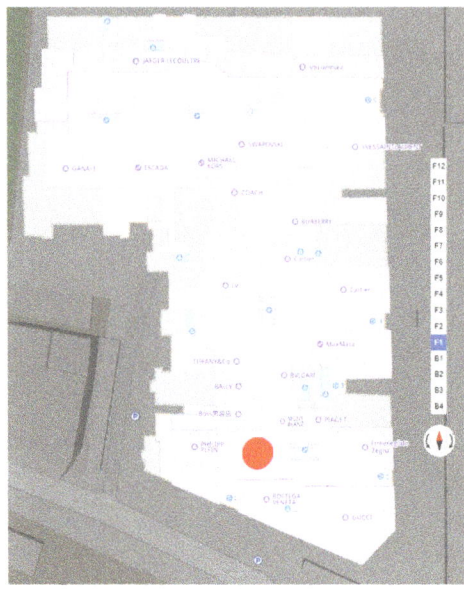

Figure 3. The AOI for self-location: the red point is the area of interest.

Three eye movement metrics (first AOI fixation time, fixation duration, and percent of fixations spent on map) were calculated. Definitions of these metrics are shown in Table 1. We assumed that people with high spatial ability could locate themselves in shorter first AOI fixation time and shorter map reading duration. We employed a two-way ANOVA to examine the differences between groups [43,44] and the results are shown in Table 2.

Table 1. Definition of metrics for analysis of map reading.

Metric	Definition
First AOI fixation time (seconds)	Time before the first fixation on AOI
Map reading duration (seconds)	Total fixation duration on the indoor map
Percent of fixations spent on map (%)	percentage of fixation count on the indoor map

Table 2. Descriptive and inferential statistics for Task 1 (Self-location).

Map reading:	MALE		FEMALE		Mean (age)		Gender ANOVA	Age ANOVA	Gender X Age ANOVA
	M	SD	M	SD	M	SD			
First AOI fixation time							$F(1,19) = 1.03$, $p > 0.05$, $\eta^2 = 0.061$	$F(1,19) = 7.25$, $p < 0.05^*$, $\eta^2 = 0.312$	$F(1,19) = 9.28$, $p < 0.01^{**}$, $\eta^2 = 0.378$
YOUNGER	18.29	5.01	21.39	7.57	19.84	6.27			
ELDERLY	28.06	11.15	33.08	10.53	30.57	10.56			
Mean (gender)	23.18	9.64	27.23	10.61					
Map reading duration							$F(1,19) = 0.87$, $p > 0.05$, $\eta^2 = 0.051$	$F(1,19) = 8.47$, $p < 0.05^*$, $\eta^2 = 0.346$	$F(1,19) = 9.69$, $p < 0.01^{**}$, $\eta^2 = 0.443$
YOUNGER	26.40	9.50	28.50	8.04	27.45	8.37			
ELDERLY	40.96	15.69	50.57	19.78	45.77	17.58			
Mean (gender)	33.68	14.44	39.54	18.39					
% of fixation on map							$F(1,19) = 0.07$, $p > 0.05$, $\eta^2 = 0.004$	$F(1,19) = 0.49$, $p > 0.05$, $\eta^2 = 0.030$	$F(1,19) = 0.93$, $p > 0.05$, $\eta^2 = 0.024$
YOUNGER	0.85	0.07	0.88	0.05	0.86	0.06			
ELDERLY	0.84	0.07	0.83	0.10	0.84	0.08			
Mean(gender)	0.85	0.07	0.85	0.08					

M = mean, SD = standard deviation. **: $p < 0.01$, *: $p < 0.05$.

Table 2 and Figure 4 shows that the first AOI fixation time for males was 23.18 seconds (SD = 9.64) and the results of this metric for females had a mean of 27.23 seconds (SD = 10.61). Males spent 33.68 seconds (SD = 14.44) on average reading the indoor map, which was shorter than the time spent by females who spent 39.54 seconds (SD = 18.39). Males and females spent the same percentage of fixations on the map (M = 0.85). Although Figures 4a and 4b show that females spent more time on first fixation and map reading, the ANOVA results reveal that the gender difference was not significant in the first AOI fixation time ($F(1,19) = 0.57, p > 0.05$). The results are similar for the map reading duration ($F(1,19)=0.63, p >0.05$) and percent of fixation on the map ($F(1,19) = 0.07, p > 0.05$).

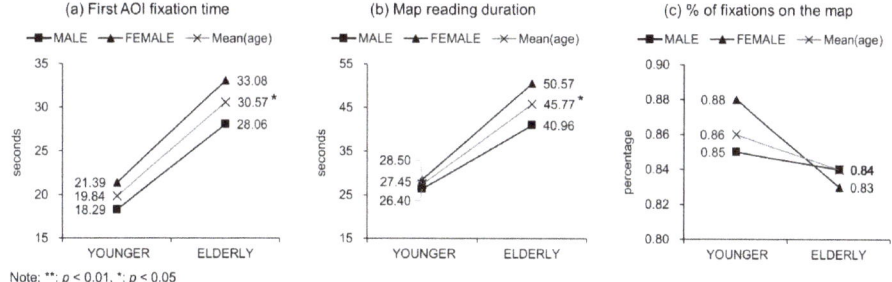

Figure 4. Results of visual attention on map reading in Task 1.

In contrast, statistically significant differences were observed between age groups. ANOVA results indicate that age differences were statistically significant in the first AOI fixation time ($F(1,19) = 7.25, p > 0.05$) and the map reading duration ($F(1,19) = 8.47, p > 0.05$). The mean values of the first AOI fixation time and the map reading duration in the younger adult group were 19.84 seconds (SD = 6.27) and 27.45 seconds (SD = 8.37) respectively, which are less than those in the elderly adult group (M = 30.57 seconds, SD = 10.56 and M = 45.77 seconds, SD=17.58). However, the difference was not significant in the percent of fixation on the map ($F(1,19) = 0.49, p > 0.05$), which indicates that younger and elderly adults spent a similar percentage of fixations on the map (M = 0.86, SD = 0.06 and M = 0.84, SD = 0.08).

Table 2 shows that gender and age difference was not significant in the percent of fixation on the map. However, the ANOVA result of the first AOI fixation time was 9.28 ($p < 0.01$) and the fixation duration was 9.69 ($p < 0.01$), which proved that the gender and age difference was significant in these variables. In order to find out which factor is differentially effective at each level of a second factor, we selected the Simple Effects Test [45]. Table 3 indicates that the only elderly and gender difference was significant in the first AOI fixation time. Yet, it is clear that both elderly and younger adults were significantly different with a gender factor in the map reading duration.

Table 3. Simple Effects Test for Task 1 (self-location).

			First AOI fixation time			Map reading duration		
Gender	Age(I)	Age(J)	MD(I-J)	SE	Sig.	MD(I-J)	SE	Sig.
female	elderly	younger	11.69	5.64	$p > 0.05$	22.07	8.90	$p > 0.05$
male	elderly	younger	9.77	5.64	$p > 0.05$	14.56	8.90	$p > 0.05$
Age	Gender(I)	Gender(J)						
elderly	female	male	5.01	5.64	$p < 0.05$*	9.61	8.90	$p < 0.05$*
younger	female	male	3.09	5.64	$p > 0.05$	2.10	8.90	$p < .05$*

MD = mean difference, SE = standard error. *: $p < 0.05$.

4.1.2. Visual Attention on Landmarks

In Task 1, all participants were asked to stand at the same position (Figure 5a, pink point). They could look around but were not allowed to walk around. A key process for self-location is to match the map objects to the corresponding landmarks in the surrounding environment. In order to analyze what landmarks the participants use to locate themselves, we divided the landmarks into four types (store, elevator, door, and others) and generated AOIs for these landmarks. Examples are shown in Figure 5. We then calculated the fixation durations (in percentage) on these four types of landmarks and the results are shown in Figure 6.

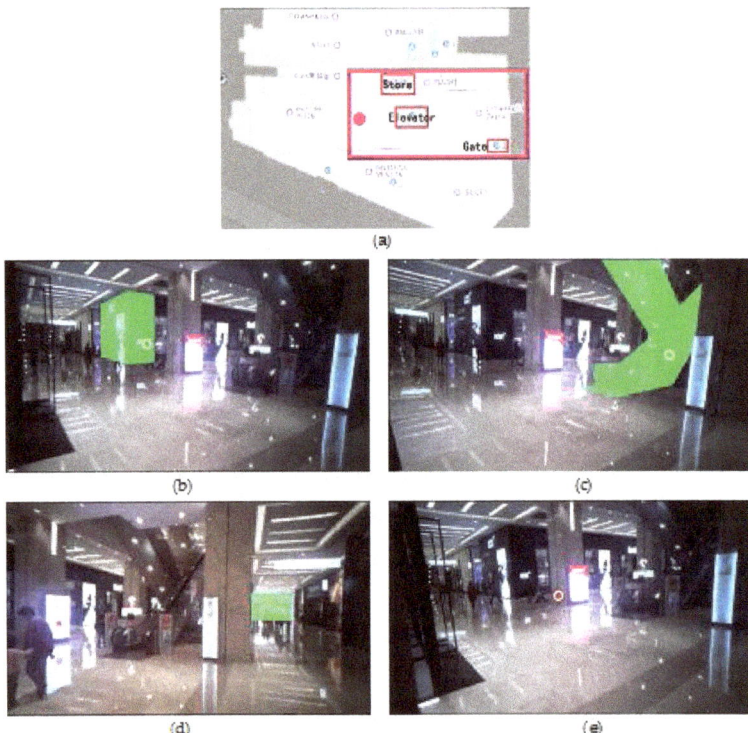

Figure 5. Experiment position and AOI divisions: (**a**) Experiment position and participant's visual field in AOIs, (**b**) AOI of store, (**c**) AOI of elevator, (**d**) AOI of the gate, and (**e**) AOI of others.

For the gender factor, the results revealed that males spent less time on the stores (M = 0.71, SD = 0.15) than females (M = 0.75, SD = 0.07) and that males fixated slightly longer on the elevator (M = 0.09, SD = 0.10) and the door (M = 0.11, SD = 0.10)) than females (M = 0.07, SD = 0.07, M = 0.10, SD = 0.06). However, no significant difference was found across the gender factor (Table 4).

In terms of the age factor, we found that younger adults paid significantly less visual attention to the stores (M = 0.68, SD = 0.12) than elderly adults (M = 0.77, SD = 0.12) with F-test statistics of 0.71, $p < 0.5$. In addition, younger adults also paid significantly less total fixation duration (M = 4.26, SD = 1.93) than elderly adults (M = 8.70, SD = 4.21) with F-test statistics of 8.01, $p < 0.5$. No significant difference was detected in other types of landmarks across age groups (Figure 6).

As for gender and age factors, the only elderly and gender difference was significant in the store fixation time (percentage), according to the Simple Effect Test results ($p < 0.05*$).

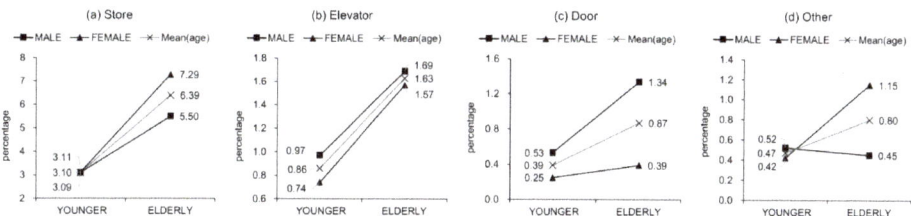

Figure 6. Results of visual attention on landmarks in Task 2.

Table 4. Descriptive and inferential statistics for visual attention on the landmark.

Visual attention on landmark	MALE		FEMALE		Mean (age)		Gender ANOVA	Age ANOVA	Gender X Age ANOVA
	M	SD	M	SD	M	SD			
Store (in percentage)							$F(1,19) = 0.41$, $p > 0.05$, $\eta^2 = 0.025$	$F(1,19) = 0.71$, $p < 0.05^*$, $\eta^2 = 0.042$	$F(1,19) = 0.46$, $p < 0.05^*$, $\eta^2 = 0.009$
YOUNGER	0.68	0.14	0.69	0.09	0.68	0.12			
ELDERLY	0.75	0.17	0.79	0.06	0.77	0.12			
Mean (gender)	0.71	0.15	0.75	0.07					
Elevator (in percentage)							$F(1,19) = 3.34$, $p > 0.05$, $\eta^2 = 0.173$	$F(1,19) = 4.68$, $p > 0.05$, $\eta^2 = 0.226$	$F(1,19) = 5.25$, $p > 0.05$, $\eta^2 = 0.247$
YOUNGER	0.10	0.13	0.08	0.09	0.09	0.10			
ELDERLY	0.08	0.07	0.06	0.07	0.07	0.06			
Mean (gender)	0.09	0.10	0.07	0.07					
Door (in percentage)							$F(1,19) = 0.05$, $p > 0.05$, $\eta^2 = 0.003$	$F(1,19) = 1.89$, $p > 0.05$, $\eta^2 = 0.106$	$F(1,19) = 0.99$, $p > 0.05$, $\eta^2 = 0.034$
YOUNGER	0.12	0.74	0.16	0.36	0.14	0.10			
ELDERLY	0.06	1.09	0.04	0.55	0.05	0.08			
Mean (gender)	0.09	0.10	0.10	0.07					
Others (in percentage)							$F(1,19) = 2.84$, $p > 0.05$, $\eta^2 = 0.151$	$F(1,19) = 1.12$, $p > 0.05$, $\eta^2 = 0.065$	$F(1,19) = 1.56$, $p > 0.05$, $\eta^2 = 0.089$
YOUNGER	0.10	0.30	0.07	0.16	0.09	0.05			
ELDERLY	0.11	0.36	0.11	1.05	0.11	0.04			
Mean (gender)	0.11	0.05	0.10	0.06					
Total fixation duration							$F(1,19) = 0.09$, $p > 0.05$, $\eta^2 = 0.006$	$F(1,19) = 8.01$, $p < 0.05^*$, $\eta^2 = 0.334$	$F(1,19) = 0.39$, $p > 0.05$, $\eta^2 = 0.024$
YOUNGER	4.60	1.91	4.12	4.43	4.26	1.93			
ELDERLY	7.98	2.15	9.42	4.37	8.70	4.21			
Mean (gender)	6.29	3.67	6.77	4.28					

M = mean, SD = standard deviation. $F(df)$, $*p < 0.05$, $p > 0.05$.

4.1.3. Visual Attention Transitions between the Map and the Landmarks

To evaluate the participants' visual attention transitions between the map and landmark, we defined the Switches: Map<–>Landmark metric as the numbers of attention switches between the map and landmark. Figure 7 shows that males made an average of 2.5 ($SD = 1.08$) switches between the map and the landmarks, which was the same with females (M = 2.5, $SD = 1.27$) with F-test statistics of 0.00, $p > 0.05$.

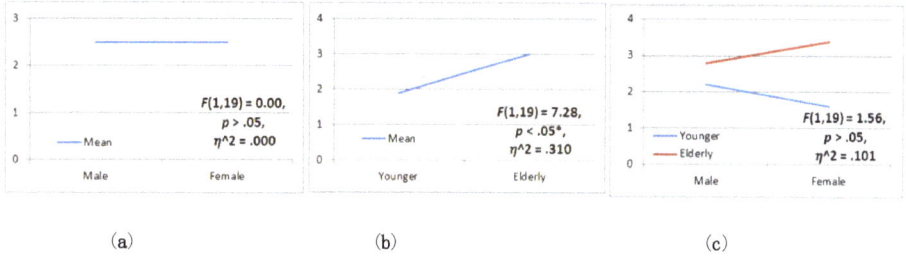

(a)   (b)   (c)

Figure 7. Visual attention transitions between map and landmark: (**a**) gender differences, (**b**) age differences, and (**c**) gender and age cross differences.

In the age groups, ANOVA results show that the age difference was significant, $F(1,19) = 7.28$, $p < 0.05$. The elderly adult group made more attention switches between the map and the landmarks ($M = 3.0$, $SD = 1.20$) than the younger adult group ($M = 1.9$, $SD = 0.74$). There was no significance between the gender and age effects on Switches: Map<–>Landmark, $F(1,19) = 1.56$, $p > 0.05$.

4.2. Task 2 (Route memorization)

We distinguished three types of AOIs: Route (blue), Landmark (brown), and Legend (yellow) (Figure 8). Route AOIs include the primary route, the start, and the end position. Store AOIs include the store symbol and the name near the route. Store AOIs and Route AOIs do not overlap with each other. However, Route AOIs include some store names such as MUSHIJIU and LALABOBO. Legend AOIs include compass and floor level icons. Fixation durations on these three types of AOIs were calculated.

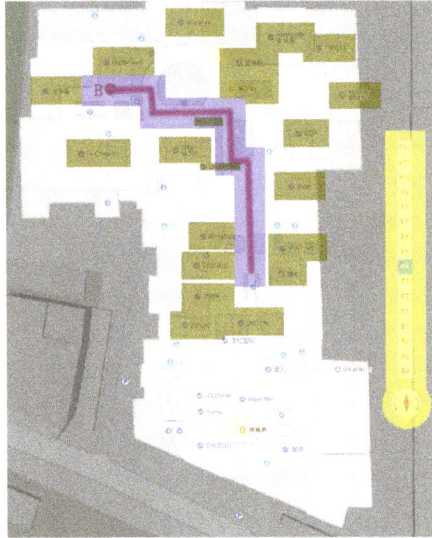

Figure 8. AOI divisions for route memorization.

Table 5 and Figure 9 show the results of fixation durations on different types of AOIs. Males spent significantly less fixation duration on Landmark ($M = 15.58$ s, $SD = 4.82$) than females ($M = 20.23$ seconds, $SD = 5.19$, $F(1, 19) = 8.17$, $p < 0.05$), less fixation duration on Legend ($M = 8.02$ seconds, $SD = 2.67$) than females ($M = 10.34$ seconds, $SD = 3.57$, $F(1, 19) = 6.31$, $p < 0.05$), but more fixation duration on Route ($M = 17.90$ seconds, $SD = 5.04$) than females ($M = 16.09$ seconds, $SD = 4.76$, $F(1, 19) = 1.22$, $p > 0.05$). In general, males spent less time on map memorization ($M = 42.21$ s, $SD = 10.35$) than females ($M = 47.46$ s, $SD = 12.36$), $F(1,19) = 2.93$, $p > 0.05$.

Differences among age groups are consistent across the three types of AOIs. Elderly adults spent more time on memorizing Landmark ($M = 21.34$ s, $SD = 5.33$), Route ($M = 20.26$ seconds, $SD = 3.65$) and Legend ($M = 11.26$ seconds, $SD = 2.59$) than younger adults (Landmark: $M = 14.47$ seconds, $SD = 2.75$, Route: $M = 13.73$ seconds, $SD = 3.60$, Legend: $M = 7.09$ seconds, $SD = 2.76$). In total, elderly adults had significantly higher fixation duration on map memorization ($M = 53.66$ seconds, $SD = 7.73$) than younger adults ($M = 36.02$ seconds, $SD = 6.53$). The ANOVA results indicate that differences between younger and elderly adults were statistically significant in these fixation durations ($p < 0.001$).

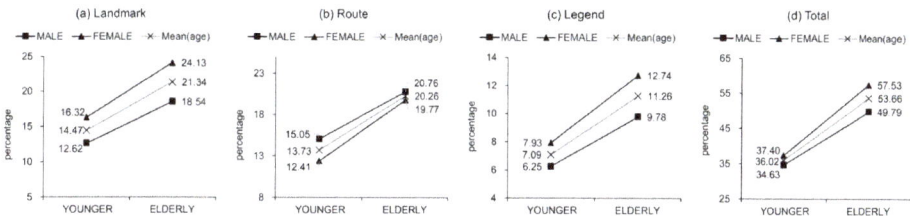

Figure 9. Results of visual attention on different types of AOIs in Task 2.

Table 5. Descriptive and inferential statistics for Task 2 (Route memorization).

Fixation duration	MALE		FEMALE		Mean (age)		Gender	Age	Gender X Age
	M	SD	M	SD	M	SD	ANOVA	ANOVA	ANOVA
Landmark									
YOUNGER	12.62	1.96	16.32	2.14	14.47	2.75	$F(1,19) = 8.17$,	$F(1,19) = 17.84$,	$F(1,19) = 14.74$,
ELDERLY	18.54	5.15	24.13	4.24	21.34	5.33	$p < 0.05*$,	$p < 0.001***$	$p < 0.001***$,
Mean (gender)	15.58	4.82	20.23	5.19			$\eta^2 = 0.338$	$\eta^2 = 0.527$	$\eta^2 = 0.512$
Route									
YOUNGER	15.05	3.58	12.41	3.46	13.73	3.60	$F(1,19) = 1.22$,	$F(1,19) = 15.81$,	$F(1,19) = 0.25$,
ELDERLY	20.76	4.90	19.77	2.30	20.26	3.65	$p > 0.05$,	$p < 0.001***$,	$p > 0.05$,
Mean (gender)	17.90	5.04	16.09	4.76			$\eta^2 = 0.071$	$\eta^2 = 0.497$	$\eta^2 = 0.015$
Legend									
YOUNGER	6.25	2.64	7.93	2.89	7.09	2.76	$F(1,19) = 6.31$,	$F(1,19) = 18.50$,	$F(1,19) = 13.45$,
ELDERLY	9.78	1.03	12.74	2.44	11.26	2.59	$p < 0.05*$,	$p < 0.001***$,	$p < 0.01**$,
Mean (gender)	8.02	2.67	10.34	3.57			$\eta^2 = 0.283$	$\eta^2 = 0.536$	$\eta^2 = 0.431$
Total									
YOUNGER	34.63	5.92	37.4	7.48	36.02	6.53	$F(1,19) = 2.93$,	$F(1,19) = 33.11$,	$F(1,19) = 15.87$,
ELDERLY	49.79	7.89	57.53	5.90	53.66	7.73	$p > 0.05$,	$p < 0.001***$,	$p < 0.01**$,
Mean (gender)	42.21	10.35	47.46	12.36			$\eta^2 = 0.155$	$\eta^2 = 0.674$	$\eta^2 = 0.378$

M = mean, SD = standard deviation. $F(df)$, *** $p < 0.001$, ** $p < 0.01$, * $p < 0.05$, $p > 0.05$.

We observed significant gender and age interaction effects on landmark (F (1, 19) = 14.74, $p < 0.001***$), legend (F (1, 19) = 13.45, $p < 0.01**$) and total fixation duration (F (1, 19) = 15.87, $p < 0.01**$) (Table 5). Based on Simple Effect Test results, age and gender differences were significant (Table 6). It could also be seen that female factors and age factors were significant in landmark and legend fixation duration.

Table 6. Simple Effects Test for Task 2 (route memorization).

			Landmark			Legend			Total		
			MD(I-J)	SE	Sig.	MD(I-J)	SE	Sig.	MD(I-J)	SE	Sig.
Gender	Age(I)	Age(J)									
female	elderly	younger	7.85	2.34	$p < 0.05*$	4.87	1.53	$p < 0.05*$	20.73	4.49	$p < 0.05*$
male	elderly	younger	6.10	2.34	$p > 0.05$	3.70	1.53	$p > 0.05$	15.12	4.49	$p > 0.05$
Age	Gender(I)	Gender(J)									
elderly	female	male	5.46	2.34	$p < 0.01**$	3.27	1.53	$p < 0.01**$	7.77	4.49	$p < 0.01**$
younger	female	male	3.71	2.34	$p < 0.05*$	2.10	1.53	$p < 0.05*$	2.17	4.49	$p < 0.01**$

MD = mean difference, SE = standard error. *: $p < .05$, **$p < .01$.

4.3. Task 3 (Route following)

4.3.1. General performance

We introduced two metrics to analyze general performance in Task 3 (route following): stop duration and error count. Definitions are shown in Table 7.

Table 7. Definitions of stop duration and error in Task 3.

Metric	Definition
stop duration	The time the participants spent to make a decision at decision points (at elevator and corner)
error count	The number of incorrect decisions the participants made at decision points (at elevator and corner)

The results of the error count at turning positions (C1 ~ C4) and elevators (E1 ~ E2) are shown in Figure 10. It is seen that participants made more errors at the end position than the starting position. They had nine errors at C4 but only two errors at C1. Females showed similar performance with males. Females made fewer errors at C3, C4, and E1 but encountered slightly more trouble at C1 and C2. The difference between the younger and elderly adults was significant. Elderly adults encountered more troubles at C1, C2, C4, E1, and E2. In addition, elderly adults especially elderly females performed the worst during wayfinding because they made errors at C1 and C2 but the others did not show any problems.

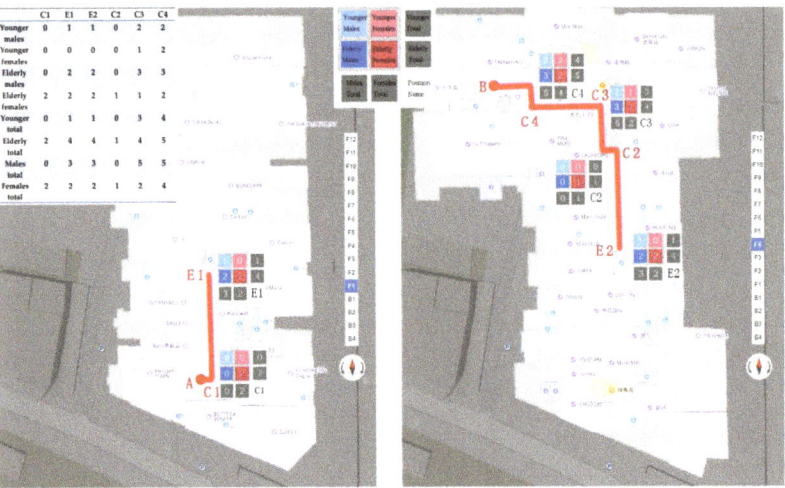

Figure 10. Error counts made by different groups (younger male, younger female, elderly male, and elderly female) at turning positions and elevator.

We further tested the differences quantitatively (Figure 11). Mean stop duration was 0.15 ($p > 0.05$) and mean error count was 0.26 ($p > 0.05$). The results revealed that a gender-related difference was not significant in the route following general performance. Males stopped for 29.89 seconds ($SD = 13.17$), and females spent 31.68 seconds ($SD = 12.85$). In addition, males had more problems at the corner position with 35.83 seconds ($SD = 6.76$) spent at corners, which is 12 seconds more than they spent at elevators ($M = 23.95$ seconds, $SD = 11.10$).

The Mean stop duration results across age groups indicated that younger adults had much better wayfinding performance than elderly adults. ANOVA results show that significant differences were shown in age-related groups. The difference in the stop duration was significant, $F(1,19) = 8.43$, $p < 0.01$. Younger adults only spent 23.86 seconds ($SD = 8.09$) in the stop duration, which is almost 15 seconds less than elderly adults ($M = 37.71$ seconds, $SD = 12.98$). However, the age-related difference was not significant in the error count, $F(1,19) = 3.88$, $p > 0.05$. Younger adults made an average of 0.9 ($SD = 0.70$) errors in corners and elderly adults made 2.0 ($SD=1.17$) errors.

For gender and age effects, there were no significant differences in the mean stop duration ($F(1,19)$ = 1.22, $p > 0.05$) and mean errors ($F(1,19)$ = 2.24, $p > 0.05$) between gender and age in the spatial orientation process (Table 8).

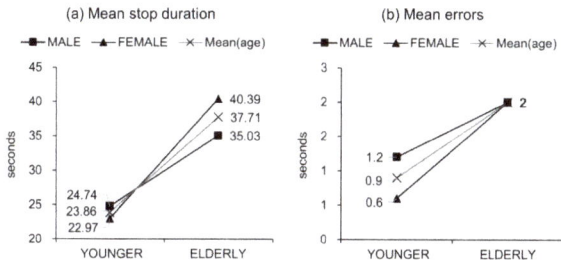

Figure 11. AOI for self-location: the red point is the area of interest.

Table 8. Descriptive and inferential statistics for Task 3 (route following).

	MALE		FEMALE		Mean(age)		Gender	Age	Gender X Age
	M	SD	M	SD	M	SD	ANOVA	ANOVA	ANOVA
General performance									
Mean stop duration							$F(1,19) = 0.15$,	$F(1,19) = 8.43$,	$F(1,19) = 1.22$,
YOUNGER	24.74	6.61	22.97	10.07	23.86	8.09	$p > 0.05$,	$p < 0.01**$,	$p > 0.05$,
ELDERLY	35.03	16.75	40.39	8.96	37.71	12.98	$\eta^2 = 0.048$	$\eta^2 = 0.493$	$\eta^2 = 0.087$
Mean (gender)	29.89	13.17	31.68	12.85					
Mean errors							$F(1,19) = 0.26$,	$F(1,19) = 3.88$,	$F(1,19) = 2.24$,
YOUNGER	1.20	0.89	0.60	0.45	0.90	0.70	$p > 0.05$,	$p > 0.05$,	$p > 0.05$,
ELDERLY	2.00	0.71	2.00	0.84	2.00	1.17	$\eta^2 = 0.020$	$\eta^2 = 0.194$	$\eta^2 = 0.036$
Mean (gender)	1.60	0.99	1.30	1.11					

M = mean, SD = standard deviation. $F(df)$, ** $p < 0.01$, $p > 0.05$.

4.3.2. Verbal Protocol

We used the verbal protocol to gain additional qualitative insight into the thoughts of the participants. All verbal reports were transcribed and translated into English. The transcripts were then segmented based on the sentence-coding protocol shown in Table 9.

Statement sentences were analyzed based on the positive and negative verbal reports. For instance, the statements were divided into S1S2 (positive statement) and S3S4 (negative statement). If the participants generated more positive sentences, they were considered more confident in their wayfinding behavior. If the participants could not express their wayfinding accurately, they were required to respond to prompts from the experimenters, which indicates that they encountered difficulty in describing their wayfinding process possibly due to a weak understanding of spatial orientation.

Table 9. Sentence classification for the verbal interaction between participants and researchers.

Statement:	Example(s)
S1: Positive statement regarding landmarks	This is the LV store near the elevator.
S2: Positive statement regarding direction	I turn left at this corner. I go west at this position.
S3: Negative statement regarding landmarks	Where is the Xian Yuxian store?
S4: Negative statement regarding direction	Should I turn left or right?
Response:	**Example(s)**
R1: Positive response regarding landmarks	Yes, I find the route by recognizing the Xian Yuxian store.
R2: Positive response regarding direction	No, I turn west at this position.
R3: Negative response regarding landmarks	Sorry, I forget the store name.
R4 Negative response regarding direction	Well, I am not sure whether to turn right or left.

The results are shown in Figure 12. We observed that males preferred to use 'left' and 'right' (S1 = 27, R1 = 20) to find their orientation rather than landmarks (S2 = 13, R2 = 10). In contrast, females preferred to use landmarks to find their routes (S2 = 22, R2 = 16) rather than direction (S1 = 14, R1 = 7). It can be assumed that females encountered similar verbal problems as males because females were asked to describe their wayfinding preference (R1 + R2 + R3 + R4 = 38) only slightly more often than males (R1 + R2 + R3 + R4 = 37). However, females had less confidence than males at decision points and females expressed 'not sure' 22 times more than males (S3 + S4 + R3 + R4).

In terms of the age factor, the wayfinding confidence difference between younger and elderly adults was significant but the wayfinding preference difference was quite small (Figure 8b). It is clear that elderly adults encountered more problems in finding their way (S3 + S4 + R3 + R4). In addition, younger adults use 'words of direction' 39 times (S1 + S3 + S5 + S7), which is only two fewer times than those who used landmarks (S2 + S4 + S6 + S8). However, the elderly group preferred to use the direction method to find their way in the experiment since they spoke 68 times about directions (S1 + S3 + S5 + S7), which is 15 times more than about landmarks (S2 + S4 + S6 + S8).

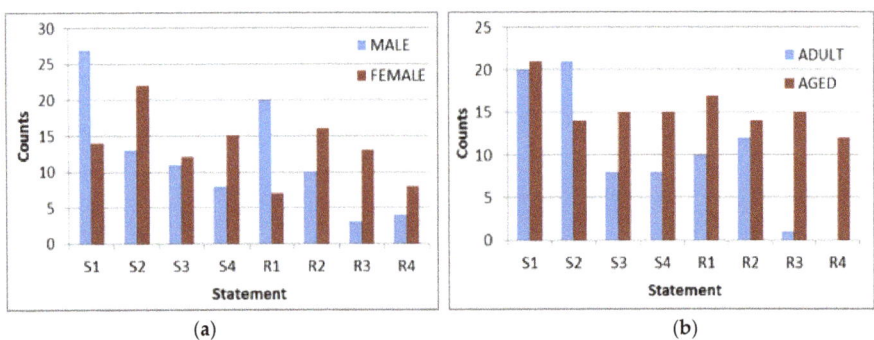

Figure 12. Retrospective verbal protocol results: (**a**) sentence counts between males and females and (**b**) age-related effects on verbal counts.

5. Discussion

In this section, we summarize experimental results and discuss findings about gender and age-related differences in indoor wayfinding.

5.1. Gender Difference

Finding 1: Males had no significant differences with females in indoor self-location, route reading, and route following. However, males paid less visual attention on landmark and legend factors than females when remembering the route.

In general, there was no significant gender difference in indoor wayfinding performance. Males and females had similar effectiveness and efficiency in self-location, route memorization, and route following (Figure 4, Figure 6, Figure 9, and Figure 11). This finding has also been reported by other researchers. For example, Coluccia, Iosue, and Brandimonte [46] found that the significant difference in wayfinding time was not directly due to gender. Harrell, Bowlby, and Hoffarth [47] reported that no gender difference was found in the use of landmarks or buildings to assist in wayfinding.

However, we have observed a difference between males and females in map reading and indoor wayfinding. Males paid significantly less attention to landmarks and legend information than females in route memorization, but they had similar total visual attention on route information (Table 5). Even though Avery [48] and Dogu [49] found that men and women searched shopping landmarks similarly, we found that females paid more visual attention to landmarks. A possible explanation for these divergent results is that females and males adopt different map reading and wayfinding strategies. Chebat and Therrien [50] reported that males tended to find their way by route and direction information, but females preferred to remember the landmarks at corners and then find the correct direction. Babin, Boles, and Griffin [51] concluded that females showed more hedonistic tendencies during wayfinding and hedonistic people were more easily distracted by stores, move more slowly, and stop more frequently. That might explain why females tend to pay more visual attention to landmarks.

5.2. Age Difference

Finding 2: Age-related differences were significant in indoor wayfinding. Younger adults generally outperformed elderly adults in wayfinding in real indoor environments.

The results indicate that younger adults performed better in indoor wayfinding than elderly adults (Table 2, Table 4, Table 5, and Table 8). Our research results clearly show significant age-related differences in self-location, route memorization, and route following in a real-world indoor environment. Such results are widely consistent with those lab-based studies in real outdoor environments [18,19]. For example, Monacelli [52] reported strong age differences in a route-learning task under real hospital conditions. Morganti and Riva [53] observed a greater age-related deficit in spatial cognitive performance.

Two factors might explain why age differences occur. First, due to decreasing spatial cognitive abilities, elderly adults encounter more map reading and wayfinding problems. Taillade, Sauzéon, and Pala [19] reported that elderly adults showed an age-related decline in spatial abilities but did not recognize these problems. Second, indoor environments that contain multiple floors and massive numbers of landmarks within small spaces increase the cognitive burden for the elderly. Adamo, Briceño, and Sindone [21] found that elderly adults might have more spatial problems under complex conditions. Thus, the complexity of the surroundings and spatial cognition decline may explain the age-related differences in indoor wayfinding.

5.3. Gender and Age Difference

Finding 3: Gender and age interactive differences were significant in self-location and route memorization. The mean differences of visual attention on self-location map reading and route memorization between males and females increased with age.

The ANOVA test results show that the interactive effects of the gender and age factors were significant in self-location and route memorization (Tables 2 and 5). Table 2 shows that the interactive effects on first AOI fixation time and map reading duration differences between adult males and females were significant. Similar results were also shown in route remembering fixation duration (Table 5). Rgw Simple Effect Test results present that elderly and younger factors had significant differences with gender factors in the self-location map reading and route memorization process (Tables 3 and 6). In addition, it is obvious that the MD (gender) in younger adults was less than the MD (gender) in elderly adults. The experimental results prove that gender and age factors should not be separated in the research of indoor map reading behavior. In addition, the result reminds designers that we should pay more attention to elderly adults.

It should also be noted that the difference between female and age factors was significant in route remembering (Table 6), but similar results were not found in the other conditions. Considering the previous finding, cartographers should pay more attentions to elderly adults especially female elderly adults in the route remembering process, which might be an important finding to develop indoor maps or navigation.

5.4. Implications to Map Design

Based on the above three findings, we can generate some implications to indoor map design. Finding 2 proves that younger adults significantly outperformed elderly adults. Thus, designers should pay more attention to methods that improve the indoor maps for elderly adults. For example, for elderly adults, cartographers should design a larger size of annotation, brighten the route, and only reserve the landmarks along the route on indoor maps. Indoor navigation systems can be designed to enlarge the size of landmark symbols, which might assist the elderly to acquire spatial knowledge efficiently. In the meantime, designers should delete task-irrelevant landmarks and increase task-relevant landmarks. In addition, Table 8 shows that elderly adults spent significant longer stop duration than younger adults at turning positions. We believe that designers should provide clear information around turning positions for the elderly.

According to Finding 3, female elderly participants spent longer fixation duration than the others in route remembering. Table 5 shows that female elderly adults paid significant longer fixation to landmark and legend factors. In order to improve the efficiency of route remembering, cartographers should decrease the complexity of landmarks and legends. For example, designers can reduce the number of landmarks and only remain essential stores at crucial positions. It might also be better for designers to brighten color or change shapes of point symbols to improve the visibility of the landmarks near the destination and the turnings, which will attract the attention of female elderly adults and assist them in remembering these crucial points.

6. Summary and Further Work

To evaluate gender-related and age-related differences in indoor wayfinding performance, this study employed eye-tracking and retrospective verbal protocol methods to analyze indoor wayfinding behaviors (self-location, route memorization, and route following). Three key findings provide insight into gender and age effects on the use of indoor maps for wayfinding in real environments. According to these findings, we have extracted several implications regarding how to improve the indoor maps' design and navigation. This study could be useful to adjust maps to aid indoor navigation in real-world environments. However, this study used a small number of participants. The participant groups were limited to studying age and gender factors. We cannot generate conclusive implications from the current experiment alone. The universal implications of indoor maps need further investigation.

Future research could include more factors (such as stress [54], culture, occupation, and spatial ability) to represent the variety of user's wayfinding behaviors of a wider variety of users in indoor environments.

Author Contributions: Conceptualization, C.W. and Y.C.; Methodology, C.W.; Formal Analysis, S.Z.; Investigation, S.Z.; Writing-Original Draft Preparation, C.W.; Writing-Review & Editing, H.L.

Funding: This research was funded by the [National Natural Science Foundations of China] grant number [41171353, 41501507] and [The National High Technology Research and Development Program of China] grant number [2012AA12A404].

Acknowledgments: The authors would like to thank all the reviewers for their helpful comments and suggestions.

Conflicts of Interest: The authors declare no conflict of interest.

References

1. Lynch, K. *The Image of the City*; M.I.T. Press: Cambridge, MA, USA, 1960; pp. 46–68.
2. Allen, G.L. Spatial abilities, cognitive maps, and wayfinding: Bases for individual differences in spatial cognition and behavior. *J. Wayfinding Behav.* **1999**, *9*, 46–80.
3. Farr, A.C.; Kleinschmidt, T.; Yarlagadda, P.; Mengersen, K. Wayfinding: A simple concept, a complex process. *J. Transp. Rev.* **2012**, *32*, 715–743. [CrossRef]
4. Liao, H.; Dong, W. An Exploratory Study Investigating Gender Effects on Using 3D Maps for Spatial Orientation in Wayfinding. *J. Int. J. Geo-Inf.* **2017**, *6*, 60. [CrossRef]
5. Gartner, G.; Huang, H.; Millonig, A.; Schmidt, M.; Ortag, F. Human-centred Mobile Pedestrian Navigation Systems. *J. Mitteilungen Osterreichischen Geogr. Ges.* **2012**, *153*, 237–250.
6. Kiefer, P.; Giannopoulos, I.; Raubal, M. Where am I? Investigating map matching during selflocalization with mobile eye tracking in an urban environment. *J. Trans. GIS* **2014**, *18*, 660–686. [CrossRef]
7. Koletsis, E.; van Elzakker, C.P.; Kraak, M.J.; Cartwright, W.; Arrowsmith, C.; Field, K. An investigation into challenges experienced when route planning, navigating and wayfinding. *J. Int. J. Cartogr.* **2017**, *3*, 4–18. [CrossRef]
8. Hund, A.M.; Padgitt, A.J. Direction giving and following in the service of wayfinding in a complex indoor environment. *J. Environ. Psychol.* **2010**, *30*, 553–564. [CrossRef]
9. Vanclooster, A.; Nico, V.D.W.; De Maeyer, P. Integrating Indoor and Outdoor Spaces for Pedestrian Navigation Guidance: A Review. *J. Trans. GIS* **2016**, *20*, 491–525. [CrossRef]
10. Lin, C.T.; Huang, T.Y.; Lin, W.J.; Chang, S.Y.; Lin, Y.H.; Ko, L.W.; Hung, D.L.; Chang, E.C. Gender differences in wayfinding in virtual environments with global or local landmarks. *J. Environ. Psychol.* **2012**, *32*, 89–96. [CrossRef]
11. Yang, Y.; Merrill, E.C. Cognitive and Personality Characteristics of Masculinity and Femininity Predict Wayfinding Competence and Strategies of Men and Women. *J. Sex Roles* **2016**, *76*, 747–758. [CrossRef]
12. Golledge, R.G. Human wayfinding and cognitive maps. In *The Colonization of Unfamiliar Landscapes*; Routledge: London, UK, 1999; pp. 5–45.
13. Meilinger, T.; Knauff, M. Ask for directions or use a map: A field experiment on spatial orientation and wayfinding in an urban environment. *J. Surv.* **2008**, *53*, 13–23. [CrossRef]
14. Montello, D.R.; Lovelace, K.L.; Golledge, R.G.; Self, C.M. Sex-Related Differences and Similarities in Geographic and Environmental Spatial Abilities. *J. Ann. Assoc. Am. Geogr.* **2015**, *89*, 515–534. [CrossRef]
15. Coluccia, E.; Louse, G. Gender differences in spatial orientation: A review. *J. Environ. Psychol.* **2004**, *24*, 329–340. [CrossRef]
16. Tlauka, M.; Brolese, A.; Pomeroy, D.; Hobbs, W. Gender differences in spatial knowledge acquired through simulated exploration of a virtual shopping centre. *J. Environ. Psychol.* **2005**, *25*, 111–118. [CrossRef]
17. Andersen, N.E.; Dahmani, L.; Konishi, K.; Bohbot, V.D. Eye tracking, strategies, and sex differences in virtual navigation. *J. Neurobiol. Learn. Mem.* **2012**, *97*, 81–89. [CrossRef] [PubMed]
18. Head, D.; Isom, M. Age effects on wayfinding and route learning skills. *J. Behav. Brain Res.* **2010**, *209*, 49–58. [CrossRef] [PubMed]
19. Taillade, M.; Sauzéon, H.; Pala, P.A.; Déjos, M.; Larrue, F.; Gross, C.; N'Kaoua, B. Age-Related Wayfinding Differences in Real Large-Scale Environments: Detrimental Motor Control Effects during Spatial Learning Are Mediated by Executive Decline? *PLoS ONE* **2013**, *8*, e67193. [CrossRef] [PubMed]
20. Taillade, M.; Sauzéon, H.; Dejos, M.; Arvind Pala, P.; Larrue, F.; Wallet, G.; Gross, C.; N'Kaoua, B. Executive and memory correlates of age-related differences in wayfinding performances using a virtual reality application. *J. Aging Neuropsychol. Cogn.* **2013**, *20*, 298–319. [CrossRef] [PubMed]
21. Adamo, D.E.; Briceño, E.M.; Sindone, J.A.; Alexander, N.B.; Moffat, S. Age differences in virtual environment and real world path integration. *J. Front. Aging Neurosci.* **2012**, *4*, 26. [CrossRef]
22. Taillade, M.; N'Kaoua, B.; Sauzéon, H. Age-Related Differences and Cognitive Correlates of Self-Reported and Direct Navigation Performance: The Effect of Real and Virtual Test Conditions Manipulation. *J. Front. Psychol.* **2016**, *6*, 2034. [CrossRef]
23. Brown, L.N.; Lahar, C.J.; Mosley, J.L. Age and Gender-Related Differences in Strategy Use for Route Information A "Map-Present" Direction-Giving Paradigm. *J. Environ. Behav.* **1998**, *30*, 123–143. [CrossRef]

24. Khanan, M.F.A. Individual differences in the tourist wayfinding decision making process. In Proceedings of the 14th International Symposium on Spatial Data Handling, Hong Kong, China, 26–28 May 2010; pp. 319–324.
25. Lawton, C.A. Individual- and gender-related differences in indoor wayfinding. *J. Environ. Behav.* **1996**, *28*, 204–219. [CrossRef]
26. Vanclooster, A.; Ooms, K.; Viaene, P.; Fack, V.; Van de Weghe, N.; De Maeyer, P. Evaluating suitability of the least risk path algorithm to support cognitive wayfinding in indoor spaces: An empirical study. *J. Appl. Geogr.* **2014**, *53*, 128–140. [CrossRef]
27. Li, H.; Giudice, N.A. The effects of 2D and 3D maps on learning virtual multi-level indoor environments. In Proceedings of the 1st ACM SIGSPATIAL International Workshop on MapInteraction, Orlando, FL, USA, 5–8 November 2013; pp. 7–12.
28. Burigat, S.; Chittaro, L.; Sioni, R. Mobile Three-Dimensional Maps for Wayfinding in Large and Complex Buildings: Empirical Comparison of First-Person versus Third-Person Perspective. *J. IEEE Trans. Hum.-Mach. Syst.* **2017**, *47*, 1029–1039. [CrossRef]
29. Trine, B.; Thorsteinn, S. Wayfinding by Means of Maps in Real-world Settings: A Critical Review. *J. Navig.* **2016**, *70*, 263–275.
30. Bedi, S.; Webb, J. Through the Students' Lens: Photographic Methods for Research in Library Spaces. *J. Evid. Based Libr. Inf. Pract.* **2017**, *12*, 15–35. [CrossRef]
31. Wang, W.; Huang, H.; Gartner, G. Considering Existing Indoor Navigational Aids in Navigation Services. In *International Conference on Spatial Information Theory*; Springer: Cham, Switzerland, 2017; pp. 179–189.
32. Mandel, L.H. Wayfinding research in library and information studies: State of the field. *J. Evid. Based Libr. Inf. Pract.* **2017**, *12*, 133–148. [CrossRef]
33. Lscher, C.; Büchner, S.J.; Meilinger, T. Adaptivity of wayfinding strategies in a multi-building ensemble: The effects of spatial structure, task requirements, and metric information. *J. Environ. Psychol.* **2009**, *29*, 208–219.
34. Zhang, H.; Ye, C. An Indoor Wayfinding System Based on Geometric Features Aided Graph SLAM for the Visually Impaired. *J. IEEE Trans. Neural Syst. Rehabil. Eng.* **2017**, *25*, 1592–1604. [CrossRef] [PubMed]
35. Kinsley, K.M.; Dan, S.; Spitler, J. GoPro as an ethnographic tool: A wayfinding study in an academic library. *J. Access Serv.* **2016**, *13*, 7–23. [CrossRef]
36. Steinke, T. Eye movement studies in cartography and related fields. *J. Cartogr.* **1987**, *24*, 197–221. [CrossRef]
37. Liao, H.; Dong, W.; Peng, C.; Liu, H. Exploring differences of visual attention in pedestrian navigation when using 2D maps and 3D geo-browsers. *J. Cartogr. Geogr. Inf. Sci.* **2017**, *44*, 474–490. [CrossRef]
38. Kiefer, P.; Straub, F.; Raubal, M. Location-Aware Mobile Eye Tracking for the Explanation of Wayfinding Behavior. In Proceedings of the AGILE'2012 International Conference on Geographic Information Science, Avignon, France, 24–27 April 2012.
39. Brügger, A.; Richter, K.; Fabrikant, S.I. Distributing Attention between Environment and Navigation System to Increase Spatial Knowledge Acquisition during Assisted Wayfinding. In *International Conference on Spatial Information Theory*; Springer: Cham, Switzerland, 2017; pp. 19–22.
40. Schrom-Feiertag, H.; Settgast, V.; Seer, S. Evaluation of indoor guidance systems using eye tracking in an immersive virtual environment. *J. Spat. Cogn. Comput.* **2016**, *17*, 163–183. [CrossRef]
41. Wechsler, D. *Wechsler Adult Intelligence Scale*; Springer: New York, NY, USA, 2013.
42. Hund, A.M.; Schmettow, M.; Noordzij, M.L. The impact of culture and recipient perspective on direction giving in the service of wayfinding. *J. Environ. Psychol.* **2012**, *32*, 327–336. [CrossRef]
43. Wenczel, F.; Hepperle, L.; StäLpnagel, R.V. Gaze behavior during incidental and intentional navigation in an outdoor environment. *J. Spat. Cogn. Comput.* **2016**, *17*, 121–142. [CrossRef]
44. Lawton, C.A.; Kallai, J. Gender Differences in Wayfinding Strategies and Anxiety about Wayfinding: A Cross-Cultural Comparison. *Sex Roles* **2002**, *47*, 389–401. [CrossRef]
45. Coulombe, D. Two-way ANOVA with and without repeated measurements, tests of simple main effects, and multiple comparisons for microcomputers. *J. Behav. Res. Methods Instrum. Comput.* **1984**, *16*, 397–398. [CrossRef]
46. Coluccia, E.; Iosue, G.; Brandimonte, M.A. The relationship between map drawing and spatial orientation abilities: A study of gender differences. *J. Environ. Psychol.* **2007**, *27*, 135–144. [CrossRef]

47. Harrel, W.A.; Bowlby, J.W.; Hall-Hoffarth, D.H. Directing wayfinders with maps: The effects of gender, age, route complexity, and familiarity with the environment. *J. Environ. Psychol.* **2000**, *140*, 169–179. [CrossRef]
48. Avery, R.J. Determinants of search for nondurable goods: An empirical assessment of the economics of information theory. *J. Consum. Aff.* **1996**, *30*, 390–421. [CrossRef]
49. Dogu, U.; Erkip, F. Spatial factors affecting wayfinding and orientation: A case study in a shopping mall. *J. Environ. Behav.* **2000**, *32*, 731–755. [CrossRef]
50. Chebat, J.C.; Gélinas-Chebat, C.; Therrien, K. Gender-related wayfinding time of mall shoppers. *J. Bus. Res.* **2008**, *61*, 1076–1082. [CrossRef]
51. Babin, B.J.; Boles, J.S.; Griffin, M. The Moderating Role of Service Environment on the Customer Share → Customer Commitment Relationship. In *New Meanings for Marketing in a New Millennium*; Springer: Cham, Switzerland, 2015; pp. 266–271.
52. Monacelli, A.M.; Cushman, L.A.; Kavcic, V.; Duffy, C.J. Spatial disorientation in Alzheimer's disease the remembrance of things passed. *Neurology* **2003**, *61*, 1491–1497. [CrossRef] [PubMed]
53. Morganti, F.; Riva, G. Virtual reality as allocentric/egocentric technology for the assessment of cognitive decline in the elderly. *J. Stud. Health Technol. Inform.* **2014**, *196*, 278–284.
54. Credé, S.; Fabrikant, S.I.; Thrash, T.; Hölsche, C. Do Skyscrapers Facilitate Spatial Learning Under Stress? On the Cognitive Processing of Global Landmarks. In *International Conference on Spatial Information Theory*; Springer: Cham, Switzerland, 2017; pp. 27–29.

© 2018 by the authors. Licensee MDPI, Basel, Switzerland. This article is an open access article distributed under the terms and conditions of the Creative Commons Attribution (CC BY) license (http://creativecommons.org/licenses/by/4.0/).

International Journal of
Geo-Information

Article

Collaborative Immersive Virtual Environments for Education in Geography

Čeněk Šašinka [1], Zdeněk Stachoň [2,*], Michal Sedlák [3,*], Jiří Chmelík [4,*], Lukáš Herman [2], Petr Kubíček [2], Alžběta Šašinková [1,5], Milan Doležal [4], Hynek Tejkl [3], Tomáš Urbánek [3], Hana Svatoňová [6], Pavel Ugwitz [2,7] and Vojtěch Juřík [3,7]

[1] Division of Information and Library Studies, Faculty of Arts, Masaryk University, 60200 Brno, Czech Republic; cenek.sasinka@mail.muni.cz (Č.Š.); st.betty@mail.muni.cz (A.Š.)
[2] Department of Geography, Faculty of Science, Masaryk University, 61137 Brno, Czech Republic; herman.lu@mail.muni.cz (L.H.); kubicek@geogr.muni.cz (P.K.); 172577@mail.muni.cz (P.U.)
[3] Department of Psychology, Faculty of Arts, Masaryk University, 60200 Brno, Czech Republic; 449327@mail.muni.cz (H.T.); tour@mail.muni.cz (T.U.); jurik.vojtech@mail.muni.cz (V.J.)
[4] Department of Visual Computing, Faculty of Informatics, Masaryk University, 60200 Brno, Czech Republic; legacycz@mail.muni.cz
[5] Department of Psychology, Faculty of Social Studies, Masaryk University, 60200 Brno, Czech Republic
[6] Department of Geography, Faculty of Education, Masaryk University, 60300 Brno, Czech Republic; svatonova@mail.muni.cz
[7] HUME Lab, Faculty of Arts, Masaryk University, 60200 Brno, Czech Republic
* Correspondence: zstachon@geogr.muni.cz (Z.S.); m.sedlak@mail.muni.cz (M.S.); jchmelik@mail.muni.cz (J.C.); Tel.: +420-549-494-925 (Z.S.); +420-549-494-382 (J.C.)

Received: 5 November 2018; Accepted: 18 December 2018; Published: 23 December 2018

Abstract: Immersive virtual reality (iVR) devices are rapidly becoming an important part of our lives and forming a new way for people to interact with computers and each other. The impact and consequences of this innovative technology have not yet been satisfactory explored. This empirical study investigated the cognitive and social aspects of collaboration in a shared, immersive virtual reality. A unique application for implementing a collaborative immersive virtual environment (CIVE) was developed by our interdisciplinary team as a software solution for educational purposes, with two scenarios for learning about hypsography, i.e., explanations of contour line principles. Both scenarios allow switching between a usual 2D contour map and a 3D model of the corresponding terrain to increase the intelligibility and clarity of the educational content. Gamification principles were also applied to both scenarios to augment user engagement during the completion of tasks. A qualitative research approach was adopted to obtain a deep insight into the lived experience of users in a CIVE. It was thus possible to form a deep understanding of very new subject matter. Twelve pairs of participants were observed during their CIVE experience and then interviewed either in a semistructured interview or a focus group. Data from these three research techniques were analyzed using interpretative phenomenological analysis, which is research method for studying individual experience. Four superordinate themes—with detailed descriptions of experiences shared by numerous participants—emerged as results from the analysis; we called these (1) Appreciation for having a collaborator, (2) The Surprising "Fun with Maps", (3) Communication as a challenge, and (4) Cognition in two realities. The findings of the study indicate the importance of the social dimension during education in a virtual environment and the effectiveness of dynamic and interactive 3D visualization.

Keywords: immersive virtual reality; collaborative immersive virtual environment; immersion; sense of presence; telepresence; Head-mounted display; cyberpsychology; human–computer interaction; collaborative learning; hypsography; contour lines; map literacy

1. Introduction

Recent rapid and continuous development of immersive VR technology has opened the possibility for a wide range of applications. Decreasing prices and easy accessibility are factors helping to distribute these devices to different institutions as well as regular households. Immersive VR finds a purpose in many fields, for example, in psychotherapy and diagnostics [1–4], cognitive training [5,6], relaxation [7,8], rehabilitation [9,10], medicine [11,12], training in the industry [13–15], tourism and cultural heritage [16–18], journalism [19], and sport [20,21]. The rich potential of immersive virtual reality is also utilized in areas that use geographical data, for example, evacuation planning [22,23], geospatial data exploration and analysis [24–27], navigation in urban areas [28,29], visualization of spatial data quality [30], and urban planning [31].

Immersive virtual reality is also significantly employed as an educational tool in many areas. We can find its educational application in domains such as engineering [32,33], biology [34,35], foreign languages [36], geometry [37], emergency management [38], physics [39], design [40], geography and earth sciences in general [41–45], and in other more singular domains such as martial arts [46] and communication skills training for individuals with autism [47]. Virtual environments including VR have a long tradition in geographical research and education [48–51], but until recently, user experiences have only been rarely reported. Several recent studies analyzed the potential benefits of immersive technologies for education in geography and task solving. Philips et al. [52] examined the usage of immersive 3D geovisualization and its usefulness in a research-based learning module (flood risk assessment). The findings of a qualitative student survey showed a range of benefits (improved orientation in the study area, higher interactivity with the data, and enhanced motivation through immersive 3D geovisualization) and suggested that an immersive 3D visualization can increase learning effectiveness in higher education. Focusing specifically on hypsography education using modern technology, Carrera et al. [53] studied the possibilities of Augmented Reality technology (AR). They experimented with 63 students and tested the usability of AR to interpret relief (maximum slope, visibility between points, contour interval, and altitude interpretation). Usability was further assessed in terms of efficiency (time to accomplish the task), effectiveness (number of mistakes) and motivation (subjective satisfaction). The results of the study confirmed the enhanced usability of an AR environment for specific tasks dealing with questions of interpreting relief. None of the aforementioned studies combined both VR and a collaborative environment.

Merchant et al. [54] distinguish three types of instruction based on virtual reality technology: simulation, games, and virtual worlds. They conducted a meta-analysis of available empirical studies using desktop-based virtual reality of all three mentioned types of educational approaches. They found that games provided the highest learning outcome gain. They defined the important attributes of educational games, also called serious games [55]. Such games should provide players with sense of autonomy, identity, and interactivity [56] and enable them to test hypotheses, strategize their moves, and solve problems [57].

Collaborative learning is a trend in modern pedagogy for improving the quality of educational outcomes and processes [58–60]. It allows two or more users to interact and solve tasks together—with a critical approach towards the overly ambiguous definitions often used— and may be defined as a situation which Dillenbourg [61] (p. 7) described as "particular forms of interaction among people are expected to occur, which would trigger learning mechanisms." Dillenbourg himself noted that the main concern of learning process designers was to find ways of raising the likelihood that certain types of interaction would occur. What we expected when designing our collaborative immersive virtual environment (CIVE) application was that students would use conversation to continually build, monitor, and repair a joint problem solution, as depicted by Dillenbourg [61]. Collaborative learning principles in college education of technical disciplines were introduced for example by Gokhale [62]. He evaluated the advantages of collaboration in a team of college students and confirmed a positive feedback of collaboration for analysis and synthesis compering to the traditional individual training. Another interesting aspect of collaboration within the VR is a distant cooperation of specialists from different disciplines solving complex problems like geohazards (tsunamis, landslides, and floods) [63,64]. Collaborative learning principles applied in college education for technical disciplines were introduced, for example, by Gokhale [62]. He evaluated the advantages of collaboration in a team of college students and confirmed the positive feedback of collaboration for analysis and synthesis compared to traditional individual training. Another interesting aspect of collaboration in VR is the remote cooperation of specialists from other disciplines engaged in solving complex problems such as geohazards (tsunamis, landslides, and floods) [63,64].

Computer-supported collaborative learning was introduced in the early 1980s as an overarching framework for various attempts to design a "technologically sophisticated collaborative learning environment designed according to cognitive principles" that "could provide advanced support for a distributed process of inquiry, facilitate advancement of a learning community's knowledge as well as transform participants' epistemic states through a socially distributed process of inquiry" [65] (p. 4). Jackson and Fagan [66] conducted a qualitative study where learning processes were explored by comparing individual users, two peer users, and student-expert modes. They used an immersive virtual environment called Global Change World, which is used to educate about concepts concerning global climate change. Other instances of collaborative learning using immersive virtual reality can be found in, for example, the domain of martial arts [67], geometry education [68], and training power system operators [69]. Innovative technologies for collaborative immersive virtual reality may be able to create a shift in the educational paradigm. Siemens [70] has challenged the traditional learning theories through his "connectivism" conception and emphasized that people in the digital age are no longer isolated individuals but located in a network where they continuously interact with human and nonhuman systems. Learning should be considered a lifelong net-building activity. Horvath [71] presents a technological solution in the form of a learning environment enabling collaboration in 3D virtual reality to teach the concept of the memristor.

The main advantage of using immersive virtual reality for educational purposes is overcoming the boundaries of a specific place and time and having a virtual experimental space [72]. This offers possibilities which are barely achievable or not possible to build in a classic classroom. Our geography learning CIVE application offers a high level of interactivity for the user, which was achieved through iterative testing and development. We also intentionally used gamification principles when creating instructional tasks in order to facilitate the learning process. Our solution incorporates immersive virtual reality, real-time social collaboration, and gamification principles. We chose hypsography as an educational topic, as it is one of the most insufficiently understood areas by our university students (according to the results of the Faculty of Science entrance exams: error rate was 86% in 2016 and 73% in 2017). The objective of this study was to describe the cognitive and social tendencies of participants during collaboration on geography learning tasks by applying the interpretative phenomenological analysis methodology.

2. Methods

2.1. Materials and Technology

This study utilized a geography education CIVE application developed by our interdisciplinary team. It makes use of the Unity cross-platform game engine version 2017.3, which facilitates data loading, real-time rendering, and communication with VR equipment. The CIVE application was built in a virtual environment described by Doležal, Chmelík & Liarokapis [73]. It is used in combination with SteamVR for the proper functionality of VR equipment. Authentic geospatial data were implemented as stimuli in the application. Digital terrain models (DTMs) were used as the main input data. A fifth-generation digital terrain model (DTM 5G) created by airborne laser scanning was acquired from the Czech Office for Surveying, Mapping and Cadastre. DTMs in the application represent various parts of the Czech Republic with a similar relief. Data were transformed by doubling the vertical values to accentuate the relatively small variation in landscape altitude. DTMs were supplemented by contour lines also generated from the DTM data as well as orthophoto images provided from a WMS (Web Map Service).

The application creates a shared virtual room for multiple users. Even though users are physically located in separate objective reality rooms, the VR headset lets them share a virtual room to collaborate on a given task. Physical movements in the objective reality room are tracked and transferred to the virtual room, which means users can walk around the room and examine geospatial material from all sides, angles and distances. In the virtual room, each participant is displayed as an avatar with virtual representations of controllers he or she is holding in objective reality (Figure 1). Controllers are used to manipulate the virtual environment and provide a laser pointer for communication. Users can also talk to each other via standard audio recording and reproduction devices. Objects added to the scene, such as houses and dams, are visualized abstractly and simply. It is considered a suitable method for highlighting task relevant objects [74].

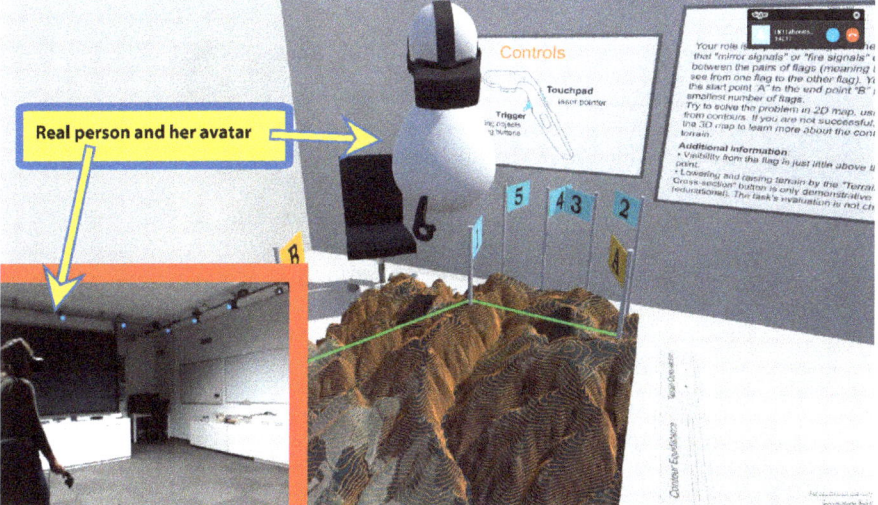

Figure 1. Objective reality (left corner) and virtual room.

The application includes two geospatial tasks. For each task, a different workplace in the room is offered. The room has a table with a map for the first task and a large map on the floor for the second task. Both geospatial tasks in the application require the user to examine contour lines on a 2D map to determine the shape of the terrain in order to find the correct solution.

The default visualization in both tasks is a 2D map. If the user cannot solve the task correctly on a 2D map, they can use various educational tools to help examine and manipulate the map. The application provides a virtual control panel (Figure 2) next to the map in the CIVE. One of the main advantages is the possibility to switch the map from 2D to 3D at any time. The map can also be switched between a white contour map and an orthophoto contour map. Contour line equidistance can be customized using a slider. Finally, when the user wants to verify their solution, they can use the Evaluate button.

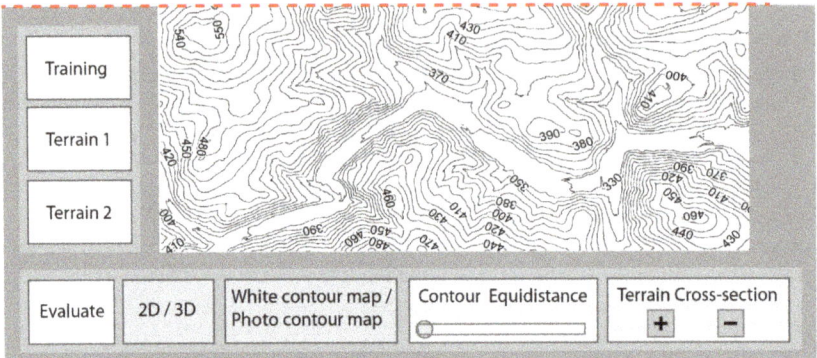

Figure 2. Virtual control panel for model manipulation.

2.2. Instructional Tasks in a CIVE Environment

For purposes of this research, two tasks were designed: Task 1—Mirror Signals and Task 2—Flooded Valley. In case of the Mirror Signals task, a map was presented to participants, with two fixed flags marking the start point (flag A) and the end point (flag B). Next to the map were five more available flags numbered 1, 2, 3, 4, and 5, which could be picked up and placed onto the map (see Figure 3). The task was to connect start point A with end point B using these additional flags in a way that mirror signals (or fire signals) could be transmitted between neighboring flags only with direct visibility. This means that the view to flag 1 from flag A, flag 2 from flag 1, and so on had to be unobstructed until an unobstructed view to flag B was obtained. The goal was to use the least number of flags possible to link the start point with the end point (see Supplement for Video S1). In the first task, the 3D model of the terrain can be dissected into individual layers and a cross-section of the terrain can be viewed.

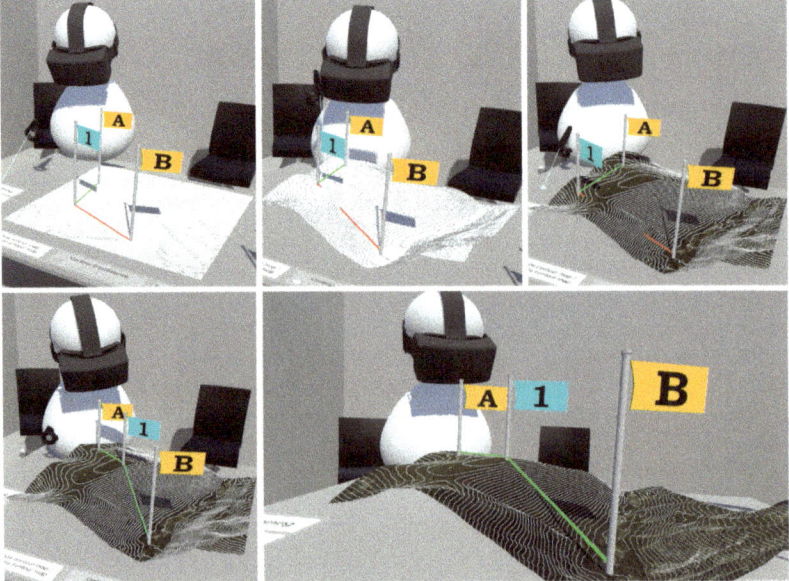

Figure 3. Incorrect (**upper**) and correct (**lower**) answers for the mirror signals task in the collaborative immersive virtual environment (CIVE).

As in Task 2—Flooded Valley, a 2D map was presented to the participants that included houses (orange rectangles) in a recognizable valley surrounded by mountain ranges and a dam (red line) (Figure 4). Just as in the previous task, five flags numbered 1, 2, 3, 4, and 5 were next to the map and could be picked up and placed onto the map. The scenario and task were as follows. *A new dam has been built to transform a valley with houses into a water reservoir. The water in the valley will gradually rise and flood the houses one by one. Use flags with numbers to mark the order in which the houses will be flooded.* After submitting the solution, the participants could watch the rising water gradually flood the houses (see Supplement for Video S2). The water level can be manipulated by user too, which lets the user gradually flood the terrain to see water flooding one contour line after another.

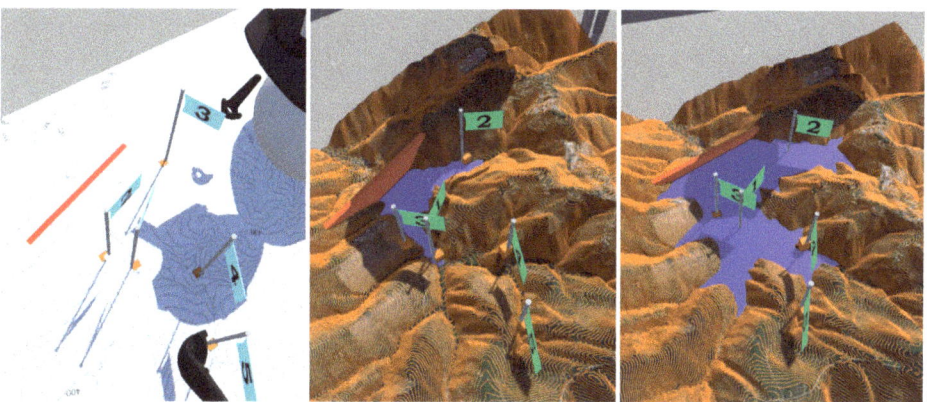

Figure 4. Flooded valley educational task in the CIVE. **Left**—flags with numbers are placed onto the 2D contour line map, **middle**—water level starts rising in the 3D visualization, and **right**—3D visualized dam is completely flooded.

2.3. Research Approach

To examine the user experience in our geography learning CIVE application, an experiential qualitative approach of Interpretative Phenomenological Analysis (IPA) was applied. This approach explores the lived experience of a person and the meaning he or she attributes to it while exposed to a specific phenomenon, for example, a short-term event or a long-term process. Its aim is to create an in-depth description of a person's lived experience during exposure to a particular phenomenon.

IPA is a frequently used strategy for research topics in weakly examined areas where the background theory has not yet been sufficiently developed. It is flexible in dealing with unexpected data that occur during research. It is therefore an ideal tool for gaining insight into and understanding the innovative use of a CIVE for geography learning or learning in general [75]. A research question in IPA is open, and although IPA is not a theory-driven approach, literature usually contributes to formulating a research question [76], as was also the case in our study. IPA does not test hypotheses and attempts to avoid creating preconditions before research. It is an inductive approach which is rather "bottom-up" than "top-down" [77].

The number of participants in IPA research depends on the richness and saturation of individual cases. Participants are experts on their own experiences and can offer the researcher an understanding of their ideas, associations, and feelings. The recommended upper limit of participants is ten [78]. Creating a research sample is based on purposive sampling and participants are selected according to relevance criteria for the research question.

Data collection in our IPA study implemented triangulation [79,80] from three research techniques (Figure 5). Using three different and complementary research techniques for data collection makes it possible to harvest the strongest aspects of all the techniques and mutually compensate their weak spots.

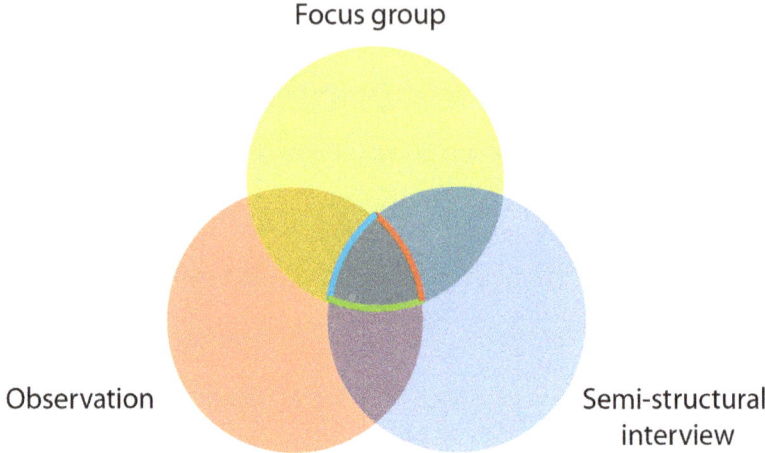

Figure 5. Triangulation of research techniques for data collection.

Half of the participants involved in the study were interviewed in pairs in a semistructured interview. The researcher sets up the key topics before interviewing, such as learning experience, gained understanding of the learning topic, and means and effectiveness of communication with a collaborator. The advantage of an individual or dyadic interview is a controlled, detailed, and deep exploration of an individual's unique experience. The other half of participants was interviewed in a focus group. As a research technique, the focus group minimizes the influence of the researcher and any preconceptions which could direct or distort the participants' statements. The researcher moderates a discussion and gives participants free space to share their individual experiences. However, some important topics can be omitted by participants, which is the most significant disadvantage of the focus group technique and the reason for our choice to use semistructured interviews to compensate for this potential weakness. Nevertheless, the key advantage of both techniques mentioned is that they bring new topics to light.

Subjectivity of the acquired data also poses a challenge. To overcome the potential risk of low validity, we conducted observations. All participants were observed and video recorded during their experience of the CIVE. We monitored voice communication, movement in objective reality and the avatars in virtual reality as tasks were completed. This data provides researchers not only with objective complementary information to the subjective reports, but also captures reactions and behavior performed unconsciously by the participants.

2.4. Research Environment and Equipment

The study took place at Masaryk University in Brno, Czech Republic, in two separate rooms. Each room was equipped with a computer (Intel® Core™ i5-6500 processor, Nvidia GeForce GTX 1080 graphics card, 16 GB RAM) connected to an HTC Vive headset (1080 × 1200 px resolution for each eye, 90 Hz refresh rate), sensors, and a controller. A participant and a researcher were present in each room. The rooms offered enough space for participants to move around and were sound insulated from the outside environment.

2.5. Participants

To design and structure the interview questions, one pair of participants was interviewed in the preparation phase. It was an in-depth phenomenological interview with a pair of "experienced" VR users conducted after collaboration in the CIVE application. Researchers themselves were involved as preparation phase participants to gain personal experience with the CIVE and educational tasks. The initial analysis resulted in a few changes to the research procedure, task setup, and virtual control panel being made. The interview with preparation phase participants also focused on their overall experience in the CIVE. Based on the information acquired, a semistructured interview schedule was created for interviewing research participants.

Research participants were recruited from the pool of volunteer students and academic teachers from the Faculty of Arts. Two exclusion criteria were applied. The first exclusion criterion was previous formal training in cartography. The second exclusion criterion was the occurrence of cybersickness in previous experiences with virtual reality or during this study. Participants were asked to report any cybersickness and were briefed on options to end participation at any moment if required.

The final research sample consisted of 12 participants who collaborated on geospatial tasks in the CIVE application in pairs. The pairs were established randomly. Seven participants were women and five were men. The mean age of the participants was 27.58 years, the minimum age was 22, and the maximum was 43. None of the participants had undergone specific GIS user training and none were significantly experienced VR users (including, for example, VR gaming).

2.6. Procedure

Participants who volunteered to this study underwent a procedure consisting of five steps: 1. Informed consent and collection of demographic data; 2. VR manipulation training; 3. Research procedure instruction and contour lines principle explanation; 4. Collaboration in the CIVE (Figure 6); and 5. Inquiry. With a pair of participants, the procedure varied from one to two hours.

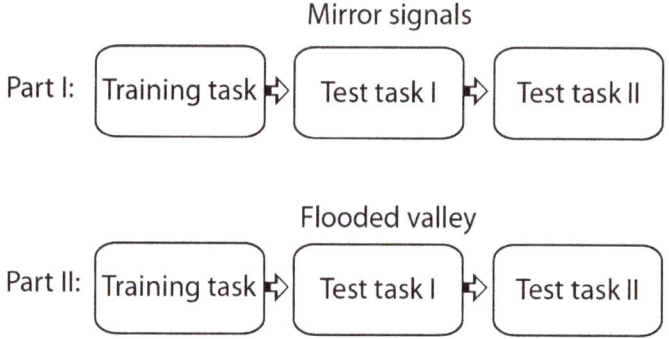

Figure 6. Step 4: collaboration in the CIVE—research tasks administration in detail.

2.7. Analysis

We employed specific idiographic case study data analysis in the IPA and the variation for multiple cases (respectively, multiple participants) as described in Smith et al. [78,81,82]. This analysis focused mainly on the shared experience (common characteristics of experience) of participants, but also mentioned significant and distinct experiences [77]. An analysis is slowly built-up by reading individual cases and creating statements about the whole group of participants. The analytic process is cyclic (iterative). The themes are reconsidered and rebuilt many times [78]. The results are transparent because they are evidenced by data examples (quotations). The results are structured according to theme. As shown in Figure 7, the analytic process cycle is as follows.

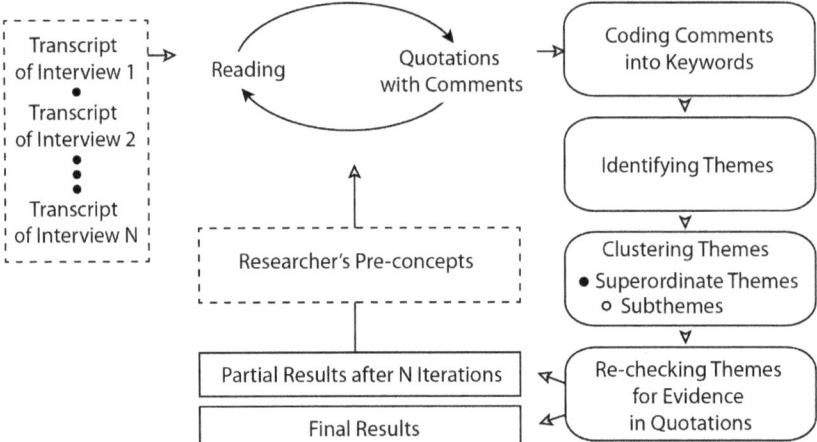

Figure 7. Scheme of the interpretative phenomenological analysis.

After transcribing the first interview, its content was read by a researcher repeatedly and significant quotations were marked and annotated (comments included preliminary interpretations and ideas from the researchers). This phase was repeated several times and the comments were then coded into keywords from which important themes were identified. These themes were then structured into a list of superordinate themes and subordinate themes belonging to each superordinate theme. Next, the themes were rechecked for evidence in verbatim excerpts (participant quotations), after which the analysis could proceed to another participant using the preliminary concepts gained from the previous interview as a framework for analysis of the next interview (Figure 7). Each participant's interview analysis was thus thoroughly considered when the next interview was analyzed, and the final list of themes applying to all participants (as described below) was based on in-depth analysis of all interviews.

3. Results

Four superordinate themes emerged from the analysis. Under these superordinate themes, several subthemes were identified, all of which are introduced in detail in the text below. The themes are well illustrated by verbatim excerpts from the data corpus, which are included in the tables. The main structure follows the most relevant topics: collaboration, learning, map literacy, communication, and cognition.

3.1. Appreciation for Having a Collaborator

The first superordinate theme relates to the thoughts and feelings of the participants towards their collaborative partners and is characterized by the appreciation of having a collaborator to solve the tasks. The collaborator motivated them and provided the opportunity to consult on the solution.

This superordinate theme includes two subthemes which we called 'Lost without a collaborator' and 'Verification and consensus with a collaborator' and are also described below.

3.1.1. Lost without a Collaborator

A key aspect prevalent throughout the accounts of collaboration was that the participants would have felt lost without a collaborator. They expressed doubt as to whether they would be able to solve the task individually. Collaboration helped them solve the tasks. They were very happy they could talk to their collaborator. Participants talked a lot, which made it easier for them to understand the task. They believed that they would have been staring at the task for a long time if they had not been working with a collaborator and would have felt uncertain and stagnated. Participants estimated that a collaborative solution was more effective than solving the task individually and did not believe that independent work on this task would have had any benefit (Table 1).

Table 1. Verbatim excerpts of statements by participants: Lost without a collaborator.

P13	"I wouldn't have managed it myself, so, like, I don't even have experience with it, so I was really glad that there was someone with me who would say to me: 'Yeah, this . . . '"
P14	"I was quite pleased to hear the other person's opinion. If I had done it like alone, it might have been a bit sad (. . .) would've had to think about whether it was correct, whether I'd made the right decision. But this way, when I had you and you helped me with it . . . "
P09	"We were looking at it together and solved it together, because we talked a lot the whole time, so . . . it seemed more, like, understandable to me."
	"It helped me a lot to have a collaborator, because I would have stared at it for a very long time and would have been very uncertain, because I was wandering a little in it, so it helped me a lot when the collaborator said: 'Let's just solve it in one minute and go to the next one' . . . and that was just great, because we just needed to try it and we tried it."
P12	"This way, it was even more fun and faster." "This interaction is always as if time always flies faster. If I had been there alone, I would have looked around more."
	"If I had been there alone, I would've looked half an hour somewhere else where something else was, but because there were two of us, I focused more on the task, because you always pulled me back to it."

3.1.2. Verification and Consensus with the Collaborator

Participants described that as they made decisions about solutions to the task, they usually consulted their collaborator to verify the answer before submitting it. They sought consensus on the right solution together. Participants discussed their viewpoints and the specifics of a particular task which could influence the answer. They talked to the collaborator about which strategy or key they should use to solve the task. The usual modus operandi among the pairs of participants was to talk about a strategy for the solution, reach an agreement on the correct answer and then submit it. They were therefore much more confident when submitting the answer and felt better about it. It also helped them to inspire each other. When anyone in the dyad discovered a useful strategy, they shared it and both then used it. Solving the task with a collaborator was reported as more effective. Participants usually discussed and decided on a solution together (Table 2).

Table 2. Verbatim excerpts of statements by participants: Verification and consensus with the collaborator.

P04	"I consider collaboration as good, because it verifies that I thought about something. I asked the collaborator whether he saw it the same way, and he said that he did, and in that case we submitted it."
P03	"We just agreed on how to do it." "It seemed to me as less ambiguous and so we found some . . . consensus about the right solution, and whether we saw something special about that case."
P09	"We discussed the task, searched the key which we would establish as a solving strategy, and using laser pointers, showed each other the things we were currently talking about."
	"We always talked nicely about it, to both agree on it before we completely submitted it."
P11	"If the collaborator was thinking the same thing I was, then it was easier to submit the answer, but individually I would maybe have thought about it more or . . . but I think it also helped me to understand it, because both of us found something relevant and then we both used it further, so we were enriching each other."
P12	"I think that thanks to the fact that we evaluated it little by little, the process was more efficient than it would have been if I had been there alone, then I would either think about it more or have made more mistakes."

3.2. The Surprising "Fun with Maps"

The second superordinate theme relates to the reported level of excitement the participants felt while working on geospatial tasks in the CIVE application, although most participants verbalized that they usually did not enjoy working with maps and considered them boring. Moreover, working in CIVE also enhanced the educational effect.

This superordinate theme includes the two subthemes. Finally, seeing what contour lines represent in reality and learning a skill to work with maps.

3.2.1. Finally Seeing What Contour Lines Represent in Reality

Many participants explained that thanks to being able to switch the 2D map to the 3D model of the terrain, which they could examine and walk around freely, an association developed in their minds between what a contour line looked like on paper and what it represented. Virtual reality helped them solve the task and see the correct answer more clearly. They found it helpful to use educational tools for visualization in 3D, for example, raising the terrain's water level to see how contour lines were flooded one by one. All of this helped them learn about contour lines and create associations between 2D maps and real 3D terrain (Table 3).

Table 3. Verbatim excerpts of statements by participants: Finally seeing what contour lines represent in reality.

P03	"On one hand it was great, because now you know where the contours are and what they look like and stuff, and then the virtual reality is turned on and then it (the 3D model) emerged, which I think is great."
P09	"It really was helpful and I could see it in that more clearly … It was like it allowed me to concentrate really well on the task."
P12	"And I think it really helped us to gain insight, so in the next task our imagination was better, that we could imagine it better, and that what we created is some model of how those contours look like in reality."
P11	"Yes, I think it helped even in understanding what contours actually are, when the person then really sees it as the real differences in height, that it's not just lines."
P14	"In fact, normally a person can't see it like this, as in that virtual reality."
	"With that flooding, certainly, like flooding, imagining that water, as it rises. When we evaluated it, it was then easier to shift it and see how the water would rise than if I had to imagine it on the table."
	"In fact, this can be utilized in many ways, even, like, only in education when a person imagines how it looks in reality. So this was great."

3.2.2. Learning a Skill to Work with Maps

An additional and clearly identifiable subtheme which emerged from the analysis relates to the new skill participants learned for working with maps. Participants explained that they had acquired a better understanding of contour lines and that if they came across similar tasks in the future, they would be able to solve it faster. Our educational application was seen as a good learning and training tool for improving map orientation skill and decreasing the time it occupied. For some participants, maps were an alien territory, but with our CIVE application, their map orientation skills improved. Their map reading speed increased and it was now easier for them to imagine terrain (Table 4).

Table 4. Verbatim excerpts of statements by participants: Learning a skill to work with maps.

P04	(if they had to solve a similar task in the future) "Well, certainly it would be better. On that level, we wouldn't be looking at it for five minutes and ... (participant laughs) ... and wouldn't be trying to understand contours."
P11	(if they had to solve a similar task in the future) "Like, I would probably be pretty much orientated in it ... such good training."
P03	"We learned to read contours much better, perceive them and search for them even in that not completely biblical environment, because neither of us is a geographer and we weren't used to using contours every day, and that ability to orientate gradually improved."
P04	"We are certainly a little, or at least I am, someone who doesn't work very often with contours. I have oriented myself in that environment, so now I'm on ... now it would take me less time to recognize, where the hills and valleys are."
	"I actually didn't see that terrain at all, so I think that actually for a long time both of us only looked at it." "Later we were faster reading the map."
P13	"Much better, I can imagine it better as, like ... now I can imagine it better."

3.3. Communication as a Challenge

The third superordinate theme relates to the effort participants made to communicate their thoughts and feelings to the collaborator. Participants described that they had to concentrate more on facilitating communication by the means they had available in the virtual environment.

It includes three subthemes: Absence of avatar faces and invisibility of emotions, limited gestures via controllers, and having an intangible body.

3.3.1. Absence of Avatar Faces and Invisibility of Emotions

Many participants felt they had limited options when it came to communicating emotions to their collaborator. One of the first things they noticed was that avatars had no faces. Some of the participants looked at their collaborator's avatar when they talked to them, and some did not. Most of the participants considered faces as important and missed them in the virtual reality environment for conveying emotion. Besides, participants considered it important to see where their collaborator was looking. This was possible in our CIVE application, but they were not surprised at being unable to look their collaborator in the eyes, as they had expected it this way. Some of the participants wondered whether it would be strange or disturbing if their collaborator's avatar had some representation of a face, as there could be discrepancies between what the person was trying to communicate and the emotions the artificial face managed to convey (Table 5).

Table 5. Verbatim excerpts of statements by participants: Absence of avatar faces and invisibility of emotions.

P10	(collaborator having no face) "It seemed terribly comic to me, like, when we talked to each other—that alone made me laugh for a long time."
P12	"Yes, I had to adjust my ways a little in communicating, for example, gestures and ... Basically, we didn't even see each other's facial expressions, and facial expressions are also quite important, so I didn't see what facial expressions she had ... when I heard her laughing, I heard that, but when you can't see the other person's eyes, it's that different."
P04	"Sometimes I missed those, like, emotions there, that I was, like, smiling (participant laughs) ... and there was no way of passing it over and then I always realized that I'm smiling in an empty room."
P03	"I considered it important to be able to see where that person was looking or what he was calculating or something."
P06	(collaborator having no face) "I probably expected it. I've seen it before." "Natural, it probably wasn't ... (participant laughs) ... but it was probably not surprising."

Table 5. *Cont.*

P10	"I wonder if it would have been stranger if it had simulated a person even more and then there was some discrepancy, even like, that it would have had a more realistic face, then it might have been even stranger."
P08	"There should rather be a square than a simulation of the shape of a head, or that, as you said, being deformed, that is probably not what a person really wants, for it to resemble a person."
P10	"Maybe it also then even evokes some emotions, and that is probably not what is intended, for people to act according to it."

3.3.2. Limited Gestures via Controllers

When participants were asked to describe their experience of communicating with their collaborator, they often described the need to modify their communications and actions because they had avatars instead of real bodies. Participants mentioned that the collaborator's representation was fine, but if the avatar had been more detailed, it would have been even better, as they wanted to see their collaborator's gestures. They would then look at their collaborator during communication more often. However participants say it was possible to read information from the posture and proximity of the collaborator's avatar. They had to think about how to depict something during communication when the collaborator could not see them fully. It was apparently demanding, but also fun. It required an unusual style of thinking which required the participants to consider the selection of gestures. They managed, however, to adapt to the visible parts of their avatar and used only those to communicate (Table 6).

Table 6. Verbatim excerpts of statements by participants: Limited gestures via controllers.

P04	"To me it seemed okay, but certainly if that avatar functioned better and I could even look at gestures, then it would be better. That probably ... like I would use more, I would try to communicate more and I would even look at him more."
P12	"That is true, I actually also gestured with my hands and ... it wasn't actually being seen ... so I had to, like, with that controller."
P04	"Sometimes I looked where you were standing, but I couldn't make out a lot from that, and yeah, I saw for example, that he was currently leaned over the numbers, yeah, and ... actually yes, when I think about it, you looked, for example, I saw, that he was currently leaned over the numbers, so I assumed he was currently solving something."
P12	"One tries out a little different way of communicating. Maybe he concentrates a little more on what he's doing with the hands, legs, what and how he moves and how to communicate something to the other person, so you have to take into consideration what he sees."
P11	"Well yeah, well, since it was a little bit more limited with those avatars, as with that, that there weren't all the details, then it was a little bit more interesting, so ... that sometimes there's too much detail." "I actually had to think about it, how to show something considering that I will not be seen as a whole, and, like, when I show something with my hands, that the hands actually were not seen."
	"Yeah, I've been able to adjust to what is actually visible and somehow just move only with those things that are visible."
P12	"So I think a person gets used to it quickly ... he learns how to work with what he sees."

3.3.3. Having an Intangible Body

All the participants dealt with the fact that their body in VR was not composed of any physical material. The situation when the avatars of both participants stood in the same virtual space or when an avatar stood "inside" a virtual object occurred. The physical area around a participant was always free, and the decision not to walk through virtual objects was always up to the participant. Participants tried to keep a usual personal distance between themselves and the collaborator, even though it was only an avatar.

Many participants mentioned the problem of obstructing or shadowing each other's view. When a collaborator stood in the map, it was quite a big problem and hard for the other person to read contour lines, but they did not realize they were doing it. Participants usually did not tell each other. They recognized the problem, but it usually only lasted a few seconds before the collaborator changed position and they could see the map again.

However, participants mostly did not mind that their avatar was not physical. It only bothered them at the beginning on account of habit (Table 7).

Table 7. Verbatim excerpts of statements by participants: Having an intangible body.

P04	"When my collaborator appeared in that first room during the first task, and when you, like, moved to the flags and I stepped out of your way, right, to like make space for you, so in that moment I was fully aware of the fact that I actually didn't have to move and that we could be both there, one through another, but, but I made a step back (participant laughs), because it seemed a little bit awkward."
P03	"I guess I would make him space, if I could. I would probably respect the personal zone even in cyberspace."
P11	"When I was looking at something and I was, like, leaned over it, like that I was thinking about something, and since she didn't see me as a whole, so I thought I wouldn't be obstructing and then I found out that I'm obstructing there with my whole body, and that she didn't see the map at all."
P12	"Well, there was such, such a funny thing, when you were standing there somehow through the table and it wasn't possible to see through it at all and it was so weird."
P04	"it was quite a big problem, but it didn't occur to me at all that I could be shadowing you, but because we both got in there, that we both walked inside that map since it was difficult to read, but then I didn't see those contour numbers or the contour heights actually in that moment, when the person was standing exactly through the map, that's true."
	"And we never said to each other: 'hey please make a step back'."
	"I was dealing with it as with a problem, certainly, but probably in the same moment you walked further on, so it didn't bother me anymore."
	"I think it was really a matter of a few seconds." "The fact that the body actually took up quite a lot of space was not okay."
	"I found it good that we could place the flags through each other in there, that you could place them here and I could place it there and you here and that we could cross over each other like this."

3.4. Cognition in Two Realities

The fourth and final superordinate theme relates to the cognitive aspects of simultaneously existing in two realities: objective and virtual reality. Participants were present in objective reality but also felt the sense of presence in virtual reality.

This superordinate theme includes three subthemes: Where are my legs? Immersion and involvement in the artificial world and confusion during the return to objective reality.

3.4.1. Where Are My Legs?

This question was asked by one of the participants, while other participants also wondered why their avatar looked so rudimentary. Many participants could not adapt to not seeing their own legs. They were strongly conscious of their absence, some even intrigued by it, as they were accustomed to seeing their legs as they looked down. Most participants would have been happier to have virtual legs in the virtual environment. By contrast, one participant did not mind that she had no legs, but did not like that the collaborator was missing legs (Table 8).

Table 8. Verbatim excerpts of statements by participants: Where are my legs?

P03	"When I put the headset on, I couldn't get used to, like, that I don't have any legs, I don't have a wristwatch. I was aware of these two things very strongly from self-perception."
	"I found it interesting not to actually see the legs. Because always when I put my glasses on and look, when a person looks down and he is walking somewhere, then he can see his legs and now I didn't see them, so that was interesting to me."
P08	"It wasn't very pleasant when I looked down, then I felt that I just have them (legs), but they're simply not there."
P11	"It was quite odd that I was actually in the table, or, like (participant laughs) . . . moving, not actually seeing my own legs, knowing that the legs are probably right where the table was (participant laughs) . . . kind of a strange feeling."
P09	"Maybe just because I didn't see the legs in there, then I didn't mind going through the table."
P11	"I was quite glad that if the legs had been displayed in there and I saw them go through the table, then it might have been even stranger."

3.4.2. Immersion and Involvement in the Artificial World

The experience of being in immersive VR was characterized by the loss of tracking objective reality and having a stronger sense of presence in the virtual environment. Immersed in VR and wholly engaged in the task, participants felt a stronger sense of presence in virtual reality. They did not perceive or think about what may have been happening around them in objective reality. While in VR, they had no need to be in touch with the outside world. Only when they bumped into something or heard the experimenter speak did they think about where someone or something was and feel disoriented (Table 9).

Table 9. Verbatim excerpts of statements by participants: Immersion and involvement in the artificial world.

P09	"On one hand, I was really, like, immersed in that task and in that activity, and on the other hand . . . so it was really, like, absorbing for me."
P13	"Well, I just bumped into something there, but otherwise I had no clue who was doing what in here." (in the objective reality room)
P11	"I was actually more in that virtual reality than in the real reality, actually. Sometimes I really didn't perceive the real reality, I put myself into it a lot."
P14	"I actually didn't have a clue what was actually happening around me."
P04	"I have to say that I didn't quite perceive that much." "Only when I took my headset off did I find out that I was terribly sweaty under it." "Then I, like, realized more that it was actually warm in there."
P12	"At first I was thinking about what it looked like from the outside, the things we were doing there, that it must have looked really funny."
	"At the back of my mind I knew that I was, like, in the real reality and that I'm doing those things others can't see, but I was also, like, quite able to put myself into it, that I'm simply in some room without a ceiling and where there's just some map on the floor."
P03	"When I was solving it, the task, I perceived more the virtual reality, but when there was nothing going on at time, then I perceived more the physical world again."

3.4.3. Confusion during the Return to Objective Reality

All of the participants liked the virtual environment and became accustomed to it, and most did not want to leave it. Although most of the participants described that they did not have any problems after taking their headsets off, some described specific feelings and perceptions which they experienced for a short time after they had returned from VR to objective reality.

For instance, one participant described how shocked he felt seeing his real hands again after leaving VR. A moment after leaving VR he felt lightweight and thought he would faint and felt strange even after some time. The time after exiting VR was more disorienting to him than the time spent in VR.

As mentioned above, though, most participants described no awkward feelings after taking their headsets off. They did not need to adapt to objective reality; it was completely normal for them to return to the objective reality room (Table 10).

Table 10. Verbatim excerpts of statements by participants: Confusion during the return to objective reality.

P08	"For me it was a shock to see my hands again after I took the headset off, and I had a clear feeling that when I was standing in that other room, I could simply walk through the person in there, that my hand could just pass through that person."
	"It's still strange. For a moment after sitting down, I felt as if I'd pass out."
	"So that one feels lightweight and just feels as if the wall isn't there, that I could walk through it. For me, it was probably a much more shocking experience after than with the headset on. And I wondered how I would feel if I layed down now, because I actually didn't even see my hands, I perceived it as those hands when I looked, like: "Wow" and I would probably, I would certainly not want to willingly go out of the room and go, for example, out onto the street, because I would be afraid that I, like, can't control it and that something could happen."
P11	"Yeah, I liked it there, that I didn't want to come back, but then when I took the headset off, then it was actually … quite strange, that it was, like, drawn, the real things. So I had to acclimatize a little bit."
	"It seemed to me that things were a little bit smaller, or as the details displayed there, like in reality, those details are displayed normally, so it was, like, more detailed."
	"Then I had problems with reality, that it's, like, too detailed and that I, like, can't perceive it. Because in the virtual reality I could perceive everything, because it was simpler, so there were, like, simple stimuli, but in the genuine reality a person has to distinguish what he actually perceives, because there's a lot of it, so that he can no longer see it as an overall picture with all the things that are actually there. It's, like, more understandable in there."
	"Yeah, yeah, a little bit yes, just only on those details, that I had to perceive reality again, as to distinguish what I would actually look at, as I already said. Well, but it was just for a moment … in about three minutes I was okay again. But it wasn't even unpleasant, so it's stupid to say 'okay', but simply, that I wasn't even perceiving it anymore after I adapted."
P12	"I didn't want to go back, I liked it there very much. It was, like, when I took the headset off, it was like, like at first unpleasant, until the eyes got used to it, that I was used to that virtual reality and to that light and to how it looked there, and then I took the headset off and it was, like, "Ouuu", a little bit unpleasant."

4. Discussion

In this section, we discuss the results of our study in the context of referenced literature and challenge it with our preliminary expectations and recommend further research and applicational options. The results are already interpretative and deeply descriptive, therefore the discussion to each subtheme will be concise.

One of the main findings of this study was that participants would have felt **lost without a collaborator** and that working in a dyad brought more entertainment and better results. From a social psychological perspective on collaborative learning [83], collaborators can be explained as providing social and emotional support to each other, enjoying mutual interaction, and having a positive effect on satisfaction and results. Participants in our study felt motivated by their collaborator. A social psychological perspective considers motivation as a precursor to effective cognitive processes during collaborative learning. Motivation in collaborative learning can be viewed from two points of view. From a socio-motivational point of view, collaborators are motivated to work together because they share the rewards for completing the task. From a social cohesion point of view, cohesiveness arises between collaborators and draws them into looking after each other and cooperating and working together. Slavin [84] and Johnson and Johnson [85] discovered that students are more motivated during collaborative learning than individual learning.

Another important finding is that collaborators debated a lot during the problem-solving process and sought **verification and consensus with their collaborator**. From a cognitive perspective on collaborative learning [86], collaboration with a peer can be explained as achieving better quality in basic information processing components such as coding, rehearsal and retrieval of information, activation of strategies and metacognition. Participants in our study claimed it would have taken them longer to solve the tasks individually. O'Donnell and Dansereau [87] explain that the presence of collaborator helps the student stay focused on a task and gives them an opportunity to verify understanding of the subject matter.

According to Webb and Farivar [88], if a student explains the task to the collaborator, it allows the student to identify flaws in their own reasoning. Collaborative learning and negotiation of meaning between people can support greater coherence in understanding subject matter [89].

Participants also explained that **finally seeing what contour lines represent in reality** helped them gain insight. From the perspective of Piaget's theory of cognitive development, specifically of the concept of mental schemas [90], the educational tools implemented in our CIVE application, which enabled participants to switch between a 2D map and 3D model or to raise water level in the terrain, served as a means to confront the participant's understanding of the subject matter. In Piaget's terms, participants underwent the process of accommodation, during which their preexisting schemas were adjusted according to the new experience. The importance of experience was emphasized both by Piaget's predecessors as Dewey [91], and his followers, who further elaborated his work: Kolb [92] understands learning as a circular process of creating knowledge via transformation of experience. Participants in our study first tried to complete the task on a 2D map. Their assumptions and understanding were then challenged by the 3D model which visualized their solution. In the case of an incorrect solution, cognitive conflict or disequilibrium occurs as a result, which drives the student to reduce this state and to renew equilibrium. The collaborator serves as another potential source of cognitive conflict. This is in accordance with the general educational approach proposed by Neale, Smith, and Johnson [93], to first give students an opportunity to create assumptions about the subject matter and then let them test it against evidence to discover contradictions. This strategy aims to make students aware of their predictions and present contradictory evidence to create cognitive conflict.

The participants expressed that they had a better understanding of contour lines after the experiment. Several aspects could contribute to **learning a skill to work with maps**. One of them is from the perspective of Vygotsky's theory of cognitive development [94]. According to his concept of the zone of proximal development, if a student receives appropriate support during interaction with another person during the task solving process, they can internalize the process, reorganize cognitive structures, and develop new competence. This concept resembles the concept of scaffolding, which, according to Hogan and Pressley [95], is a support enabling a student to solve new tasks, teaches competence and fades over time. Modern usage of this term often incorporates not only interpersonal support but also software based educational tools. Our CIVE application provided scaffolding for learning through problem solving, which according to Guzdial et al. [96] helps students acquire deep understanding of subject matter and new competence. Our application was also a case of scientific discovery learning, which Chen and Zhang [97] consider as a learning process during which students generate and test their hypothesis. In their study, they found a prominent effect of collaborative scientific discovery learning in VR on intuitive understanding and discovery outcomes. The results of the study by Okada & Simon [98] show that collaborative discovery learning in pairs is more effective compared to individual discovery learning.

Participants had problems with the **absence of avatar faces and invisibility of emotions**. According to Ekman and Friesen [99], people gather information about another person from four main sources in the visual informational channel: the face, tilts of the head, body posture, and skeletal muscle movements. They described that during conversation people do not continuously look at a listener but look to determine the listener's emotions or find out whether they are paying attention, agreeing, or attempting to respond with their own speaking. The participants of our study did not have a virtual face and could not make these distinctions. Some of them therefore did not even look at their collaborator's face while they were speaking. Most participants, however, missed having a face as a channel of information and did not know how to substitute its role.

Participants described their experiences with **limited gestures via controllers** and how they had to learn to work with it. Tu [100] explained that virtual communication differs from communication in objective reality. According to him, because of the limited communication channels, participants miss the clues for social context, and communication may be impersonal or cold. Virtual communication therefore requires different communication styles and strategies to maintain personal and social communication. In our study, we observed that participants sought personal contact with their collaborator, and even though the communication channels were limited, found innovative ways of using controllers and avatars for communication.

Participants described that **having an intangible body** created situations of obstructing each other's view but did not influence the proximity and personal space rules they followed. Bailenson et al. [101,102] discovered in several studies that participants seek to maintain the same interpersonal distance in immersive virtual reality as in objective reality. This is in accordance with our observations and what participants expressed in the focus group and interviews. They used their avatars as nonverbal communication tools and kept the same proximity to the collaborator as they would in objective reality. However, because they did not have full control over the avatar's movements and position, obstruction of each other's view sometimes occurred.

Some participants described strange sensations related to the cognitive discrepancy between their tactile sensations of objective reality and their visual perception of virtual reality. Some of them asked themselves **Where are my legs?** It is important, though, that this was not a case of cybersickness, which, according to LaViola [103] and Davis, Nesbitt, and Nalivaiko [104], is a type of motion sickness caused by cognitive discrepancy between the tactile sensations of a static position and the visual perception of movement. It seems, however, to be based on the same principle of cognitive discrepancy.

A common experience shared by participants was **immersion and involvement in the artificial world**. Witmer and Singer [105] describe immersion and involvement as preconditons for a sense of presence. Immersion as a psychological state can be characterized as perceiving the particular environment which surrounds us and perceiving self as a part of that environment. In the context of virtual reality, it means ignoring the medium and being absorbed by the simulation [106]. The participants of our study described losing track of objective reality and not knowing what was happening around them in objective reality. Involvement occurs as a result of being engaged in a meaningful task and focusing attention on specific content. Csikszentmihalyi's [107] well-known psychological concept of flow describes a similar state characterized by being fully involved and absorbed in a task, feeling energized focus and enjoyment, and losing a sense of time and space. The participants of our study described the task as capturing their whole attention and eliminating the perception of external stimuli. According to Witmer and Singer [105], participants feel a stronger sense of presence in virtual reality than objective reality as result of both immersion and involvement, which is precisely what out participants described.

Several participants in our study described their **confusion during the return to objective reality**. Two of the participants described states of derealization, which is defined by DSM-5 [83] as the detachment from a person's surroundings (world, people, or objects) and experience of the surroundings as unreal, dreamlike, or visually distorted. Research conducted by Aardema et al. [108] demonstrated that exposure to immersive VR induces a dissociative experience and temporarily increases the symptoms of depersonalization and derealization from objective reality.

5. Conclusions

In this study, we explored the experience of geography learning in a CIVE. The experiment centered on collaborative learning, development of geography competences and cognitive and social aspects. The objective was to broaden knowledge and understanding of these areas in the specific context of a CIVE. Using a uniquely-developed geography learning CIVE application, twelve participants experienced an educational intervention during which they collaborated in pairs on geospatial tasks. By means of observation, semistructured interviews, a focus group, and an interpretative phenomenological analysis, we gained deep insight into the participants' experiences. From these data, four superordinate themes emerged, each including the above depicted subthemes.

From these superordinate themes, we concluded the following:

1. Appreciation for having a collaborator. Collaborative educational interventions have previously been shown as more efficient than individual task solving [85–87] (among others). Whether this applies to a VR environment is yet to be empirically tested at a quantitative level, but based on our study's results, we may conclude that collaborative VR education has great potential both in terms of improving learning outcomes and decreasing task related anxiety.
2. The Surprising "Fun with Maps". Motivational potential is believed to be one of the greatest expected advantages of VR educational interventions. As far as we can estimate from the qualitative analyses, when the topic of the educational session is well chosen, VR offers ways of exciting learners and making them interested in a topic they would find (or expect to be) boring. However, such a qualified choice needs to be based on the necessary knowledge of the lesson's subject (geography in our case), educational principles and VR technology specifics.
3. Communication as a challenge. As some participants reported that communication with their partner was challenging when no facial expressions were transmittable and because gestures were not precisely transferred into VR, the means of communication in a CIVE appear to be one of the key topics for future research. However, since we observed that many of the participants managed to innovate ways of communicating within a relatively short time (approx. 60–120 min), we believe that in a long-term educational intervention (for example, a regular semester course) learners would likely adapt and communication would no longer feel challenging. This is also yet to be confirmed experimentally.
4. Cognition in two realities. Since some of the participants reported negative or confused feelings after the VR session during their return to objective reality, some future research challenges have emerged. The first will be to eliminate the negative impact of VR immersion in some participants. Predictors of the depersonalization and derealization states need to be identified in order to provide special care to those learners at risk (or to exclude them from the intervention before they are allowed to begin). The second and a worthwhile consideration will be to search for ways of adapting the VR environment or sessions to decrease the risk of such states. However, most of the participants showed no indications of negative feelings, and hence, the overall results of our study are more than motivating for further elaboration of the CIVE intervention design.

This IPA-based study identified key areas that may play a key role in using collaborative iVR technology and suggested its potential benefits and limits in the field of education. In future studies, quantitative confirmation of the findings will be extensive and include effectiveness comparisons with traditional tools such as GIS (Parong & Mayer) [109]. Broadening the list of learning tasks is also yet to be done. Challenges for further research will include the impact of intervening variables such as the level of user experience with iVR, educational intervention length (repeated measurements), and interindividual differences (e.g., cognitive style or map literacy).

Supplementary Materials: The following are available online at http://hci.fi.muni.cz/CIVE-papers/Task_1_Mirror_signals.mp4 (Video S1—task 1) http://hci.fi.muni.cz/CIVE-papers/Task_2_Flooded_valley.mp4 (Video S2—task 2).

Author Contributions: Only the substantial activities are listed for each author. Conceptualization, Č.Š., Z.S., J.C., V.J. and P.K.; Data Curation, H.T.; Formal Analysis, M.S.; Funding Acquisition, H.S.; Investigation, H.T.; Methodology, Č.Š., Z.S., M.S. and T.U.; Project Administration, P.K.; Resources, L.H.; Software, J.C. and M.D.; Supervision, Č.Š., Z.S. and J.C.; Visualization, P.U.; Writing—Original Draft, M.S.; Writing—Review & Editing, A.Š.

Funding: This research was funded by Masaryk University, Czech Republic, Grant No. MUNI/M/0846/2015, "Influence of cartographic visualization methods on the success of solving practical and educational spatial tasks".

Acknowledgments: The authors would like to thank all students and colleagues who participated in this study. This work was supported by the research infrastructure of the HUME Lab Experimental Humanities Laboratory, Faculty of Arts, Masaryk University.

Conflicts of Interest: The authors declare no conflict of interest.

References

1. Romano, D.M. Virtual Reality Therapy. *Dev. Med. Child Neurol.* **2005**, *47*, 580. [CrossRef] [PubMed]
2. Botella, C.; García-Palacios, A.; Villa, H.; Baños, R.; Quero, S.; Alcañiz, M.; Riva, G. Virtual Reality Exposure in the Treatment of Panic Disorder and Agoraphobia: A controlled Study. *Clin. Psychol. Psychother.* **2007**, *14*, 164–175. [CrossRef]
3. Garcia-Palacios, A.; Hoffman, H.; Kwong See, S.; Tsai, A.; Botella, C. Redefining Therapeutic Success with Virtual Reality Exposure Therapy. *CyberPsychol. Behav.* **2001**, *4*, 341–348. [CrossRef] [PubMed]
4. Bertella, L.; Marchi, S.; Riva, G. Virtual Environment for Topographical Orientation (VETO): Clinical Rationale and Technical Characteristics. *Presence Teleoperators Virtual Environ.* **2001**, *10*, 440–449. [CrossRef]
5. Cho, B.H.; Ku, J.; Jang, D.P.; Kim, S.; Lee, Y.H.; Kim, I.Y.; Lee, J.H.; Kim, S.I. The Effect of Virtual Reality Cognitive Training for Attention Enhancement. *Cyberpsychol. Behav.* **2002**, *5*, 129–137. [CrossRef] [PubMed]
6. Anderson-Hanley, C.; Arciero, P.; Brickman, A.; Nimon, J.; Okuma, N.; Westen, S.; Merz, M.; Pence, B.; Woods, J.; Kramer, A.; et al. Exergaming and Older Adult Cognition. *Am. J. Prevent. Med.* **2012**, *42*, 109–119. [CrossRef]
7. Moller, H.J.; Bal, H.; Sudan, K.; Potwarka, L.R. Recreating Leisure: How Immersive Environments can Promote Wellbeing. In *Interacting with Presence: HCI and the Sense of Presence in Computer-Mediated Environments*; Riva, G., Waterworth, J., Murray, D., Eds.; De Gruyter Open Ltd.: Warsaw/Berlin, Germany, 2014; pp. 102–122.
8. Waterworth, J.; Waterworth, E.L. Relaxation Island: A Virtual Tropical Paradise. In Proceedings of the British Computer Society HCI Conference 2004: Designing for Life, Leeds, UK, 6–10 September 2004.
9. Keefe, F.; Huling, D.; Coggins, M.; Keefe, D.; Rosenthal, Z.; Herr, N.; Hoffman, H. Virtual Reality for Persistent Pain: A New Direction for Behavioral Pain Management. *Pain* **2012**, *153*, 2163–2166. [CrossRef]
10. Mirelman, A.; Maidan, I.; Herman, T.; Deutsch, J.; Giladi, N.; Hausdorff, J. Virtual Reality for Gait Training: Can It Induce Motor Learning to Enhance Complex Walking and Reduce Fall Risk in Patients With Parkinson's Disease? *J. Gerontol. Ser. A Biol. Sci. Med. Sci.* **2010**, *66*, 234–240. [CrossRef]
11. Huber, T.; Paschold, M.; Hansen, C.; Wunderling, T.; Lang, H.; Kneist, W. New Dimensions in Surgical Training: Immersive Virtual Reality Laparoscopic Simulation Exhilarates Surgical Staff. *Surg. Endosc.* **2017**, *31*, 4472–4477. [CrossRef]
12. Kilmon, C.A.; Brown, L.; Ghosh, S.; Mikitiuk, A. Immersive Virtual Reality Simulations in Nursing Education. *Nurs. Educ. Perspect.* **2010**, *31*, 314–317.
13. Ordaz, N.; Romero, D.; Gorecky, D.; Siller, H. Serious Games and Virtual Simulator for Automotive Manufacturing Education & Training. *Procedia Comput. Sci.* **2015**, *75*, 267–274. [CrossRef]
14. Matsas, E.; Vosniakos, G. Design of a Virtual Reality Training System for Human–robot Collaboration in Manufacturing Tasks. *Int. J. Interact. Design Manuf.* **2015**, *11*, 139–153. [CrossRef]
15. El-Mounayri, H.; Rogers, C.; Fernandez, E.; Satterwhite, J. Assessment of STEM e-Learning in an Immersive Virtual Reality (VR) Environment. In Proceedings of the 2016 ASEE Annual Conference & Exposition Proceedings, ASEE Conferences, New Orleans, LA, USA, 26–29 June 2016. [CrossRef]
16. Guttentag, D. Virtual Reality: Applications and implications for tourism. *Tour. Manag.* **2010**, *31*, 637–651. [CrossRef]

17. Callieri, M.; Chica, A.; Dellepiane, M.; Besora, I.; Corsini, M.; Moyés, J.; Ranzuglia, G.; Scopigno, R.; Brunet, P. Multiscale Acquisition and Presentation of very Large Artifacts. *J. Comput. Cultural Heritage* **2011**, *3*, 1–20. [CrossRef]
18. Jung, T.H.; tom Dieck, M.C. Augmented Reality, Virtual Reality and 3D Printing for the Co-Creation of Value for the Visitor Experience at Cultural Heritage Places. *J. Place Manag. Dev.* **2017**, *10*, 140–151. [CrossRef]
19. De la Peña, N.; Weil, P.; Llobera, J.; Spanlang, B.; Friedman, D.; Sanchez-Vives, M.; Slater, M. Immersive Journalism: Immersive Virtual Reality for the First-Person Experience of News. *Presence Teleoperators Virtual Environ.* **2010**, *19*, 291–301. [CrossRef]
20. Bideau, B.; Kulpa, R.; Vignais, N.; Brault, S.; Multon, F.; Craig, C. Virtual reality, a Serious Game for Understanding Performance and Training Players in Sport. *IEEE Comput. Gr. Appl.* **2009**. [CrossRef]
21. Staurset, E.; Prasolova-Førland, E. Creating a Smart Virtual Reality Simulator for Sports Training and Education. *Smart Innov. Syst. Technol.* **2016**, *59*, 423–433.
22. Mól, A.C.; Jorge, C.A.; Couto, P.M. Using a Game Engine for VR Simulations in Evacuation Planning. *IEEE Comput. Gr. Appl.* **2008**, *28*, 6–12. [CrossRef]
23. Shen, S.; Gong, J.; Liang, J.; Li, W.; Zhang, D.; Huang, L.; Zhang, G. A Heterogeneous Distributed Virtual Geographic Environment—Potential Application in Spatiotemporal Behavior Experiments. *ISPRS Int. J. Geo-Inf.* **2018**, *7*, 54. [CrossRef]
24. Cook, D.; Cruz-Neira, C.; Kohlmeyer, B.D.; Lechner, U.; Lewin, N.; Nelson, L.; Olsen, A.; Pierson, S.; Symanzik, J. Exploring Environmental Data in a Highly Immersive Virtual Reality Environment. *Environ. Monit. Assess.* **1998**, *51*, 441–450. [CrossRef]
25. Kreylos, O.; Bawden, G.; Bernardin, T.; Billen, M.I.; Cowgill, E.S.; Gold, R.D.; Hamann, B.; Jadamec, M.; Kellogg, L.H.; Staadt, O.G.; et al. Enabling scientific workflows in virtual reality. In Proceedings of the 2006 ACM international conference on Virtual reality continuum and its applications, VRCIA '06, Hong Kong, China, 14–17 June 2006; ACM: New York, NY, USA, 2006; pp. 155–162. [CrossRef]
26. Lin, H.; Gong, J. Exploring Virtual Geographic Environments. *Geogr. Inf. Sci.* **2001**, *7*, 1–7. [CrossRef]
27. Kubíček, P.; Šašinka, Č.; Stachoň, Z.; Herman, L.; Juřík, V.; Urbánek, T.; Chmelík, J. Identification of altitude profiles in 3D geovisualizations: The role of interaction and spatial abilities. *Int. J. Dig. Earth* **2017**, 1–17. [CrossRef]
28. Carbonell-Carrera, C.; Saorín, J. Geospatial Google Street View with Virtual Reality: A Motivational Approach for Spatial Training Education. *ISPRS Int. J. Geo-Inf.* **2017**, *6*, 261. [CrossRef]
29. Virtanen, J.; Hyyppä, H.; Kämäräinen, A.; Hollström, T.; Vastaranta, M.; Hyyppä, J. Intelligent Open Data 3D Maps in a Collaborative Virtual World. *ISPRS Int. J. Geo-Inf.* **2015**, *4*, 837–857. [CrossRef]
30. Zanola, S.; Fabrikant, S.I.; Çöltekin, A. The Effect of Realism on the Confidence in Spatial Data Quality in Stereoscopic 3D Displays. In Proceedings of the 24th International Cartography Conference, ICC 2009, Santiago, Chille, 15–21 November 2009; pp. 15–21.
31. Zhang, S.; Moore, A. The Usability of Online Geographic Virtual Reality for Urban Planning. *ISPRS—International Archives of the Photogrammetry. Remote Sens. Spat. Inf. Sci.* **2013**, *XL-2/W2*, 145–150. [CrossRef]
32. Abulrub, A.; Attridge, A.; Williams, M. Virtual Reality in Engineering Education: The Future of Creative Learning. *Int. J. Emerg. Technol. Learn.* **2011**, *6*. [CrossRef]
33. Dinis, F.M.; Guimaraes, A.S.; Carvalho, B.R.; Martins, J.P.P. Development of Virtual Reality Game-based Interfaces for Civil Engineering Education. In Proceedings of the 2017 IEEE Global Engineering Education Conference, EDUCON, Athens, Greece, 26–28 April 2017; pp. 1195–1202. [CrossRef]
34. Lalley, J.P.; Piotrowski, P.S.; Battaglia, B.; Brophy, K.; Chugh, K. A Comparison of V-Frog[C] to Physical Frog Dissection. *Int. J. Environ. Sci. Educ.* **2010**, *5*, 189–200.
35. Ai-Lim Lee, E.; Wong, K.; Fung, C. How Does Fesktop Virtual Reality Enhance Learning Outcomes? A Structural Equation Modeling Approach. *Comput. Educ.* **2010**, *55*, 1424–1442. [CrossRef]
36. Lee, B.W.; Shih, H.Y.; Chou, Y.T.; Chen, Y.S. Educational Virtual Reality Implementation on English for Tourism Purpose Using Knowledge-based Engineering. In Proceedings of the 2017 International Conference on Applied System Innovation, ICASI, Sapporo, Japan, 13–17 May 2017; pp. 792–795. [CrossRef]
37. Lai, C.; McMahan, R.P.; Kitagawa, M.; Connolly, I. Geometry Explorer: Facilitating Geometry Education with Virtual Reality. In *Virtual, Augmented and Mixed Reality*; Springer International Publishing: Cham, Switzerland, 2016; pp. 702–713. [CrossRef]

38. Molka-Danielsen, J.; Prasolova-Førland, E.; Fominykh, M.; Lamb, K. Reflections on Design of Active Learning Module for Training Emergency Management Professionals in Virtual Reality. In *NOKOBIT—Norsk Konferanse for Organisasjoners Bruk av Informasjonsteknologi*; NOKOBIT, Bibsys Open Journal Systems: Oslo, Norway, 2017; Volume 25, p. 1.
39. Van der Linden, A.; van Joolingen, W. A Serious Game for Interactive Teaching of Newton's Laws. In Proceedings of the 3rd Asia-Europe Symposium on Simulation & Serious Gaming—VRCAI '16, New York, NY, USA, 3–4 December 2016; pp. 165–167. [CrossRef]
40. Ştefan, L. Immersive Collaborative Environments for Teaching and Learning Traditional Design. *Procedia Soc. Behav. Sci.* **2012**, *51*, 1056–1060. [CrossRef]
41. Hirmas, D.; Slocum, T.; Halfen, A.; White, T.; Zautner, E.; Atchley, P.; Liu, H.; Johnson, W.; Egbert, S.; McDermott, D. Effects of Seating Location and Stereoscopic Display on Learning Outcomes in an Introductory Physical Geography Class. *J. Geosci. Educ.* **2014**, *62*, 126–137. [CrossRef]
42. Stojšić, I.; Ivkov Džigurski, A.; Maričić, O.; Ivanović Bibić, L.; Đukičin Vučković, S. Possible Application of Virtual Reality in Geography Teaching. *J. Subj. Didact.* **2017**, *1*, 83–96. [CrossRef]
43. Konečný, M. Cartography: Challenges and Potential in the Virtual Geographic Environments Era. *Ann. GIS* **2011**, *17*, 135–146. [CrossRef]
44. Herman, L.; Kvarda, O.; Stachoň, Z. Cheap and Immersive Virtual Reality: Application in Cartography. In *ISPRS Archives of the Photogrammetry, Remote Sensing and Spatial Information Sciences*; Zlatanova, S., Dragicevic, S., Sithole, G., Eds.; Copernicus GmbH: Gottingen, Germany, 2018; Volume XLII-4, pp. 261–266. [CrossRef]
45. Masrur, A.; Zhao, J.; Wallgrün, J.O.; LaFemina, P.; Klippel, A. Immersive Applications for Informal and Interactive Learning for Earth Science. In Proceedings of the Workshop on Immersive Analytics, Exploring Future Interaction and Visualization Technologies for Data Analytics, VIS2017, Phoenix, AZ, USA, 1–6 October 2017; pp. 1–5.
46. Hsu, W.C.; Lin, H.C.K.; Lin, Y.H. The research of applying Mobile Virtual Reality to Martial Arts learning system with flipped classroom. In Proceedings of the 2017 International Conference on Applied System Innovation, ICASI, Sapporo, Japan, 13–17 May 2017; pp. 1568–1571. [CrossRef]
47. Halabi, O.; Abou El-Seoud, S.; Alja'am, J.; Alpona, H.; Al-Hemadi, M.; Al-Hassan, D. Design of Immersive Virtual Reality System to Improve Communication Skills in Individuals with Autism. *Int. J. Emerg. Technol. Learn.* **2017**, *12*, 50. [CrossRef]
48. Fisher, P.; Unwin, D. *Virtual Reality in Geography*; Taylor and Francis Ltd.: London, UK, 2001.
49. Batty, M. Virtual Reality in Geographic Information Systems. In *The Handbook of Geographic Information Science*; Wilson, J.P., Fotheringham, A.S., Eds.; Blackwell Publishing: Oxford, UK, 2008; pp. 317–334.
50. Lin, H.; Chen, M.; Lu, G.; Zhu, Q.; Gong, J.; You, X.; Wen, Y.; Xu, B.; Hu, M. Virtual Geographic Environments (VGEs): A New Generation of Geographic Analysis Tools. *Earth-Sci. Rev.* **2013**, *126*, 74–84. [CrossRef]
51. Lin, H.; Batty, M.; Jorgensen, S.E.; Fu, B.; Konečný, M.; Voinov, A.A.; Torrens, P.; Lu, G.; Zhu, A.X.; Wilson, J.P.; et al. Virtual Environments Begin to Embrace Process-based Geographic Analysis. *Trans. GIS* **2015**, *19*, 493–498. [CrossRef]
52. Philips, A.; Walz, A.; Bergner, A.; Graeff, T.; Heistermann, M.; Kienzler, S.; Korup, O.; Lipp, T.; Schwanghart, W.; Zeilinger, G. Immersive 3D Geovisualization in Higher Education. *J. Geogr. Higher Educ.* **2015**, *39*, 437–449. [CrossRef]
53. Carbonell Carrera, C.; Saorin, J.L.P.; de la Torre Cantero, J. Teaching with AR as a Tool for Relief Visualization: Usability and Motivation Study. *Int. Res. Geogr. Environ. Educ.* **2017**, *27*, 69–84. [CrossRef]
54. Merchant, Z.; Goetz, E.; Cifuentes, L.; Keeney-Kennicutt, W.; Davis, T. Effectiveness of Virtual Reality-based Instruction on Students' Learning Outcomes in K-12 and Higher Education: A Meta-analysis. *Comput. Educ.* **2014**, *70*, 29–40. [CrossRef]
55. Zyda, M. From Visual Simulation to Virtual Reality to Games. *Computer* **2005**, *38*, 25–32. [CrossRef]
56. Gee, J. *What Video Games Have to Teach us About Learning and Literacy*; Palgrave Macmillan: Basingstoke, UK, 2008.
57. Ang, C.S.; Rao, G.S.V.R.K. Computer Game Theories for Designing Motivating Educational Software: A Survey Study. *Int. J. E-Learn.* **2008**, *7*, 181–199.

58. Kyndt, E.; Raes, E.; Lismont, B.; Timmers, F.; Cascallar, E.; Dochy, F. A Meta-analysis of the Effects of Face-to-face Cooperative Learning. Do Recent Studies Falsify or Verify Earlier Findings? *Educ. Res. Rev.* **2013**, *10*, 133–149. [CrossRef]
59. Harding-Smith, T. *Learning Together: An Introduction to Collaborative Learning*; HarperCollins College Publishers: New York, NY, USA, 1993.
60. Vygotsky, L. *Interaction between Learning and Development*; W.H. Freeman and Company: New York, NY, USA, 1997.
61. Dillenbourg, P. *Collaborative Learning: Cognitive and Computational Approaches*; Advances in Learning and Instruction Series; Elsevier Science, Inc.: New York, NY, USA, 1999.
62. Gokhale, A.A. Collaborative Learning Enhances Critical Thinking. *J. Technol. Educ.* **1995**, *7*, 22–30. [CrossRef]
63. Havenith, H.-B.; Cerfontaine, P.; Mreyen, A.-S. How Virtual Reality Can Help Visualise and Assess Geohazards. *Int. J. Digit. Earth* **2017**. [CrossRef]
64. Lin, H.; Chen, M.; Lu, G. Virtual Geographic Environment: A Workspace for Computer-Aided Geographic Experiments. *Ann. Assoc. Am. Geogr.* **2013**, *103*, 465–482. [CrossRef]
65. Lehtinen, E.; Hakkarainen, K.; Lipponen, L.; Veermans, M.; Muukkonen, H. Computer Supported Collaborative Learning: A Review. *JHGI Giesbers Rep. Educ.* **1999**, *10*, 1999.
66. Jackson, R.L.; Fagan, E. Collaboration and learning within immersive virtual reality. In *Proceedings of the 3rd International Conference on Collaborative Virtual Environments*; Churchill, E., Reddy, M., Eds.; ACM: New York, NY, USA, 2000; pp. 83–92. [CrossRef]
67. He, T.; Chen, X.; Chen, Z.; Li, Y.; Liu, S.; Hou, J.; He, Y. Immersive and Collaborative Taichi Motion Learning in Various VR Environments. In Proceedings of the 2017 IEEE Virtual Reality (VR), Los Angeles, CA, USA, 18–22 March 2017; IEEE: Los Angeles, CA, USA, 2017; pp. 307–308. [CrossRef]
68. Kaufmann, H.; Schmalstieg, D. Designing Immersive Virtual Reality for Geometry Education. In Proceedings of the IEEE Virtual Reality Conference (VR 2006), Alexandria, VA, USA, 25–29 March 2006; pp. 51–58. [CrossRef]
69. Dos Reis, P.R.; Matos, C.E.; Diniz, P.S.; Silva, D.M.; Dantas, W.; Braz, G.; de Paiva, A.C.; Araújo, A.S. An Immersive Virtual Reality Application for Collaborative Training of Power Systems Operators. In Proceedings of the 2015 XVII Symposium on Virtual and Augmented Reality, Sao Paulo, Brazil, 25–28 May 2015; pp. 121–126. [CrossRef]
70. Siemens, G. Connectivism: A Learning Theory for the Digital Age. *Int. J. Instruct. Technol. Distance Learn.* **2014**, *2*, 1–8.
71. Horvath, I. Innovative Engineering Education in the Cooperative VR Environment. In Proceedings of the 2016 7th IEEE International Conference on Cognitive Infocommunications, CogInfoCom, Wroclaw, Poland, 16–18 October 2016; pp. 359–364. [CrossRef]
72. Hew, K.; Cheung, W. Use of Three-dimensional (3-D) Immersive Virtual Worlds in K-12 and Higher Education Settings: A Review of the Research. *Br. J. Educ. Technol.* **2010**, *41*, 33–55. [CrossRef]
73. Doležal, M.; Chmelík, J.; Liarokapis, F. An Immersive Virtual Environment for Collaborative Geovisualization. In Proceedings of the 9th International Conference on Virtual Worlds and Games for Serious Applications, VS-Games 2017, Athens, Greece, 6–8 September 2017; pp. 272–275. [CrossRef]
74. Juřík, V.; Herman, L.; Kuníček, P.; Stachoň, Z.; Šašinka, Č. Cognitive Aspects of Collaboration in 3D Virtual Environments. In *ISPRS Archives of the Photogrammetry, Remote Sensing and Spatial Information Sciences*; Halounova, L., Ed.; Copernicus GmbH: Gottingen, Germany, 2016; Volume XLI-B2, pp. 663–670. [CrossRef]
75. Symeonides, R.; Childs, C. The Personal Experience of Online Learning: An Interpretative Phenomenological Analysis. *Comput. Hum. Behav.* **2015**, *51*, 539–545. [CrossRef]
76. Smith, J.A.; Flowers, P.; Larkin, M. *Interpretative Phenomenological Analysis: Theory, Method and Research*; Sage Publications Ltd.: London, UK, 2009.
77. Reid, K.; Flowers, P.; Larkin, M. Exploring Lived Experience. *Psychologist* **2005**, *18*, 20–23.
78. Smith, J.A.; Jarman, M.; Osborn, M. Doing Interpretative Phenomenological Analysis. In *Qualitative Health Psychology*; Murray, M., Chamberlain, K., Eds.; Sage Publications Ltd.: London, UK, 1999; pp. 218–240.
79. Gorard, S.; Taylor, C. *Combining Methods in Educational and Social Research*; Open University Press: Berkshire, UK, 2004.
80. Brannen, J. Combining Qualitative and Quantitative Approaches: An Overview. In *Mixing Methods: Qualitative and Quantitative Research*; Brannen, J., Ed.; Avebury: Aldershot, UK, 1992.

81. Smith, J.A.; Osborn, M. Interpretative Phenomenological Analysis. In *Qualitative Psychology: A Practical Guide to Research Methods*; Smith, J.A., Ed.; Sage Publications Ltd.: London, UK, 2003; pp. 53–80.
82. Smith, J.A. Reflecting on the Development of Interpretative Phenomenological Analysis and its Contribution to Qualitative Research in Psychology. *Qual. Res. Psychol.* **2004**, *1*, 39–54.
83. O'Donnell, A.M.; Hmelo-Silver, C.E. Introduction What is Collaborative Learning?: An Overview. In *The International Handbook of Collaborative Learning*; Routledge: New York, NY, USA, 2013; pp. 13–28.
84. Slavin, R. When Does Cooperative Learning Increase Student Achievement? *Psychol. Bull.* **1983**, *94*, 429–445. [CrossRef]
85. Johnson, D.; Johnson, R. Making Cooperative Learning Work. *Theory Pract.* **1999**, *38*, 67–73. [CrossRef]
86. O'Donnell, A.M.; Dansereau, D.F.; Hythecker, V.I.; Larson, C.O.; Rocklin, T.R.; Lambiotte, J.G.; Young, M.D. The Effects of Monitoring on Cooperative Learning. *J. Exp. Educ.* **1986**, *54*, 169–173. [CrossRef]
87. O'Donnell, A.M.; Dansereau, D.F. Scripted Cooperation in Student Dyads: A Method for Analyzing and Enhancing Academic Learning and Performance. In *Interaction in Cooperative Groups: The Theoretical Anatomy of Group Learning*; Hertz-Lazarowitz, R., Miller, N., Eds.; Cambridge University Press: Cambridge, UK, 1992; pp. 120–141.
88. Webb, N.; Farivar, S. Promoting Helping Behavior in Cooperative Small Groups in Middle School Mathematics. *Am. Educ. Res. J.* **1994**, *31*, 369. [CrossRef]
89. Duschl, R.; Osborne, J. Supporting and Promoting Argumentation Discourse in Science Education. *Stud. Sci. Educ.* **2002**, *38*, 39–72. [CrossRef]
90. Piaget, J. *The Psychology of Intelligence*; Taylor & Francis: London, UK, 2005; ISBN 0-203-98152-9.
91. Dewey, J. *Experience and Education*; Macmillan: New York, NY, USA, 1938.
92. Kolb, D. *Experiential Learning*, 2nd ed.; Pearson Education: Upper Saddle River, NJ, USA, 2015.
93. Neale, D.; Smith, D.; Johnson, V. Implementing Conceptual Change Teaching in Primary Science. *Elem. Sch. J.* **1990**, *91*, 109–131. [CrossRef]
94. Vygotsky, L.S. *Mind in Society: The Development of Higher Psychological Processes*; Harvard University Press: Cambridge, MA, USA, 1979.
95. Hogan, K.; Pressley, M. Scaffolding Scientific Competencies within Classroom Communities of Inquiry. In *Advances in Learning & Teaching. Scaffolding Student Learning: Instructional Approaches and Issues*; Hogan, K., Pressley, M., Eds.; Brookline Books: Cambridge, MA, USA, 2017; pp. 74–107.
96. Guzdial, M.; Kolodner, J.; Hmelo, C.; Narayanan, H.; Carlson, D.; Rappin, N.; Hübscher, R.; Turns, J.; Newstetter, W. Computer support for learning through complex problem solving. *Commun. ACM* **1996**, *39*, 43–45. [CrossRef]
97. Chen, Q.; Zhang, J. 2 Collaborative Discovery Learning Based on Computer Simulation. In *Collaborative Learning, Reasoning and Technology*, 2nd ed.; O'Donnell, A., Hmelo-Silver, C.E., Erkens, G., Eds.; Routledge: New York, NY, USA, 2012; pp. 154–196.
98. Okada, T.; Simon, H. Collaborative Discovery in a Scientific Domain. *Cognit. Sci.* **1997**, *21*, 109–146. [CrossRef]
99. Ekman, P.; Friesen, W. *Unmasking the Face*; Malor Books: Cambridge, MA, USA, 2003.
100. Tu, C.H. *Online Collaborative Learning Communities: Twenty-one Designs to Building an Online Collaborative Learning Community*; Libraries Unlimited: Westport, Ireland, 2004.
101. Bailenson, J.; Blascovich, J.; Beall, A.; Loomis, J. Equilibrium Theory Revisited: Mutual Gaze and Personal Space in Virtual Environments. *Presence Teleoperators Virtual Environ.* **2001**, *10*, 583–598. [CrossRef]
102. Bailenson, J.; Blascovich, J.; Beall, A.; Loomis, J. Interpersonal Distance in Immersive Virtual Environments. *Personal. Soc. Psychol. Bull.* **2003**, *29*, 819–833. [CrossRef] [PubMed]
103. LaViola, J. A Discussion of Cybersickness in Virtual Environments. *ACM Sigchi Bull.* **2000**, *32*, 47–56. [CrossRef]
104. Davis, S.; Nesbitt, K.; Nalivaiko, E. A Systematic Review of Cybersickness. In Proceedings of the 2014 Conference on Interactive Entertainment, IE2014, Newcastle, Australia, 2–3 December 2014; Blackmore, K., Nesbitt, K., Smith, S.P., Eds.; ACM: New York, NY, USA, 2014. [CrossRef]
105. Witmer, B.; Singer, M. Measuring Presence in Virtual Environments: A Presence Questionnaire. *Presence Teleoperators Virtual Environ.* **1998**, *7*, 225–240. [CrossRef]
106. Cruz-Neira, C.; Sandin, D.; DeFanti, T.; Kenyon, R.; Hart, J. The CAVE: Audio Visual Experience Automatic Virtual Environment. *Commun. ACM* **1992**, *35*, 64–72. [CrossRef]

107. Csikszentmihaiyi, M. *Flow: The Psychology of Optimal Experience*; Harper & Row Publishers: New York, NY, USA, 1990.
108. Aardema, F.; O'Connor, K.; Côté, S.; Taillon, A. Virtual Reality Induces Dissociation and Lowers Sense of Presence in Objective Reality. *Cyberpsychol. Behav. Soc. Netw.* **2010**. [CrossRef] [PubMed]
109. Parong, J.; Mayer, R.E. Learning Science in Immersive Virtual Reality. *J. Educ. Psychol.* **2018**, *110*, 785–797. [CrossRef]

© 2018 by the authors. Licensee MDPI, Basel, Switzerland. This article is an open access article distributed under the terms and conditions of the Creative Commons Attribution (CC BY) license (http://creativecommons.org/licenses/by/4.0/).

International Journal of
isprs Geo-Information

Article

Evaluation of User Performance in Interactive and Static 3D Maps

Lukáš Herman [1],*, **Vojtěch Juřík [2]**, **Zdeněk Stachoň [1]**, **Daniel Vrbík [3]**, **Jan Russnák [1]** and **Tomáš Řezník [1]**

1. Department of Geography, Faculty of Science, Masaryk University, 611 37 Brno, Czech Republic; zstachon@geogr.muni.cz (Z.S.); daniel.vrbik@tul.cz (D.V.); russnak@mail.muni.cz (J.R.); tomas.reznik@sci.muni.cz (T.Ř.)
2. Department of Psychology, Faculty of Arts, Masaryk University, 602 00 Brno, Czech Republic; jurik.vojtech@mail.muni.cz
3. Department of Applied Mathematics, Faculty of Science, Humanities and Education, Technical University of Liberec, 461 17 Liberec, Czech Republic
* Correspondence: herman.lu@mail.muni.cz; Tel.: +420-549-49-7608

Received: 4 September 2018; Accepted: 23 October 2018; Published: 26 October 2018

Abstract: Interactive 3D visualizations of geospatial data are currently available and popular through various applications such as Google Earth™ and others. Several studies have focused on user performance with 3D maps, but static 3D maps were mostly used as stimuli. The main objective of this paper was to identify differences between interactive and static 3D maps. We also explored the role of different tasks and inter-individual differences of map users. In the experimental study, we analyzed effectiveness, efficiency, and subjective preferences, when working with static and interactive 3D maps. The study included 76 participants and used a within-subjects design. Experimental testing was performed using our own testing tool 3DmoveR 2.0, which was based on a user logging method and open web technologies. We demonstrated statistically significant differences between interactive and static 3D maps in effectiveness, efficiency, and subjective preferences. Interactivity influenced the results mainly in 'spatial understanding' and 'combined' tasks. From the identified differences, we concluded that the results of the user studies with static 3D maps as stimuli could not be transferred to interactive 3D visualizations or virtual reality.

Keywords: 3D geovisualizations; 3D map; 3DmoveR; level of interactivity; map tasks; map users; OSIVQ; user's performance; user study

---

1. Introduction

3D visualization of geospatial data is employed today in many fields and in relation to many specific issues. Some universal applications, such as Google Earth™ or Virtual Earth®, and many domain specific solutions can be applied in several areas. An overview of these are presented, for example, by Shiode [1], Abdul-Rahman and Pilouk [2], or Biljecki et al. [3]. Despite the wide dissemination of 3D visualization applications, relatively little is known about their theoretical background. We can still agree with the notion of Wood et al. [4], who claimed that we do not know enough about how 3D visualizations can be used appropriately and effectively.

Buchroithner and Knust [5] distinguished between two basic types of 3D visualization: Real-3D and pseudo-3D visualization. Real-3D visualizations engage both binocular and monocular depth cues into geovisualizations using the principles of stereoscopy. Pseudo-3D visualizations are usually displayed on planar media (e.g., computer screens or widescreen projections), and are perceived by engaging only monocular depth cues [5]. In general, pseudo-3D visualization is considered a cheaper and more disseminated type of visualization, since it has no further demands on peripheral technology to provide stereoscopy. This paper examines pseudo-3D visualization in more detail, specifically studying 3D maps presented on planar media.

Many different definitions of 3D maps exist. Some of them, for example, Hájek, Jedlička, and Čada [6], concentrate mainly on map content, where 3D maps are understood to include Digital Terrain Models, 2D data draped onto terrain, 3D models of objects, or 3D symbols. Other definitions describe the specifics of the 3D map creation process (generalization, symbolization). Haeberling, Bär, and Hurni [7] define a 3D map as the generalized representation of a specific area using symbolization to illustrate its physical features. Finally, some definitions are more complex and consider the characteristics of the resulting 3D map. Bandrova [8] defines a 3D map as a computer generated, mathematically defined, three-dimensional, highly-realistic virtual representation of the world's surface, which also includes the objects and phenomena in nature and society. Schobesberger and Patterson [9] characterize a 3D map as the depiction of terrain with faux three-dimensionality containing perspective that diminishes the scale of distant areas.

We understand a 3D map as a pseudo-3D or real-3D depiction of the geographic environment and its natural or socio-economic objects and phenomena using a mathematical basis (geographical or projection coordinate systems with a Z-scale of input data and graphical projection, such as perspective or orthogonal projection) and cartographical processes (generalization, symbolization, etc.). 3D maps usually employ a bird's eye view. We define an interactive 3D map as a 3D map which allows, at least, navigational (or viewpoint) interactivity [10], whilst static maps are most often perspective views. Static 3D maps can be also tangible (for example printed by 3D printer), but in this paper, we deal only with 3D virtual maps that are displayed on the computer screen

This paper consists of a theoretical section, which is a literature review, and an empirical section, which is an experimental study. The literature review is divided into three parts, according to three fundamental factors important in cartography user studies: Stimuli, task, and user [11,12]. The main objectives of the empirical section relate to these three dimensions. First, we want to find out the differences between interactive and static 3D maps. Second, we want to explore the role of different types of tasks performed on the 3D maps, and the individual and group differences between 3D map users.

2. Related Concepts and Research

The differences between interactive and static 3D maps are based on the different psychological processes underlying their perception. From this point of view, we can discuss the concept of information and computational equivalence [13]. Larkin and Simon [13] suggested that two different visualizations are information equivalent when the information contained in one visualization is derivable from the other. However, the processes of derivation may require a different level of computation, since visualizations may be depicted by using different graphics or interfaces. Two different external representations (in our case 3D maps) are considered computationally equivalent if a person needs to perform the same number of mental processes (computations) when reading them to achieve the same information. The issue of interactivity in 3D maps is also discussed in the field of cartography, as interactive visualization solves the problems with overall visibility and readability of complex and informationally rich areas [14].

Complex terrain models and 3D maps can be identical in terms of the information they contain; however, specific options to interact with them may promote, or conversely, hinder the number of computations when reading them. This implies that two equivalent 3D maps may not be comparable when considering only their content. It is necessary to consider the process of interaction with the specific interface (which can be characterized as physical computation), and based on this interaction, we need to measure the mental processes required to achieve specific information (mental computations). Following the work of Vygotsky and later Leontiev, human activity is stated as the core aspect of the process of perception and directly structures the user's cognitive functions [15]. Leontiev [16] understood human activity as a "circular structure" including: Initial afforestation →

effector processes regulating contact with the objective environment → correction and enrichment by means of reverse connections of the original afferent image.

Boy [15] noted the importance of the actionists' perspective, seeing the human mental reflection of the world as not exclusively created by external influences, but also by the processes through which users/people come into practical contact with the objective world. Neisser adopts a similar point of view when he suggests his cyclic model [17]. We must consider the fact that the user/operator is no longer considered as a passive cognitive system experiencing the stimuli given by the external environment (as it usually was in a traditional experimental research paradigm). The user is an active scout, exploring the environment or system and engaging his or her inner intentions, and can influence the situation with specific activities or by following specific goals [15]. From this point of view, the effectiveness of interactive visualizations can be tested against static visualizations (also in terms of the type and quantity of interactions).

2.1. Static versus Interactive 3D Maps

Most of the recent user studies in cartography use either only static 3D maps or interactive 3D maps as stimuli, not both. Static stimuli have been used, for example, by Schobesberger and Patterson [9], Engel et al. [18], Niedomysl et al. [19], Popelka and Brychtová [20], Seipel [21], Popelka and Doležalová [22], Preppernau and Jenny [23], Rautenbach et al. [24], Zhou et al. [25], and Liu et al. [26], whilst interactive stimuli have been used by Abend et al. [27], Wilkening and Fabrikant [28], Treves et al. [29], Špriňarová et al. [30], McKenzie and Klippel [31], Carbonell-Carrera and Saorín [32], and Herman et al. [33].

Some studies have been conducted comprising two successive parts using interactive stimuli in one part and static stimuli in the other, for example, Juřík et al. [34]. A direct comparison of static versus interactive visualizations was conducted by Bleisch, Dykes, and Nebiker [35], Herbert and Chen [36] or Kubíček et al. [37]. Bleisch, Dykes, and Nebiker [35] compared the reading of bar chart heights in static 2D visualizations and bar charts placed in a 3D environment. Interaction in a 3D environment was enabled, but it was not monitored or analyzed, and we do not know whether participants used the interactive capabilities of the 3D stimuli to achieve a better solution or whether they made decisions solely on the basis of visual information. Herbert and Chen [36] tried to identify whether users preferred 2D maps and plans or interactive geovisualizations from the ArcScene software in matters of spatial planning. In both of these studies, two independent variables were not distinguished as separate (level of interactivity and dimensionality of visualization), and it is not possible to identify their true effect.

Kubíček et al. [37] investigated the roles of both types of 3D visualization (pseudo-3D versus real-3D) and the level of navigational interactivity (static versus interactive) when working with terrain profiles. The results of this study indicated that the type of 3D visualization does not affect the performance of users significantly, but the level of navigational interactivity has a significant influence on the usability of a particular 3D visualization. Previous experiments met several methodological limitations (e.g., untreated primary effect when solving tasks in the early phase may influence better performance in the later phase), and in regard to this work, we suggested a design that focuses exclusively on comparing interactive and non-interactive 3D maps. In this study, we focused on designing a test that would make undertaking a comparison of static and interactive 3D maps as objective as possible.

The test battery and data collection procedure for comparing static and interactive 3D maps were evaluated in a pilot study conducted by Herman and Stachoň [38]. In the present study, we emphasize the importance of measuring and analyzing the process of interaction in its entire complexity (i.e., as deeply as possible) while controlling all the residual variables.

2.2. The Nature of Tasks in 3D Maps

3D maps can be used for different purposes, and these specific purposes predetermine the nature of the tasks that would be solved. Interactivity represents only one of the possible factors; other factors may be represented by task complexity. The increasing complexity of the task changes the quality of cognitive processes included in the process of task solving. In the language of mathematics, we do not speak of addition but rather multiplication or squaring. We can suppose that as the complexity of the task grows, the significance of interactivity will be distinctly emphasized—in a more complex task, interactivity will be more helpful, and therefore we suppose a significant and larger effect will be found in the interactive condition. For this question, it is necessary to determine a typology of tasks for 3D maps in terms of their complexity. Various taxonomies of tasks for 3D maps have been used, for example, Kjellin et al. [39], Boér, Çöltekin, and Clarke [40] or Rautenbach et al. [41]. The basic tasks describing the interaction with a specific interface or environment are called interaction primitives (IPs) [10]. IPs represent the elementary activities that can be performed during the process of interaction. The applicable taxonomy of IPs (tasks) for 3D maps was proposed by Juřík, Herman, and Šašinka [42]. A generalized version of this taxonomy is shown in Table 1.

Table 1. Taxonomy of tasks in empirical research of 3D maps (ranked from the simplest to the most complex task according to Juřík, Herman and Šašinka [42]) with the given number of studies using this type of task.

Task	Number of User Studies	User Studies
Search	16	[9,18–20,22–24,27–30,32,39,41,43]
Pattern recognition	0	-
Spatial understanding	18	[18–21,23–26,28,30,31,33–35,37,38,41,44]
Quantitative estimation	2	[18,24]
Shape description	3	[9,28,32]
Combined tasks	1	[34]
Planning	3	[23,30,34]

The frequency of use of individual types of task varies considerably in the papers analyzed. Some are used very often (search and spatial understanding), while others are used relatively less. We selected tasks related to pattern recognition, spatial understanding, and combined tasks. The simplest search tasks were not tested exclusively as they form a part of the more complex tasks. Pattern recognition tasks have not been used in any previous user study with 3D maps and testing this type of task was a challenge for this reason. Spatial understanding tasks, which have been used in most studies, were selected to make the results of our study comparable. We did not consider planning or shape description tasks because their evaluation can be difficult and largely subjective. Combined tasks have not been used often, but they lead to more complex cognitive processes and emulate user interaction, so this type of tasks was applied.

2.3. Users of 3D Maps and Their Spatial Abilities

Some previous studies suggested that the use of 3D maps may promote the realistic perception of spatial arrangement of the scene, making it easier for laypersons to form an impression of the scene without the necessity for any symbolic language [37]. By contrast, some studies supported the claim that some forms of 3D visualization may increase the time required to solve tasks and create visual discomfort during their use [21,45]. For experts experienced in map reading, 3D visualization may lower the clarity of depicted content and increase the chance of making an error [34].

These inconsistencies in map depiction have still not been explored very deeply, as several important factors contribute. Besides the type of visualization, interactivity and task type (discussed above), a level of (geo) expertise, and innate spatial ability (or better cognitive style) is involved when dealing with map content. The observer's focus on an object in a scene or on the overall spatial arrangement of the scene plays an important role in computational processes. Individual spatial abilities determine the efficiency in remembering and understanding the spatial arrangement of the scene, and based on the mental image of this scene, they can be more or less successful when dealing with specific tasks [46,47].

The existence of people who are more spatially oriented, those who are more object oriented, and those mainly verbally oriented has been explored in many psychological studies [48–50]. This orientation of a person is measured, for example, with the Object-Spatial Imagery and Verbal Questionnaire (OSIVQ) developed by Blazhenkova and Kozhevnikov [51]. From this point of view, these three factors must be considered as part of the experimental design in evaluating geographical products. In the study presented, we involved experts and laypersons in the field of geography (to compare the results of these two groups of users) and measured their object-spatial orientation using the OSIVQ. These people were tested on interactive and static 3D maps.

3. Experimental Study

The aim of the study is to analyze the differences between effectiveness (correctness) [52], efficiency (response times) [53], and subjective preferences [52] when working with static and interactive 3D maps. Correctness, response times, and subjective preferences were dependent variables. Independent variables were the level of interactivity, level of expertise, and task type. We addressed three research questions (RQ), which were further defined by nine hypotheses (H). The research questions and hypotheses were defined based on literature and our pilot studies. Hypothesis H1, H2, and H3 were based on Kubíček et al. [37] and Herman and Stachoň [38]. Hypothesis H4 and H5 were based on Špriňarová et al. [30] and Juřík et al. [34]. Hypothesis H6 and H7 were based on Bowman et al. [54] and Herman et al. [55]. Hypothesis H8 and H9 were based on Štěrba et al. [56] and Stachoň et al. [57].

- RQ1: Does user performance differ between interactive and static 3D maps?

    - H1: Participants solve interactive tasks with greater accuracy than static tasks.
    - H2: Participants solve static tasks faster than interactive tasks.
    - H3: Participants subjectively prefer interactive tasks to static tasks.

- RQ2: Does user performance differ regarding different task types?

    - H4: Static and interactive tasks have significant differences in accuracy in all three task subcategories (spatial understanding, pattern recognition, combined tasks).
    - H5: Static and interactive tasks have significant differences in the time required to complete the tasks in all three task subcategories (spatial understanding, pattern recognition, combined tasks).

- RQ3: Does user performance differ between experts and laypersons?

    - H6: Experts solve the tasks with greater accuracy than laypersons.
    - H7: Experts solve the tasks faster than laypersons.
    - H8: Accuracy and speed of user response in laypersons significantly correlates with the high spatial factor score detected in the OSIVQ questionnaire.
    - H9: Accuracy and speed of user response in experts does not correlate with the high spatial factor score detected in the OSIVQ questionnaire.

3.1. Methods

3.1.1. Participants

A total of 76 participants took part in the study. Testing was conducted in May and June 2018. The participants were recruited via email, social networks, and personal contact. The overwhelming majority of the participants were students and graduates of Masaryk University and Technical University Liberec. Masaryk University's ethics committee approved this research. The majority of the participants could be considered to be experts as they were either geography or cartography graduates or students who had obtained at least a bachelor's degree. A smaller number of participants were members of the general public. For more details about gender, age, self-reported experiences, and field of education, see Table 2. The participants agreed to the experimental procedure, participated voluntarily, and could withdraw freely from the experiment at any time. All the participants had normal or corrected-to-normal vision. The environmental conditions (including lighting conditions and other environmental factors) were kept constant for all the participants.

Table 2. Participant's characteristics.

			Laypersons		Experts	
Total		N	32		44	
Females		N	19		18	
Males		N	13		26	
Age		Min	18		20	
		Mean	26.875		26.795	
		Stdv	7.602		4.203	
		Median	23.500		26.000	
		Max	42		46	
Self-reported experiences (How often you work with …?	PC	Median	1	daily	1	daily
	Maps	Median	3	occasionally	2	regularly
	3D visualizations	Median	4	singularly	3	occasionally
Field of education		N	6	foreign languages	23	geography
			5	psychology	12	cartography
			4	economy	8	geoinformatics
			4	informatics	1	geodesy
			3	pedagogy		
			2	laws		
			8	other humanities		

3.1.2. Procedure

A mixed factorial (2 × 3 × 2) design [58] was chosen for the study. Level of interactivity (static vs interactive) and task type (spatial understanding tasks, pattern recognition tasks, and combined tasks) were the within-subject factors to indicate the expected differences. Level of expertise (experts and laypersons) was the between-subject factor. To maximize the internal validity of the study, four versions of the test battery (Figure 1—I, II, III, and IV) were created to counterbalance the static and interactive tasks. The geographical stimuli could not be artificially designed, so the geographical nature of specific tasks was also counterbalanced (regarding the specific region used and its difficulty, as discussed). The tasks in the test battery were counterbalanced to prevent a primacy/learning effect and to reduce the potential diversity of tasks. Equal numbers of experts and laypersons were assigned to each of these four versions.

The test battery comprised an introductory questionnaire on personal information and previous 3D visualization experience. Two training tasks followed (static and interactive, in which participants attempted all three possible types of virtual movement). After training, 24 testing tasks were completed with 3D maps. Finally, the OSIVQ questionnaire was given. Testing tasks with 3D maps were divided into six blocks. Blocks were introduced with detailed instructions and ended with a brief, subjective evaluation. Before testing, participants were instructed that the correctness of responses was important and that their response times would be recorded, and that it would be ideal to solve tasks accurately, as well as quickly.

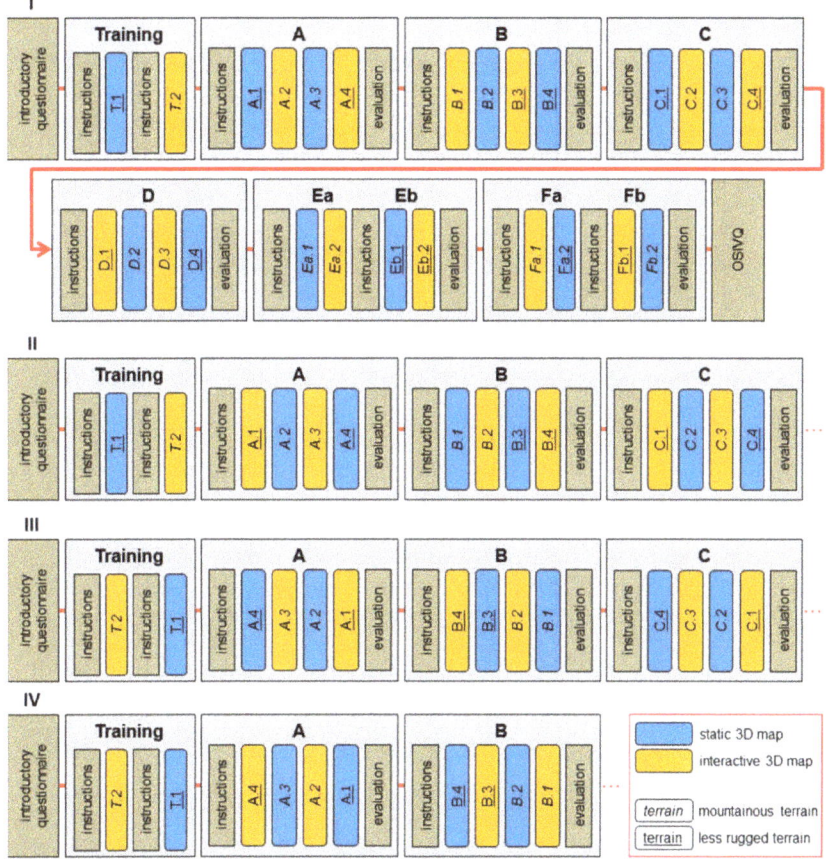

Figure 1. Design of the experiment (four versions of the test battery are marked as I, II, III, and IV).

For this outline of 3D map tasks, we created tasks that engaged elementary cognitive processes, as in Reference [59]. We selected spatial understanding tasks (A, B, C), pattern recognition tasks (E), and combined tasks (D, F). Specifically, we formulated the tasks as follows:

A. Select which of four buildings is at the lowest altitude.
B. Select which of four buildings is in the location with lowest signal intensity.
C. Determine which of four buildings are visible from the top of the signal transmitter.
D. Determine which of four buildings are visible from the top of the signal transmitter and are also in the location with lowest signal intensity.
E. Determine whether the spatial distribution of signal intensity depends on altitude or terrain slope.

    a. Determine whether signal intensity depends on altitude.
    b. Determine whether signal intensity depends on terrain slope.

F. Comparison of average altitudes and average terrain slope in highlighted areas.

    a. Determine which of the four areas is located at the highest average altitude.
    b. Determine which of the four areas is characterized by the highest average terrain slope.

Signal intensity (in tasks B, D, and E) was depicted with an orange color scale (color intensity). Participant responses to the all the above-mentioned tasks required choosing from four options. Most of the tasks (A, B, D, E, F) indicated only one correct answer. Only task C required more than one correct answer to complete it correctly.

3.1.3. Apparatus

3DmoveR (3D Movement and Interaction Recorder), which is our original application developed at the Faculty of Sciences, Masaryk University [55] and can be optimized to record the process of user interaction with 3D maps, was employed for user testing. The 3DmoveR was based on the combination of a user logging approach and online questionnaire engaging practical spatial tasks. This application is freely available to any interested person under a BSD (Berkeley Software Distribution) license. Open web technologies (JavaScript, jQuery, WebGL and PHP) were used for its implementation. All user interaction data and user responses were recorded and stored on the server for later analysis. The 3DmoveR and two derived variants, 3DtouchR (3D Touch Interaction Recorder) and 3DgazeR (3D Gaze Recorder), have been used in several user studies [31,38,42–44,55,60].

For the empirical part of this study, 3DmoveR version 2.0 was used. The main shift from the previous version lay in replacing the X3DOM library for rendering 3D geospatial data with the equally focused Three.js library. This change extended support for various types of devices (mouse-controlled desktop PCs, laptops with touchpads, or tablets) and across all operating system platforms and web browsers. In addition to better hardware and software support, this change had other benefits, such as automated, and therefore, faster stimuli preparation (using open source GIS—QGIS 2.18 and Qgis2threejs plugin), more precise stimuli control settings (assigning specific movements to different keys or prohibiting all types of movement for static stimuli), and customization of user movement in 3D scenes, for better control and greater accuracy than the previous 3DmoveR version.

Although 3DmoveR is primarily designed to test 3D geospatial data, it is also possible to create slides containing classic questionnaires (e.g., OSIVQ) with this tool. Based on the results of a previous survey described in Juřík et al. [60], the testing interface comprised a classic PC with keyboard and mouse, monitor (screen resolution 1920 × 1080 px), and Windows OS. The application was launched via the Google Chrome web browser, as the survey in Juřík et al. [60] found that this software configuration was the most commonly used by respondents. It also contributed to the increase of the environmental validity of the results.

3.1.4. Materials

Digital terrain models formed the principal part of stimuli in this experiment. Terrain models from the EU-DEM [61], which is a freely available data source, were the primary data input for stimuli. Four homogenous areas from different parts of Europe were chosen for processing. Two areas represented mountainous terrain (southeastern France, borderland of Italy and Austria), and another two areas represented less rugged, rather hilly terrain (southern Norway, borderland of the Czech Republic, Poland and Germany). Each area was divided into six rectangles (20 × 20 km), and two equal squares were prepared for training tasks. These digital terrain models were processed in QGIS 2.18 with the Qgis2threejs plugin. Objects required for each task were created and edited manually in QGIS. Moreover, textures for tasks from blocks B, D, and E were created in QGIS. The symbology and visualization style were set in the Qgis2threejs plugin, as well as Z-factor (1.5, which is the default value).

HTML and JavaScript files were than exported from the plugin. The graphical user interface (GUI) to enter responses was created in HTML (Figure 2). All 3D scene controls were defined within one JavaScript file and modified to be controlled only by a mouse in the interactive variants and not to allow any navigational interactivity in the static variants of 3D scenes. The first (initial) position of the virtual camera in the interactive version corresponded in all tasks to the positions of the virtual camera in the static version of corresponding tasks. See available online video for a detailed description of experimental testing (https://youtu.be/Xat0slCx-Yg).

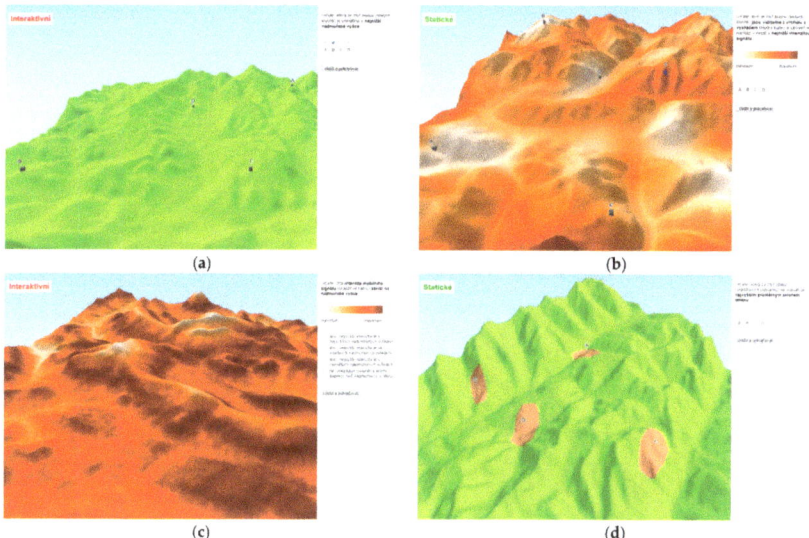

Figure 2. Examples of 3DmoveR user interface: (**a**) Task A—selecting which of four buildings is at the lowest altitude—interactive variant; (**b**) Task D—determining which of four buildings are visible from the top of the signal transmitter and are also in the location with lowest signal intensity—static variant; (**c**) Task Ea—determining whether signal intensity depends on terrain slope—interactive variant; (**d**) Task Fb—determining which of the four areas is characterized by the highest average terrain slope—static variant.

3.2. Results

The research design included three main factors, so we performed three-way analysis of variance (ANOVA) as Warne [62] to gain a complex picture of the research issue first. We analyzed the influence of the observed factors (level of interactivity, level of expertise, and task type) and the interaction effects of the factors on the participants' performance (i.e., correctness and response times). The factor of interactivity had two levels (interactive and static), the task type factor had three levels (spatial understanding tasks, pattern recognition tasks, and combined tasks), and the expertise factor had two levels (laypersons and experts). See descriptive statistics in Table 3 and results of ANOVA in Table 4. Regarding the hypotheses outlined, we further analyzed the data using Levene's *t*-test [63] or Mann Whitney U test [64] (depending on whether the data had a normal distribution), to more closely look at the discussed research questions.

Regarding task response times, the dataset did not show a normal distribution, so we transformed the time responses to a normal distribution using Box-Cox transformation ($\lambda = 0.3$), as recommended for working with specific variables such as time [65].

Table 3. Correctness of user responses and time demands in individual tasks according to level of interactivity, level of expertise, and task type.

		Correctness per One Task [0–1]				Response Time for One Task [s]			
		Interactive		Static		Interactive		Static	
		Laypersons	Experts	Laypersons	Experts	Laypersons	Experts	Laypersons	Experts
Combined tasks	Median	1.000	1.000	1.000	1.000	26.670	24.725	17.290	17.835
	Mean	0.907	0.949	0.519	0.559	31.673	29.553	19.371	20.616
	Stdv	0.289	0.219	0.498	0.495	22.978	23.713	10.278	12.989
Spatial understanding	Median	1.000	1.000	1.000	1.000	26.705	22.680	17.520	18.155
	Mean	0.751	0.740	0.565	0.630	34.450	31.138	19.982	21.509
	Stdv	0.431	0.438	0.495	0.482	27.660	25.524	11.416	15.428
Pattern recognition	Median	1.000	1.000	1.000	1.000	35.740	30.780	27.265	25.610
	Mean	0.862	0.865	0.738	0.921	36.594	32.740	31.342	28.201
	Stdv	0.343	0.340	0.436	0.268	18.714	19.758	18.556	14.839

Table 4. ANOVA results—correctness and response times.

Predictor		Df	Sum of Squares	Mean Square	F-Value	p-Value	Significance
Correctness per one task [0–1]	Interactivity	1	19.2	19.172	106.015	<2e−16	***
	Task type	2	7.5	3.753	20.752	1.23e−09	***
	Expertise	1	0.8	8.440	4.666	0.0309	*
	Interactivity × task type	2	8.8	4.391	24.281	3.92e−11	***
	Interactivity × expertise	1	0.5	0.524	2.897	0.0889	.
	Task type × expertise	2	0.3	0.128	0.706	0.4937	
	Interactivity × task type × expertise	2	0.4	0.212	1.171	0.3101	
Response time for one task [s]	Interactivity	1	22,243	22,243	114.173	<2e−16	***
	Task type	2	7375	3687	18.927	7.32e−09	***
	Expertise	1	598	598	3.069	0.0800	.
	Interactivity × task type	2	1156	578	2.966	0.0518	.
	Interactivity × expertise	1	732	732	3.760	0.0527	.
	Task type × expertise	2	116	58	0.298	0.7420	
	Interactivity × task type × expertise	2	75	38	0.193	0.8244	

Significance codes: *** significance level = 0.001, * significance level = 0.05, significance level = 0.1.

We found statistically significant differences in task type and interactivity for task-solving times and in expertise, task type, and interactivity for correctness. Only the interaction of interactivity and the task types factor was found to be statistically significant for both correctness and response times (see Table 4 and Figure 3).

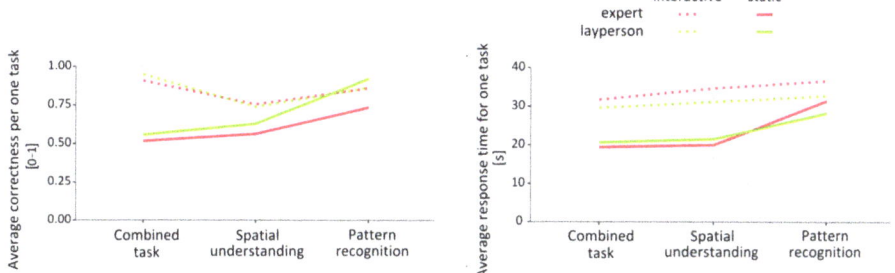

Figure 3. Average correctness (**left**) and average response times (**right**) by task type.

3.2.1. RQ1. Does User Performance Differ between Interactive and Static 3D Maps?

Correctness

To answer the general research question, whether interactivity influenced user performance on maps, we compared the overall performance of all the participants for the interactivity factor (static vs interactive tasks, regardless of task type, see Figure 4). The assumption of normal distribution was not fulfilled in correctness, and the Shapiro-Wilk test (as in Reference [66]) of normality did not assume normal distribution of the correct answers for interactive and static tasks (see Table 5). Therefore, we conducted the Mann-Whitney U test to measure the differences in the correct answers between static and interactive tasks. Significant differences were found as static tasks were solved with less accuracy than interactive tasks, as shown in Figure 4 and Table 5.

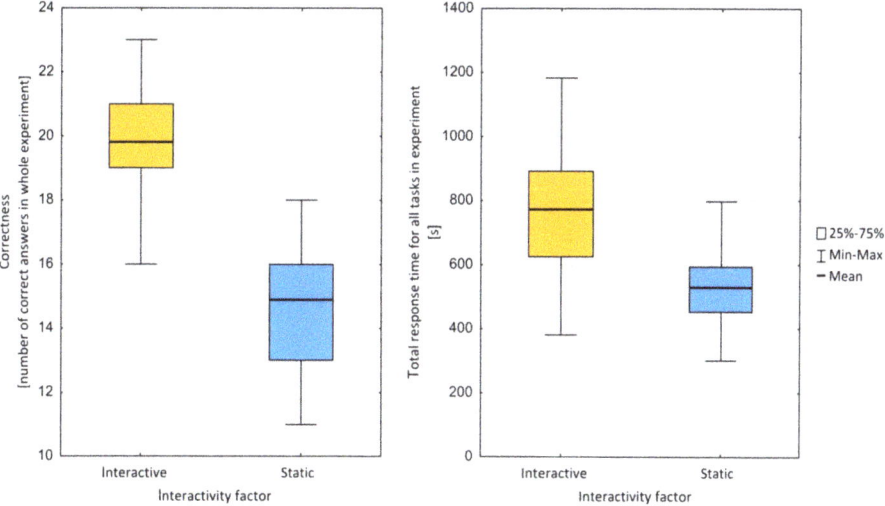

Figure 4. Total correctness (**left**) and total response time (**right**) of user responses in terms of the interactivity factor.

Table 5. Overall measures (correctness and response time) and analyses results for the interactivity factor.

Correctness [Number of Correct Answers in Whole Experiment]		Median	Mean	Stdv	Shapiro-Wilk Test		Mann Whitney U test	
					p-Value		U	p-Value
Interactivity	Interactive	20.000	19.816	1.522	0.023		25.500	0.000
	Static	15.000	14.895	1.689	0.035			

Total response time for all tasks in experiment [s]		Median	Mean	Stdv	Shapiro-Wilk test		Levene's t-test		
					p-value	T	Df	p-value	
Interactivity	Interactive	777.370	772.165	199.075	0.627	6.412	59.314	2.61e−08	
	Static	526.750	529.675	115.305	0.916				

Response Times

Similar to accuracy, we compared the time the participants needed to complete all the tasks. The assumption of normal distribution in time required for task-solving was fulfilled (see Shapiro-Wilk test, Table 5), so we used Levene's *t*-test for equality of variances to assess the differences between static and interactive tasks. For more details, see Table 5 and Figure 4.

Subjective Preferences

The subjective preferences of the participants indicated that most considered interactivity in maps to be a helpful feature to solve the given tasks. In all the experimental tasks, 89% of the users reported that interactive task-solving was easier, as they agreed or strongly agreed with the claim that task solving was easier with interactive conditions. Figure 5 presents a detailed summary of the specific answers for each of the six task blocks.

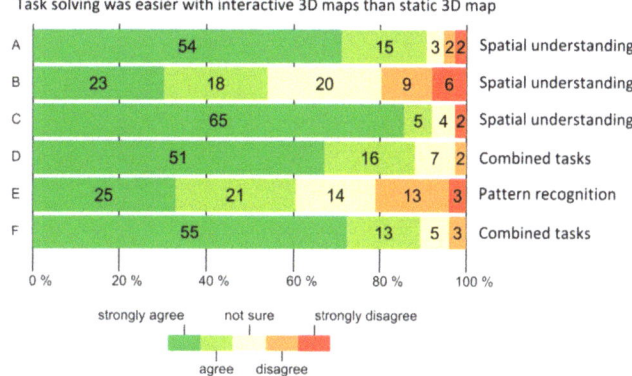

Figure 5. Subjective preferences of interactive 3D maps for individual task types.

3.2.2. RQ2: Does User Performance Differ Regarding Different Task Types?

Correctness

To gain deeper insights into the role of task complexity, we compared user performance across specific task types divided into three categories: Spatial understanding, pattern recognition, and combined tasks. Accuracy in the spatial understanding and combined tasks categories showed statistically significant differences between the static and interactive conditions. The pattern recognition tasks showed no significant differences. The values of the central tendency are summarized in Table 6.

Table 6. Overall measures (correctness and response time) and analyses results for the task types factor.

	Correctness per One Task [0–1]		Median	Mean	Stdv	Shapiro-Wilk Test	Mann Whitney U Test	
						p-Value	U	p-Value
Task type	Combined tasks	Interactive	1.000	0.931	0.253	0.000	4.500	0.000
		Static	1.000	0.541	0.498	0.000		
	Spatial understanding	Interactive	1.000	0.744	0.436	0.002	201.000	0.000
		Static	1.000	0.602	0.489	0.002		
	Pattern recognition	Interactive	1.000	0.863	0.343	0.000	661.000	0.000
		Static	1.000	0.843	0.362	0.000		

	Response time for one task [s]		Median	Mean	Stdv	Shapiro-Wilk test	Levene's t test		
						p-value	T	Df	p-value
Task type	Combined tasks	Interactive	25.745	30.463	23.504	0.915	−5.732	60.295	3.38e−07
		Static	17.595	20.100	11.954	0.135			
	Spatial understanding	Interactive	25.745	32.549	26.552	0.038	6.572	57.045	1.64e−08
		Static	18.030	20.872	13.928	0.077			
	Pattern recognition	Interactive	32.515	34.369	19.539	0.178	2.018	66.906	0.048
		Static	26.245	29.545	16.692	0.252			

Response Times

Differences in the task categories were also found in the time required to complete the given tasks. Similar to accuracy, differences were found in both spatial understanding tasks and combined tasks, while pattern recognition tasks showed no significant differences. The central tendency values are summarized in Table 6. The data showed that combined tasks were solved the fastest, while pattern recognition tasks were solved the slowest.

3.2.3. RQ3: Does User Performance Differ between Experts and Laypersons?

Expertise

The normal distribution of the data was assumed (see Table 7), so we conducted t-tests to measure the exact differences between experts' and laypersons' response times and correctness. The empirical evidence supported our expectation that experts would have higher accuracy than laypersons when solving cartographic tasks. However, experts were not significantly faster or slower than laypersons. For more details, see Table 7 and Figure 6.

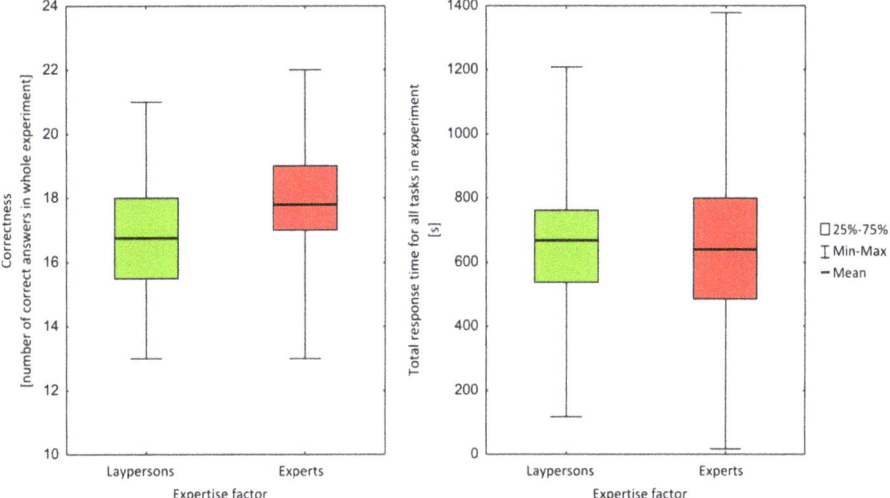

Figure 6. Comparison of correctness of responses (left) and response times (right) by laypersons and experts.

Table 7. The overall measures (correctness and response time) and analyses report in terms of expertise factor.

Correctness [Number of Correct Answers in Whole Experiment]		Median	Mean	Stdv	Shapiro-Wilk Test		T	Levene's t-Test	
					p-Value			Df	p-Value
Expertise	Experts	18.000	17.795	1.961	0.266		2.253	74	0.027
	Laypersons	17.000	16.750	1.984	0.357				
Total response time for all tasks in experiment [s]		Median	Mean	Stdv	Shapiro-Wilk test		T	Levene's t-test	
					p-value			Df	p-value
Expertise	Experts	605.095	638.979	242.324	0.221		0.520	74	0.605
	Laypersons	635.950	667.339	216.389	0.398				

Cognitive Style

We investigated whether the objective performance (correctness and response time) of individual participants was related to cognitive styles detected via the OSIVQ questionnaire. Correctness and response times were both aggregated according to task type by addition. Table 8 shows the correlation coefficients calculated for task types and all three cognitive styles (spatial, object, and verbal) from OSIVQ. No significant correlation was found at this level. When we analyzed these data at a more detailed level, positive correlation was found only between correctness and spatial cognitive style for experts in task block B ($r = 0.347$; p-value $= 0.021$), which was spatial understanding task type.

Table 8. Correlation coefficient (significance level α = 0.05) for correctness, response times, and cognitive styles measured via Object-Spatial Imagery and Verbal Questionnaire (OSIVQ) (spatial, object, and verbal).

		Laypersons						Experts					
		Object		Spatial		Verbal		Object		Spatial		Verbal	
		R	p-Value	R	p-Value	R	p-Value	R	p-Value	R	p-Value	R	p-Value
Correctness	Combined tasks	−0.155	0.396	0.057	0.756	−0.013	0.943	0.082	0.598	−0.167	0.277	−0.070	0.651
	Spatial under-standing	0.013	0.942	−0.111	0.545	−0.018	0.924	0.137	0.376	0.018	0.908	−0.145	0.348
	Pattern recognition	−0.110	0.548	−0.155	0.398	−0.089	0.629	0.041	0.793	0.076	0.625	−0.088	0.569
	Overall	−0.114	0.535	−0.119	0.518	−0.056	0.760	0.147	0.340	−0.045	0.770	−0.162	0.295
Response times	Combined tasks	0.201	0.269	0.013	0.944	−0.104	0.572	0.065	0.675	−0.071	0.648	0.108	0.486
	Spatial under-standing	0.108	0.557	0.069	0.707	−0.130	0.479	−0.008	0.957	−0.096	0.533	0.226	0.141
	Pattern recognition	0.348	0.051	0.092	0.616	−0.085	0.645	0.127	0.413	−0.036	0.817	0.262	0.085
	Overall	0.208	0.253	0.064	0.726	−0.127	0.488	0.042	0.789	−0.085	0.582	0.215	0.161

4. Discussion

The ANOVA results suggested that significant main effects existed in the correctness of answers for the factors of interactivity, task type, and expertise, and for the interaction of the task type and interactivity factors at the significance level of 0.001 (except for expertise, $p < 0.05$). For response times, only the factors of interactivity and task type were found to have significant differences, also at the significance level of 0.001. According to these results, all the mentioned factors significantly influenced user performance when evaluating the altitude of objects placed in virtual 3D visualizations. It should be mentioned that the factor of expertise, which had a significant effect only for correctness, implied that when working with virtual 3D visualizations, the role of expertise may be less. The data also strongly emphasized the advantage of interactivity when working with this type of stimuli, which grew significantly with more complex (combined) tasks (see Section 3.2.1).

4.1. Research Question 1

Based on the given data, H1, H2, and H3 were confirmed. These hypotheses related to the results of the entire test (user response accuracy and speed were aggregated for all 24 tasks and participants). As expected, we found significant differences in overall user response accuracy and speed between interactive and static 3D maps. Interactive tasks were solved with greater accuracy (H1), while static tasks were solved faster (H2). Interactivity in tasks offered users a good option to explore content more precisely and identify the best solution (accuracy) but required more time. In the subjective comparison of interactive and static 3D maps, 89% of the participants strongly agreed or agreed with the statement that task solving was easier with interactive 3D maps. This unequal proportion also corroborated the other hypothesis that users preferred interactive tasks (H3).

4.2. Research Question 2

We hypothesized that interactivity had the same effect in all three subcategories of applied tasks (spatial understanding, pattern recognition, and combined tasks). For accuracy (H4) and speed (H5), the effect in combined tasks and spatial understanding tasks favored interactivity, although in pattern recognition tasks, no significant differences between interactive and static 3D maps were found. In pattern recognition tasks, accuracy and required time were quite high despite interactivity. The data suggested that pattern recognition tasks were probably more difficult than the other types because the participants took longer to solve them, though this greater effort led them to the correct answers. In future research, we should also consider that the experiment contained fewer pattern recognition tasks (in the number of each trial) than tasks in the other subcategories and that an existing effect may not have been seen.

The significant improvement of accuracy in interactive combined tasks—suggested to be the most complex of the three subcategories—indicated the real value added to interactive versions of 3D maps. In complex 3D tasks, where all the necessary data could not be depicted in easily accessible ways, the importance of interactivity grew significantly.

4.3. Research Question 3

The examination of the effect of expertise confirmed H6, which predicted greater accuracy by experts (geography students or graduates). However, H7 was refused as we did not find any statistically significant difference in response time between experts and laypersons. We also investigated the suggested relationship between cognitive styles measured in the OSIVQ questionnaire and user performance in tasks (H8 and H9). We could discern no relationship between specific cognitive styles and specific task types. Therefore, H8 was refuted, and H9 was confirmed. We can assume that all the cognitive strategies represented in the OSIVQ questionnaire were involved in the process of solving complex cartographic tasks (which 3D map tasks certainly are).

4.4. General Discussion

We discuss some limitations of our experimental design and procedure. Individual task types (RQ3) were somewhat difficult to compare due to the unequal numbers of experimental tests, especially pattern recognition tasks, of which there were only four in each test variant (two interactive and two static). However, in our opinion, it is possible to compare combined tasks (8 in each test variant) and spatial understanding tasks (12 in each test variant). For this reason, we analyzed the correctness and response times for all the test answers to RQ 1 (H1, H2, and H3) and RQ3 (H6 and H7). Another possible limitation is related to the number of tested participants. In general, it can be stated that a higher number of participants generates more representative results. However, in the experimental testing of 3D maps, the number of participants is usually lower (e.g., the average number of participants in the studies listed in Table 1 is 49), and these studies have produced significant results (i.e., References [20,28,35]).

In general, some authors have stated that comparing static and interactive maps can be problematic from the perspectives of cartography (e.g., Roth et al. [67]) and psychology (as discussed by Juřík et al. [60]). However, as mentioned in Section 2.3, other authors have made such comparisons, particularly to explore the process of perception and decision making [36–69]. From the perspective of traditional experiments, spatial data represent noisy, ambiguous stimuli, which are hard to control and adjust as sets of controlled test tasks. To research this issue, we needed a well-controlled, balanced experimental design with the maximum possible range of measurable variables. This condition was an objective in the present study. Importantly, from the literature review, we recognized that the results of previous user studies used as stimuli for static 3D maps cannot be generalized or transmitted to interactive 3D maps or virtual reality, as a fundamental component of virtual reality is 3D visualization of spatial data and navigational interactivity.

5. Conclusions and Future Work

In this study, we investigated the influence of interactivity in virtual 3D maps on user performance (accuracy and speed). The users consisted of both experts and laypersons. The participants completed an online testing battery with various task types including both interactive and static geovisualizations. We found significant differences in both accuracy and speed. Our data indicated that various tasks in 3D maps were solved more accurately in the presence of interactivity, and that users subjectively preferred to solve interactive tasks. However, tasks were solved faster with static visualizations. Further analysis indicated some differences between specific types of task-solving. Differences between experts and laypersons in overall task-solving accuracy were also identified.

Despite the limited number of available participants, our results can contribute to the development of new systems using 3D maps designed for landscape management, precision farming, environmental protection, and crisis management, where tasks that consider both terrain (altitudes and slopes) and thematic information are performed on 3D geovisualizations using color intensity as the main variable. Such 3D maps have been used, for example, by Jedlička and Charvát [70] to visualize yield potential, Herman and Řezník [71] to map noise, Christen et al. [72] to visualize avalanche simulations, and Dübel et al. [73] and Sieber et al. [74] to represent hazardous weather.

Specifically, the benefits of interactive 3D maps are influenced by factors contributed by the purpose of the map, which are map use conditions, type (and complexity) of map tasks, and potential map users.

- Interactive 3D maps are suitable for purposes where more accurate solution/decision is required, and no/less time pressure exists on the speed of this decision.
- Interactive 3D maps are more suitable for complex tasks (see Section 2.2 for more on task complexity).
- Interactive 3D maps are more suitable for geospatial data experts (geographers, spatial, and urban planners, etc.). It is necessary to carefully consider the use of 3D maps for laypersons.

For user studies, one clear recommendation can be made: If experimental results are to be generalized for interactive 3D maps and virtual reality, interactive 3D maps should be used as stimuli.

From a technological point of view, it is now possible to perform user testing directly with interactive 3D maps, which may be more appropriate regarding the transferability of results into practice in the design and implementation of 3D geovisualizations (see Juřík et al. [60]). Technologies that permit testing in controlled [38] and non-controlled conditions [56] can be connected to eye-tracking devices [33] and various interfaces, such as a touch screens [43,44] or the Wii Remote Controller [30], and other technologies for stereoscopic (real-3D) visualization with different immersion levels [34,37,57].

We would like to continue testing and will be working directly on interactive 3D testing. Importantly, user interaction and movement in the virtual environment can be described, analyzed, and compared, for example, with the results of the OSIVQ questionnaire, or inspected if any relationship exists between the results of the OSIVQ questionnaire and navigation in photorealistic and immersive virtual environments.

We also want to focus on more complex tasks that include advanced types of interaction. However, the difficulty of each task is also affected by the shape and complexity of the terrain or the distance between objects inserted into this terrain. Therefore, it must also be mentioned that 3D maps (and GIS data in general) represent complex stimuli which do not allow us to create a strict experimental design (as usually required in experimental studies). Regarding this, comprehensive data collection is required in interactive 3D maps to acquire better insight into the processes of decision making and task solving.

Supplementary Materials: A video documenting an experimental battery can be accessed at: https://youtu.be/Xat0slCx-Yg.

Author Contributions: L.H. was responsible for the literature review (cartographical and geoinformatics aspects), implementation of the testing tool, design of the experimental study, data analysis and interpretation and discussion of the results. L.H. also conducted the experimental study and coordinated whole paper preparation. V.J. collaborated on the literature review (psychological aspects), data analysis and discussion of the results. Z.S. advised on experimental design and collaborated on interpretation and discussion of the results. D.V. and J.R. collaborated on execution of the experimental study and data analysis. T.Ř. advised on implementation of the testing tool and collaborated on interpretation of the results.

Funding: This research was supported by the grants of the Masaryk University "The influence of cartographic visualization methods in the success of solving practical and educational spatial tasks" (Grant No. MUNI/M/0846/2015), "Integrated research on environmental changes in the landscape sphere of Earth III" (Grant No. MUNI/A/1251/2017) and by the grant of the Ministry of Education, Youth and Sports of the Czech Republic (Grant No. LTACH-17002) "Dynamic Mapping Methods Oriented to Risk and Disaster Management in the Era of Big Data". This research was supported also by the research infrastructure HUME Lab Experimental Humanities Laboratory, Faculty of Arts, Masaryk University.

Acknowledgments: We are grateful to Dajana Snopková for helping us with statistical analysis. Finally, we would like to thank the participants for their time and efforts

Conflicts of Interest: The authors declare no conflict of interest.

References

1. Shiode, N. 3D Urban Models: Recent Developments in the Digital Modelling of Urban Environments in Three-dimensions. *GeoJournal* **2001**, *52*, 263–269. [CrossRef]
2. Abdul-Rahman, A.; Pilouk, M. *Spatial Data Modelling for 3D GIS*, 1st ed.; Springer: Berlin, Germany, 2008; 289p, ISBN 978-3-540-74166-4.
3. Biljecki, F.; Stoter, J.; Ledoux, H.; Zlatanova, S.; Çöltekin, A. Applications of 3D city models: State of the art review. *ISPRS Int. J. Geo Inf.* **2015**, *4*, 2842–2889. [CrossRef]
4. Wood, J.; Kirschenbauer, S.; Döllner, J.; Lopes, A.; Bodum, L. Using 3D in Visualization. In *Exploring Geovisualization*, 1st ed.; Dykes, J., MacEachren, A.M., Kraak, M.-J., Eds.; Elsevier: Amsterdam, The Netherlands, 2005; pp. 295–312.
5. Buchroithner, M.F.; Knust, C. True-3D in Cartography—Current Hard and Softcopy Developments. In *Geospatial Visualisation*, 1st ed.; Moore, A., Drecki, I., Eds.; Springer: Berlin, Germany, 2013; pp. 41–65.

6. Hájek, P.; Jedlička, K.; Čada, V. Principles of Cartographic Design for 3D Maps Focused on Urban Areas. In Proceedings of the 6th International Conference on Cartography and GIS, Albena, Bulgaria, 13–17 June 2016; Bandrova, T., Konečný, M., Eds.; Bulgarian Cartographic Association: Sofia, Bulgaria, 2016; pp. 297–307.
7. Haeberling, C.; Bär, H.; Hurni, L. Proposed Cartographic Design Principles for 3D Maps: A Contribution to an Extended Cartographic Theory. *Cartogr. Int. J. Geogr. Inf. Geovisual.* **2008**, *43*, 175–188. [CrossRef]
8. Bandrova, T. Innovative Technology for the Creation of 3D Maps. *Data Sci. J.* **2006**, *4*, 53–58. [CrossRef]
9. Schobesberger, D.; Patterson, T. Evaluating the Effectiveness of 2D vs. 3D Trailhead Maps. In Proceedings of the 6th ICA Mountain Cartography Workshop Mountain Mapping and Visualisation, Lenk, Switzerland, 1–15 February 2008; pp. 201–205.
10. Roth, R. Cartographic Interaction Primitives: Framework and Synthesis. *Cartogr. J.* **2012**, *49*, 376–395. [CrossRef]
11. Šašinka, Č. Interindividuální Rozdíly v Percepci Prostoru a Map. Ph.D. Thesis, Masaryk University, Brno, Czech Republic, 2012.
12. Lokka, I.-E.; Çöltekin, A. Simulating Navigation with Virtual 3D Geovisualizations—A Focus on Memory Related Factors. In *ISPRS Archives of the Photogrammetry, Remote Sensing and Spatial Information Sciences*; Halounová, L., Ed.; Copernicus GmbH: Gottingen, Germany, 2016; Volume XLI-B2, pp. 671–673.
13. Larkin, J.H.; Simon, H.A. Why a Diagram is (Sometimes) Worth Ten Thousand Words. *Cogn. Sci.* **1987**, *11*, 65–100. [CrossRef]
14. Shepherd, I. Travails in the Third Dimension: A Critical Evaluation of Three Dimensional Geographical Visualization. In *Geographic Visualization: Concepts, Tools and Applications*, 1st ed.; Dodge, M., McDerby, M., Turner, M., Eds.; John Wiley & Sons, Ltd.: Chichester, UK, 2008; pp. 199–222. ISBN 978-0-470-51511-2.
15. Boy, G.A. *The Handbook of Human-Machine Interaction: A Human-Centered Design Approach*, 1st ed.; Ashgate: Farnham, UK, 2011; 478p, ISBN 9781138075825.
16. Leontiev, A. Activity and Consciousness. 1977. Available online: https://www.marxists.org/archive/leontev/works/activity-consciousness.pdf (accessed on 15 August 2018).
17. Neisser, U. *Cognition and Reality: Principles and Implications of Cognitive Psychology*, 1st ed.; W. H. Freeman & Company: San Francisco, CA, USA, 1976; 230p, ISBN 13-978-0716704775.
18. Engel, J.; Semmo, A.; Trapp, S.; Döllner, J. Evaluating the Perceptual Impact of Rendering Techniques on Thematic Color Mappings in 3D Virtual Environments. In Proceedings of the 18th International Workshop on Vision, Modeling and Visualization (VMV 2013), Lugano, Switzerland, 11–13 September 2013; The Eurographics Association: Geneve, Switzerland, 2013.
19. Niedomysl, T.; Elldér, E.; Larsson, A.; Thelin, M.; Jansund, B. Learning Benefits of Using 2D versus 3D Maps: Evidence from a Randomized Controlled Experiment. *J. Geogr.* **2013**, *112*, 87–96. [CrossRef]
20. Popelka, S.; Brychtová, A. Eye-tracking Study on Different Perception of 2D and 3D Terrain Visualization. *Cartogr. J.* **2013**, *50*, 240–375. [CrossRef]
21. Seipel, S. Evaluating 2D and 3D Geovisualisations for Basic Spatial Assessment. *Behav. Inf. Technol.* **2013**, *32*, 845–858. [CrossRef]
22. Popelka, S.; Doležalová, J. Non-Photorealistic 3D Visualization in City Maps: An Eye-Tracking Study. In *Modern Trends in Cartography*, 1st ed.; Brus, S., Vondráková, A., Voženílek, V., Eds.; Springer: Berlin, Germany, 2015; pp. 357–367. ISBN 978-3-319-07925-7.
23. Preppernau, C.A.; Jenny, B. Three-dimensional versus Conventional Volcanic Hazard Maps. *Nat. Hazards* **2015**, *78*, 1329–1347. [CrossRef]
24. Rautenbach, V.; Coetzee, S.; Çöltekin, A. Investigating the Use Of 3D Geovisualizations for Urban Design in Informal Settlement Upgrading in South Africa. In *ISPRS Archives of the Photogrammetry, Remote Sensing and Spatial Information Sciences*; Halounová, L., Ed.; Copernicus GmbH: Gottingen, Germany, 2016; Volume XLI-B2, pp. 425–431.
25. Zhou, Y.; Dao, T.H.D.; Thill, J.-C.; Delmelle, E. Enhanced 3D Visualization Techniques in Support of Indoor Location Planning. *Comput. Environ. Urban Syst.* **2016**, *50*, 15–29. [CrossRef]
26. Liu, B.; Dong, W.; Meng, L. Using Eye Tracking to Explore the Guidance and Constancy of Visual Variables in 3D Visualization. *ISPRS Int. J. Geo Inf.* **2017**, *6*, 274. [CrossRef]

27. Abend, P.; Thielmann, T.; Ewerth, R.; Seiler, D.; Műhling, M.; Dőring, J.; Grauer, M.; Freisleben, B. Geobrowsing Behaviour in Google Earth—A Semantic Video Content Analysis of On-Screen Navigation. In *GI_Forum 2012: Geovisualization, Society and Learning*; Jekel, T., Car, A., Griesebner, G., Eds.; Wichmann: Berlin, Germany, 2012; pp. 2–13.
28. Wilkening, J.; Fabrikant, S.I. How Users Interact with a 3D Geo-Browser under Time Pressure. *Cartogr. Geogr. Inf. Sci.* **2013**, *40*, 40–52. [CrossRef]
29. Treves, R.; Viterbo, P.; Haklay, M. Footprints in the Sky: Using Student Tracklogs from a "Bird's Eye View" Virtual Field Trip to Enhance Learning. *J. Geogr. High. Educ.* **2015**, *39*, 97–110. [CrossRef]
30. Špriňarová, K.; Juřík, V.; Šašinka, Č.; Herman, L.; Štěrba, Z.; Stachoň, Z.; Chmelík, J.; Kozlíková, B. Human-computer Interaction in Real 3D and Pseudo-3D Cartographic Visualization: A Comparative Study. In *Cartography—Maps Connecting the World: 27th International Cartographic Conference 2015—ICC2015*, 1st ed.; Sluter, C.R., Ed.; Springer: Berlin, Germany, 2015; pp. 59–73. ISBN 978-3-319-17737-3.
31. McKenzie, G.; Klippel, A. The Interaction of Landmarks and Map Alignment in You-Are-Here Maps. *Cartogr. J.* **2016**, *53*, 43–54. [CrossRef]
32. Carbonell-Carrera, C.; Saorín, J. Geospatial Google Street View with Virtual Reality: A Motivational Approach for Spatial Training Education. *ISPRS Int. J. Geo Inf.* **2017**, *6*, 261. [CrossRef]
33. Herman, L.; Popelka, S.; Hejlová, V. Eye-tracking Analysis of Interactive 3D Geovisualizations. *J. Eye Mov. Res.* **2017**, *10*, 1–15. [CrossRef]
34. Juřík, V.; Herman, L.; Šašinka, Č.; Stachoň, Z.; Chmelík, J. When the Display Matters: A Multifaceted Perspective on 3D Geovisualizations. *Open Geosci.* **2017**, *9*, 89–100. [CrossRef]
35. Bleisch, S.; Dykes, J.; Nebiker, S. Evaluating the Effectiveness of Representing Numeric Information Through Abstract Graphics in 3D Desktop Virtual Environments. *Cartogr. J.* **2008**, *45*, 216–226. [CrossRef]
36. Herbert, G.; Chen, X. A Comparison of Usefulness of 2D and 3D Representations of Urban Planning. *Cartogr. Geogr. Inf. Sci.* **2015**, *42*, 22–32. [CrossRef]
37. Kubíček, P.; Šašinka, Č.; Stachoň, Z.; Herman, L.; Juřík, V.; Urbánek, T.; Chmelík, J. Identification of Altitude Profiles in 3D Geovisualizations: The Role of Interaction and Spatial Abilities. *Int. J. Digit. Earth* **2017**. [CrossRef]
38. Herman, L.; Stachoň, Z. Comparison of User Performance with Interactive and Static 3D Visualization—Pilot Study. In *ISPRS Archives of the Photogrammetry, Remote Sensing and Spatial Information Sciences*, Halounová, L., Ed.; Copernicus GmbH: Gottingen, Germany, 2016; Volume XLI-B2, pp. 655–661.
39. Kjellin, A.; Pettersson, L.W.; Seipel, S. Evaluating 2D and 3D Visualizations of Spatiotemporal Information. *ACM Trans. Appl. Percept.* **2010**, *7*, 1–23. [CrossRef]
40. Boér, A.; Çöltekin, A.; Clarke, K.C. An Evaluation of Web-based Geovisualizations for Different Levels of Abstraction and Realism—What do users predict? In Proceedings of the International Cartographic Conference, Dresden, Germany, 25–30 August 2013.
41. Rautenbach, V.; Coetzee, S.; Çöltekin, A. Towards Evaluating the Map literacy of Planners in 2D Maps and 3D Models in South Africa. In Proceedings of the AfricaGEO 2014 Conference, Cape Town, South Africa, 1–3 July 2014.
42. Juřík, V.; Herman, L.; Šašinka, Č. Interaction Primitives in 3D Geovisualizations. In In *Useful Geography: Transfer from Research to Practice.* Proceedings of the 25th Central European Conference, Brno, Czech Republic, 2–13 October 2017; Svobodová, H., Ed.; Masaryk University: Brno, Czech Republic, 2018; pp. 294–303.
43. Herman, L.; Stachoň, Z. Controlling 3D Geovisualizations through Touch Screen—The Role of Users Age and Gesture Intuitiveness. In Proceedings of the 7th International Conference on Cartography and GIS, Sozopol, Bulgaria, 18–23 June 2018; Bandrova, T., Konečný, M., Eds.; Bulgarian Cartographic Association: Sofia, Bulgaria, 2018; Volume 1, pp. 473–480.
44. Herman, L.; Stachoň, Z.; Stuchlík, R.; Hladík, J.; Kubíček, P. Touch Interaction with 3D Geographical Visualization on Web: Selected Technological and User Issues. In *ISPRS Archives of the Photogrammetry, Remote Sensing and Spatial Information Sciences*; Dimopoulou, E., Van Oosterom, P., Eds.; Copernicus GmbH: Gottingen, Germany, 2016; Volume XLII-2/W2, pp. 33–40.
45. Livatino, S.; De Paolis, L.T.; D'Agostino, M.; Zocco, A.; Agrimi, A.; De Santis, A.; Bruno, L.V.; Lapresa, M. Stereoscopic Visualization and 3-D Technologies in Medical Endoscopic Teleoperation. *IEEE Trans. Ind. Electron.* **2015**, *62*, 525–535. [CrossRef]

46. Hayes, J.; Allinson, C.W. Cognitive Style and its Relevance for Management Practice. *Br. J. Manag.* **1994**, *5*, 53–71. [CrossRef]
47. Kozhevnikov, M. Cognitive Styles in the Context of Modern Psychology: Toward an Integrated Framework of Cognitive Style. *Psychol. Bull.* **2007**, *133*, 464–481. [CrossRef] [PubMed]
48. Peterson, E.R.; Deary, I.J.; Austin, E.J. A New Measure of Verbal–Imagery Cognitive Style: VICS. *Pers. Individ. Differ.* **2005**, *38*, 1269–1281. [CrossRef]
49. Blajenkova, O.; Kozhevnikov, M.; Motes, M.A. Object-spatial imagery: A new self-report imagery questionnaire. *Appl. Cogn. Psychol.* **2006**, *20*, 239–263. [CrossRef]
50. Jonassen, D.H.; Grabowski, B.L. *Handbook of Individual Differences, Learning, and Instruction*; Routledge: Abingdon, UK, 2012; 512p, ISBN 978-0805814132.
51. Blazhenkova, O.; Kozhevnikov, M. The New Object-Spatial-Verbal Cognitive Style Model: Theory and Measurement. *Appl. Cogn. Psychol.* **2009**, *23*, 638–663. [CrossRef]
52. Rubin, J.; Chisnell, D.; Spool, J. *Handbook of Usability Testing: How to Plan, Design, and Conduct Effective Tests*, 2nd ed.; Wiley: Hoboken, NJ, USA, 2008; 384p, ISBN 978-0-470-18548-3.
53. EEE 610:1990. *IEEE Standard Computer Dictionary: A Compilation of IEEE Standard Computer Glossaries*; IEEE: Piscataway, NJ, USA, 1990. [CrossRef]
54. Bowman, D.A.; Kruijff, E.; Poupyrev, I.; LaViola, J.J. *3D User Interfaces: Theory and Practice*, 1st ed.; Addison Wesley Longman Publishing: Redwood City, CA, USA, 2004; 512p, ISBN 978-0321980045.
55. Herman, L.; Řezník, T.; Stachoň, Z.; Russnák, J. The Design and Testing of 3DmoveR: An Experimental Tool for Usability Studies of Interactive 3D Maps. *Cartogr. Perspect.* **2018**, *90*, 31–63. [CrossRef]
56. Štěrba, Z.; Šašinka, Č.; Stachoň, Z.; Štampach, R.; Morong, K. *Selected Issues of Experimental Testing in Cartography*, 1st ed.; Masaryk University, MuniPress: Brno, Czech Republic, 2015; 120p, ISBN 978-80-210-7909-0.
57. Stachoň, Z.; Kubíček, P.; Málek, F.; Krejčí, M.; Herman, L. The Role of Hue and Realism in Virtual Reality. In Proceedings of the 7th International Conference on Cartography and GIS, Sozopol, Bulgaria, 18–23 June 2018; Bandrova, T., Konečný, M., Eds.; Bulgarian Cartographic Association: Sofia, Bulgaria, 2018; Volume 1, pp. 932–941.
58. Howell, D. *Statistical Methods for Psychology*, 7th ed.; Cengage Wadsworth: Belmont, CA, USA, 2010; 793p, ISBN 978-0-495-59784-1.
59. Anderson, W.; Krathwohl, D.R.; Bloom, B.S. *A Taxonomy for Learning, Teaching, and Assessing: A Revision of Bloom's Taxonomy of Educational Objectives*, 1st ed.; Longman: New York, NY, USA, 2001; 352p, ISBN 978-0801319037.
60. Juřík, V.; Herman, L.; Šašinka, Č.; Stachoň, Z.; Chmelík, J.; Strnadová, A.; Kubíček, P. Behavior Analysis in Virtual Geovisualizations: Towards Ecological Validity. In Proceedings of the 7th International Conference on Cartography and GIS, Sozopol, Bulgaria, 18–23 June 2018; Bandrova, T., Konečný, M., Eds.; Bulgarian Cartographic Association: Sofia, Bulgaria, 2018; Volume 1, pp. 518–527.
61. European Environment Agency. Copernicus Land Monitoring Service—EU-DEM. Available online: https://www.eea.europa.eu/data-and-maps/data/copernicus-land-monitoring-service-eu-dem (accessed on 15 September 2018).
62. Warne, R.T. A Primer on Multivariate Analysis of Variance (MANOVA) for Behavioral Scientists. *Pr. Assess. Res. Eval.* **2014**, *17*, 1–10.
63. Levene, H. Robust Tests for Equality of Variances. In *Contributions to Probability and Statistics: Essays in Honor of Harold Hotelling*, 1st ed.; Olki, I., Ed.; Stanford University Press: Palo Alto, CA, USA, 1960; pp. 278–292.
64. Mann, H.B.; Whitney, D.R. On a Test of Whether one of Two Random Variables is Stochastically Larger than the Other. *Ann. Math. Stat.* **1947**, *1*, 50–60. [CrossRef]
65. Box, G.E.; Cox, D.R. An Analysis of Transformations. *J. R. Stat. Soc. Ser. B* **1964**, *2*, 211–252.
66. Shapiro, S.S.; Wilk, M.B. An Analysis of Variance Test for Normality (Complete Samples). *Biometrika* **1965**, *3/4*, 591–611. [CrossRef]
67. Roth, R.E.; Çöltekin, A.; Delazari, L.; Filho, H.F.; Griffin, A.; Hall, A.; Korpi, J.; Lokka, I.-E.; Mendonça, A.; Ooms, K.; et al. User Studies in Cartography: Opportunities for Empirical Research on Interactive Maps and Visualizations. *Int. J. Cartogr.* **2017**, *3*, 61–89. [CrossRef]

68. Keskin, M.; Çelik, B.; Doğru, A.Ö.; Pakdil, M.E. A Comparison of Space-Time 2D and 3D Geovisualization. In Proceedings of the 27th International Cartographic Conference, Rio de Janeiro, Brazil, 23–28 August 2015; pp. 1–17.
69. Bogucka, E.P.; Jahnke, M. Feasibility of the Space–Time Cube in Temporal Cultural Landscape Visualization. *ISPRS Int. J. Geo Inf.* **2018**, *7*, 209. [CrossRef]
70. Jedlička, K.; Charvát, K. Visualisation of Big Data in Agriculture and Rural Development. In Proceedings of the IST-Africa Week Conference, Gaborone, Botswana, 9–11 May 2018; Cunningham, P., Cunningham, M., Eds.; IEEE: Piscataway, NJ, USA, 2018; pp. 1–8.
71. Herman, L.; Řezník, T. Web 3D Visualization of Noise Mapping for Extended INSPIRE Buildings Model. In *Environmental Software Systems. Fostering Information Sharing, Proceedings of theIFIP Advances in Information and Communication Technology, Neusiedl am See, Austria, 9–11 October 2013*; Hřebíček, J., Schimak, G., Kubásek, M., Rizzoli, A.E., Eds.; Springer: Berlin/Heidelberg, Germany, 2013; Volume 413, pp. 414–424.
72. Christen, M.; Bűhler, Y.; Bartelt, P.; Leine, R.; Glover, J.; Schweizer, A.; Graf, C.; McArdell, B.W.; Gerber, W.; Deubelbeiss, Y.; et al. Integral Hazard Management Using a Unified Software Environment: Numerical Simulation Tool "RAMMS" for Gravitational Natural Hazards. In Proceedings of the 12th Congress INTERPRAEVENT 2012, Grenoble, France, 23–26 April 2012; Koboltschnig, G., Hübl, J., Braun, J., Eds.; International Research Society INTERPRAEVENT: Klagenfurt, Austria, 2012; Volume 1, pp. 77–86.
73. Dübel, S.; Röhlig, M.; Tominski, C.; Schumann, H. Visualizing 3D Terrain, Geo-Spatial Data, and Uncertainty. *Informatics* **2017**, *4*, 6. [CrossRef]
74. Sieber, R.; Hollenstein, L.; Eichenberger, R. Concepts and Techniques of an Online 3D Atlas—Challenges in Cartographic 3D Visualization. In Proceedings of the Leveraging Applications of Formal Methods, Verification and Validation, Applications and Case Studies, Heraklion, Greece, 15–18 October 2012; Margaria, T., Steffen, B., Eds.; Springer: Berlin/Heidelberg, Germany, 2012; pp. 325–326. [CrossRef]

© 2018 by the authors. Licensee MDPI, Basel, Switzerland. This article is an open access article distributed under the terms and conditions of the Creative Commons Attribution (CC BY) license (http://creativecommons.org/licenses/by/4.0/).

Communication

Determining Optimal Video Length for the Estimation of Building Height through Radial Displacement Measurement from Space

Andrew Plowright, Riccardo Tortini *,† and Nicholas C. Coops

Integrated Remote Sensing Studio, Department of Forest Resources Management, University of British Columbia, 2424 Main Mall, Vancouver, BC V6T 1Z4, Canada; andrew.plowright@alumni.ubc.ca (A.P.); nicholas.coops@ubc.ca (N.C.C.)
* Correspondence: rtortini@ucla.edu or riccardo.tortini@ubc.ca; Tel.: +1-310-993-5201
† Current address: Department of Geography, University of California, Los Angeles, CA 90095, USA

Received: 14 August 2018; Accepted: 14 September 2018; Published: 18 September 2018

Abstract: We presented a methodology for estimating building heights in downtown Vancouver, British Columbia, Canada, using a high definition video (HDV) recorded from the International Space Station. We developed an iterative routine based on multiresolution image segmentation to track the radial displacement of building roofs over the course of the HDV, and to predict the building heights using an ordinary least-squares regression model. The linear relationship between the length of the tracking vector and the height of the buildings was excellent ($r^2 \leq 0.89$, RMSE ≤ 8.85 m, $p < 0.01$). Notably, the accuracy of the height estimates was not improved considerably beyond 10 s of outline tracking, revealing an optimal video length for estimating the height or elevation of terrestrial features. HDVs are demonstrated to be a viable and effective data source for target tracking and building height prediction when high resolution imagery, spectral information, and/or topographic data from other sources are not available.

Keywords: high definition video; International Space Station (ISS); multiresolution segmentation; building tracking; height estimate

1. Introduction

The earliest examples of using videos from space in Earth Observation (EO) dates back to the 1970s, with the Return Beam Vidicon (RBV) sensor carried aboard the first three Landsat satellites [1]. However, the RBV operated along the ground track of the satellite, providing a video with a similar footprint as the 2D multispectral imagery.

Recent directional videos acquired from space orbit, provide a potentially novel viewing perspective at high spatial and temporal resolutions. While previous studies have used video image sequences in combination with digital maps and high resolution topographic data, such as Light Detection and Ranging (LiDAR), to generate 3D building models [2], the extraction of topographic metrics from directional videos remains less explored. In addition, although unsupervised video segmentation techniques date back to the 1990s [3,4], this approach has yet to be applied to videos from space.

As the nadir of non-geostationary earth-observing sensors moves across the Earth's surface, the angle of incidence between terrestrial features and the sensor changes (e.g., Figure 1). Consequently, when recorded to video, vertical objects such as trees or buildings appear to 'lean' away from a sensor's isocenter. This effect, known as radial displacement, is more pronounced with taller objects, whose apexes will appear to shift away from the isocenter more rapidly than objects closer to the ground. This principle is used for a wide variety of photogrammetric applications, including the generation of digital elevation models [5], detecting and measuring urban objects [6], mapping forest structure and regeneration [7,8], and improving geo-positioning accuracy [9]. The accuracy of this approach has been compared to terrestrial laser scanning [10], and has been demonstrated to be an effective complement to airborne laser scanning for the reconstruction of 3D landscape features [11]. Photogrammetric measurement techniques are frequently used in conjunction with image analysis and feature extraction routines [12], and are particularly important in the development of unmanned aerial vehicle positioning and navigational systems [13].

Figure 1. Example of radial displacement of buildings over the course of a high definition video from space.

In this paper, we examine the potential for extracting useful landscape information from this effect using a High Definition Video (HDV) of Vancouver, British Columbia, Canada, recorded from space. We analyze the relationship between the height above ground of thirty buildings of various sizes, and the radial displacement of their rooftops over the course of the video. The degree to which the duration of the video, and consequently the magnitude of the displacement, affects the relationship is also assessed.

2. Materials and Methods

2.1. Data Collection

The HDV dataset 'grss_dfc_2016' [14] covering an urban and harbor area in downtown Vancouver, Canada (49°15′ N, 123°06′ W), was provided by Deimos Imaging and UrtheCast. The full color HDV (~34 s total) was acquired on 2 July 2015, using the high-resolution camera Iris installed onboard the Zvezda module of the International Space Station (ISS). The ISS operates in a sun-synchronous orbit with an inclination angle of 51.6°, covering the same area 15 times per day [15]. This unique orbit undergoes a precession of approximately 6° per day, providing a wide range of sun illumination angles for earth observation. Iris utilizes a 14MPixel Complementary Metal Oxide Semiconductor (CMOS) detector to capture RGB HDVs at 3 frame per second (fps) and converted to 30 fps before delivery to the user, with a nominal footprint at nadir of 3.8 km × 5.7 km for 400 km altitude [16]. The Iris HDV frames utilized in this study were fully orthorectified and resampled to 1 m, with a total frame format of 3840 × 2160 pixels (approximately 3.8 km × 2.1 km).

A total of 1032 frames were extracted from the entire length of the HDV, and a sample of 30 buildings from the downtown area were selected through a stratified random sampling process. A dataset of georeferenced building footprints for the area was acquired [17], which included each building's height above ground. A height threshold of 10 m and a minimum roof area of 500 m^2 were applied to eliminate the high number of buildings that were (i) likely to be shadowed by the area's taller structures, and/or (ii) commercial row buildings that could not be visually distinguished at the video's resolution. Furthermore, the thinness ratio k [18], a measurement quantifying the intricacy of a shape's outline, was computed for all building footprints. Samples of ten buildings were then drawn from the following three height classes: 10–40 m, 40–70 m, and >70 m, and they represented an equal number of evenly (k > 0.7) and irregularly shaped (k ≤ 0.7) roofs.

2.2. Roof Tracking Algorithm

Over the course of the video, the movement of the satellite's nadir causes the radial displacement of the buildings to gradually increase. From an initial near-orthogonal view, the buildings appeared to gradually 'tilt' as the video progressed. This effect was measured by tracking the apparent movement of rooftops within the scene. To this end, an iterative frame-by-frame tracking routine based on image segmentation was developed and implemented.

A multiresolution segmentation algorithm was applied to each HDV frame in the eCognition® software environment (Trimble Navigation Ltd., Sunnyvale, CA, USA). The composition of homogeneity criterion for shape and compactness were set to 0.8 and 0.5, respectively, and the scale parameter was set to 40. Beginning with the geo-referenced footprint of a given building (which is assumed to have roughly the same shape as the building's rooftop), the following process was then iterated over the video frames in chronological order. The segment with the greatest degree of overlap with the building's outline was extracted. If the segment was within 30% of the size of the outline, then the outline of the building was replaced with that segment. If not, the frame was skipped (Figure 2). The radial displacement of the outline was quantified by measuring the Euclidian distance between the outline's centroid (i.e., geometric center) and the centroid of the original building footprint.

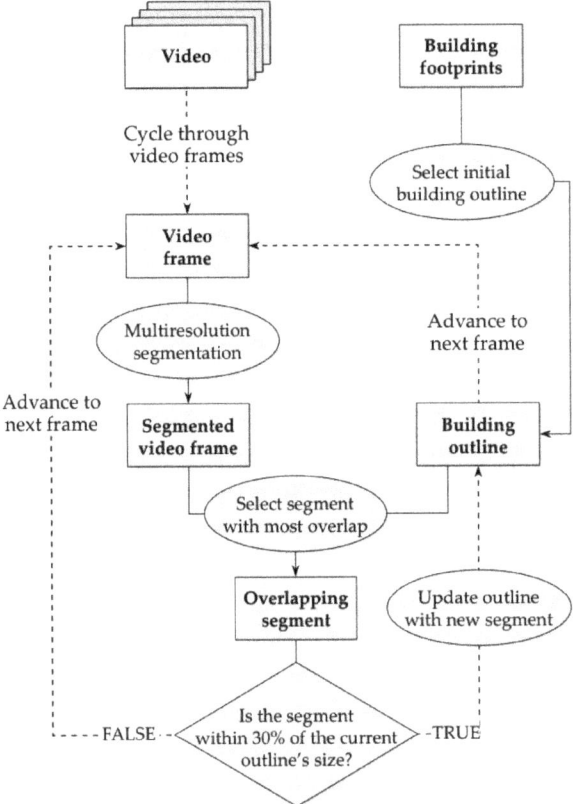

Figure 2. Flowchart of the proposed rooftop tracking method.

2.3. Building Height Prediction

Given that radial displacement was greater for taller features than smaller ones, the displacement distance of the outlines was used as a predictor of the buildings' height above ground. Using the 30 sample buildings, the relationship between the two variables was tested using the ordinary least-squares (OLS) regression.

Displacement increased over the course of the HDV, and so the predictive power of the relationship may change with time. To investigate this possibility, an OLS regression model was fit at every 0.10 s interval (i.e., 3 frames). The r^2 of each model was recorded and then plotted against time.

3. Results

3.1. Roof Tracking Algorithm

Figure 3 shows an example of the rooftop tracking routine over the course of the HDV. Though the rooftops are initially in line with the buildings' footprints, the roofs gradually shift away as the effects of radial displacement are made evident.

Irregularities in the image segmentation and distortions of the target due to changing viewing angles, may cause a high degree of variation in the shape of the rooftop outlines. Using centroids to measure the displacement of the outlines could compensate for these variations.

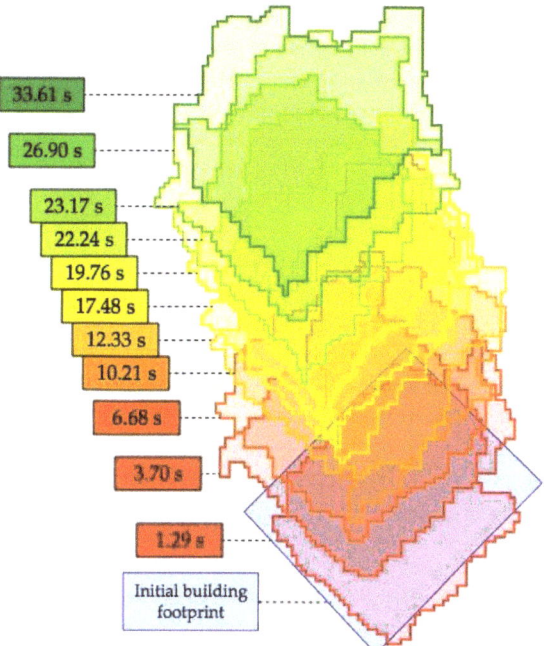

Figure 3. Example of building rooftop tracking over the course of the high definition video (HDV). Outlines are colored according to the video time at which they were extracted.

Figure 4 shows the radial displacement of the sample buildings over the course of the video. Of the 30 sample building rooftops, all but three were successfully tracked to the end of the video (i.e., within the last 20 frames). These three targets were lost in the tracking process at different times: 31.92 s, 32.02 s, and 18.24 s from the beginning of the video. Potential causes for tracking failures, include the gradual distortion of the rooftops' shape or shadowing effects from neighboring buildings.

Figure 4. Radial displacement of building rooftops in pixels, measured by tracking the movement of rooftop outlines over the course of the video. Initial building rooftop outlines appear as green polygons. Green targets represent the centroids of the tracked outlines' final positions. Green vectors represent the radial displacement of the outlines. Red polygons represent three buildings that were lost during the tracking progress.

3.2. Building Height Prediction

The relationship between the sample buildings' radial displacement and their height above ground was evaluated over the course of the video by fitting OLS regression models to the two variables every 0.10 s. Figure 5 shows the change in the r^2 of these models over time. Outlying points with lower r^2 values (e.g., ~8 s; 15–20 s) are principally due to irregularities in the HDV frame sequence, leading to gaps between the times when the building outlines were updated. An improved tracking algorithm capable of updating outlines at every frame would likely yield fewer low outliers, and the curve itself would reach its plateau earlier. This plateau represents the optimal video length required for accurately estimating building height. Prior to reaching this plateau, the low degree of radial displacement is insufficient for computing building heights, whereas the height estimates are no longer improved once this plateau has been attained. The best model fit achieved through this process was r^2 = 0.89 (RMSE ≤ 8.85 m, $p < 0.01$).

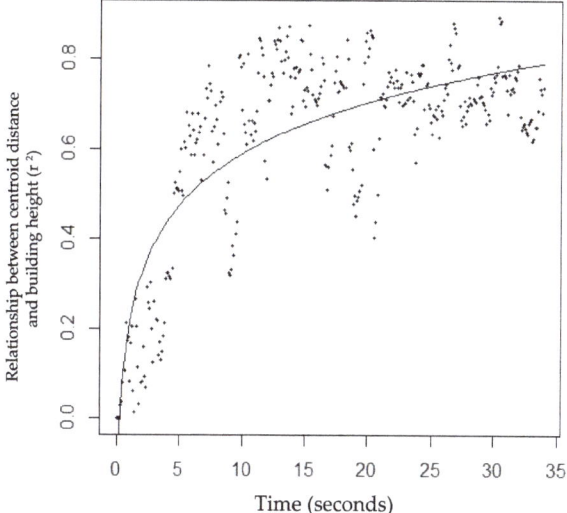

Figure 5. Temporal change in the relationship between buildings' radial displacement and height above ground as measured by the r^2 of least-squares regression models.

4. Discussion and Conclusions

In this paper, we presented a methodology for estimating building height in downtown Vancouver, British Columbia, Canada, using a HDV recorded from the ISS. We developed an iterative routine based on multiresolution image segmentation to track the radial displacement of building roofs over the course of the HDV.

The degree of radial displacement, as measured by the tracking algorithm, gradually increased over the course of the video. As the displacement increased, so too did its potential for estimating building height, achieving an r^2 of up to 0.89 (Figure 5). However, after having attained a plateau at ~10 s, the accuracy of the height estimates did not considerably improve. This result is of fundamental importance in situations where only shorter clips may be available. Furthermore, attempts to track targets for longer periods may also lead to tracking failures, as demonstrated in Figure 4. This study therefore suggests that an optimal video length exists for the purpose of estimating the height or elevation of terrestrial features when using HDVs shot from space.

The ISS completes an orbit around the Earth every 90 min, offering videos with unprecedentedly high spatial and temporal resolution. In addition, the large area covered by its frame (i.e., approximately 3.8 km × 2.1 km) makes monitoring highly dynamic situations possible at broad spatial scales. As the availability of these videos becomes more widespread, demand for maximizing their value will increase. Whilst top-down HDVs are typically used for tracking the horizontal movement of targets, radial displacement allows analysts to extract additional vertical information from a scene. This work contributes to the establishment of optimal video parameters for this task, which are crucial for cost-effect acquisition planning. Not limited to spaceborne sensors, the proposed methodology may be applied to other sources of top-down HDVs, such as those acquired by conventional aircraft or unmanned aerial vehicles.

Author Contributions: A.P. and R.T. designed the study, processed the data, and wrote the manuscript supervised by N.C.C. All authors analyzed the results and proofread the manuscript.

Funding: This research received no external funding.

Acknowledgments: The authors would like to thank Deimos Imaging for acquiring and providing the data used in this study, and the IEEE GRSS Image Analysis and Data Fusion Technical Committee. We are also thankful to the three anonymous reviewers for their comments on an earlier version of the manuscript.

Conflicts of Interest: The authors declare no conflict of interest.

References

1. Schade, O.H., Jr. Electron Optics and Signal Readout of High-Definition Return-Beam Vidicon Cameras. In *Photoelectronic Imaging Devices*; Biberman, L.M., Nudelman, S., Eds.; Springer US: New York, NY, USA, 1971; pp. 345–399.
2. Zhang, Y.; Zhang, Z.; Zhang, J.; Wu, J. 3D Building Modelling with Digital Map, LiDAR Data, and Video Image Sequences. *Photogramm. Rec.* **2005**, *20*, 285–302. [CrossRef]
3. Hampapur, A.; Jain, R.; Weymouth, T.E. Production Model Based Digital Video Segmentation. In *Multimedia Tools and Applications*; Furht, B., Ed.; Springer US: New York, NY, USA, 1995; pp. 9–46.
4. Wang, D. Unsupervised Video Segmentation Based on Watersheds and Temporal Tracking. *IEEE Trans. Circuits Syst. Video Technol.* **1998**, *8*, 539–546. [CrossRef]
5. Usyal, M.; Toprak, A.S.; Polat, N. DEM generation with UAV Photogrammetry and accuracy analysis in Sahitler hill. *Measurement* **2015**, *73*, 539–543. [CrossRef]
6. Suliman, A.; Zhang, Y. Stereo-Based Building Roof Mapping in Urban Off-Nadir VHR Satellite Images: Challenges and Solutions. In *Urban Remote Sensing*; Weng, Q., Quattrochi, D., Gamba, P.E., Eds.; CRC Press Inc.: Boca Raton, FL, USA, 2018; p. 53.
7. Rahlf, J.; Breidenbach, J.; Solberg, S.; Næsset, E.; Astrup, R. Digital aerial photogrammetry can efficiently support large-area forest inventories in Norway. *Forestry* **2017**, *90*, 710–718. [CrossRef]
8. Goodbody, T.R.; Coops, N.C.; Hermosilla, T.; Tompalski, P.; Crawford, P. Assessing the status of forest regeneration using digital aerial photogrammetry and unmanned aerial systems. *Int. J. Remote Sens.* **2018**, *39*, 5246–5264. [CrossRef]
9. Tang, S.; Wu, B.; Zhu, Q. Combined adjustment of multi-resolution satellite imagery for improved geo-positioning accuracy. *ISPRS J. Photogramm. Remote Sens.* **2016**, *114*, 125–136. [CrossRef]
10. Lichti, D.D.; Gordon, S.J.; Stewart, M.P.; Franke, J.; Tsakiri, M. Comparison of digital photogrammetry and laser scanning. *Proc. Int. Soc. Photogramm. Remote Sens.* **2002**, 39–44.
11. Habib, A.; Ghanma, M.; Morgan, M.; Al-Ruzouq, R. Photogrammetric and LiDAR data registration using linear features. *Photogramm. Eng. Rem. Sens.* **2005**, *71*, 699–707. [CrossRef]
12. Gruen, A.; Baltsavias, E.P.; Henricsson, O. (Eds.) *Automatic Extraction of Man-Made Objects from Aerial and Space Images*, 2nd ed.; Birkhäuser: Basel, Switzerland, 2012.
13. Burdziakowski, P.; Przyborski, M.; Janowski, A.; Szulwic, J. A vision-based unmanned aerial vehicle navigation method. In Proceedings of the 1st International Conference on Innovative Research and Maritime Applications of Space Technology (IRMAST), Gdańsk, Poland, 23–24 April 2015.
14. 2016 IEEE GRSS Data Fusion Contest. Available online: http://www.grss-ieee.org/community/technical-committees/data-fusion (accessed on 17 May 2018).
15. DeLucas, L.J. International Space Station. *Acta Astronaut.* **1996**, *38*, 613–619. [CrossRef]
16. Beckett, K. UrtheCast Second-Generation Earth Observation Sensors. In *The International Archives of the Photogrammetry—Remote Sensing and Spatial Information Sciences, Proceedings of the 36th International Symposium on Remote Sensing of Environment, Berlin, Germany, 11–15 May 2015*; Schreier, G., Skrovseth, P.E., Staudenrausch, H., Eds.; Copernicus Publications: Göttingen, Germany, 2015; pp. 1069–1073.
17. Metro Vancouver Open Data Catalogue. Available online: http://data.vancouver.ca/datacatalogue/buildingFootprints.htm (accessed on 17 May 2018).
18. Da Fontoura Costa, L.; Marcondes Cesar, R., Jr. *Shape Classification and Analysis: Theory and Practice*, 2nd ed.; CRC Press Inc.: Boca Raton, FL, USA, 2009; pp. 449–504.

© 2018 by the authors. Licensee MDPI, Basel, Switzerland. This article is an open access article distributed under the terms and conditions of the Creative Commons Attribution (CC BY) license (http://creativecommons.org/licenses/by/4.0/).

International Journal of
isprs Geo-Information

Article

4D Time Density of Trajectories: Discovering Spatiotemporal Patterns in Movement Data

Yebin Zou [1,*], Yijin Chen [1,*], Jing He [1], Gehu Pang [2] and Kaixuan Zhang [1]

1. College of Geoscience and Surveying Engineering, China University of Mining and Technology, Beijing 100083, China; tbp1600202040@student.cumtb.edu.cn (J.H.); tsz1600205086q@student.cumtb.edu.cn (K.Z.)
2. Changjiang Chongqing Waterway Engineering Bureau, Chongqing 401121, China; panggehu@sina.com
* Correspondence: tbp1600202041@student.cumtb.edu.cn (Y.Z.); y.j.chen@cumtb.edu.cn (Y.C.); Tel.: +86-130-4116-8400 (Y.Z.)

Received: 10 April 2018; Accepted: 27 May 2018; Published: 4 June 2018

Abstract: Modern positioning and sensor technology enable the acquisition of movement positions and attributes on an unprecedented scale. Therefore, a large amount of trajectory data can be used to analyze various movement phenomena. In cartography, a common way to visualize and explore trajectory data is to use the 3D cube (e.g., space-time cube), where trajectories are presented as a tilted 3D polyline. As larger movement datasets become available, this type of display can easily become confusing and illegible. In addition, movement datasets are often unprecedentedly massive, high-dimensional, and complex (e.g., implicit spatial and temporal relations and interactions), making it challenging to explore and analyze the spatiotemporal movement patterns in space. In this paper, we propose 4D time density as a visualization method for identifying and analyzing spatiotemporal movement patterns in large trajectory datasets. The movement range of the objects is regarded as a 3D geographical space, into which the fourth dimension, 4D time density, is incorporated. The 4D time density is derived by modeling the movement path and velocity separately. We present a time density algorithm, and demonstrate it on the simulated trajectory and a real dataset representing the movement data of aircrafts in the Hong Kong International and the Macau International Airports. Finally, we consider wider applications and further developments of time density.

Keywords: 4D time density; 3D data cube; movement data; trajectory datasets; visual data exploration; space use intensity; spatiotemporal movement patterns

1. Introduction

Recent ubiquity and widespread use of modern positioning and context-aware devices have enabled the acquisition of movement positions and attributes of almost any type of moving object, and thus, have produced large amounts of trajectories data [1]. These data are usually collected as a series of trajectories; that is, when an object moves in the basic 3D geographic space of our physical world, the movement of each object can be presented as a tilted 3D polyline in space [2]. Analysis and exploration of large movement datasets is of great significance to many fields, such as the exploration of the movement laws of a particle, the analysis of human behavior, and the search for 'bottlenecks' in transportation networks [3]. They study the movement of groups or individuals on different spatial scales, different time scales, and with varying degrees of complexity [1,4].

In wildlife ecology, the decreased size and widespread use of animal tracking labels allow animal ecologists to collect large amounts of trajectory data describing animal movements. These data are usually composed of trajectories in space and time [1,5], which are commonly analyzed and visualized using the methods for home range/utilization distribution estimation [6]. Home range is defined as an area within which animals usually confine their normal activities (foraging, mating and taking care of young) [7]. Another concept associated with the home range is the utilization distribution [8], which is a probability surface on the 2D region that represents the possibility of finding animals in a particular area [1,9,10]. The home range is usually defined by the probabilistic contour of a certain value of the utilization distribution surface. It usually uses a 0.95 probability, but the choice is subjective and can vary depending on the study [1]. However, these two concepts often focus on the spatial distribution of the measured positions only in 2D space and ignore the time series of the measurements.

One notion that has persisted in wildlife ecology is the space usage patterns of animals' movement. Animals prefer to spend more time at particular locations, or visit a given place frequently, or move slowly/quickly in some areas, making their living environment uneven [11–13]. Ecologists are particularly interested in exploring the role of time in this heterogeneous behavior [1,14]. However, most of the methods for home range/utilization distribution estimation [15–19] are only associated with two spatial dimensions, and seldom consider the time dimension; this makes it difficult to visually discover the spatiotemporal patterns of movement.

Thus, another potential development we can see is to extend the calculation of home range/utilization distribution into a real 3D geographical space (i.e., using elevation as the third dimension). This is of great significance to animals moving in the air or in water, and animals often changing their vertical distribution relative to external environmental factors [1,20,21]. We expect that the movement range of birds or marine creatures can be viewed as a 3D geographic space [1,22], and time, specifically the function of time (3D analogy of utilization distribution), would now represent the fourth dimension. A 3D space, with three spatial axes, forms a three-dimensional geographic space, and is used to visualize the spatial aggregation of the collected movement trajectories. This is where the data cube is incorporated into the trajectory data visualization.

We propose 4D time density as an effective method for analyzing and identifying spatiotemporal movement patterns in large trajectory datasets. This approach was inspired by the space-time density of trajectories [1,2] and the home range/utilization distribution concept in wildlife ecology [10,17]. However, we changed the algorithm for density calculation, incorporating the fourth dimension-4D time density into 3D geographic space, instead of the 2D geographic space. The 4D time density is derived by dividing the normalized path length by aggregated velocity. In addition, time density and utilization distribution are conceptually slightly different. Time density is a measure of the frequency and intensity of a space use of a species, which is associated with the concept of utilization distribution, since the space use intensity is large for places with a large probability of finding a given species. We subsequently describe the trajectory division and cube cell construction methods to establish the computational range of time density, where the traveled distance and aggregated velocity are calculated. The method yields results of space use intensity that are highly correlated with the true probabilities of occurrence (i.e., utilization distribution), and successfully depicts temporal variations in density of occurrence [22]. In a real application case, we present an application of the 4D time density of trajectories on a real dataset that represents the movement data of the aircrafts at the Hong Kong International and the Macau International Airports. The results show that the proposed approach produces density volumes that successfully capture temporal variations in the density of occurrence, and visually identify the specific spatiotemporal patterns of the movement of aircrafts.

2. Related Works

In computer programming contexts, a data cube is a multidimensional array of values, generally used to describe multidimensional data, such as time series of image data [23], spatiotemporal sensor data [24], statistical data [25,26], geographic data [27], and simulation data [28]. Even though it is called a 'cube', it can be 1-, 2-, or 3-dimensional, or even higher dimensional, and the semantic of the dimension is not necessarily spatial or temporal (https://en.wikipedia.org/wiki/Data_cube). Each dimension of the data cube typically represents an attribute of the datasets, and the cells of the data cube represent the facts of interest [29,30]. As a form of organizing data, a data cube can thus be used to describe a large volume of trajectory data. However, on the one hand, as larger movement datasets become available, the display of a data cube quickly becomes unsatisfactory, especially when there are many trajectories [2]. On the other hand, it is difficult to illustrate the trajectory attributes in space and time, as they involve many aspects. It is therefore necessary to aggregate or simplify such data, and visually explore their attributes [2,31].

Kaya et al. [32] proposed an experimental study to verify whether the advantages and limitations of 2D and 3D representations are valid for spatiotemporal data visualization. They conducted an experiment that identified different scenarios of spatiotemporal data analysis, each of which is visualized with both a density map and density cube techniques. The experimental results revealed that 3D representations perform better than 2D representations when analyzing spatiotemporal data.

Demšar and Virrantaus [2] used the space-time density to solve the problem of overlapping and clutter of trajectories when there is a large amount of data displayed in the space-time cube. However, they provided information about traffic and routes but did not display other movement attributes.

Spretke et al. [33] applied color coding to multiple trajectory segments on a 2D map based on differences in attributes, in order to display different categories of segments. This helped to separate migratory birds' daytime flight from the night flight and stops. However, over-plotting hindered the detection of spatial behavior along each trajectory.

Ware et al. [34] developed the GeoZui4D system to show the multiple attributes of 3D trajectories of whale underwater movement by using color, texture, and glyphs, but there were still deficiencies, such as over-rendering and view occlusion.

Kraak and Huisman [35] used a combination of a time graph, scatter chart, cartographic map, and space-time cube to identify interesting events. The colored trajectory segments were used to represent the selected attributes through a map and a data cube. However, it only considered a single trajectory, despite their collection.

Gao [36] presented a spatiotemporal analysis framework to explore human mobility patterns and internal urban dynamics. Based on large-scale detailed records of mobile phone calls in a city, the combination of space-time density estimation, spatiotemporal visualization and spatiotemporal autocorrelation analysis not only helped to visually represent spatiotemporal data, but also provided a quantitative analysis to determine the spatiotemporal patterns of human mobility. Therefore, the above methods often focused on a particular attribute, and do not provide sufficient visualization support to study the spatial, temporal, and attribute components of trajectories in real 3D geographical space, according to our research.

Static methods for home range and utilization distribution derivation calculate these two concepts from the sampled locations of animal movement. However, they do not take into account the temporal aspect of the data [1]. The concept of home range was first proposed by Burt [37] as follows: the normal area of daily activity for animals foraging, mating, and taking care of young. The definition, however, is vague about the application of "normality", and was later revised by other scholars. Kernohan et al. [38] proposed a more comprehensive concept of home range, namely, an area where a certain animal appears with a certain probability (e.g., 95%) over a period of time. Three methods are commonly used to calculate the home range: polygonal methods, such as the minimum convex polygon (MCP); grid cell methods, such as the grid cell counting method; and probabilistic methods such as kernel density estimation (KDE) [39]. In 1949, Hayne [40] introduced the concept of the "activity center", and emphasized that the biological connotation of home range should emphasize the utilization intensity of animals at different parts within the range of activity.

Since the 1980s, the concept of utilization distribution has been widely utilized in the study of home range [11]. Utilization distribution is a probability distribution surface constructed from the discrete activity sites of individuals acquired at different times [41]. Kernel density estimation is most commonly used to generate a probabilistic surface from animal location measurements [1], which usually uses a standard 2D point kernel density estimation to place a probability decay function at each point, and then incorporates them into the surface, thereby generating a probability estimation of the animal being in each position [42]. In most cases, the decay function is a symmetric Gaussian kernel, and other decay functions are sometimes used [1,17], such as linear, bisquare, Epanechnikov, and Brownian. As mentioned above, most of the methods for deriving home range/utilization distribution were generally based on two-dimensional kernel functions in geographic space, and seldom accounted for time. However, Demšar et al. [1] proposed an alternative geographic visualization approach that extended the concept of home range/utilization distribution into three-dimensional space-time (x-y + t), based on the concept of the space-time cube. However, it only regards time as the third dimension upon a 2D space (i.e., two-dimensional plane x-y) to estimate the home range/utilization distribution.

We thus utilize the ideas of calculating the home range/utilization distribution in 2D space (x-y) or 3D space (x-y + t) to derive our 4D time density (x-y-z + t) in 3D geographic space, which seeks to solve the problems of the cluttered data cube by aggregating trajectories via calculation of their time density. This paper is mainly a methodology article that proposes a new method for geographic visualization. As mentioned above, it is partly inspired by the methodology of home range/utilization distribution; we therefore chose to introduce it in the context of wildlife ecology. However, the above issues exist not only in the research field of wildlife ecology, but also in the many studies of moving objects (e.g., humans). Since this article endeavors to develop a common visualization method for most types of movement objects, we try to dilute the concept of home range/utilization distribution in the following sections of this work.

3. Method of Calculating 4D Time Density

This section describes the algorithm for time density. The simulated trajectories are used to demonstrate the generation, stacking, and normalization of time density in Matlab™ 8.5 software. In Voxler™ 4 software, volume rendering (direct volume rendering) and volume slicing are used to present the density volumes.

3.1. Algorithm for Calculating 4D Time Density of Trajectories

Time density is a measure of the frequency and intensity of space use of a species. Imagine a data cube, as shown in Figure 1, where the coordinate axis X, Y, and Z of the space Cartesian coordinate system serve as its three dimensions. The position thus at coordinate (x, y, z) is recorded as a point, and the movement of each object can be presented as a tilted 3D polyline (left view of Figure 1) [43]. If such a polyline is accurately mapped, we can find the corresponding trajectory segment in one of the 3D geographic spaces, i.e., the cube cell Va, where the time density of the trajectory is calculated. The trajectory $P_1 - P_2 - \ldots - P_m - P_{m+1} - \ldots - P_n$ is thus divided and assigned to each cube cell. Here, line segments $P_m - P_{m+1} - \ldots - P_{m+i} (i = 1, 2, 3 \ldots)$ fall into the data cube Va, where $P_m = (x_m, y_m, z_m)$ is the point coordinate and x_m, y_m, z_m are the geographic coordinates. $P_{(Va)1}$ and $P_{(Va)2}$ are the intersections of the cube cell and trajectory. It is specified that the trajectory segments $P_m - P_{m+1} - \ldots - P_{m+i}$ pass through the centroid (center) of the cube cell Va, and all cube cells do not intersect and are parallel to the axes of the established Cartesian coordinate system.

The time density around each trajectory in 3D space is calculated as a volume (i.e., the 3D cube cells in Figure 1), the density of which indicates the frequency and intensity of the space use of the moving objects in the cube cell Va. This is associated with the concept of home range/utilization distribution. The time density in the cube cell Va is given by Formula (1).

$$\check{d}_{xyzt}(Va) = \frac{\check{L}_{(Va)}\ [m/m^3]}{\check{v}_{(Va)}\ [m/s]} = [s/m^3], \qquad (1)$$

where $\check{d}_{xyzt}(Va)$ is the time density of the cube cell Va, and $\check{v}_{(Va)}$ is the aggregated velocity. $\check{L}_{(Va)}$ is the normalized path length in $[m/m^3]$ and is computed as Formula (2).

$$\check{L}_{(Va)} = \frac{L_{(Va)}}{A_{(Va)}}, \qquad (2)$$

where $L_{(Va)}$ is the total path length within the cube cell Va, and $A_{(Va)}$ is the volume of Va in m³. The final output graphs can be explained as follows—high values indicate the areas that are frequently visited or where the objects spend more time; low values represent the areas that are not frequently visited or where the objects move faster.

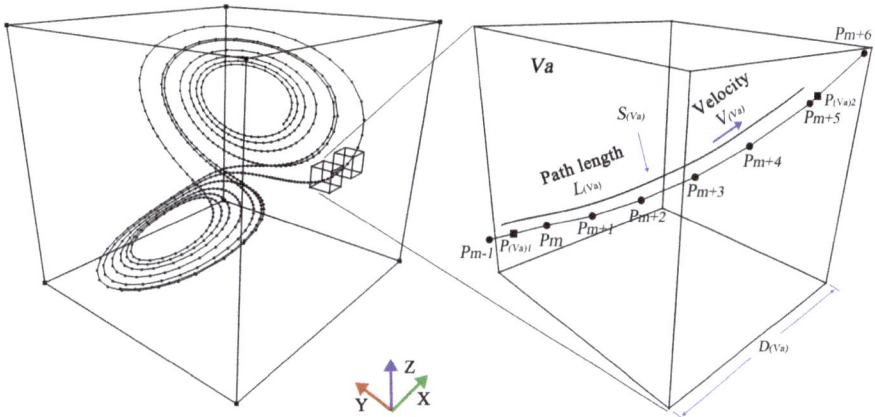

Figure 1. Basic principle of time density estimation. Some points and trajectories (polylines) of the Lorenz model is displayed in the data cube.

There is another method to calculate time density. If the point records are sampled using an equal time interval Δt, and no observations are lost, the velocity is inversely proportional to the time $t_{(Va)}$, as given by Formula (3).

$$\check{v}_{(Va)} = \frac{L_{(Va)}}{t_{(Va)}} = \frac{L_{(Va)}}{\sum_{i=0}^{m} n_{i(Va)} \cdot \Delta t}, \qquad (3)$$

where $n_{i(Va)}$ is the weight of the i-th point. This will produce a simple time-density estimation given by Formula (4); it produces the same result as Formula (1).

$$\check{d}_{xyzt}(Va) = \frac{L_{(Va)} \cdot \sum_{i=0}^{m} n_i(Va) \cdot \Delta t}{L(Va)} = \frac{L(Va) \cdot \sum_{i=0}^{m} n_i(Va) \cdot \Delta t}{A(Va) \cdot L(Va)} = \frac{\sum_{i=0}^{m} n_i(Va) \cdot \Delta t}{A(Va)} \left[s/m^3\right], \qquad (4)$$

Here, the time density is calculated by two methods, namely Formulas (1) and (2), and Formulas (3) and (4). Two methods are given and compared in the article. The first method uses Newton's formula, $t = s/v$, to calculate the density indirectly, which derives 4D time density by dividing the normalized path length by the aggregated velocity.

We can clearly see that the time density actually indicates the time consumed by moving objects in the spatial region represented by the unit cube cell. Therefore, it is possible to directly sum the time differences between adjacent sampling points to obtain the total consumed time. The second method (i.e., Formulas (3) and (4)) is exactly such a derivation process. If the point records are sampled using a regular time interval Δt, the time density can be calculated by summing the weighted time within the cube cell via Formula (4), which considers the weight of time at each point in calculating the total consumed time. There is similar conclusion for irregular sampling intervals. The derivation of Formula (4) is simple and intuitive. However, the advantages of using Formula (1) instead of Formula (4) are as follows:

(1) Since we use the path length and aggregated velocity to calculate the time density in Formula (1), the density should always be at the same scale, which allows us to compare the analytical output for different sampling intervals. Therefore, it is disadvantageous to create the time

density directly through the time difference between adjacent points, because the calculated time density is nonuniform (i.e., not at the same scale) for the different sampling intervals in a trajectory datasets.

(2) Individual modeling of path length and velocity can provide more possibilities to include various explanatory variables to explain the behavior of the moving objects. In kinematics, the velocity can be the function of various environmental conditions (e.g., elevation, terrain, season, wind, obstacles, road conditions, etc.) [44–47]. If the velocity and actual movement trajectory are modelled more accurately by using additional movement attributes, we should be able to generate a finer time density map for a given spatial region.

However, as this is the first expansion of the trajectory data considering the time dimension in 3D space, these advantages will not be discussed in detail herein. In the following sections, we present the detailed algorithm for calculating the time density. The pseudocode of the algorithm is shown in the following text.

Algorithm: 4D time density algorithm

arrange point records by time sequence and convert them to curves;
calculate cube cell size $D_{(Va)}$ depend on the sampling resolution and spatial extent;
TotalTimeDensity = 0; AverageTimeDensity = 0;
for each trajectory
  TrajectoryTimeDensity = 0;
  allocate cube cells around the trajectory;
  for each cube cell
    calculate NormalizedLength of the trajectory curve;
    calculate AggregatedVelocity by aggregating the velocities;
    TrajectoryTimeDensity = normalized (NormalizedLength/AggregatedVelocity);
  end
  TotalTimeDensity = TotalTimeDensity + TrajectoryTimeDensity;
end
TotalTimeDensity = normalized TotalTimeDensity;
AverageTimeDensity = normalized (TotalTimeDensity/Number of trajectories);

3.1.1. Curve Fitting of the Trajectory

The trajectory of a moving object in 3D space is usually a continuous curve, but the actual sampling process produces a series of discrete points $P_1, P_2, \ldots, P_m, P_{m+1}, \ldots, P_n$ [2,48]. The original continuous trajectory is thus usually approximated by a series of straight lines between the sampling points, which is not a real movement path. For our algorithm, we read the point records through the time sequence to generate a trajectory polyline $P_1 - P_2 - \ldots - P_m - P_{m+1} - \ldots - P_n$, and then use the cubic spline function in the Matlab™ software to fit the polyline into a continuous curve $S_{(Va)}$. The algorithm reads each trajectory sequentially, i.e., one after the other. We use the cubic spline method instead of inserting multi-lines directly, based on the following considerations:

(1) The fitted path passes through all the sampling points, and is maximally in accordance with the actual trajectory path.
(2) As mentioned above, 4D time density is derived by dividing the NormalizedLength by the AggregatedVelocity. If the velocity and actual movement trajectory are modelled more accurately, we should be able to generate a finer time density map for a given spatial region.

3.1.2. Estimation of the Size of Cube Cell

The time density is derived in each cube cell. Consequently, we need to choose a suitable size $D_{(Va)}$ of the cube cell to provide maximal information content while meeting the goals of spatial analysis.

On the one hand, it is clear that the higher the resolution, the higher the accuracy of the rendered path. On the other hand, if the size of the cube cell is too small, there are not enough observations, and the output of the analysis will become noisy since it only emphasizes a part of the point, which is difficult to interpret visually [28]. Recall that we need more points in a cube cell to calculate the path length and velocity of the points accurately. To meet these two requirements, we propose the following geometric principle: the algorithm reads all trajectories sequentially, calculates the distance between adjacent points on the trajectories, and selects the third quartile as the cube cell size. This means that for approximately 75% of the points in the datasets, there will be at least two points within a cube cell. The remaining 25% are interpolated by dichotomy, until there are at least two points in the cube cell. According to this heuristic, we estimate the appropriate cube cell size $D_{(Va)}$.

3.1.3. Calculation of the Normalized Path Length

Our algorithm allocates the cube cells around the trajectory from the first point of a trajectory. Once the size of the cube cell is estimated, we can derive the length of the trajectory curve within each cube cell Va. It is first necessary to calculate the intersection coordinate $P_{(Va)}$ of the trajectory $S_{(Va)}$ and the cube cell Va. The calculation of intersection uses the function on each segment, since the cubic spline function is a piecewise function. We calculate the length $L_{(Va)}$ of the trajectory curve $S_{(Va)}$, which yields the distance traveled by the object in the cube cell Va. The NormalizedLength is then calculated by using Formula (2).

3.1.4. Calculation of the Aggregated Velocity

The next step is to calculate the AggregatedVelocity in the cube cell Va. Therefore, the velocities at the intersections $P_{(Va)1}$ and $P_{(Va)2}$ need to be interpolated by the adjacent points. Since this is the first realization of time density, we use the simplest interpolation function, linear interpolation, to insert velocities at the intersections. The AggregatedVelocity for each cell is subsequently obtained by averaging the velocities at all points within the cube cell. However, we can use other, more complex functions, such as kriging interpolation. In geostatistics, this interpolates predictions at unsampled locations according to the spatial correlation between adjacent geographic objects.

3.1.5. Derivation of the Time Density

In the final step, the estimation of the time density is obtained by dividing the NormalizedLength $\check{L}_{(Va)}$ by the AggregatedVelocity $\check{v}_{(Va)}$. The algorithm calculates the density of each trajectory separately, and in the meantime sums their corresponding densities to TotalTimeDensity—the time density for the entire set of trajectories. This process is implemented using 3D map algebra (i.e., voxel-by-voxel). A new trajectory is added once the moving object accesses the cube cell. Therefore, the TotalTimeDensity is the sum of the densities of multiple trajectories. When the number of trajectories is large, the corresponding TotalTimeDensity is large, due to the stacking effect of time density. The final step in calculating both AverageTimeDensity and TotalTimeDensity is to normalize the density to the range of [0, 1]. Section 3.2 demonstrates the generation of AverageTimeDensity and TotalTimeDensity in detail.

We propose a technique to estimate time density by separately modeling movement path and velocity in an established cube cell. In summary, time density can be derived from the following six steps:

- Generate trajectories from point records (arrange point records by time sequence, and convert them to curves);
- Calculate the appropriate cube cell size based on the sampling density and the spatial extent;
- Derive the total length of the trajectory in the cube cell, and normalize it;
- Interpolate the velocities at intersections by using linear interpolation, and aggregate the velocities to obtain the average velocity of each cube cell;

- Derive the time density by dividing the normalized path length by the aggregated velocity using Formula (1);
- Generate the total time density volume by using 3D map algebra, and normalize it.

3.2. 4D Time Density of Simulated Trajectories

Figure 2 shows the TrajectoryTimeDensity (i.e., 3D cube cells as described above) of four simulated trajectories. The grayscale value of each cube cell represents the time density of the trajectory. The higher the grayscale value, the higher the corresponding density. The density of each trajectory is gradually increasing along the positive direction of the Z axis, from 0.1 to 1. The internal trajectory curves are visualized by setting the transparency of the cube cells surface.

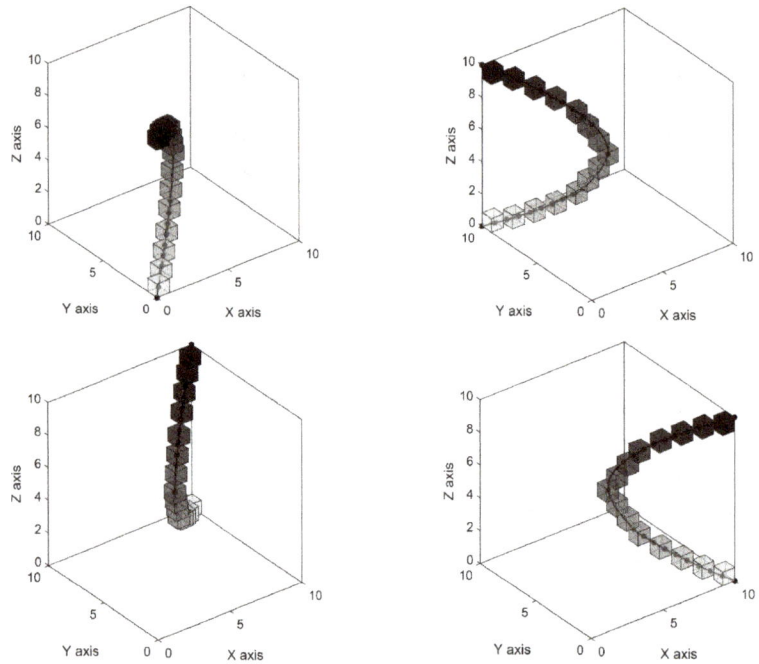

Figure 2. TrajectoryTimeDensity around the four simulated trajectories. Each view shows the time density around a single trajectory.

When the algorithm handles all trajectories, their densities are added to TotalTimeDensity. This process is implemented using 3D map algebra (i.e., voxel-by-voxel). Figure 3 shows the time density for four simulated trajectories. In Figure 3a, the TotalTimeDensity volume is shown using the same 3D cube cell as in Figure 2. The grayscale value of some cubes becomes larger, while others decrease. In Figure 3b, the trajectories are overlaid on the TotalTimeDensity volume. In these two views, there is a time density hot spot in the central region of the simulated area due to the stacking effect of density. The TotalTimeDensity is large in this region, which represents the trajectory convergence phenomenon and implies that many objects have visited the area. However, it should be noted that visitors have only accessed the area, but the time of their visit is not known.

In Figure 3a,b, the time density of the stacking region is the sum of the densities of multiple trajectories that entered the region. It can also be explained as the product of the AverageTimeDensity and the number of trajectories (i.e., the number of visits). The number of trajectories is calculated from the GPS positioning data of the trajectory dataset, which is the number of times that the object enters a certain spatial region (i.e., cube cell) during the statistical period. The AverageTimeDensity represents the overall average of the time that visitors spend in the region. The relationship between them can be expressed as Formula (5).

$$\check{d}_{xyzt}(\text{Va}) = \sum_{i=0}^{n} \check{d}_{xyzti} = n \cdot \bar{d}_{xyzt}, \qquad (5)$$

where $\check{d}_{xyzti}$ is the density of the i-th trajectory, n is the number of trajectories in the density stacking region, and $\bar{d}_{xyzt}$ represents the AverageTimeDensity. A new trajectory is added once the object revisited the cube cell every time; therefore, the number of visits and number of trajectories mentioned later are the same concept. In Figure 3c, the TotalTimeDensity of the stacking region is decreased after it is normalized by the number of trajectories, and is even smaller than the density of the nonstacked trajectories in the upper half region of the simulated area. Therefore, in the two factors that affect the TotalTimeDensity, the number of visits occupies a larger weight, but the average time occupies a smaller weight; that is, the number of visits is large, but the average time spent by visitors is relatively short, resulting in the obvious contrast between Figure 3b,c. This is an interesting movement pattern which we need to explore. In Section 4, we present the visual and analytic capabilities of TotalTimeDensity and AverageTimeDensity through a real application case.

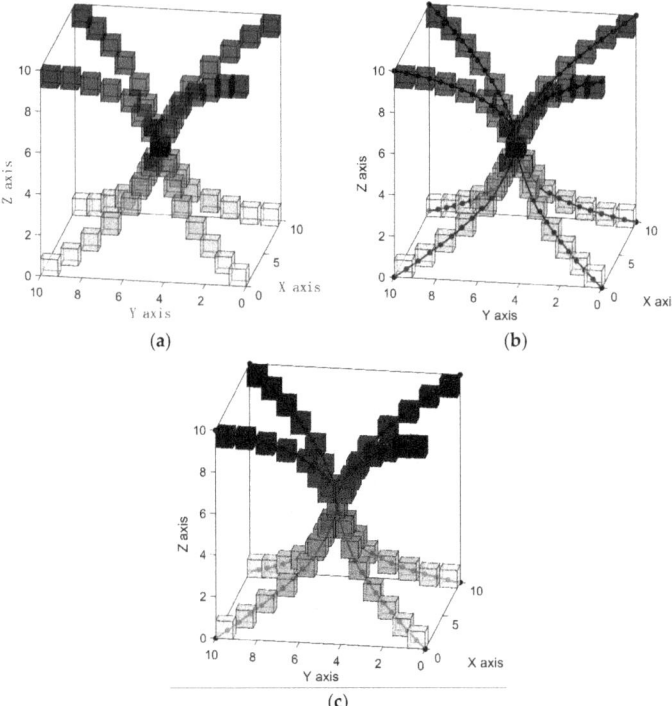

Figure 3. Time Density of four simulated trajectories. (a) The TotalTimeDensity of the simulated trajectories; (b) the TotalTimeDensity volume stacked with the simulated trajectory; and (c) AverageTimeDensity volume—the resulting density volume obtained by normalizing the TotalTimeDensity volume by the number of trajectories.

3.3. Visualizing the Time Density Volume

When studying the distribution of temperature, pressure, or humidity of a certain space in the physical system, it necessary to describe them only by the algebraic quantity in mathematics. The field determined by these algebraic quantities (i.e., scalar functions) is called a scalar field (https://en.wikipedia.org/wiki/Scalar_field). The time density of the trajectories is a volume in which the value of each point can be uniquely described by a scalar calculated from NormalizedLength and AggregatedVelocity. For one trajectory, the density of a certain cube cell is unique, but for the stacked trajectories, the density is the sum of the densities of multiple trajectories. Therefore, many density volumes will produce visual relationships such as inclusion, occlusion, and masking, making it difficult to visualize on a two-dimensional display [2,48]. Volume visualization is an important research field of information visualization; it is common in the medical domain (e.g., a 3D CT lesion distribution images and 3D ultrasound vision) [49] and in the fields of geology [50], mining (e.g., 3D map of the location, direction, length, and depth of an underground mine) [51,52], and meteorology (e.g., 3D representation of the atmosphere, such as cold air masses, hurricanes, and haze) [53]. The three main techniques of volume visualization are direct volume rendering, volume slicing, and isosurfaces [2]. In the following, we use the first two methods to visualize the time density volume in Voxler™ 4 software, which is a professional 3D data visualization system that provides a new way of visualizing volumetric data.

Direct volume rendering is a set of techniques for displaying 2D projections of 3D discrete sampled datasets (usually 3D scalar fields). The technique assumes that the volume is semitransparent, and maps the discrete 3D data field to the corresponding 2D image by controlling the color, light, and observation direction of the volume. We can visualize volume data from different angles by selecting different lighting models and viewing directions [54]. The classical algorithms for direct volume rendering include splatting, maximum intensity projection, shear-warp, volume-ray casting, etc., among which volume-ray projection is a classic algorithm. It emits projected light from each point of the projection plane, passes through the 3D data field, and subsequently calculates the intensity of the attenuated light by the light equation, and then draws it into an image [55].

Volume slicing or visualization with clipping planes (not necessarily a plane) is a surface that is colored, based on the value of the volume data in the region of the slice position [54]. The clipping plane is useful for detecting the interior of the volume data, which removes those unimportant regions to expose the internal patterns [56]. Volume slices are widely used in the medical industry. For example, the physician can easily display the 3D distribution of tumor lesions or of the brain's blood stasis by using the 3D CT image [57].

The TotalTimeDensity volume and the AverageTimeDensity volume are visualized using these two methods in Figure 4. In Figure 4a–c, the time density volumes are displayed by direct volume rendering using the grayscale color and rainbow color schemes. Figure 4a shows the intersection of cube cells of the four trajectories of Figure 3. The non-intersecting parts are set to be invisible here. Obviously, the intersection parts are symmetrical about the center point. In Figure 4d,e, the density volumes are sliced in different directions, some of which are generated using two slicing planes in two different directions. These different volume visualizations can help visually identify the space usage patterns.

As mentioned above, the TotalTimeDensity is determined by the AverageTimeDensity and the number of visits. In different spatial regions, there may be significant differences between these two factors, which in turn reflect the differences (e.g., social, economic, cultural or ecological aspects) of different spatial regions. Examples include a central business district (CBD) and a residential area, an animal's habitat and breeding ground, as well as a troposphere and stratosphere. Based on these two factors, we can therefore explore the behavioral characteristics and space usage patterns of moving objects in different scenarios. Potential applications across a wide range of fields include marketing promotion, advertisement serving, urban planning and construction, ecological and species conservation, etc. [58].

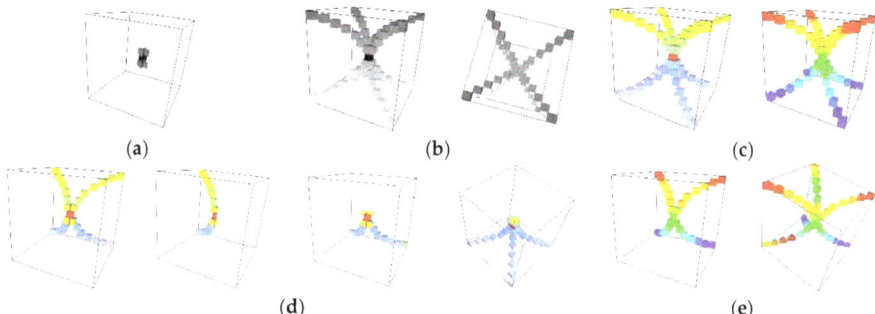

Figure 4. Visualizing the TotalTimeDensity volume and the AverageTimeDensity volume. (**a**) direct volume rendering of the trajectory stacking region using the grayscale color scheme; (**b**) two views of direct volume rendering of the TotalTimeDensity volume using the grayscale color scheme; (**c**) comparison of volume rendering of (**left**) TotalTimeDensity volume and (**right**) AverageTimeDensity volume using rainbow color scheme; (**d**) volume slicing of TotalTimeDensity volume in different directions and (**e**) volume slicing of AverageTimeDensity volume in different directions.

4. Application: 4D Time Density of the Aircraft Movement Trajectories

This section presents an application of time density on a real dataset that represents the movement trajectories of aircrafts at the Hong Kong International and Macau International Airports. We will subsequently explore the space use patterns and characteristics of the aircrafts of the two airports for the Pearl River Delta airspace.

4.1. Study Area

The Hong Kong International and Macau International Airports are located in the Pearl River Delta Metropolitan Region (PRD) in the southeast of Guangdong Province, China. PRD is the low-lying area surrounding the Pearl River estuary, where the Pearl River flows into the South China Sea. It has convenient land, sea, and air transportation, and is known as the "South Gate" of China [59].

The specific location of the Hong Kong International Airport (ICAO: VHHH; IATA: HKG) * is Chek Lap Kok, Lantau Island, New Territories, Hong Kong, with geographical coordinates: 22°18′32″ N and 113°54′52″ E. There are two runways in the airport with azimuths of 70 degrees and 250 degrees, respectively, both of which are 3800 m in length and 9 m in elevation. Hong Kong is the third largest financial center in the world, and an important international financial, trade, and shipping center. In 2016, VHHH handled 70.5 million passengers and 4.52 million tons of air cargo. At present, more than 100 airlines provide more than 1100 flights per day from the airport, to over 190 cities across the globe [60]. The geographical coordinates of the Macau International Airport (ICAO: VMMC; IATA: MFM) are 22°08′58f″ N and 113°35′30″ E, which is approximately 40 kilometers from the Hong Kong International Airport. There are two runways in the airport: Runway 16/34 is 3360 m long, and the taxiing runway is 1460 m long, both of which are 6 meters in elevation. Its designated passenger traffic is 6 million per year [61].

* ICAO: International Civil Aviation Organization; IATA: International Air Transport Association. VHHH and HKG are the ICAO airport code and IATA airport code for Hong Kong International Airport respectively.

4.2. Data Description

We collected trajectory data for 30 days and 1235 take off and landing flights at VHHH and VMMC. The research data was purchased and downloaded from the flight real-time tracking website. The data service agreement allows researchers to use these data for personal research, as opposed to commercial, purposes. The raw dataset contains movement attributes, such as the call sign, latitude, longitude, elevation, UTC, speed, and azimuth of the flight. The time resolution is approximately 20 s. However, the position (latitude, longitude, and elevation) and velocity attributes only are used for our experiments. According to the source/destination and departure/arrival conditions of the flights, the datasets is divided into different subsets to calculate the time density of different subsets of flight data. Here, we have removed the sampling points generated when aircrafts move on the apron, in order to avoid affecting the time density calculation.

Figure 5 shows the flight trajectory points in two different ways. Figure 5a is a 2D map of 1 day of flight data (12 December 2017) for the two airports. This display ignores the elevation information of the sampling points, and the 3D spatial patterns cannot be identified. We place these trajectory points in a three-dimensional data cube (Figure 5b), where we can clearly see the 3D spatial position of the points. There is also a map of the study area attached to the x-y plane of the cube, as a geographical background of the movement trajectories. The location of the two airports is also marked on the map, where position A represents VHHH and position B represents VMMC. The geographical coverage of the flight trajectory is 177 km × 186 km in the E-W and the N-S directions. Since the elevation difference of the flights' movement range is too small compared to its length and width, the elevation difference is properly amplified to better observe the changes of the movement patterns in the vertical direction. However, this does not affect the overall view. Considering the spatial sampling resolution and the movement range of the flights, the appropriate cube cell size is estimated to be 800 m (see the principle in Section 3).

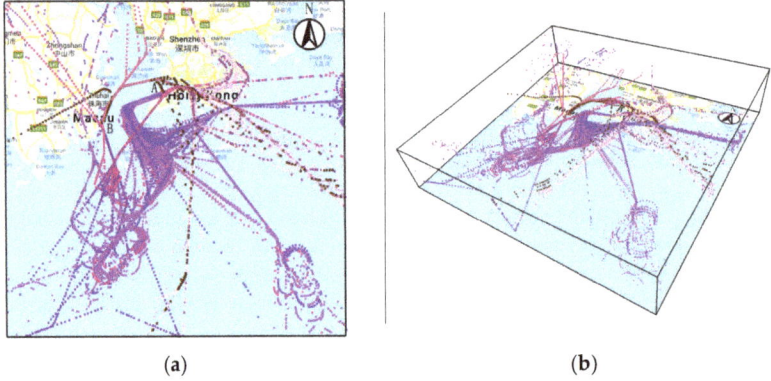

Figure 5. Trajectories of flights on 12 December, 2017, shown in (**a**) a traditional 2D map and (**b**) a 3D data cube.

4.3. Results: Identification of Movement Patterns from Density Volumes

We apply direct volume rendering and volume slicing techniques to generate time density volumes for the flight trajectory. As expected, we are able to visually identify the specific movement patterns of aircraft movement in the density volume.

Figure 6 shows the visualization of different TotalTimeDensity volumes. Figure 6a,b are the TotalTimeDensity volumes of arrival and departure flights, shown with direct volume rendering, respectively. The display in Figure 5b is cluttered with a high amount of overprinting, especially in the airspace near the airport. Both these displays are clearer than the traditional data cube (Figure 5), and the spatial-temporal patterns are more visually recognizable. The runways of VHHH are approximately in the east-west direction; therefore, the flights followed a trajectory from the south to the airport, then turned right at position a (Figure 6a), and finally entered the airport from the west and landed on the runway. However, the departing flights leave the airport from the east. The runways of VMMC are approximately in the north-south direction. All flights enter the airport from the south and take off from the north (position b in Figure 6b). These movement patterns and characteristics are clearly shown in Figure 6a,b.

The hot spots of time density are even more eye-catching when the TotalTimeDensity volume is displayed using a horizontal clipping plane through the average elevation of the VHHH and VMMC (Figure 6c). It can be clearly seen that VHHH is busier than VMMC, because VHHH has a large number of daily flights, resulting in the high-density areas in red near the VHHH. Compared with VHHH, VMMC has fewer flights per day, so it is shown in Figure 6c as areas with low-density that are light green to blue. These patterns can also be observed in Figure 6d, which visualizes the TotalTimeDensity volume with multiple clipping planes in different orientations (mainly vertical clipping planes).

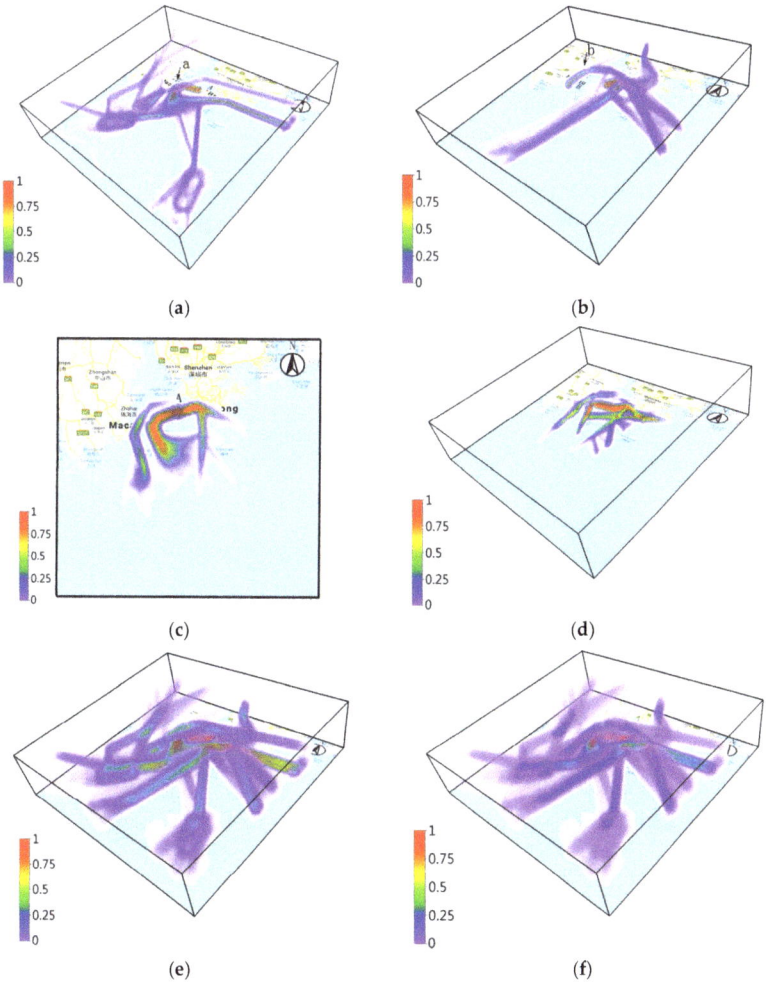

Figure 6. Time density volume of flight movement trajectory at VHHH and VMMC. TotalTimeDensity volume of (**a**) arrival flights and (**b**) departure flights shown with direct volume rendering. TotalTimeDensity volume of flight movement trajectory shown with (**c**) a horizontal clipping plane and (**d**) multiple clipping planes in different orientations. Density volume of (**e**) the number of visits and (**f**) AverageTimeDensity.

Figure 6e,f shows the density volume of the number of visits and AverageTimeDensity. The number of visits is the number of times that the flights enter the region Va within 30 days. In the airspace near the airport, all flights generally land and take off along the fixed air routes. In the meantime, flights have low speed and encounter heavy traffic, resulting in the accumulation of a large number of trajectories (the number of visits) and a high AverageTimeDensity. As the distance of the aircrafts from the airport increases, the air routes of the flight gradually become radial, and in the meantime, the flights move at a higher speed, resulting in spatial areas with low-density, i.e., low values of the number of visits and AverageTimeDensity values occur.

Figure 7 shows the TotalTimeDensity for all flights displayed from four different angles. All four panels show the same time density volume, where the top-left image sets the map transparency to 35% and looks up at the cube. In Figure 7, the time density by direct volume rendering is shown in red near the runway of the airport, on the approaching routes before landing, and on the departing routes just after takeoff, indicating that there are spatial regions with high time densities. As the distance from the airport increases, the TotalTimeDensity gradually decreases, and the corresponding volume rendering colors gradually change from orange to green to blue. These phenomena can be clarified by Figure 6e,f. According to Formula (5), TotalTimeDensity is regarded as the product of the AverageTimeDensity and the number of visits. In the airspace near the airport, the number of flights is large, but the flight speed is low; the corresponding TotalTimeDensity, therefore, is large. Similarly, in the airspace far from the airport, these two phenomena are exactly opposite, resulting in a low TotalTimeDensity value. There are two circles (c and d) in Figure 7a, where c is the trajectory of the planes that make an 8-shaped hovering maneuver, and d is the trajectory of the aircrafts that hover a circle. They are hovering arrival flights that are waiting for other planes to land or takeoff. These two movement features can also be confirmed in Figure 6a.

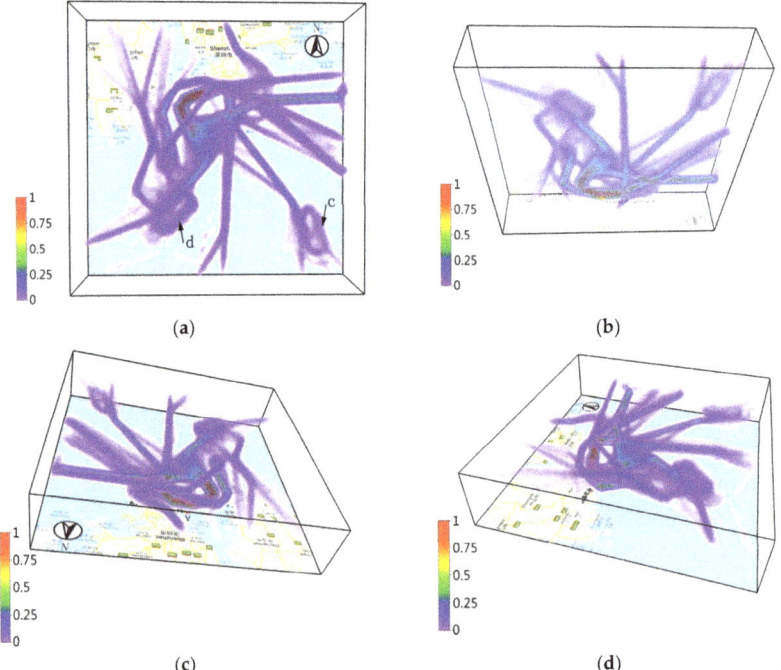

Figure 7. TotalTimeDensity of flights' movement data displayed in different directions. TotalTimeDensity observed from (a) the top view; (b) the bottom of the cube and (c,d) the side views. The map transparency in (b) is set to 35%.

5. Discussion

We use the dynamic properties of the spatial trajectories to derive the 4D time density, and visually analyze and explore the movement patterns of the moving objects in 3D geographical space. Achieving this goal is becoming increasingly easier, as the new sensor and data collection infrastructure supports better access to the context properties (speed, acceleration, direction, curvature, barometric pressure, humidity, altitude, etc.) of movement [62].

There are several issues worthy of further consideration, which can be divided into three categories:

1. *Complexity of the algorithm.* At present, our algorithm uses the calculated cube cell size to partition each trajectory. We specify that all trajectories pass through the cubes' centroid (center), and the cube cells are parallel to the established Cartesian coordinate system (Figure 1). The time density is then derived by dividing the NormalizedLength by the AggregatedVelocity. Therefore, the generation of cube cells and the calculation of density are somehow complicated. Note that the time density calculation of vehicle movement in the real application case is computationally expensive, i.e., calculation time may take several hours on a standard PC, depending on the spatial extent of the area and the predefined data sampling resolution. In this case, it is not possible to use this method for real-time visualization. We plan to implement different types of density calculation methods to gradually develop this algorithm. For example, we can refer to Demšar and Virrantaus [2] to use a cylinder around the 3D trajectory as a calculation range for time density, while the radius of the cylinder can be adjusted. This is a less computationally demanding solution.

2. *Visualization techniques of volume data.* Time density is a volume, a data type that is difficult to visualize and explore. A typical 3D dataset is a set of 2D slices obtained by MRI, CT, or 3D ultrasound scanners, which can be 1GB in size. Generally, these data are obtained in a regular pattern (e.g., one slice per millimeter), and typically have a regular number of image pixels in the regular pattern [63,64]. We are considering other volume visualization techniques, rather than the previously proposed methods. One alternative is hardware-accelerated volume rendering. Starting with programmable pixel shaders that originated in approximately 2000, people were increasingly aware of the power of multipoint parallel computing, and began to perform general-purpose calculations on graphics chips [65]. With such capabilities, any algorithm with parallel execution steps (e.g., volume ray projection or tomographic reconstruction) can be implemented with great acceleration [66]. Based on the current programmable graphics hardware technologies, the algorithm can use a programmable graphics processing unit (GPU) for hardware acceleration. Another alternative is the optimization technique of volume rendering, including early ray termination, volume segmentation, empty space skipping, etc. [65]. The main objective of the optimization is to skip as many voxels as possible and handle less information. The premise of using these methods is to meet the resolution requirement of the application without affecting the overall view. These methods produce volume visualizations in which patterns can be more pronounced and more quickly manifested, and that can therefore be used to explore our density volume.

3. *Applications and user-related evaluation.* Last but not least, the time density algorithm and all these visualization techniques should be developed with intended users, and should be evaluated for strengths and limitations in a variety of situations. For example, visual validation aimed at different users, experts, and application scenarios (e.g., marketing, urban planning, rescue services, ecological protection, etc.) can be explored. Further research can focus on the empirical analysis of the resulting time density, in which the users and experts can approve or adjust these theories and technologies.

6. Conclusions

We present a 4D time density algorithm, apply the volume visualization techniques to visualize the resulting density volume, and explore the movement patterns of moving objects in space and time through a real application case. The method is based on the concept of a data cube. It regards the movement range of the objects as a 3D geographical space, and displays the resulting density volume in it. The 4D time density is derived by dividing the NormalizedLength by the AggregatedVelocity.

This is a new method for geographical visualization inspired by the aggregated space-time density of trajectories in the space-time cube [2] and the home range/utilization distribution concept in wildlife ecology; however we changed the density algorithm. The ideas of calculating home range/utilization distribution in 2D space (x-y) or 3D space (x-y + t) are utilized to derive 4D time density (x-y-z + t) in real 3D geographic space. As mentioned above, time density has the following geographical indications: high values indicate the areas that are frequently visited, or where the objects spend more time; low values represent the areas that are not frequently visited, or where the objects move faster. It is therefore associated with the concept of utilization distribution, and can be seen as a 3D analogy of the utilization distribution, since the space use intensity is highly positively correlated with the probabilities of occurrence.

The time density of trajectories is tested on a real datasets that represents the movement data of flights at VHHH and VMMC. We expect this method can be used for all types of trajectory analysis. In our test of movement datasets, the time density is suited for trajectories in regions with soft constraints (e.g., seasonal migration of animals in the ocean or sky). It can also be applied to the trajectories in areas with hard constraints (e.g., road traffic or people's indoor activity).

In addition, time density indicates that the moving objects have visited the place, but the exact visit time (order) is not known. Actually, it presents the resulting view of the time function (Formula (1)), rather than reflecting the time (order) of visit. The space-time cube [2] could, however, embody the chronological order, since it explicitly employs time as its third dimension, representing the moment at which the movement occurs. We suggest two alternative solutions to the problem of the ignored time dimension in the data cube. The first solution is to use the time frame. The position of the moving object can be observed in the movement snapshot at each moment. In other words, we can see the distribution of moving objects at times $t_1, t_2, \ldots, t_n$. Therefore, by changing the time frame, the sampling point at that moment, or the movement trajectory before that moment, can be displayed. We can manually pull the scroll bar (setting a scroll bar) or play an animation to show the trajectory changes over time in the data cube. Another solution is to introduce a classical space-time cube into our approach, where the space-time density is calculated for each trajectory based on the x-y plane position and time attribute of the trajectory points. Space-time density explicitly employs time as its third dimension, which represents the moment at which the movement occurs. Therefore, we can associate these two visualizations to show space usage at each specific moment. We can also calculate and display the time density directly in the space-time cube. For spatial analyses with explicit temporal patterns as their focus, this method can be used as an alternative.

This work seeks to make a scientific contribution to spatiotemporal analysis of trajectories in large movement datasets. The technology can potentially be used for the analysis of movement data in GIS science and related disciplines. Potential research objects include humans, vehicles, ships, fish or other wild animals, etc. Future work can focus on extending its application to a wider range of scenarios in geographic analysis and GIS science.

Author Contributions: Y.Z. conducted the research, performed the experiments and wrote the paper; Y.C. offered helpful suggestions and reviewed the manuscript; J.H. conceived and designed the experiments; and G.P. & K.Z. contributed to the data analysis and literature search. All authors have read and approved the submitted manuscript and have agreed to be listed.

Acknowledgments: The authors would like to thank the reviewers for their comments. This research is supported by "the Fundamental Research Funds for the Central Universities" (Grant No. 2010YD06).

Conflicts of Interest: The authors declare that they have no conflict of interest.

References

1. Demšar, U.; Buchin, K.; van Loon, E.E.; Shamoun-Baranes, J. Stacked space-time densities: A geovisualisation approach to explore dynamics of space use over time. *Geoinformatica* **2015**, *19*, 85–115. [CrossRef]
2. Demšar, U.; Virrantaus, K. Space-time density of trajectories: Exploring spatiotemporal patterns in movement data. *Int. J. Geogr. Inf. Sci.* **2010**, *24*, 1527–1542. [CrossRef]
3. Tominski, C.; Schumann, H.; Andrienko, G.; Andrienko, N. Stacking-based visualization of trajectory attribute data. *IEEE Trans. Vis. Comput. Gr.* **2012**, *18*, 2565–2574. [CrossRef] [PubMed]
4. Holden, C. Inching toward wildlife ecology. *Science* **2006**, *313*, 779–782. [CrossRef] [PubMed]
5. Bridge, E.S.; Thorup, K.; Bowlin, M.S.; Chilson, P.B.; Diehl, R.H.; Flacron, R.W.; Hartl, P.; Kays, R.; Kelly, J.F.; Robinson, W.D.; et al. Technology on the move: Recent and forthcoming innovations for tracking migratory birds. *Bioscience* **2011**, *61*, 689–698. [CrossRef]
6. Steiniger, S.; Hunter, A.J.S. A scaled line-based kernel density estimator for the retrieval of utilization distributions and home ranges from GPS movement tracks. *Ecol. Inf.* **2013**, *13*, 1–8. [CrossRef]
7. Long, J.A.; Nelson, T.A. Time geography and wildlife home range delineation. *J. Wildl. Manag.* **2011**, *76*, 407–413. [CrossRef]
8. Van Winkle, W. Comparison of several probabilistic home-range models. *J. Wildl. Manag.* **1975**, *39*, 118–123. [CrossRef]
9. Kie, J.G.; Matthiopoulos, J.; Fieberg, J.; Powell, R.A.; Cagnacci, F.; Mitchell, M.S.; Gaillard, J.M.; Moorcroft, P.R. The home-range concept: Are traditional estimators still relevant with modern telemetry technology? *Philos. Trans. R. Soc.* **2010**, *365*, 2221–2231. [CrossRef] [PubMed]
10. Worton, B.J. Kernel methods for estimating the utilization distribution in home-range studies. *Ecology* **1989**, *70*, 164–168. [CrossRef]
11. Benhamou, S.; Riotte-Lambert, L. Beyond the utilization distribution: Identifying home range areas that are intensively exploited or repeatedly visited. *Ecol. Model.* **2012**, *227*, 112–116. [CrossRef]
12. Austin, D.; Bowen, W.D.; McMillan, J.I. Intraspecific variation in movement patterns: Modeling individual behaviour in a large marine predator. *Oikos* **2004**, *105*, 15–30. [CrossRef]
13. Kranstauber, B.; Kays, R.; LaPoint, S.D.; Wikelski, M.; Safi, K. A dynamic brownian bridge movement model to estimate utilization distributions for heterogeneous animal movement. *J. Anim. Ecol.* **2012**, *81*, 738–746. [CrossRef] [PubMed]
14. Riotte-Lambert, L.; Benhamou, S.; Chamaillé-Jammes, S. Periodicity analysis of movement recursions. *J. Theor. Biol.* **2013**, *317*, 238–243. [CrossRef] [PubMed]
15. Downs, J.A.; Horner, M.W. Analysing infrequently sampled animal tracking data by incorporating generalized movement trajectories with kernel density estimation. *Comput. Environ. Urban* **2012**, *36*, 302–310. [CrossRef]
16. Downs, J.A.; Horner, M.W.; Tucker, A.D. Time-geographic density estimation for home range analysis. *Ann. GIS* **2011**, *17*, 163–171. [CrossRef]
17. Getz, W.M.; Fortmann-Roe, S.; Cross, P.C.; Lyons, A.J.; Ryan, S.J.; Wilmers, C.C. Locoh: Nonparameteric kernel methods for constructing home ranges and utilization distributions. *PLoS ONE* **2007**, *2*, e207. [CrossRef] [PubMed]
18. Getz, W.M.; Wilmers, C.C. A local nearest-neighbour convex-hull construction of home ranges and utilization distributions. *Ecography* **2004**, *27*, 489–505. [CrossRef]
19. Downs, J.A.; Horner, M.W. A characteristic-hull based method for home range estimation. *Trans. GIS* **2009**, *13*, 527–537. [CrossRef]
20. Yan, R.C.; Beaulieu, M.; Hanuise, N.; Kato, A. Diving into the world of biologging. *Endanger. Species Res.* **2009**, *10*, 21–27. [CrossRef]
21. Shamoun-Baranes, J.; van Loon, E.V.; van Gasteren, H.; Belle, J.V.; Bouten, W.; Buurma, L. A comparative analysis of the influence of weather on the flight altitudes of birds. *Bull. Am. Meteorol. Soc.* **2006**, *87*, 47–61. [CrossRef]
22. Keating, K.A.; Cherry, S. Modeling utilization distributions in space and time. *Ecology* **2009**, *90*, 1971–1980. [CrossRef] [PubMed]
23. Small, C. Spatiotemporal dimensionality and time-space characterization of multitemporal imagery. *Remote Sens. Environ.* **2012**, *124*, 793–809. [CrossRef]

24. Li, J.; Meng, L.; Wang, F.Z.; Zhang, W.; Cai, Y. A Map-Reduce-enabled SOLAP cube for large-scale remotely sensed data aggregation. *Comput. Geosci.* **2014**, *70*, 110–119. [CrossRef]
25. Xu, Z.; Lee, J.; Park, D.; Chung, Y. Multidimensional analysis model for highly pathogenic avian influenza using data cube and data mining techniques. *Biosyst. Eng.* **2017**, *157*, 109–121. [CrossRef]
26. Kamp, V.; Sitzmann, L.; Wietek, F. A spatial data cube concept to support data analysis in environmental epidemiology. In Proceedings of the 9th International Conference on Scientific and Statistical Database Management, Olympia, WA, USA, 11–13 August 1997; pp. 100–103. [CrossRef]
27. Afonso, A.P.; Martins, B. Visualizing human trajectories: Comparing space-time cubes and static maps. In Proceedings of the 28th International BCS Human Computer Interaction Conference, Southport, UK, 9–12 September 2014; pp. 207–212. [CrossRef]
28. Hengl, T.; van Loon, E.E.; Shamoun-baranes, J.; Bouten, W. Geostatistical analysis of GPS trajectory data: Space-time densities. In Proceedings of the 8th International Symposium on Spatial Accuracy Assessment in Natural Resources and Environmental Sciences, Shanghai, China, 25–27 June 2008; pp. 17–24.
29. Morfonios, K.; Konakas, S.; Ioannidis, Y.; Kotsis, N. ROLAP Implementations of the data cube. *ACM Comput. Surv.* **2007**, *39*, 12. [CrossRef]
30. Gary, J.; Chaudhuri, S.; Bosworth, A.; Layman, A.; Reichart, D.; Venkatrao, M.; Pellow, F.; Pirahesh, H. Data Cube: A relational aggregation operator generalizing group-by, cross-tab, and sub-totals. *Data Min. Knowl. Discov.* **1997**, *1*, 29–53. [CrossRef]
31. Shen, J.W.; Liu, X.T.; Chen, M. Discovering spatiotemporal patterns from taxi-based floating car data: A case study from Nanjing. *GISci. Remote Sens.* **2017**, *54*, 617–638. [CrossRef]
32. Kaya, E.; Eren, T.; Doger, C.; Balcisoy, S. Do 3D Visualizations Fail? An Empirical Discussion on 2D and 3D Representations of the Spatiotemporal Data. In Proceedings of the Eurasia Graphics, Istanbul, Turkey, 14 October 2014; pp. 1–12.
33. Spretke, D.; Bak, P.; Janetzko, H.; Kranstauber, B.; Mansmann, F.; Davidson, S. Exploration through enrichment: A visual analytics approach for animal movement. In Proceedings of the ACM Sigspatial International Symposium on Advances in Geographic Information Systems, Chicago, IL, USA, 1–4 November 2011; pp. 421–424. [CrossRef]
34. Ware, C.; Arsenault, R.; Plumlee, M.; Wiley, D. Visualizing the underwater behavior of humpback whales. *IEEE Comput. Graph.* **2006**, *26*, 14–18. [CrossRef]
35. Kraak, M.J.; Huisman, O. Beyond exploratory visualization of space-time paths. In *Geographic Data Mining and Knowledge Discovery*; CRC Press: Boca Raton, FL, USA, 2009; pp. 431–443. [CrossRef]
36. Gao, S. Spatiotemporal analytics for exploring human mobility patterns and urban dynamics in the mobile age. *Spat. Cognit. Comput.* **2015**, *15*, 86–114. [CrossRef]
37. Burt, W.H. Territoriality and home range concepts as applied to mammals. *J. Mammal.* **1943**, *24*, 346–352. [CrossRef]
38. Kernohan, B.J.; Gitzen, R.A.; Millspaugh, J.J. Analysis of animal space use and movements. In *Radio Tracking and Animal Populations*; Milspaugh, J.J., Marzluff, J.M., Eds.; Academic Press: New York, NY, USA, 2001; pp. 125–166. ISBN 9780124977815. [CrossRef]
39. Zhang, J.D.; Hull, V.; Ouyang, Z.Y. A review of home range studies. *Acta Ecol. Sin.* **2013**, *33*, 3269–3279. [CrossRef]
40. Hayne, D.W. Calculation of size of home range. *J. Mammal.* **1949**, *30*, 1–18. [CrossRef]
41. Silverman, B.W. *Density Estimation for Statistics and Data Analysis*; Chapman and Hall: New York, NY, USA, 1986; pp. 296–309. ISBN 0-412-24620-1. [CrossRef]
42. Silva, L.D.; de Azevedo, E.B.; Elias, R.B.; Silva, L. Species distribution modeling: Comparison of fixed and mixed effects models using INLA. *ISPRS Int. J. Geo-Inf.* **2017**, *6*, 391. [CrossRef]
43. Pelekis, N.; Kopanakis, I.; Marketos, G.; Ntoutsi, I.; Andrienko, G.; Theodoridis, Y. Similarity search in trajectory databases. In Proceedings of the 14th International Symposium on Temporal Representation and Reasoning, Alicante, Spain, 28–30 June 2007; pp. 129–140. [CrossRef]
44. Beguería, S.; van Asch, T.W.J.; Malet, J.P.; Gröndahl, S.A. GIS-based numerical model for simulating the kinematics of mud and debris flows over complex terrain. *Nat. Hazard Earth Syst.* **2009**, *9*, 1897–1909. [CrossRef]
45. Shamoun-Baranes, J.; van Loon, E.V.; Liechti, F.; Bouten, W. Analyzing the effect of wind on flight: Pitfalls and solutions. *J. Exp. Biol.* **2007**, *210*, 82–90. [CrossRef] [PubMed]

46. Belle, J.V.; Shamoun-Baranes, J.; Loon, E.V.; Bouten, W. An operational model predicting autumn bird migration intensities for flight safety. *J. Appl. Ecol.* **2007**, *44*, 864–874. [CrossRef]
47. Benhamou, S.; Cornélis, D. Incorporating movement behavior and barriers to improve kernel home range space use estimates. *J. Wildl. Manag.* **2010**, *74*, 1353–1360. [CrossRef]
48. Laube, P.; Imfeld, S.; Weibel, R. Discovering relative motion patterns in groups of moving point objects. *Int. J. Geogr. Inf. Sci.* **2005**, *19*, 639–668. [CrossRef]
49. Karadayi, K.; Managuli, R.; Kim, Y. Three-dimensional ultrasound: From acquisition to visualization and from algorithms to systems. *IEEE Rev. Biomed. Eng.* **2009**, *2*, 23–39. [CrossRef]
50. Hsieh, T.J.; Yang, Y.S. Visualizing the seismic spectral response of the 1999 chi-chi earthquake using volume rendering technique. *J. Comput. Civ. Eng.* **2012**, *26*, 225–235. [CrossRef]
51. Li, C. A ray-casting algorithm based approach to 3D visualization of underground Mines. *China Min. Mag.* **2005**, *14*, 4–7. [CrossRef]
52. Jin, B.X.; Fang, Y.M.; Song, W.W. 3D visualization model and key techniques for digital mine. *Trans. Nonferr. Metal. Soc.* **2011**, *21*, 748–752. [CrossRef]
53. Liu, P.; Gong, J.H.; Yu, M. Visualizing and analysing dynamic meteorological data with virtual globes. *Environ. Model. Softw.* **2015**, *64*, 80–93. [CrossRef]
54. Drebin, R.A.; Carpenter, L.; Hanrahan, P. Volume rendering. *Comput. Graph.* **1988**, *22*, 65–74. [CrossRef]
55. Callahan, S.P.; Callahan, J.H.; Scheidegger, C.E.; Silva, C.T. Direct volume rendering: A 3D plotting technique for scientific data. *Comput. Sci. Eng.* **2007**, *10*, 88–92. [CrossRef]
56. Weiskopf, D.; Engel, K.; Ertl, T. Interactive clipping techniques for texture-based volume visualization and volume shading. *IEEE Trans. Vis. Comput. Graph.* **2003**, *9*, 298–312. [CrossRef]
57. Kumar, E.P.; Sumithra, M.G.; Kumar, P.S. Abnormality detection in brain MRI/CT using segmentation algorithm and 3D visualization. In Proceedings of the Fifth International Conference on Advanced Computing, Portland, OR, USA, 22–26 October 2006; pp. 56–62. [CrossRef]
58. Andrew, M.E.; Wulder, M.A.; Nelson, T.A.; Coops, N.C. Spatial Data, analysis approaches, and information needs for spatial ecosystem service assessments: A review. *GISci. Remote Sens.* **2015**, *52*, 344–373. [CrossRef]
59. Yao, H.S.; Xu, X.Q. Reviews and Prospects of Geographical Studies on the Pearl River Delta since China's Opening-up and Reforms. *World Reg. Stud.* **2010**, *2*, 162–169.
60. Passengers—Hong Kong International Airport. Available online: http://www.hongkongairport.com/ (accessed on 5 September 2017).
61. Home | Macau International Airport. Available online: http://www.macau-airport.com/en/ (accessed on 5 September 2017).
62. Li, Z.; Yue, J.; Li, H.; Li, D.; Fu, Z. Individual Identification from 3D Captured Movement Data. *Sens. Lett.* **2012**, *10*, 335–340. [CrossRef]
63. Zhang, Z.M.; Lu, W.; Shi, Y.Z.; Yang, T.L.; Liang, S.L. An improved volume rendering algorithm based on voxel segmentation. In Proceedings of the IEEE International Conference on Computer Science & Automation Engineering, Zhangjiajie, China, 25–27 May 2012; pp. 372–375. [CrossRef]
64. Pokrajac, D.; Megalooikonomou, V.; Lazarevic, A.; Kontos, D.; Obradovic, Z. Applying spatial distribution analysis techniques to classification of 3D medical images. *Artif. Intell. Med.* **2005**, *33*, 261–280. [CrossRef] [PubMed]
65. Rodríguez, M.B.; Gobbetti, E.; Guitián, J.A.I.; Makhinya, M.; Marton, F.; Pajarola, R.; Suter, S.K. State-of-the-art in compressed GPU-based direct volume rendering. *Comput. Graph. Forum* **2015**, *33*, 77–100. [CrossRef]
66. He, F.; Li, X. A Rendering Method for Visualization of Medical Data. *Mod. Appl. Sci.* **2010**, *4*, 43–50. [CrossRef]

© 2018 by the authors. Licensee MDPI, Basel, Switzerland. This article is an open access article distributed under the terms and conditions of the Creative Commons Attribution (CC BY) license (http://creativecommons.org/licenses/by/4.0/).

Article

2DPR-Tree: Two-Dimensional Priority R-Tree Algorithm for Spatial Partitioning in SpatialHadoop

Ahmed Elashry [1,*], Abdulaziz Shehab [2], Alaa M. Riad [2] and Ahmed Aboul-Fotouh [2]

1. Department of Information Systems, Kafr El-Sheikh University, Kafr El-Sheikh 33511, Egypt
2. Department of Information Systems, Mansoura University, Mansoura 35516, Egypt; abdulaziz_shehab@mans.edu.eg (A.S.); amriad2000@gmail.com (A.M.R.); elfetouh@gmail.com (A.A.-F.)
* Correspondence: Ahmed_Elashry@fci.kfs.edu.eg

Received: 23 March 2018; Accepted: 7 May 2018; Published: 9 May 2018

Abstract: Among spatial information applications, SpatialHadoop is one of the most important systems for researchers. Broad analyses prove that SpatialHadoop outperforms the traditional Hadoop in managing distinctive spatial information operations. This paper presents a Two Dimensional Priority R-Tree (2DPR-Tree) as a new partitioning technique in SpatialHadoop. The 2DPR-Tree employs a top-down approach that effectively reduces the number of partitions accessed to answer the query, which in turn improves the query performance. The results were evaluated in different scenarios using synthetic and real datasets. This paper aims to study the quality of the generated index and the spatial query performance. Compared to other state-of-the-art methods, the proposed 2DPR-Tree improves the quality of the generated index and the query execution time.

Keywords: SpatialHadoop; spatial data processing; cloud computing; PR-Tree; geospatial data

1. Introduction

The rapid and continuous growth of geospatial information generated from devices such as smartphones, satellites, and other Internet of Things (IoT) devices means that traditional Geographic Information System (GIS) cannot support such a large amount of data [1,2]. GIS is insufficient in this situation because of poor adaptability of the basic incorporated frameworks. Therefore, blending both GIS and cloud computing represents a new era for the advancement of data storage and processing, and their applications in GIS [3,4].

Recently, Hadoop [5,6] has become the most well-known open source cloud-computing platform. Hadoop provides a solution for the problem of data processing of huge datasets in many fields. Hadoop employs MapReduce [7–10] to produce an efficient data processing framework. MapReduce is a simplified distributed processing programming paradigm that has been utilized for a variety of applications, such as constructing indexes, data classification and clustering, and different types of information analysis [11]. MapReduce was developed to give an effective distributed parallel processing paradigm with a high degree of fault tolerance and adequate scalability mechanisms. However, Hadoop has some deficiencies in terms of effectiveness, especially when dealing with geospatial data [8]. A primary inadequacy is the absence of any indexing mechanism that could support specific access to spatial information in particular areas due to the demands for effective query processing. Because of this issue, an expansion of Hadoop, called SpatialHadoop, has been developed. SpatialHadoop [12,13] is a Hadoop system that is suited for spatial operations. It adds spatial constructs and geospatial information into the Hadoop core functionality.

In SpatialHadoop, spatial data are purposely fractioned and distributed to Hadoop cluster nodes. From that point, information that has spatial nearness is congregated in the same partition, which will be indexed later. All SpatialHadoop indexing structures are based on a set of partitioning techniques. All of these partitioning techniques are built-in to the Hadoop Distributed File System

(HDFS). Consequently, SpatialHadoop provides efficient query processing algorithms that access just a particular area of the information and give the correct query result. As exhibited in the paper by Ahmed Eldawy and Mohamed Mokbel [12], many spatial operations are proposed, such as range query [14–16], kNN query [17,18], spatial joins [19–21], and skyline query [22].

The contributions of this paper are summarized as follows: (1) the Two-Dimensional Priority R-Tree (2DPR-Tree) is proposed as a version of the PR-Tree with some enhancements that make it applicable in SpatialHadoop. (2) Unlike other techniques, the 2DPR-Tree algorithm achieves simultaneous partitioning of the input shapes into the desired number of partitions and highly preserved spatial proximity of these shapes. (3) A broad arrangement of experiments on different datasets (synthetic and real) was executed to illustrate the efficiency and scalability of the 2DPR-Tree indexing technique. (4) Compared to other techniques, the 2DPR-Tree has a superior performance and functionality for range and kNN queries.

The rest of the paper is organized as follows: Section 2 discusses related works on SpatialHadoop and SpatialHadoop indexing techniques. Section 3 illustrates the overall architecture of SpatialHadoop. Section 4 presents a description of the Priority R-Tree (PR-Tree). Section 5 presents a description of the proposed 2DPR-Tree partitioning technique in SpatialHadoop. Section 6 presents the experimental setup, configurations, and the performance measures. The representative results of the extensive experimentation performed are also included in this section. Finally, Section 7 concludes the work and discusses future research directions.

2. Related Work

Since files in Hadoop are not indexed, they must be sequentially filtered and scanned. To overcome this issue SpatialHadoop utilizes spatial indexes inside the Hadoop Distributed File System as a method for the efficient recovery of spatial information [23]. Indexing is the key difference of SpatialHadoop in terms of achieving a better execution than Hadoop and the other systems [24].

SpatialHadoop provides various indexing algorithms that mainly differ in data partitioning techniques. As shown in Table 1, SpatialHadoop provides space partitioning techniques such as a grid and Quadtree, space-filling curve (SFC) partitioning techniques such as the Z-curve and Hilbert curve, and data partitioning techniques such as Sort-Tile-Recursive (STR), STR+, and KD-Tree [23].

Table 1. A general classification of SpatialHadoop partitioning techniques.

Dimension	Category	Grid	Quad Tree	Z Curve	Hilbert Curve	STR	STR+	KD-Tree	2DPR-Tree
Partition Boundary	overlapping	✓	✓				✓	✓	
	non-overlapping			✓	✓	✓			✓
Search Strategy	top-down	N/A	N/A					✓	✓
	bottom-up	N/A	N/A	✓	✓	✓	✓		
Split Criterion	space-oriented	✓	✓						
	space-filling curve (SFC)-oriented			✓	✓				
	data-oriented					✓	✓	✓	✓

The grid technique [25] is a uniform data partitioning technique. This technique divides the spatial space into equal-sized rectangles using a uniform grid of $\sqrt{P_N} \times \sqrt{P_N}$ cells, where P_N is the desired number of partitions, and data located on the boundaries between partitions are redundantly allocated to those overlapping partitions. The simple process and calculations of the grid technique allow a minimal index creation time. The grid partitioning technique is simple to implement, however it causes non-uniform data distribution through the cluster nodes. This affects load balancing and therefore the efficiency of the query. The spatial query efficiency is not optimal because of the unorganized data, and the consequent time taken to search the data for the query [26].

The Quadtree technique is a Quadtree-based data partitioning technique. It preserves the adjacent relationship of objects and provides a space uniform recursive decomposition into partitions (four partitions in each iteration) until each partition has the object's defined number limit. Therefore, there is no way to control the generated partition number to satisfy the desired number of partitions. Similar to the grid partitioning technique, data located on the partition boundaries are redundantly allocated to those overlapping partitions. The Quadtree technique is extremely suited for parallel processing. However, high data transfer and high I/O costs are required, and it is hard to apply in higher dimensions [27].

The Z-curve technique sorts the input points based on their order on the Z-curve and then separates the curve into P_N partitions. Boundary objects that overlap in different partitions are assigned to the partition with maximal overlap. The Z-curve technique generates almost equal sized partitions with a linear complexity of the mapper's input, but the spatial neighborhood relationships are not always well preserved as it generates a high degree of overlap between partitions [26,28].

The Hilbert curve is a space-filling curve technique that uses the Hilbert-curve to bulk-load the R-Tree on MapReduce [29]. The partitioning function puts objects in the same partition to keep spatial proximity by using the sorted minimum boundary rectangle (MBR) values of object nodes from the Hilbert-curve, and transforms them into a standard and proven multi-dimensional index structure—R-Tree—through parallelization in MapReduce. Hilbert packing reduces the data transfer overhead through the network and thersefore the query response time [30]. Similar to the Z-curve, boundary objects that overlap in more than one partition are assigned to the maximal overlap partition.

The STR technique is an R-Tree packing algorithm [31,32]. It divides the input spatial data based on a random sample into an R-Tree [33,34] and each node in the tree has k/P_N objects, where k is the random sample size and P_N is the desired number of partitions. All leaf node boundaries are used as partition boundaries. Boundary objects that overlap in more than one partition are assigned to the maximal overlap partition.

The STR+ technique is the same as the STR technique. However, boundary objects that overlap in more than one partition are redundantly assigned to the overlapping partitions [35].

The KD-Tree technique transforms multidimensional location information into one-dimensional space. SpatialHadoop utilizes the KD-Tree partitioning method in the paper by Jon Louis Bentle [36] to partition the input dataset into P_N partitions. The KD-Tree technique begins with the input MBR as one partition and partitions it $P_N - 1$ times to produce n partitions. Boundary objects that overlap in more than one partition are redundantly assigned to overlapping partitions.

3. The Overall Architecture of SpatialHadoop

A SpatialHadoop cluster has one master node that divides a map-reduce job into smaller tasks, distributed to and executed by slave nodes. As shown in Figure 1, users access SpatialHadoop through The Pigeon Language in the Language layer to process their datasets. The Pigeon is an SQL-like language that supports the Open Geospatial Consortium (OGC) standard that was developed to simplify spatial data processing [37].

The operations layer consists of the various computational geometry operations, as mentioned in the paper by Ahmed Eldawy, et al. [9], and a set of spatial queries such as the range query and kNN query. The range query [14] takes the spatial input dataset SR and a query area QA as information and returns all objects in SR that are located within QA. In Hadoop, the input dataset is stored as a sequential heap file. Thus, all spatial input objects must be examined to get the result. SpatialHadoop attains a faster performance by exploiting the spatial index. In SpatialHadoop, the range query executes in two stages. In the first stage, the file blocks that should be handled are chosen. This stage exploits the index to choose blocks that are located within the specified area QA. Blocks that are completely located in the area QA are considered a part of the result without needing further processing. The other blocks, which are partially located in the specified area, are sent to a second stage that searches the index to get objects covered by the specified area. Each block that needs to be processed is assigned to a map function that searches its index to get the matching records [12]. The kNN query [14,18] takes a query point Q and an integer k to find the k closest points to Q in the input dataset. In Hadoop, the kNN query checks all the input points in the input dataset, finds the distances between them and Q, and then the top-k points are returned as the result [7]. In SpatialHadoop, the kNN query is performed in three stages. The first stage returns an initial answer of the k nearest points to Q within the same partition (the same file block). First, a filter function, which obtains only the covering partition, is utilized to locate the partition that includes Q. At that point, the initial result is found by applying the traditional kNN to the chosen partition index. The second stage checks if the initial result can be considered a final result by sketching a test circle centered on the query point with a span equivalent to the distance from the query point to its k_{th} remotest neighbor from the initial result. On the off chance that the test circle does not cover any partition other than the query point partition, the initial result is considered the final result. Otherwise, we continue to the third stage. The third stage runs a range query to find all points inside the MBR of the test circle. At that point, the final result is prepared by gathering the initial result from the first stage and the result from the second stage to get the nearest k points [23].

The MapReduce layer has two new components: the SpatialFileSplitter removes file blocks that are not part of the result utilizing the global index, while the SpatialRecordReader gets the partial result efficiently from each file block utilizing local indexes [12].

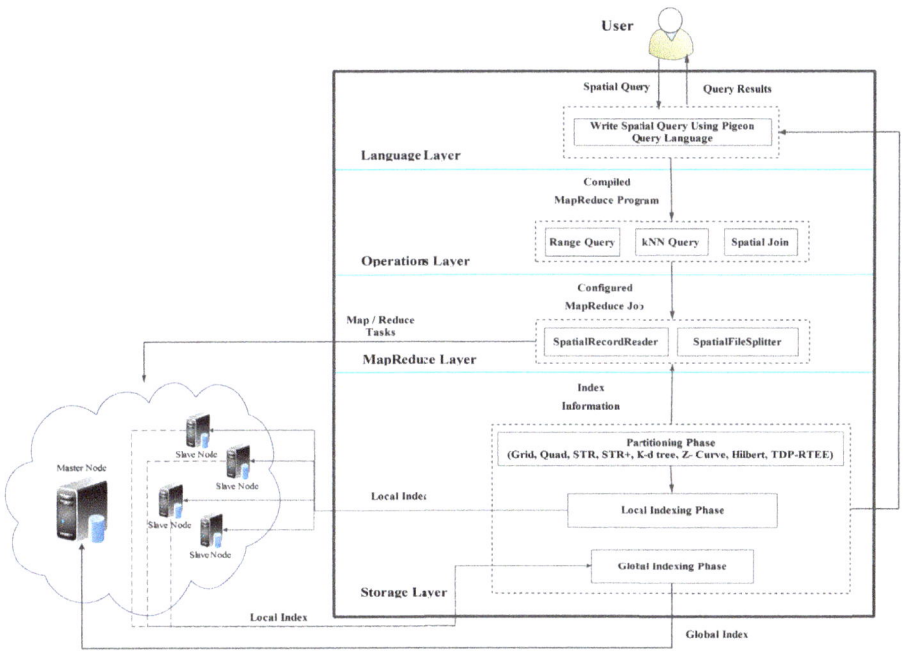

Figure 1. SpatialHadoop system architecture [12].

In the storage layer, the MapReduce job constructs the SpatialHadoop index in three phases: partitioning, local indexing, and global indexing [23]. In the partitioning phase, a file is spatially parceled into the desired number of partitions. Each partition is represented in a rectangle with a size equal to one file block (64 MB) as the default. This phase runs in three stages; the initial stage is fixed, and the other two stages are repeated for each partitioning technique. The initial stage figures out the number of partitions needed, which is fixed for all partitioning techniques. The second stage takes an arbitrary specimen and examines the proportion P_N of the partitions to such an extent that the number of arbitrary specimen points in each partition is at most k/P_N, where k is the arbitrary specimen size. The third stage segments the input file by allocating every record to at least one partition. In the local indexing phase, a local index is constructed for each partition separately according to the index type and saved to a file with one HDFS block, which is defined by the MBR of the partition. In the global indexing phase, the local index files are grouped into one file. The global index is stored in the master node main memory to index all partitions utilizing their MBRs as keys [23].

4. The Priority R-Tree

The PR-Tree is considered one of the best R-Tree variants for distributed extreme data. The PR-Tree is the first R-Tree variant that can answer any window query in the optimal $O(\sqrt{N/D_b} + T/D_b)$ I/Os, where N is the number of d-dimensional (hyper) rectangles stored in the R-Tree, D_b is the disk block size, and T is the output size [38].

The PR-Tree works by considering each rectangle as a four dimensional point $(x_{min}, y_{min}, x_{max}, y_{max})$ in a KD-Tree. The PR-Tree has a structure like the original R-Tree in which the input rectangles are stored in the leaves, and each interior node $\mathcal{V}$ contains the MBR for each of its children $\mathcal{V}_c$. However, the PR-Tree structure is different from the original R-Tree in that not all the leaves are on the same level of the tree and the interior nodes only have six degrees [38].

The idea of the PR-Tree is to deal with the input rectangle $((x_{min}, y_{min}); (x_{max}, y_{max}))$ as a four-dimensional point $(x_{min}, y_{min}, x_{max}, y_{max})$. The PR-Tree is then only a KD-Tree on N rectangles that are sampled at N points. Aside from that, four additional leaves are included underneath each interior node; these leaves have the most extraordinary B rectangles in each of the four dimensions, where B is the number of rectangles that fit one partition (leaf). These leaves are called priority leaves [39].

The definition of the structure of the PR-Tree is as follows: If S is a set of N rectangles, $R_i^* = (x_{min}(R_i), y_{min}(R_i), x_{max}(R_i), y_{max}(R_i))$ is defined as the representation of a rectangle, $R_i = ((x_{min}(R_i), y_{min}(R_i)); (x_{max}(R_i), y_{max}(R_i)))$ is a four dimensional point, and S* is the N four dimensional points corresponding to S.

As mentioned in the paper by Lars Arge, et al. [38], Algorithm 1 illustrates how to construct a PR-Tree T_S on a set of four dimensional points S*. It is characterized recursively: If S* contains four-dimensional points less than B then T_S consists of a solitary leaf. Otherwise, T_S consists of a node $\mathcal{V}$ with six children, four priority leaves, and two recursive PR-Trees. The node $\mathcal{V}$ and the priority leaves beneath it are created as follows:

- Extract the B four-dimensional points in S* with minimal x_{min}-coordinates and store them in the first priority leaf $\mathcal{V}_p^{x_{min}}$.
- Extract the B four-dimensional points among the rest of the points with minimal y_{min}-coordinates and store them in the second priority leaf $\mathcal{V}_p^{y_{min}}$.
- Extract the B four-dimensional points among the rest of the points with maximal x_{max}-coordinates and store them in the third priority leaf $\mathcal{V}_p^{x_{max}}$.
- Finally, extract the B four-dimensional points among the rest of the points with maximal y_{max}-coordinates and store them in the fourth priority leaf $\mathcal{V}_p^{y_{max}}$.

Consequently, the priority leaves contain the extraordinary four-dimensional points in S*. In the wake of building the priority leaves, the set S_r^* of the remaining four-dimensional points are partitioned into two subsets; S*< and S*>. These are of a roughly similar size and recursively develop the PR-Trees $T_S<$ and $T_S>$. The division is performed utilizing the x_{min}; y_{min}; x_{max}, or y_{max}-coordinates in a round-robin model, as if building a four-dimensional KD-Tree on S_r^*. Table 2 shows the description of symbols that are used in the presented algorithms.

Table 2. Description of symbols that are used in the algorithms.

Symbol	Description
S	Set of rectangles in the working file
N	Rectangles number in S.
n_p	The number of shapes/points to be indexed
P_N	Partition number calculated by dividing the size of working file by the file block size as each partition should fit into only one file block
B	Number of shapes/points assigned for each partition or file block calculated as n_p/P_N
S^*	Set of 4D points (a point for each rectangle in S)
S^*_{2D}	Set of 2D points (a 2D point for each rectangle in S)
R_N	Initial node (root) with start index = 0 and end index = S^*.length and depth = 0
μ	Median (the divider that splits the rest of the points into two almost equal sized subsets)

Algorithm 1 PR-tree index creation working steps.

1 **Function PRTreeIndex**(S, P_N)
2   **Input:** S = {R_1, ..., R_N}, P_N
3   **Output:** A priority search tree (Stack of nodes)
4 **Method:**
5   B ← n_p / P_N
6   **Foreach** rectangle R ∈ S **do**   // prepare S^*
7   R^* ← (Rx_{min}, Ry_{min}, Rx_{max}, Ry_{max})
8   S^* ← R^* // store R^* in S^*
9   **End For**
10   R_N ← Initial node with start_index = 0, end_index = S^*.length and depth = 0
11   STACK.push(R_N)
12   **While** (STACK is not empty)
13   Nd ← pop(STACK)
14   **If** (Nd.size ≤ B)   // where Nd.size = Nd.end_index − Nd.start_index
15   leaf ← create a single leaf   // T_S consists of a single leaf;
16   **Else If** (Nd.size ≤ 4B)
17   b ← ⌈(Nd.size)/4⌉
18   Recursively sort and extract the B points in S^* in a leaf node according to x_{min}, y_{min}, x_{max} and y_{max}
19   **Else**
20   Recursively sort and extract the B points in S^* in a leaf node according to x_{min}, y_{min}, x_{max}, and y_{max}
21   μ ← (Nd.size − 4B)/2
22       $T_{S<}$ (Nd.start_index + (4*B), Nd.start_index + (4*B) + μ, Nd.depth+1)
23       $T_{S>}$ (Nd.start_index + (4*B) + μ, Nd.end_index, Nd.depth+1)
24   STACK.push ($T_{S<}$ and $T_{S>}$)
25   **End if**
26   **End while**

5. The 2DPR-Tree Technique in SpatialHadoop

Within all of the various SpatialHadoop partitioning techniques, all records from the input dataset, no matter the spatial data type (point, line, or polygon), are changed into 2D points as they are sampled to make the in-memory bulk-loading step unsophisticated and more effective [23]. This operation of approximation of all input shapes into points is achieved by getting the MBR of each shape, converting the input dataset to a set of rectangles, and then getting the center point of each rectangle. Motivated by this observation, Algorithm 2 was proposed to develop the 2DPR-Tree Technique—a PR-Tree that has its index points on the two-dimensional plane [40]—in SpatialHadoop, as a new partitioning and indexing technique.

The 2DPR-Tree employs a top-down approach to bulk loading an R-Tree with the input shapes. The tree may have sub-trees that contain fewer than four nodes or empty sub-trees with no nodes at all, so this was handled in the search procedure.

Algorithm 2 begins with calculating B by dividing the total number of shapes in the input dataset by the desired number of partitions, starting from the root node that contains the MBR of all data shapes. If the number of shapes is less than or equal to B, a scalar priority leaf V_p is created. Otherwise, the priority leaf V_p^{xmin} is created and stores the left-extreme B shapes with minimal x-coordinates. After that, if the rest of the shapes are less than or equal to B, then the second priority leaf V_p is created and stores the remaining shapes. Otherwise, the second priority leaf V_p^{ymin} is created and stores the bottom-extreme B shapes with minimal y-coordinates. Again, the rest of the shapes are checked for if they are less than or equal to B and, if so, the third priority leaf V_p is created and stores the remaining shapes. Otherwise, the third priority leaf V_p^{xmax} is created and stores the right-extreme B shapes with maximal x-coordinates and the fourth priority leaf V_p^{ymax} stores the remaining top-extreme B shapes with maximal y-coordinates.

On the other hand, if the number of shapes under the root node is higher than 4B, a four-priority leaf and two sub-P-Trees are created, as follows:

1. The first priority leaf V_p^{xmin} stores the left-extreme B shapes with minimal x-coordinates.
2. The second priority leaf V_p^{ymin} stores the bottom-extreme B shapes with minimal y-coordinates.
3. The third priority leaf V_p^{xmax} stores the right-extreme B shapes with maximal x-coordinates.
4. The fourth priority leaf V_p^{ymax} stores the top-extreme B shapes with maximal y-coordinates.
5. In separating the rest of the n-4B shapes into two parts in light of our present tree depth, the first part contains the number of shapes equal to μ calculated as in line 32, and the second part contains the rest of the n-4B shapes. The same plan is utilized in finding the KD-Tree:

    (a) If ((depth % 4) == 0) split based on the ascending order of the x-coordinate (left extraordinary).
    (b) If ((depth % 4) == 1) split based on the ascending order of the y-coordinate (bottom extraordinary).
    (c) If ((depth % 4) == 2) split based on the descending order of the x-coordinate (right extraordinary).
    (d) If ((depth % 4) == 3) split based on the descending order of the y-coordinate (top extraordinary).

Recursively applying this calculation will make two sub-trees in the parceled parts. Stop when no shapes remain to be filed (e.g., stop when n-4B? 0).

The proposed 2DPR-Tree in Algorithm 2 is different from the traditional PR-Tree described in Algorithm 1 in two situations. The first is when the Nd.size is less than 4B. In line 17 in Algorithm 1 the Nd.size is divided by four to generate four leaves with a capacity less than B, which will cause the generated leaves to be partially filled with shapes. On the other hand, lines 12–30 in Algorithm 2 guarantee that all generated leaves are filled with shapes. The second situation occurs while calculating μ, which determines the number of shapes in each of the generated subtrees. In Algorithm 1, μ is calculated to produce two subtrees with shapes of roughly similar sizes. In Algorithm 2, μ is calculated as multiples of 4B. As a result, the proposed Algorithm 2 fills all available leaves with shapes except in the worst case scenario in which one leaf is partially filled. This in turn guarantees that the number of generated leaves satisfies the desired number of partitions P_N and achieves 100% space utilization.

As an example, assuming that a file has 1.5 M records and B—the maximum capacity of the partition—is equal to 100,000 records, the desired number of partitions P_N should be 15 partitions. Figure 2 shows the structure of the traditional PR-Tree of the file using Algorithm 1. It generates 12 partitions with a full capacity (100,000 records) and 16 partitions with 18,750 records each. Therefore, the traditional PR-Tree divides the input file into 28 partitions. Figure 3 shows the structure of the 2DPR-Tree for the same file. It generates 15 partitions at full capacity, achieving 100% space utilization and satisfying the desired number of partitions P_N.

Algorithm 2 2DPR-Tree index creation working steps.

```
1    Function 2DPRTreeIndex (S, P_N)
2    Input: S = {R_1, ...., R_N}, P_N
3    Output: A 2DPR-tree(Stack of nodes)
4    Method:
5    B ← n_p / P_N
6    Foreach rectangle R ∈ S do          // prepare S*
7        R* ← R.getCenterPoint(); // converting each rectangle to a 2D point
8        S*_{2D} ← R*                    // store R* in S*
9    End For
10   R_N ← Initial node with start_index = 0 and end_index = S*. length and depth = 0
11   STACK.push (R_N)
12   While (STACK is not empty)
13   Nd ← pop (stack)
14   If(Nd.size ≤ B)    //where Nd.size = Nd.end_index - Nd.start_index
15   leaf ← create a single leaf    //T_S comprises a single leaf;
16   Else If (Nd.size ≤ 4B)
17       Sort (the S* points, X, ASC)
18       Extract (the B points in S* with the minimal X coordinate, leaf $\mathcal{V}_p^{Xmin}$)
19       If ((Nd.size – B) ≤ B)
20       Sort (the rest S* points, Y, ASC)
21       leaf $\mathcal{V}_p^{Ymin}$ ← create a leaf with the rest S* points
22       Else
23          Sort (the rest S* points, Y, ASC)
24          Extract (the B points in S* with the minimal Y coordinate, leaf $\mathcal{V}_p^{Ymin}$)
25          If ((Nd.size – 2B) ≤ B)
26             Sort (the rest S* points, X, DESC)
27             leaf $\mathcal{V}_p^{Xmax}$ ← create a leaf with the rest S* points
28          Else
29             Sort (the rest S* points, X, DESC)
30             Extract (the B points in S* with the maximal X coordinate, leaf $\mathcal{V}_p^{Xmax}$)
31             Sort (the rest S* points, Y, DESC)
32             leaf $\mathcal{V}_p^{Ymax}$ ← create a leaf with the rest S* points
33          End if
34       End if
35   Else
36       $\mu \leftarrow \left\lfloor \left( \frac{\lfloor (n-4B)/(4B) \rfloor}{2} \right) \right\rfloor \times 4B$
37       If ((Nd.depth % 4) == 0)
38          split by the x coordinate (left extraordinary)
39       Else If ((Nd.depth % 4) == 1)
40          split by the y coordinate (bottom extraordinary)
41       Else If ((Nd.depth % 4) == 2)
42          split by the x coordinate backward (right extraordinary)
43       Else
44          split by the y coordinate backward (top extraordinary)
45       End If
46       T_{S<} (Nd.start_index + (4*B), Nd.start_index + (4*B) + μ, Nd.depth+1)
47       T_{S>} (Nd.start_index + (4*B) + μ, Nd.end_index, Nd.depth+1)
48       STACK.push (T_{S<} and T_{S>})
49   End if
50   End while
```

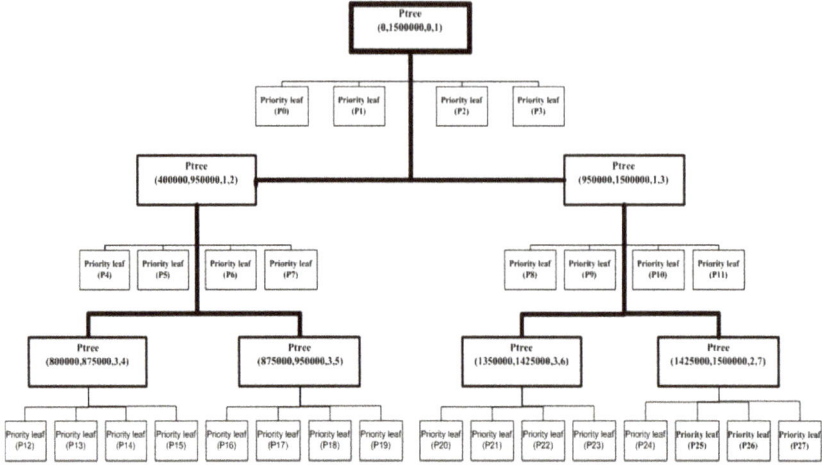

Figure 2. PR-Tree structure for a file with a 1.5 M rectangle.

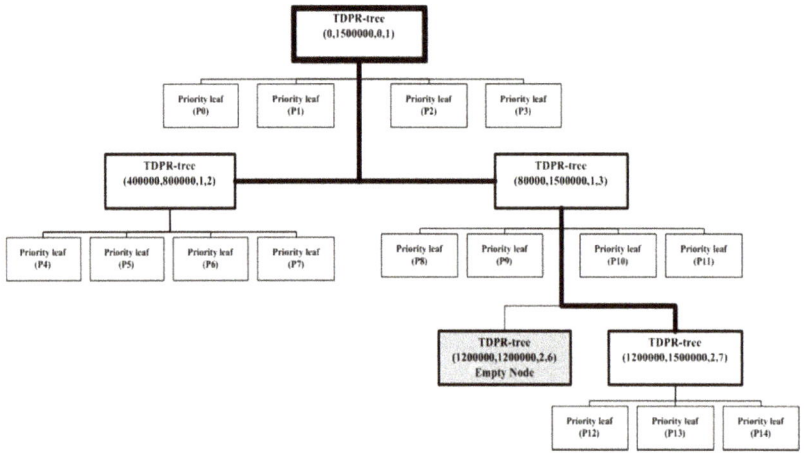

Figure 3. 2DPR-Tree structure for a file with a 1.5 M rectangle.

6. Experimentation

6.1. Experimental Setup

All experiments were performed on an EMR Amazon cluster of five 'm3.xlarge' nodes, which have a high-frequency 4vCPU Intel Xeon processor, 15 GB of main memory, 2 × 40 GBSSD storage running a Linux operating system, Hadoop2.7.2, and Java 8 [41]. We used synthetic datasets with a uniform distribution in 1 M × 1 M units of area. Each object in the datasets is a rectangle. The synthetic datasets consist of several files with different sizes (1, 2, 4, 8, and 16 GB) that were generated using the SpatialHadoop built-in uniform generator [24]. Additionally, we used real datasets, representing non-uniformly distributed and skewed data, that was extracted from OpenStreetMap, specifically a Buildings data file that had 115 M records of buildings, a Cities data file that had 171 K records of the boundaries of postal code areas (mostly cities), and a Sports data file that had 1.8 M records of sporting areas [12]. Table 3 shows a detailed description of the real datasets.

Table 3. Real spatial datasets.

Name	Data Size	Records No.	Average Record Size	Description
Buildings	28.2 GB	115 M	263 bytes	Boundaries of all buildings
Cities	1.4 GB	171 K	8.585 KB	Boundaries of postal code areas (mostly cities)
Sports	590 MB	1.8 M	343 bytes	Boundaries of sporting areas

6.2. Experimental Results

An experimental study comparing the performances of different SpatialHadoop indexing algorithms and the 2DPR-Tree is presented. The experiments show that spatial query processing is very reliant on the size and nature of the dataset, and the indexes demonstrate diverging performance with the alternative dataset types.

Figure 4a shows the graphical representation of the Cities dataset that has been partitioned and indexed into 14 partitions by the 2DPR-Tree using Algorithm 2. Figure 4b–f shows its representation with the other partitioning techniques. It is noted that the spatial locality in the Hilbert and Z-curve techniques is not always well preserved as they generate a high degree of overlap between partitions.

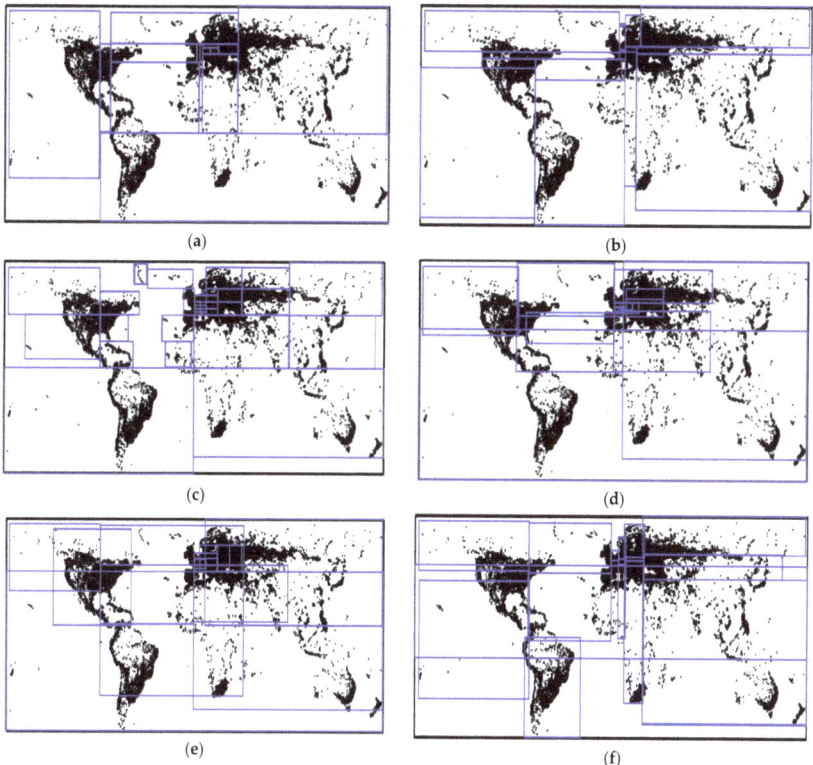

Figure 4. The Cities dataset indexed with different SpatialHadoop indexing techniques: (**a**) Cities indexed with the 2DPR-Tree; (**b**) Cities indexed with the KD-Tree; (**c**) Cities indexed with the Quadtree; (**d**) Cities indexed with the Hilbert-Curve; (**e**) Cities indexed with the Z-Curve; (**f**) Cities indexed with the STR and STR+.

From applying the different partitioning techniques to the uniformly distributed synthetic datasets, an interesting finding is that although all partitioning techniques should partition the input dataset into the same specific number of partitions as mentioned in Section 3, the Quadtree, STR, and STR+ techniques have divided the input datasets into a different number of partitions that are much bigger than desired (Table 4). Table 5 shows that Quadtree divided the Sports, Cities, and Buildings datasets into 25, 34, and 705 partitions, respectively, when the desired number of partitions are 6, 14, and 252 partitions. On the other hand, the 2DPR-Tree, KD-Tree, Z-curve, and Hilbert techniques adhered to the desired number of partitions.

Figure 5 shows the performance measures that assess the indexing time for uniformly distributed synthetic datasets using different techniques. All techniques have approximately the same indexing time for the datasets that are 1, 2, and 4 GB in size. The KD-Tree and Quadtree have the best indexing time for the 8 GB dataset and the 2DPR-Tree has the best indexing time for the 16 GB dataset. For real datasets, Figure 6 shows that 2DPR-Tree has the better indexing time for the datasets of Cities and Buildings.

Table 4. Partition number generated by indexing techniques in the synthetic datasets.

File Size (GB)	Partitions NO				
	1 GB	2 GB	4 GB	8 GB	16 GB
2DPR-Tree	10	20	39	77	154
KD-Tree	10	20	39	77	154
Quadtree	16	64	64	256	256
Z-curve	10	20	39	77	154
Hilbert	10	20	39	77	154
STR & STR+	12	20	42	81	156

Table 5. Partition number generated by indexing techniques in the real datasets.

Real Dataset	Partitions NO		
	Sports	Cities	Buildings
2DPR-Tree	6	14	252
KD-Tree	6	14	252
Quadtree	25	34	705
Z-curve	6	14	252
Hilbert	6	14	252
STR & STR+	6	18	252

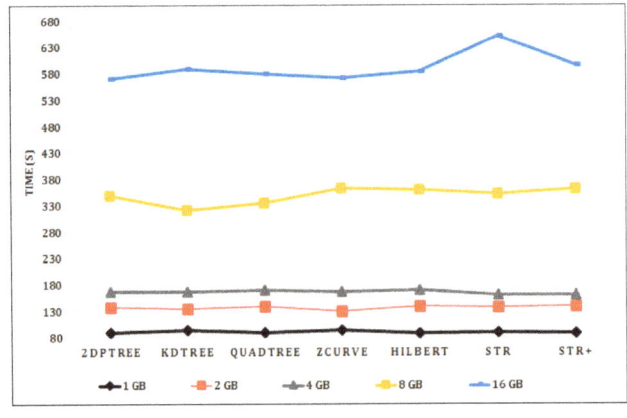

Figure 5. Indexing time for the synthetic datasets.

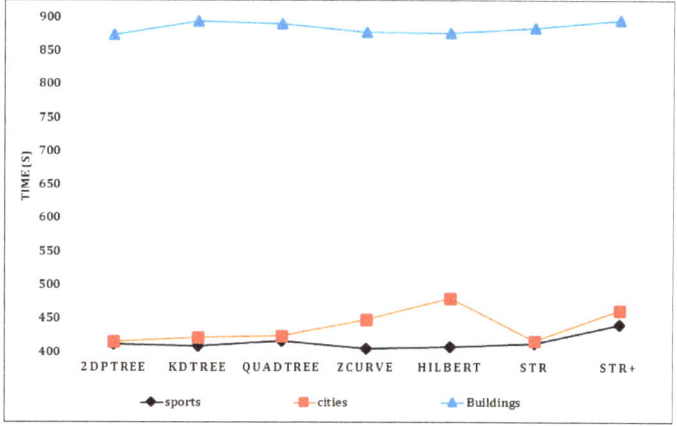

Figure 6. Indexing time for the real datasets (Sports, Cities, and Buildings).

The range and kNN queries, as presented in the paper by Ahmed Eldawy and Mohamed Mokbel [12], were performed on the partitioned data to quantify and examine the performance of the diverse partitioning strategies. For the range query, the rectangular area A is revolved over arbitrary records from the input dataset. The measure of A is balanced with the end goal that the query area is equal to the selection ratio (σ) multiplied by the total area of the working file, as shown in Equation (1):

$$A = \sigma * Area(InMBR), \tag{1}$$

where the choice proportion $\sigma \in (0, 1]$ is a parameter we change in our analysis and Area(*InMBR*) is the region of the MBR of the working file.

Figure 7a shows the range query processing performance on the indexed synthetic datasets with a query window area equal to 0.01% of the input dataset area. The performance of the 2DPR-Tree and KD-Tree is stable and roughly unchanged through different dataset sizes. On the other hand, the Quadtree, Z-curve, Hilbert, and STR techniques showed varying performances with the change of the input dataset sizes. Figure 7b shows that changing the query window area to 1% of the input dataset area did not have an effect on the performance of the different partitioning techniques for the small size datasets of 1 GB, 2 GB, and 4 GB. For the 8 GB and 16 GB datasets, the range query takes a long time as it must access a greater number of partitions to obtain the query answer. The 2DPR-Tree and KD-Tree take 101 and 103 s, respectively, to answer the range query with 1% query window area on a 16 GB input dataset, which is an excellent result compared to the Quadtree, Z-curve, and Hilbert methods that take 132.5, 127.5, and 112 s, respectively, to answer the same query.

In order to show the effect of changing the size of the query window area on the performance of different partitioning techniques, a range query with a query window area equal to the input dataset area was performed. That query returned all objects in the input dataset and requires the indexing and partitioning technique to access all dataset partitions to obtain the query answer. By comparing results from Figure 7b,c, we find that answering a range query with a query window area equal to the whole input dataset area takes only three times the length of time that it takes to answer a range query with a query window area equal to 1% of the input dataset area. Therefore, the query window area does not have a significant effect on the performance of the range query with different indexing and partitioning techniques. The size of the input dataset, the number of partitions that are generated by the partitioning techniques, and the number of partitions that need to be accessed to get the result have the largest effect on the performance of the range query with different partitioning techniques. As shown in Figure 7b,c, the Quadtree method that divides the 8 GB and 16 GB input datasets into

256 partitions takes much more time to answer the query than the other techniques that divide the 8 GB and 16 GB input datasets into 77,154 partitions.

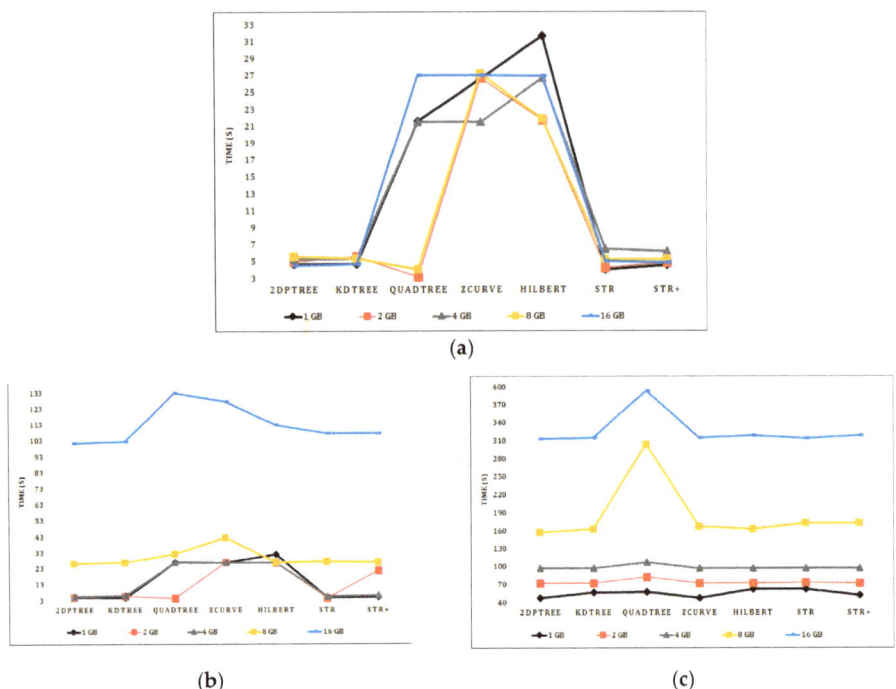

Figure 7. Range query execution time on indexed synthetic datasets: (**a**) Range query with a 0.0001 query window area; (**b**) range query with a 0.01 query window area; (**c**) range query with a query window area equal to the file area.

Figure 8a,b shows the range query processing performance on the Sports and Cities datasets with different query window areas. Quadtree has the best time performance for the range queries with small query window areas equal to 0.01% and 1% of the input dataset area. However, for the range queries with larger query window areas equal to 10% and 50% of the input dataset area, the Quadtree performance rapidly decreased. This is because when the query window area is increased, the number of partitions that is required to be processed to answer the range query is increased, especially for the Quadtree as it partitions the input datasets into a greater number of partitions than the other techniques. On the other hand, the 2DPR-Tree has the best time performance for the range query with query window areas equal to 10% and 50% of the input dataset area, as the 2DPR-Tree divides the input dataset into the desired number of partitions and the spatial proximity of the input shapes is always well preserved. The results shown in Figure 8c confirm our earlier claims as the 2DPR-Tree and the KD-Tree answer the range query with a query window area equal to 50% of the Buildings dataset area in 111 and 120 s, respectively, and Quadtree takes approximately twice the time to answer the same query.

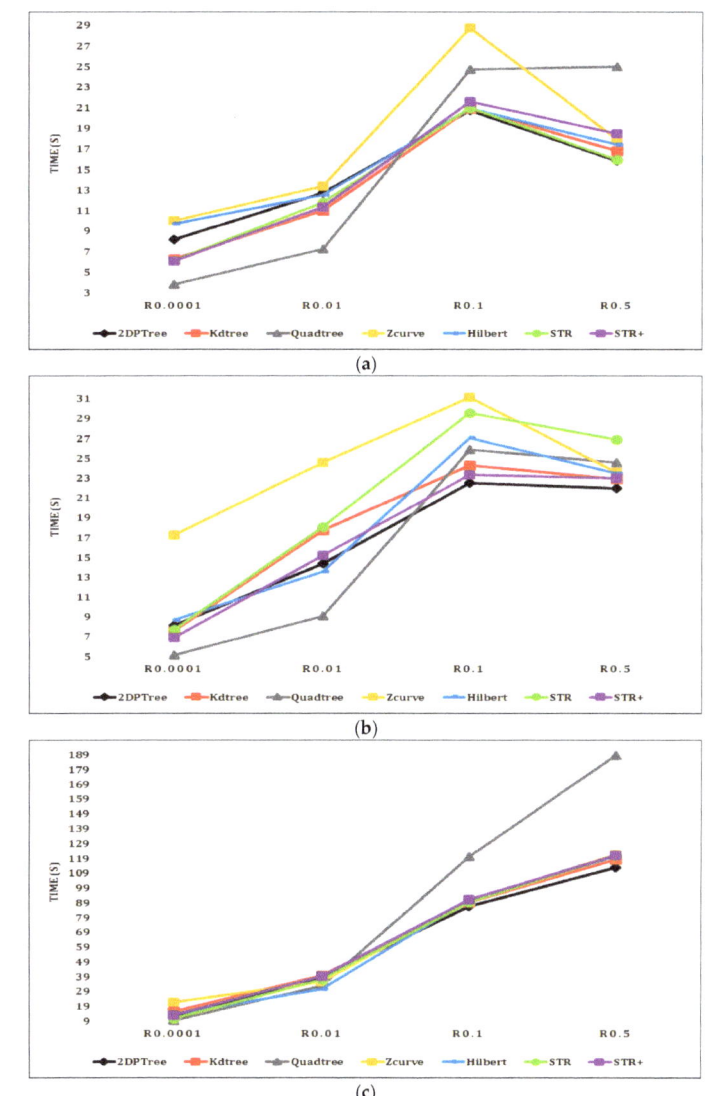

Figure 8. Range query execution time for indexed real datasets: (**a**) Query window area equal to 0.01%, 1%, 10%, and 50% of the Sports dataset area; (**b**) query window area equal to 0.01%, 1%, 10%, and 50% of the Cities dataset area; (**c**) query window area equal to 0.01%, 1%, 10%, and 50% of the Buildings dataset area.

For the kNN query, query locations are arbitrarily chosen from points sampled from the input dataset. Figure 9a–d shows the kNN query performance over the indexed synthetic datasets as the input file size is increased from 1 to 16 GB and k varied from 1–1000. In the uniformly distributed synthetic data, all algorithms have roughly the same performance with different k values. The 2DPR-Tree and KD-Tree techniques, respectively, have the best query execution time for the synthetic datasets.

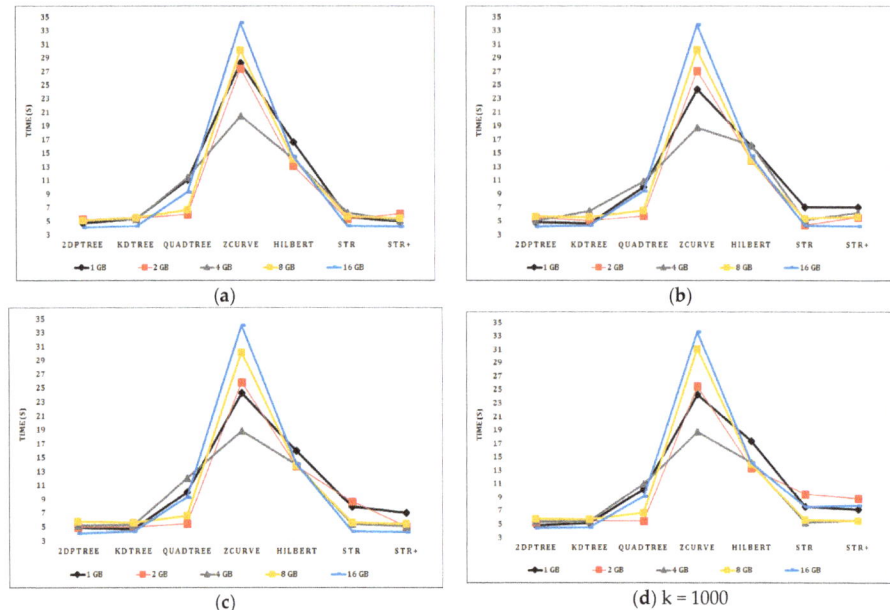

Figure 9. kNN query execution time for indexed synthetic datasets: (**a**) With k = 1; (**b**) with k = 10; (**c**) with k = 100; (**d**) with k = 1000.

Figure 10a shows the kNN query performance on the Sports dataset as k is varied from 1 to 10,000. Quadtree outperforms the other techniques in performing the kNN queries as it divides the Sports dataset into 25 smaller partitions, in contrast with the other techniques that divide the Sports dataset into six larger partitions. The partition access time of Quadtree is therefore much lower than that of the other techniques, and the kNN query requires a smaller number of partitions to be accessed to get the query result. However, the 2DPR-Tree performs best at the level of techniques that are committed to the desired number of partitions, which is calculated in the initial stage of the partitioning phase and should be fixed for all partitioning techniques. Figure 10b shows the 2DPR-Tree has the best performance for the kNN queries on the Cities dataset with different k values. For the Buildings dataset, Figure 10c shows that Quadtree outperforms the other techniques. However, the KD-Tree has the best kNN query execution time for k equal to 1, 10, and 100 points and the 2DPR-Tree has the best kNN query execution time for k equal to 1000 and 10,000 points, among the techniques that are committed to the desired number of partitions.

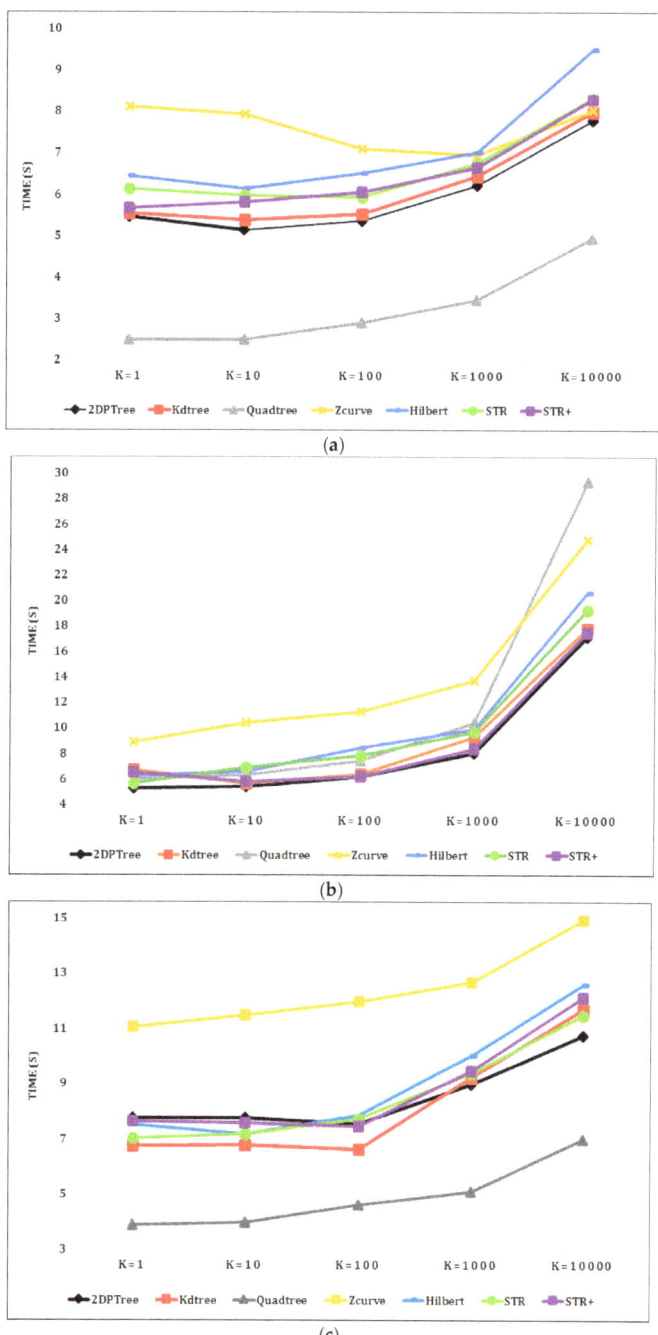

Figure 10. kNN query execution times for indexed real datasets: (**a**) kNN on the Sports dataset with k equal to 1, 10, 100, 1000, and 10,000 points; (**b**) kNN on the Cities dataset with k equal to 1, 10, 100, 1000, and 10,000 points; (**c**) kNN on the Buildings dataset with k equal to 1, 10, 100, 1000, and 10,000 points.

7. Conclusions

In this paper, we presented the 2DPR-Tree as a new partitioning technique in SpatialHadoop. An extensive experimental study was performed to compare the proposed 2DPR-Tree with state-of-the-art SpatialHadoop techniques. Various techniques were experimentally evaluated using different types of datasets (synthetic and real) with different distributions (uniformly and non-uniformly distributed data). The Quadtree, STR, and STR+ techniques were not restricted with the desired number of partitions, so they required much more time to build the index. The proposed 2DPR-Tree outperforms other techniques in indexing time for a 16 GB synthetic dataset and for the Cities and Buildings real datasets. For the range query, the performance of the 2DPR-Tree and KD-Tree was stable and roughly unchanged throughout use of the different synthetic datasets. On the other hand, the Quadtree, Z-curve, Hilbert, and STR showed varying performances with the changing of the synthetic dataset sizes. For the real datasets, Quadtree performed best for the range queries with small query window areas equal to 0.01% and 1% of the input dataset area. However, for range queries with larger query window areas equal to 10% and 50% of the input dataset area, the performance of this method rapidly decreased. On the other hand, the 2DPR-Tree performed best for range queries with large query window areas. The 2DPR-Tree and KD-Tree answer the range query with a query window area equal to 50% of the Buildings dataset area in 111 and 120 s, respectively, and Quadtree takes approximately twice the amount of time to answer the same query. For the kNN query, all partitioning techniques have roughly the same performance with different k values for the synthetic datasets. For real datasets, Quadtree outperforms other techniques as it divides the input datasets into a large number of small partitions, in contrast with the other techniques that are restricted to a specific number of larger partitions. Therefore, the partition access time of Quadtree is much lower than that of the other techniques. In addition, the kNN query requires a small number of partitions to be accessed to achieve the result. However, the 2DPR-Tree performs best for the kNN queries with high k values among the techniques that are committed to the desired number of partitions. Therefore, the proposed 2DPR-Tree is significantly better than the other partitioning techniques. As part of our future work, we will develop new multi-dimensional spatial data types on SpatialHadoop, and a new indexing technique for these data types will be developed with the goal of further enhancing query response time and query result accuracy.

Author Contributions: A.E. came up with the original research idea; A.M.R. advised A.E., A.S., and A.A.-F. on the experiment design and paper structure; A.E. and A.S. designed the experiments, deployed the experiment environment, developed the scripts for experiments, and conducted the experiments. Al.M.R. and A.A.-F. analyzed the experiment results; all authors drafted the manuscript; and read and approved the final manuscript.

Acknowledgments: The authors would like to thank the editor and the anonymous reviewers for their systematic reviews, valuable comments and suggestions to improve the quality of the paper.

Conflicts of Interest: The authors declare no conflict of interest.

References

1. Cary, A.; Yesha, Y.; Adjouadi, M.; Rishe, N. Leveraging cloud computing in geodatabase management. In Proceedings of the IEEE International Conference on Granular Computing, San Jose, CA, USA, 14–16 August 2010.
2. Li, Z.; Hu, F.; Schnase, J.L.; Duffy, D.Q.; Lee, T.; Bowen, M.K.; Yang, C. A spatiotemporal indexing approach for efficient processing of big array-based climate data with mapreduce. *Int. J. Geogr. Inf. Sci.* **2017**, *31*, 17–35. [CrossRef]
3. Haynes, D.; Ray, S.; Manson, S. Terra populus: Challenges and opportunities with heterogeneous big spatial data. In *Advances in Geocomputation: Geocomputation 2015–the 13th International Conference*; Griffith, D.A., Chun, Y., Dean, D.J., Eds.; Springer International Publishing: Cham, Switzerland, 2017; pp. 115–121.
4. Katzis, K.; Efstathiades, C. Resource management supporting big data for real-time applications in the 5g era. In *Advances in Mobile Cloud Computing and Big Data in the 5g Era*; Mavromoustakis, C.X., Mastorakis, G., Dobre, C., Eds.; Springer International Publishing: Cham, Switzerland, 2017; pp. 289–307.

5. White, T. *Hadoop: The Definitive Guide*; O'Reilly Media: Scbastopol, CA, USA, 2015.
6. Thusoo, A.; Sarma, J.S.; Jain, N.; Shao, Z.; Chakka, P.; Anthony, S.; Liu, H.; Wyckoff, P.; Murthy, R. Hive: A warehousing solution over a map-reduce framework. *Proc. VLDB Endow.* **2009**, *2*, 1626–1629. [CrossRef]
7. Li, F.; Ooi, B.C.; Ozsu, M.T.; Wu, S. Distributed data management using mapreduce. *ACM Comput.* **2014**, *46*, 31–42. [CrossRef]
8. Doulkeridis, C.; Nrvag, K. A survey of large-scale analytical query processing in mapreduce. *VLDB J.* **2014**, *23*, 355–380. [CrossRef]
9. Eldawy, A.; Li, Y.; Mokbel, M.F.; Janardan, R. Cg_hadoop: Computational geometry in mapreduce. In Proceedings of the 21st ACM SIGSPATIAL International Conference on Advances in Geographic Information Systems, Orlando, FL, USA, 5–8 November 2013; pp. 294–303.
10. Dean, J.; Ghemawat, S. Mapreduce: Simplified data processing on large clusters. *Commun. ACM* **2008**, *51*, 107–113. [CrossRef]
11. Wang, K. Accelerating spatial data processing with mapreduce. In Proceedings of the 2010 IEEE 16th International Conference on ICPADS, Shanghai, China, 8–10 December 2010.
12. Eldawy, A.; Mokbel, M.F. Spatialhadoop: A mapreduce framework for spatial data. In Proceedings of the ICDE Conference, Seoul, Korea, 13–17 April 2015; pp. 1352–1363.
13. Maleki, E.F.; Azadani, M.N.; Ghadiri, N. Performance evaluation of spatialhadoop for big web mapping data. In Proceedings of the 2016 Second International Conference on Web Research (ICWR), Tehran, Iran, 27–28 April 2016; pp. 60–65.
14. Aly, A.M.; Elmeleegy, H.; Qi, Y.; Aref, W. Kangaroo: Workload-aware processing of range data and range queries in hadoop. In Proceedings of the Ninth ACM International Conference on Web Search and Data Mining, San Francisco, CA, USA, 22–25 February 2016; pp. 397–406.
15. Zhang, S.; Han, J.; Liu, Z.; Wang, K.; Feng, S. Spatial queries evaluation with mapreduce. In Proceedings of the 2009 Eighth International Conference on Grid and Cooperative Computing, Lanzhou, China, 27–29 August 2009; pp. 287–292.
16. Ma, Q.; Yang, B.; Qian, W.; Zhou, A. Query processing of massive trajectory data based on mapreduce. In Proceedings of the First International Workshop on Cloud Data Management, Hong Kong, China, 2 November 2009; pp. 9–16.
17. Akdogan, A.; Demiryurek, U.; Banaei-Kashani, F.; Shahabi, C. Voronoi-based geospatial query processing with mapreduce. In Proceedings of the 2010 IEEE Second International Conference on Cloud Computing Technology and Science, Indianapolis, IN, USA, 30 November–3 December 2010; pp. 9–16.
18. Nodarakis, N.; Rapti, A.; Sioutas, S.; Tsakalidis, A.K.; Tsolis, D.; Tzimas, G.; Panagis, Y. (a)knn query processing on the cloud: A survey. In *Algorithmic Aspects of Cloud Computing: Second International Workshop, Algocloud 2016, Aarhus, Denmark, August 22, 2016, Revised Selected Papers*; Sellis, T., Oikonomou, K., Eds.; Springer International Publishing: Cham, Switzerland, 2017; pp. 26–40.
19. Ray, S.; Simion, B.; Brown, A.D.; Johnson, R. A parallel spatial data analysis infrastructure for the cloud. In Proceedings of the 21st ACM SIGSPATIAL International Conference on Advances in Geographic Information Systems, Orlando, FL, USA, 5–8 November 2013; pp. 284–293.
20. Ray, S.; Simion, B.; Brown, A.D.; Johnson, R. Skew-resistant parallel in-memory spatial join. In Proceedings of the 26th International Conference on Scientific and Statistical Database Management, Aalborg, Denmark, 30 June–2 July 2014; pp. 1–12.
21. Vo, H.; Aji, A.; Wang, F. Sato: A spatial data partitioning framework for scalable query processing. In Proceedings of the 22nd ACM SIGSPATIAL International Conference on Advances in Geographic Information Systems, Dallas, TX, USA, 4–7 November 2014; pp. 545–548.
22. Pertesis, D.; Doulkeridis, C. Efficient skyline query processing in spatialhadoop. *Inf. Syst.* **2015**, *54*, 325–335. [CrossRef]
23. Eldawy, A.; Alarabi, L.; Mokbel, M.F. Spatial partitioning techniques in spatialhadoop. In Proceedings of the International Conference on Very Large Databases, Kohala Coast, HI, USA, 31 August–4 September 2015.
24. Eldawy, A.; Mokbel, M.F. The ecosystem of spatialhadoop. *SIGSPATIAL Spec.* **2015**, *6*, 3–10. [CrossRef]
25. Randolph, W.; Chandrasekhar Narayanaswaml, F.; Kankanhalll, M.; Sun, D.; Zhou, M.-C.; Yf Wu, P. Uniform Grids: A Technique for Intersection Detection on Serial and Parallel Machines. In Proceedings of the Auto Carto 9, Baltimore, Maryland, 2–7 April 1989; pp. 100–109.

26. Singh, H.; Bawa, S. A survey of traditional and mapreduce based spatial query processing approaches. *SIGMOD Rec.* **2017**, *46*, 18–29. [CrossRef]
27. Tan, K.-L.; Ooi, B.C.; Abel, D.J. Exploiting spatial indexes for semijoin-based join processing in distributed spatial databases. *IEEE Trans. Knowl. Data Eng.* **2000**, *12*, 920–937.
28. Zhang, R.; Zhang, C.-T. A brief review: The z-curve theory and its application in genome analysis. *Curr. Genom.* **2014**, *15*, 78–94. [CrossRef] [PubMed]
29. Meng, L.; Huang, C.; Zhao, C.; Lin, Z. An improved hilbert curve for parallel spatial data partitioning. *Geo-Spat. Inf. Sci.* **2007**, *10*, 282–286. [CrossRef]
30. Liao, H.; Han, J.; Fang, J. Multi-dimensional index on hadoop distributed file system. In Proceedings of the 2010 IEEE Fifth International Conference on Networking, Architecture, and Storage, Macau, China, 15–17 July 2010; pp. 240–249.
31. Guttman, A. R-trees: A dynamic index structure for spatial searching. *SIGMOD Rec.* **1984**, *14*, 47–57. [CrossRef]
32. Beckmann, N.; Kriegel, H.-P.; Schneider, R.; Seeger, B. The r*-tree: An efficient and robust access method for points and rectangles. *SIGMOD Rec.* **1990**, *19*, 322–331. [CrossRef]
33. Leutenegger, S.T.; Lopez, M.A.; Edgington, J. Str: A simple and efficient algorithm for r-tree packing. In Proceedings of the 13th International Conference on Data Engineering, Birmingham, UK, 7–11 April 1997; pp. 497–506.
34. Giao, B.C.; Anh, D.T. Improving sort-tile-recursive algorithm for r-tree packing in indexing time series. In Proceedings of the the 2015 IEEE RIVF International Conference on Computing & Communication Technologies–Research, Innovation, and Vision for Future (RIVF), Can Tho, Vietnam, 25–28 January 2015; pp. 117–122.
35. Sellis, T. The r+-tree: A dynamic index for multidimensional objects. In Proceedings of the 13th International Conference on Very Large Data Bases, Brighton, UK, 1–4 September 1987; pp. 507–518.
36. Bentley, J.L. Multidimensional binary search trees used for associative searching. *Commun. ACM* **1975**, *18*, 509–517. [CrossRef]
37. Olston, C.; Reed, B.; Srivastava, U.; Kumar, R.; Tomkins, A. Pig latin: A not-so-foreign language for data processing. In Proceedings of the 2008 ACM SIGMOD International Conference on Management of Data, Vancouver, BC, Canada, 9–12 June 2008; pp. 1099–1110.
38. Arge, L.; Berg, M.D.; Haverkort, H.J.; Yi, K. The priority r-tree: A practically efficient and worst-case optimal r-tree. *ACM Trans. Algorithms* **2008**, *4*, 9. [CrossRef]
39. Agarwal, P.K.; Berg, M.D.; Gudmundsson, J.; Hammar, M.; Haverkort, H.J. Box-trees and r-trees with near-optimal query time. *Discre. Comput. Geom.* **2002**, *28*, 291–312. [CrossRef]
40. Davies, J. Implementing the Pseudo Priority r-Tree (pr-tree), a Toy Implementation for Calculating Nearest Neighbour on Points in the x-y Plane. Available online: http://juliusdavies.ca/uvic/report.html (accessed on 18 August 2017).
41. Amazon. Amazon ec2. Available online: http://aws.amazon.com/ec2/ (accessed on 10 January 2018).

© 2018 by the authors. Licensee MDPI, Basel, Switzerland. This article is an open access article distributed under the terms and conditions of the Creative Commons Attribution (CC BY) license (http://creativecommons.org/licenses/by/4.0/).

Article

Estimating the Performance of Random Forest versus Multiple Regression for Predicting Prices of the Apartments

Marjan Čeh [1], Milan Kilibarda [2], Anka Lisec [1] and Branislav Bajat [2,*]

1. Faculty of Civil and Geodetic Engineering, University of Ljubljana, Jamova cesta 2, 1000 Ljubljana, Slovenia; marjan.ceh@fgg.uni-lj.si (M.Č.); anka.lisec@fgg.uni-lj.si (A.L.)
2. Faculty of Civil Engineering, University of Belgrade, Bulevar kralja Aleksandra, 73, 11000 Belgrade, Serbia; kili@grf.bg.ac.rs
* Correspondence: bajat@grf.bg.ac.rs; Tel.: +381-11-3218-579

Received: 5 April 2018; Accepted: 30 April 2018; Published: 2 May 2018

Abstract: The goal of this study is to analyse the predictive performance of the random forest machine learning technique in comparison to commonly used hedonic models based on multiple regression for the prediction of apartment prices. A data set that includes 7407 records of apartment transactions referring to real estate sales from 2008–2013 in the city of Ljubljana, the capital of Slovenia, was used in order to test and compare the predictive performances of both models. Apparent challenges faced during modelling included (1) the non-linear nature of the prediction assignment task; (2) input data being based on transactions occurring over a period of great price changes in Ljubljana whereby a 28% decline was noted in six consecutive testing years; and (3) the complex urban form of the case study area. Available explanatory variables, organised as a Geographic Information Systems (GIS) ready dataset, including the structural and age characteristics of the apartments as well as environmental and neighbourhood information were considered in the modelling procedure. All performance measures (R^2 values, sales ratios, mean average percentage error (MAPE), coefficient of dispersion (COD)) revealed significantly better results for predictions obtained by the random forest method, which confirms the prospective of this machine learning technique on apartment price prediction.

Keywords: random forest; OLS; hedonic price model; PCA; Ljubljana

1. Introduction

Over the last twenty years, there has been an increase in the number of empirical studies analysing prediction techniques for real estate property value. Recent years have brought a great interest in applying spatial statistics to hedonic price modelling, which was partially caused by increasing Geographic Information Systems (GIS) development and the applications of big data. The use of GIS tools has been particularly significant for the evaluation of the impact of environmental/spatial attributes in property values [1–3]. This has resulted in the introduction of advanced geostatistical methods and Geographically Weighted Regression (GWR) as efficient methodologies for capturing spatial heterogeneity and spatial autocorrelation in housing markets versus multiple regression as a global model [4,5]. Further developments in hedonic models of spatial housing economics that can be potentially facilitated with the GIS data environment include elements with extended spatial econometrics, neighbourhood and segregation models, housing market areas, models of segregation, migration, agent-based models and utilization of recently developed machine learning and data mining techniques [6].

In the last decade of the twentieth century, machine learning (ML) techniques were recognized as an alternative to the classical hedonic model [7–9]. These approaches are based on empirical models that determine transition rules and link correlations that are based on data input/output values as well as dependent/independent continual and categorical variables.

Most of the machine learning applications in real estate price estimation are based on Artificial Neural Networks (ANN) algorithms [2,10,11]. Fan et al. [12] used the decision tree technique for exploring the relationship between house prices and housing characteristics, which aided the determination of the most important variables of housing prices and predicted housing prices. In recent studies, there have also been other examples based on recent machine learning techniques, such as support vector machines (SVM) [13]. Improved performance of the SVM algorithm, when compared to the ANN algorithm, was achieved by Kontrimas and Verikas [14], although the multilayer perceptron ANN algorithm used in their study was outperformed by ordinary least square (OLS) regression. The authors of those studies found that the performance of the ML-based techniques was considerably higher than the official real estate models. These results were often accompanied with the conclusion that real estate price estimation is a nonlinear problem [14,15].

Lately, an ML technique known as random forest [16] was developed to represent the superstructure of a ready-made decision tree data mining technique. A variety of researchers have attempted to use random forest as a potential technique for real estate mass appraisal in recent times [17,18].

In this study, besides coupling GIS and ML techniques, we also focused on several issues: (a) how to employ diverse available data (mostly open access) that can be used as explanatory variables in mass appraisal processes concerning expected problems with collinearity, residual heteroscedasticity, and spatial dependency—especially when faced with typically nonlinear tasks in apartment value prediction; (b) the proposition of a more flexible explanatory variable selection procedure in an ML modelling environment; and (c) a discussion of the performance of models with respect to structural characteristics of apartments and their spatial amenities.

This paper is organized as follows: the next section reports the case study area and details of its real estate market followed by a description of how the data is utilized. The following sections present descriptions of two modelling techniques: (1) the ordinary least squares (OLS) linear regression as a benchmark method and (2) the random forest (RF) method, which is a novel technique in the domain of real estate value estimation as well as a Principal Component Analysis (PCA) solution for dealing with multicollinearity in multiple regression and the review of model validation measures. Hereafter, the interpretation of PCAs and their semantic relationships with the most informative predictive variables selected by RF are discussed. Conclusions and recommendations for future research are given in the closing section.

2. Case Study and Data Description

Ljubljana is the capital city of the Republic of Slovenia and is situated at the confluence of the Ljubljanica River and Sava River in central Slovenia. The administrative boundary of the city of Ljubljana encompasses 275 km^2 and has nearly 300,000 inhabitants in 40 settlements. The city morphology is very complex, since green wedges of forests and meadows on low hills, which serve as two large city parks, are incised towards the Central Business District (CBD) from the west and southeast (Figure 1). Regions of semi-agricultural, small gardens and recreational areas extend towards densely urbanised settlements in the center from the northeast and northwest.

Slovenian real estate prices peaked in the first half of 2008. In the study period of this analysis, which is from the year 2008 to the end of 2013, the prices of apartments in Ljubljana declined by a total of 28%, which represents the deepest fall in the Slovenian real estate market.

The original data set of 7407 records of apartment transactions, provided by the Mass Real Estate Valuation Office at the Surveying and Mapping Authority of the Republic of Slovenia, refers to real estate sales from 2008–2013, a period of six consecutive years. The transaction records are geocoded and include total transaction prices (€) and structural, time, environmental and neighbourhood information. The mean value of observed transactions is 2415 €, the minimum is 711 € and the maximum is 4934 € with a standard deviation of 575 € per square meter.

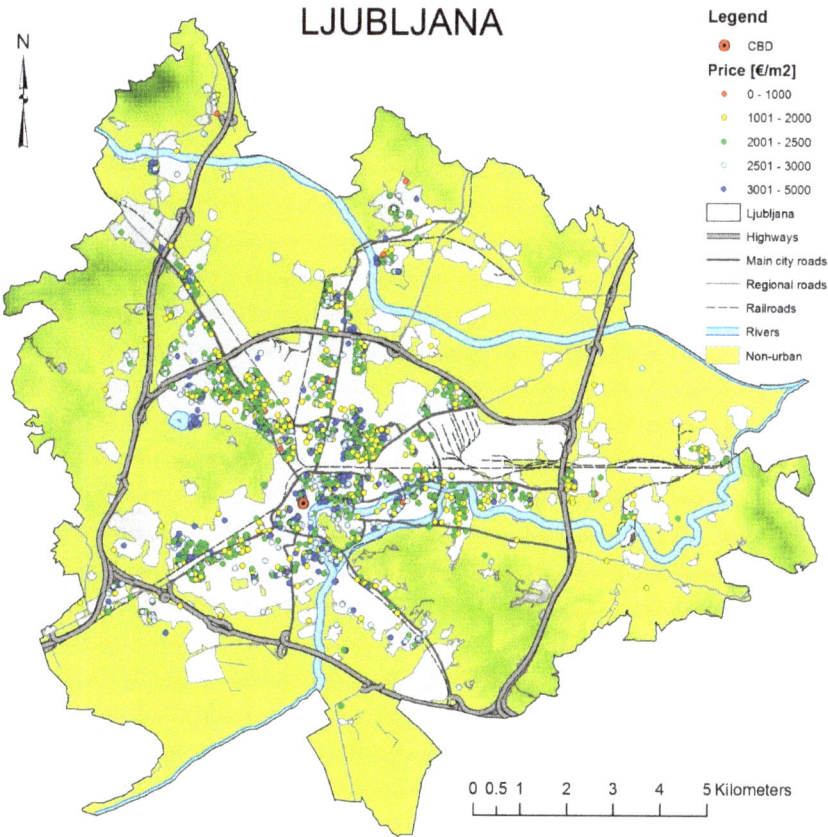

Figure 1. Observed transactions of apartments in Ljubljana in the period from 2008–2013.

Explanatory Variables

When predicting prices as a dependent variable in the real estate market, the determinants of apartment prices can be divided into four groups [19]: (1) time/structural variables (e.g., age, the number of rooms in each house, etc.); (2) accessibility variables (e.g., the proximity of schools, bus routes, railway stations, shops, parks, and the Central Business District); (3) neighbourhood variables (e.g., local unemployment rates); (4) environmental variables (e.g., road noise and visibility impact).

In accordance with this apportionment, all available explanatory variables in our study were divided into those four groups (Table 1). The explanatory variables referring to accessibility and environment could be considered to be spatial determinants [5]. They were prepared as input grids with 20 m resolution using a proximity function within the SAGA (System for Automated Geoscientific Analyses) GIS environment (http://www.saga-gis.org/). The values assigned to each of the grid cells were calculated as Euclidean distances between each cell and the input features (airport, roads, recreation areas, etc.).

Table 1. The list of explanatory variables used in study with corresponding variance inflation factor (VIF) values.

Variables	Description	Type	VIF
ID_cadas_com	Unique cadastral community ID	neighborhood	2.0803
ID_building	Building ID within cadas. community	neighborhood	1.6505
ID_appartment	Apartment ID within a building	structural	1.3362
floors_total	Total number of floors in the building	structural	4.2064
year built	Year of construction	time/structural	1.1748
year_ren_roof	Year of roof replacement	time/structural	3.1731
year_ren_face	Year of facade insulation	time/structural	1.4340
constr_type	Construction type (brick, concrete, wood)	structural	2.0259
Elevator	Elevator	structural	1.0439
house_type	Housing type (single, double, raw)	structural	2.8378
no_appart	Number of apartments in building	structural	1.0815
Northing	N coordinate (mathematical)	neighborhood	2.4851
Easting	E coordinate (mathematical)	neighborhood	667.249 *
trans_date	Date of transaction (contract)	time	46.5974 *
market zone	Real estate market zone	neighborhood	1.0117
floor_appartment	Apartment floor number	structural	1.8006
position_type	Position in building (basement, ground, middle, penthouse)	structural	7.4933 *
Duplex	Apartment in 2 floors	structural	1.4334
Rooms	Number of rooms in apartment	structural	1.0680
living_area	Apartment living area	structural	2.5412
total area	Apartment total area	structural	11.3511 *
year_ren_wind	Year of windows replacement	time/structural	9.6525 *
year_ren_inst	Year of installation replacement	time/structural	2.0041
floor_above_ground	Apartment above ground floor	structural	2.4321
dist_Airport	Prox. (Euclidian distance) to airport	accessability	5.2100 *
dist_Public transport	Prox. to city bus station	accessability	726.2465 *
Elevation	Elevation above sea level	environmental	2.1488
dist_Schools	Prox. to university facilities	accessability	6.8582 *
dist_Highway entr.	Prox. to highway entrance	accessability	1.2613
dist_Highway	Prox. to highway lane	environmental	68.622 *
dist_Railway	Prox. to railway	environmental	67.061 *
dist_Recreation	Prox. to green areas, forest	accessability	2.0475
dist_Main roads	Prox. to main city roads	accessability	3.5815
dist_Regional road	Prox. to regional roads	accessability	5.5086 *
dist_River	Prox. to river banks	environmental	3.3402

* VIF > 5; variable indicates high multicollinearity.

3. Methods

3.1. Hedonic Price Model

The theoretical foundation of the hedonic model is based on Lancaster's theory of consumer demand [20]. Consumers make their purchasing decisions based on the number of good characteristics as well as the per unit cost of each characteristic. Rosen [21] was the first to present a theory of hedonic pricing. An item can be valued by its characteristics; an item's total price can be considered as a sum of the price of each of its homogeneous attributes, where each attribute has a unique implicit price in an equilibrium market. This implies that an item's price can be regressed on the characteristics to determine the way in which each characteristic uniquely contributes to the overall composite unit price.

The ordinary least squares (OLS) linear regression is the standard method used to build hedonic price models. The basic hedonic price function can be represented as [22]:

$$Y = f(S\beta, N\gamma) + \varepsilon \tag{1}$$

where Y is a vector of observed housing values; S is a matrix of structural characteristics of properties; N is a matrix of time/structural variables, accessibility variables, neighbourhood variables and environmental variables; β and γ are the parameter vectors corresponding to S and N; and ε is a vector of random error terms.

The given formula can be expressed like a common regression function:

$$Y = X\beta + \varepsilon \tag{2}$$

where Y represents n × 1 vector of n observed apartment prices, X is an n × m matrix containing explanatory variables. β is an m × 1 vector of unknown regression coefficients, and ε is a vector representing the error term.

By using an ordinary least squares solution (OLS), the unknown regression coefficients are calculated as:

$$\hat{\beta} = (X^T X)^{-1} X^T Y \qquad (3)$$

3.2. Principal Component Analysis

An indicator of multicollinearity between explanatory variables was inspected prior to performing the regression analysis. The variance inflation factor (VIF) test [23] indicates the presence of multicollinearity between predictors (Table 1). High multicollinearity might be a problem since it increases the variance of coefficient estimates and makes the estimates very sensitive to minor changes in the model. The resulting instability of coefficient estimates makes it difficult to interpret models. Principal Components Analysis (PCA) is often used with the aim of transforming a dataset with many intercorrelated variables (that are probably redundant) into a dataset consisting of a smaller number of uncorrelated variables, which are known as principal components (PCs) [19]. However, the main shortcoming of using PCA is that the newly generated components complicate the interpretation of the influence of the original variables. In our study, the interpretations of newly generated components of the original variables were expressed with the general real estate concepts (type of construction, age—quality of building and apartment, floors, topography and environment, size, accessibility, zoning and density)

Based on the Kaiser–Harris principle [24], only PCs with eigenvalues greater than 1 were retained, whereas the PCs with eigenvalues less than 1 explain less variance than a single explanatory variable.

3.3. Random Forest

Random forest [16] is a classification and regression algorithm based on the bagging [25] and random subspace methods [26]. The idea of bagging is to construct an ensemble of learners, each trained on a bootstrap sample (Db) obtained from the original dataset (D) using the following sampling procedure: given a D with N examples, one creates a Db by randomly choosing k examples from D with replacement (after selecting an example, it is immediately returned to D and can be selected again). After removing duplicates, if N is large and $k = N$, it is expected that Db contains approximately two-thirds of examples from D. The prediction of the ensemble is constructed from the separate decisions by majority voting (classification) or averaging (regression). It has been shown that bagging can reduce the variance in the final model when compared to the base models and can also avoid overfitting [25].

Regression trees are used as base learners in the RF regression algorithm. After selecting the number of trees in the forest, each regression tree is grown on a separate bootstrap sample derived from the initial training data. Each node in a tree represents a binary test against the selected predictor variable. The variable is selected to minimize the residual sum of squares for the examples flowing down both branches (left and right) (Figure 2). Terminal nodes contain no more than the specified maximal number of examples from which the target value is obtained by averaging. In order to avoid high correlations among the trees in a forest, a procedure of selecting the best splitting predictor in each node of a tree is modified to choose between only m randomly selected predictors—selecting a random subspace of the original n-dimensional problem. For a fixed parameter, m ($m \ll n$), the R package *randomForest* [27] uses $m = n/3$ by default when dealing with regression problems.

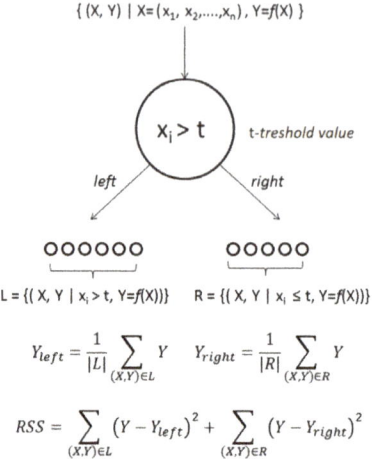

Figure 2. Regression tree node.

RF does not require an external cross-validation procedure to estimate the model accuracy. The example in the training data is not in the bootstrap sample containing about one third of the trees (the example is "out of bag"—OOB). Averaging the predictions of these trees produces the RF prediction on the example. The mean squared error (MSE) on the OOB samples gives the estimate for the general MSE on a separate test set. In addition, OOB can be used to estimate the i-th predictor variable's importance by the following manner: (1) make a random permutation of values for the variable concerning the examples from the OOB, and then (2) record the increase in the MSE for the permuted OOB when compared to the original one. Here, an assumption is made that a more important variable, when permuted, will produce a greater increase in MSE when using the same regression model.

3.4. Model Performance Measures

The predicted prices of the apartments obtained by both models were compared with the observed prices in order to determine which model gives better prediction. In real estate valuation, the average sales ratio is often used as a basic measure for the evaluation of the model's performance. The sales ratio (SR) represents the quotient between the predicted price and actual sale price for the particular apartment. However, due to the lack of normality distribution of SRs, the coefficient of dispersion (COD) is recommended for the assessment of the model prediction's accuracy [28].

COD assesses the accuracy of the predictive model by measuring how closely each sales ratio is arrayed around the median sales ratio. The COD can be calculated using

$$\text{COD} = \frac{100}{SR_m}\left(\frac{\sum_{i=1}^{n}|SR_i - SR_m|}{n}\right) \qquad (4)$$

where SR_i is the sales ratio for each apartment, SR_m is the median sales ratio and n is the number of predicted apartment prices. The agreeable COD values for single-family homes and condominiums, according to the Guidance on International Mass Appraisal and Related Tax Policy document [29] range from 5% to 15%.

The mean average percentage error (MAPE) was also used to appraise the performance of the considered models:

$$\text{MAPE} = \frac{100}{n}\sum_{t=1}^{n}\left|\frac{A_t - F_t}{F_t}\right|, \qquad (5)$$

where A_t is the actual price value, and F_t is the predicted value.

3.5. R Language Environment

All of the utilized methods were implemented using the open-source R statistical computing environment with the following packages: *randomForest* [27] for classification and regression based on a forest of trees using random inputs, *caret* [30] for data splitting and generating stratified bootstrap samples, *gstat* for cross validation, *psych* for principal component analysis, as well as the *sp* package which provides classes and methods for dealing with spatial data in R. The results obtained in R can easily be converted into any of the standard GIS formats, which enables the manipulation and analysis of the results in commercial GIS packages afterwards.

4. Results and Discussion

4.1. OLS Model Interpretation

Before performing PCA on the set of explanatory variables, the whole data set was preprocessed, which included scaling, standardization and label encoding transformation of each categorical variable with *n* possible values into *n* binary values. The PC predictors were derived, and 10 PCs were selected in accordance with expected eigenvalues higher than 1 (Kaiser–Harris principle). The list of retained principal components is given in Table 2.

The column labelled PCi contains the component loadings, which represent the correlations of the observed explanatory variables with the principal components. Component loadings are used to interpret the meaning of the components. The dark shaded table cells indicate strong correlations (over 0.60), while light shaded cells specify high or moderate correlations between the PCi and explanatory variable. The column labelled h2 contains the component communalities, which represent the amount of variance in a variable explained by the components (the proportion of each variable's variance can be explained by the principal components).

The row labelled *SS loadings* contains the eigenvalues associated with the components. An eigenvalue is the standardized variance associated with a particular component (in this case, the value for the first component is 3.44). The row labelled *Proportion Var* represents the amount of variance accounted for by each component. Here, it can be seen that the first principal component, PCA1, includes a number of variables with high loadings and accounts for 10 percent of the variance in the 36 variables.

Component loadings indicate the relative contribution of the observed variables to each principal component, which can help in the interpretation of the meaning of PCAs in real-word settings.

Concerning component loadings for PC1 and strong correlations with predictors such as year of installations (pipelines, wires) replacement, year of construction, year of window replacement, year of facade insulation and year of roof replacement, PC1 could be interpreted as "age—quality of building and apartment".

Due to its strong correlation to the apartment floor number, total number of floors in the building, apartment floor number (starting above the ground floor) and number of apartments in the building, PC2 is interpreted as "floors".

PC3 is strongly positively correlated with the elevation of the building itself above sea level, the northing Y coordinate and the proximity to river banks, and negatively correlated with the easting X coordinate and the proximity to the airport.

The threat of flooding has been noted in Ljubljana, and buildings above common flood levels are highly valued. The main city business development axis is directed towards the north, which is followed by spatial price trends of housing. On the other hand, the Eastern part of the city is more industrialized, and a huge railway arrangement area extends from the downtown core to the Eastern direction. Distance to an airport (noise), as an environmental element, influences the prices negatively.

The proximity to riverbanks and the lake shore, as an environmental amenity, influences apartment prices positively. PC3 is interpreted as "topography and general Environment".

Due to its high component loadings on the apartment living area, apartment total area and number of rooms in an apartment, PC4 is recognized as the "Size" context.

PC5 has a high positive correlation with proximity to main city roads, distance to green areas such as forests, proximity to "city bus lines" stations, distance to university facilities, and its negative correlation with the distance from regional roads, and for that reason, can be interpreted as "accessibility within the city".

PC6 is interpreted as the recreation rivers and forests context with respect to its high component loadings of distances to river banks and distances to green areas and forest. The river courses and forest boundaries coincide with cadastral community boundaries and for that reason, this principal component also has a strong correlation with cadastral community IDs.

An exceptionally high correlation (>0.9) with the distance to highway entrances and the distance to highway lane makes PC7 the "regional accessibility" context.

Provided that railway corridors represent the boundaries of real estate market zones in Ljubljana and that PC8 has a high correlation with the real estate market zoning and the distance to the railway, PCA8 is interpreted as "RE market zoning".

PC9 is interpreted as "apartment density in the building" due to its correlation with the number of apartments in a building and the apartment ID within a building. Apartments IDs grow from the bottom to the top of a building.

PC10 is interpreted as the "construction" context owing to its component loading values of construction type (brick, concrete, wood) and housing type (single, double, raw houses).

The date of transaction is a time specific variable and indicates no significant correlation to any of the PCA components, which implies that the regression model in our case does not take into account the price differences over the considered time period. The summary output of the multiple regression model on the PCAs shows that the model explains only 23% of the variability and is statistically significant.

Table 2. The list of component loadings (PCis) and correlations to observed explanatory variables.

Variables	PC1	PC2	PC3	PC4	PC5	PC6	PC7	PC8	PC9	PC10	h2
ID_cadas_com	−0.04	0.01	−0.05	0	0.09	0.84	0.09	−0.03	0	0.02	0.72
ID_builing	0.27	0.1	−0.25	0.05	0.1	0.16	−0.12	0.31	−0.6	−0.02	0.65
ID_appartment	0.07	0.23	−0.07	0	−0.06	0.02	−0.05	0.22	0.52	0.01	0.39
floors_total	0.05	0.83	0.05	−0.09	−0.14	0.1	0.03	−0.02	0.22	−0.08	0.78
floor_entrance	0	0.27	0.25	0	−0.22	0.05	0.17	−0.1	−0.05	0.22	0.28
year built	0.85	0.11	0	−0.03	0.13	0.04	−0.12	0	0.04	−0.01	0.76
year_ren_roof	0.62	−0.04	0.02	0.05	0.04	−0.09	−0.05	0.02	−0.08	−0.04	0.41
year_ren_face	0.75	0.1	0.06	−0.01	0.09	−0.12	−0.08	0.07	−0.02	−0.05	0.62
constr_type	−0.05	0.03	−0.06	−0.05	−0.02	0	0.04	−0.07	−0.1	0.64	0.44
elevator	0.28	0.7	0.07	0.01	−0.03	0.06	0.15	0.02	0.05	−0.09	0.61
house_type	−0.03	−0.07	0.12	0.04	−0.08	−0.04	0.09	−0.03	−0.08	0.51	0.31
no_appart	0.13	0.55	−0.11	−0.15	−0.07	0.01	−0.11	0.19	0.53	−0.14	0.71
northing	0.08	0.07	0.84	−0.03	0.3	0.09	−0.1	−0.16	0.14	−0.03	0.88
easting	−0.04	0.09	−0.49	−0.06	0.19	0.19	0.25	−0.41	0.42	0.05	0.73
trans_date	−0.03	0.02	0.07	−0.03	−0.03	−0.05	0.09	−0.04	−0.16	−0.46	0.26
market zone	−0.02	0.05	−0.07	−0.12	−0.09	0.16	−0.19	0.71	0.01	−0.09	0.6
floor_appartment	−0.03	0.91	0.02	−0.02	−0.05	0.02	−0.01	−0.02	0.02	−0.01	0.83
postion_type	−0.04	0.4	−0.02	0.05	−0.02	−0.06	−0.02	0	−0.29	0.15	0.28
duplex	0.02	−0.02	0	0.32	0.03	0	−0.02	−0.01	−0.1	0.05	0.12
rooms	0.02	−0.03	−0.01	0.85	0.02	−0.01	0	−0.02	0.06	−0.02	0.73
living_area	−0.02	−0.01	0	0.95	−0.02	−0.02	0.08	−0.02	0.02	−0.02	0.92
total area	0.02	−0.02	0	0.94	−0.01	−0.02	0.09	0	0.02	−0.02	0.89
year_ren_wind	0.83	0.01	0.01	0	0.02	0.06	−0.02	−0.05	0.04	0.05	0.7
year_ren_inst	0.86	0	0.01	0.02	0.06	0.03	−0.02	−0.02	0.05	0.06	0.75
floor_above_ground	−0.05	0.81	0	−0.03	−0.01	−0.03	−0.07	−0.01	0.04	−0.04	0.67
dist_Airport	−0.07	−0.06	−0.92	0.01	−0.17	−0.06	0.13	0.06	−0.04	0.04	0.91
dist_Public transport	0.1	−0.04	0.06	0.01	0.72	−0.02	0.11	−0.12	−0.12	−0.07	0.59
Elevation	−0.02	−0.01	0.82	0.04	−0.09	0.05	−0.22	0.29	−0.16	0.02	0.84
dist_Schools	0.15	−0.09	−0.07	0.05	0.34	−0.08	−0.05	0.26	−0.02	0.34	0.35
dist_Highway entr.	−0.13	−0.01	−0.24	0.08	0.05	−0.01	0.92	−0.13	−0.01	0.02	0.94

Table 2. Cont.

Variables	PC1	PC2	PC3	PC4	PC5	PC6	PC7	PC8	PC9	PC10	h2
dist_Highway	−0.14	0.02	−0.24	0.06	−0.02	0.01	0.91	−0.12	0.01	0.02	0.93
dist_Railway	0.04	−0.09	0.26	0.06	0.21	−0.29	−0.02	0.54	0.2	0.08	0.54
dist_Recreation	0.08	−0.04	0.07	−0.01	0.75	0.33	−0.2	−0.05	0.01	−0.06	0.73
dist_Main roads	0.12	−0.17	0.2	0.05	0.82	−0.22	0.09	0.12	0.04	0.04	0.84
dist_Regional road	−0.23	0.07	0.09	0	−0.49	−0.07	0.5	0.5	0.04	0	0.81
dist_River	−0.07	0.08	0.42	−0.06	−0.13	0.74	−0.17	0.08	0	0	0.79
SS loadings	3.44	3.38	3.07	2.71	2.49	2.34	1.67	1.66	1.4	1.15	
Proportion Var	0.1	0.09	0.09	0.08	0.07	0.07	0.05	0.05	0.04	0.03	

4.2. Random Forest Model Interpretation

Similar to the application method of the multiple regression model, we examined the importance of the predicting variables calculated from permuting the OOB data. We decided to only use the first ten ranked predictors (Figure 3) out of 36 by using a trial and error method to build the RF model on training data (70% bootstrap sample).

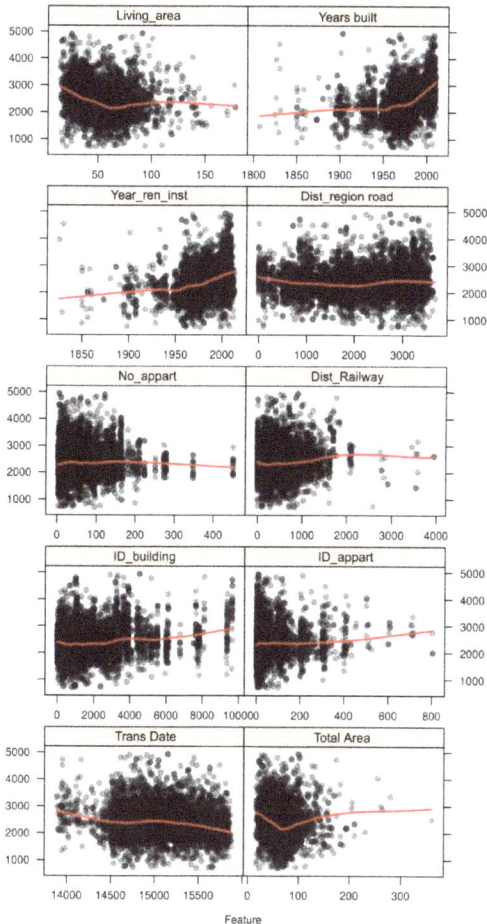

Figure 3. The scatter plots of predictor values versus price/m² values.

The scatter plots (Figure 3) were used in order to depict a bivariate relationship (predictors' values versus price/m²). Since the overlap of data points in scatter plots makes it difficult to discern the relationship, a smoothed curve through the cloud of points was fitted to describe the general relationship between the variables and apartment prices.

The interpretation of the relationships between particular variables and apartment price is given in ranked order of importance:

1. Year built (year of construction): recently built apartments have higher prices per m², in general. Nowadays, prices for apartments in buildings built from the year 1900 to the period before the end of World War II (WW2) have risen. The prices are lower for apartments in the buildings built in the period just after WW2 as the economic standard of living at that period was low and consequently, a lower quality of construction generally appeared in Slovenia and in Ljubljana. Apartment prices of buildings built after 1950, rising from an average of 2100 €/m² up to 3200 €/m² for newly-built buildings.

2. Living_area (apartment living area): smaller apartment living areas (studios and one room apartments for young couples or single households are most frequently exchanged on the market) indicate a higher price per square meter. The price per m² of an apartment declines from around 3000 €/m² to about 2100 €/m² for smaller living area between 20 m² and 65 m² in Ljubljana (19.5 €/m² for each additional m² on above mentioned interval). Apartment prices then rapidly rise per each additional m² of living area, up to 2300 €/m² (for 115 m² apartments), which might indicate the apartment market of higher income households of families with kids and both parents employed. Larger apartments (from 115 m² to 200 m²) decline in their value per square meter for each additional m².

3. Trans_date (date of transaction): represents the change in price/m² in time (days) on the relative timescale from the beginning of 2008 until the middle of 2013 (1989 days)—a period of recession in Slovenia. The graph of price changes corresponds to the reported decline of the market price, from about 3000 €/m² to about 2000 €/m² in four and a half years.

4. Total_area (Aaartment total area): represents the sum of an apartment's living area and the additional area for storage and the balcony. It is highly correlated by the predictor, apartment living area. For that reason, changes in price/m² have approximately the same trend as the apartment living area but the influence of an enlarged area is reduced by about 200 €/m².

5. Year_ren_inst (year of installations' replacement): The utilities and installations in the apartment physically deteriorate or depreciate over time and must be replaced. The younger the replacements are, the higher the average price/m² of apartments in the sample is. Apartments with old installations have an average price of 1700 €/m², whereas apartments with new replacements of gas, electrical and plumbing installations have an average price of 2800 €/m².

6. Dist_Reginal road (proximity to regional roads) Regional roads bring traffic to the city of Ljubljana from surrounding regions and are connected to the ring motorway built around the city. Their influence on the housing price decreases slightly at up to 2 km of distance and then increases to a distance of approximately 3 km. The price then decreases again over larger distances from the ring motorway.

The decline in average prices from 2600 €/m² to 2300 €/m² compared to the growing distance from regional roads might be understood as a negative influence of increased walking distances to public transportation flow, which is usually located along regional roads.

7. ID_apartment (apartment ID within a building): apartments in Slovenia are strictly numbered from the bottom to the top of the building. The prices are fairly constant with the growing number of apartment ID but begin to plateau at around ID number 300. Only high rise condominiums have apartment IDs over 300. Slightly growing prices above building unit 300 represent top floor positions of apartments in the buildings and penthouse positions with excellent views over lower condominiums. In Ljubljana, these higher positions mean beautiful views over the Kamnik–Savinja Alps mountain range to the north or views onto the nice medieval city centre and Castle Hill, surrounded by the river Ljubljanica. This predictor is, as expected, correlated with the predictors, nu_flt_in_build (number of apartments in the building), flt_floor (apartment floor number) and flt_floor_base (number of

apartments above the ground floor). There are some underground and half underground apartments which are not desirable on the market and therefore, they do not reach high prices.

8. Dist_Railway (proximity to railway) In general, apartments closer to railroad yield lower prices; the average price/m² closer to railroads is about 2250 €/m² and the (environmental noise) influence of railroad proximity to housing disappears after about 1.5 km, where the average prices are above 2.700 €/m² in Ljubljana. However, there is special situation in Ljubljana, where degraded land and abandoned buildings in several locations close to railroads were recently replaced by modern condominiums with high quality construction with the average price at around 2400 €/m².

9. No_apart (Number of apartments in the building): the price/m² grows from 2100 €/m² to about 2300 €/m² for buildings with up to 20 apartments. In this building size, about 83% of the 1550 buildings are not equipped with an elevator. The remaining 17% of the buildings have higher apartment prices. From 20 to about 100 apartments per building, the price is almost stabilised. However, the price/m² declines for buildings with huge numbers of apartments.

10. ID_building (building ID within cadastral community): new buildings have the largest available number in the sequence within the cadastral community, and apartment prices/m² for newly built structures are higher than older ones. However, there is an anomaly in the graph for the interval from approximately ID 3000 to ID 5000, which is the result of random chance. The ID numbers of buildings from the abovementioned interval (in four cadastral communities) correspond to the neighbourhoods of higher prices (Zupančičeva jama, Trnovski bloki, Vič south of Cesta na Brdo and Šiška elite settlement Koseze pond).

Comparing, semantically, the set of interpretations of the top ten PCAs with the set of top ten ranked predictors selected by RF (importance calculated from permuting OOB data), we can conclude that the two models have equivalent ratings for 7 out of 10 variables (Figure 4).

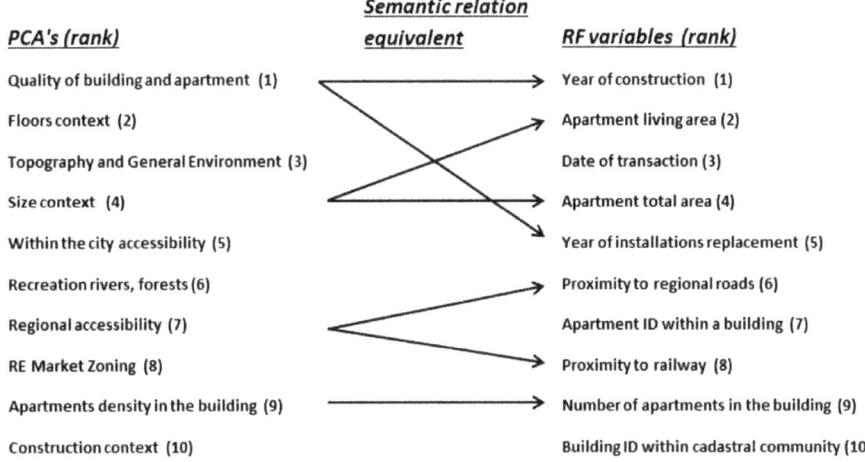

Figure 4. Semantic comparison of the top ten Principal Components (PCs) with the set of top ten ranked predictors selected by random forest (RF).

4.3. The Comparison of OLS and RF Performance

The comparison of OLS and RF performance was conducted in an out of sample prediction context using a stratified five-fold cross validation procedure with training sets consisting of 70% of all transactions and test sets consisting of 30% of all transactions. In "stratified" cross-validation, training and test sets have the same spatial and price value distribution as the full dataset [31]. In addition, "stratified" is a variant of the k-fold within training data and also ensures that each fold has the right proportion of samples in regard to spatial location and price values.

Predefined performance measures for both sets of data are given in Table 3. All performance measures (SR, MAPE, COD) indicate that significantly better results were obtained by RF in comparison to OLS. Considering the R^2 values for OLS and RF (0.23 and 0.57, respectively) and the noticeably lower MAPE and COD values for the RF model, it can be concluded that we are facing a non-linear problem. RF outperforms the OLS model in this non-linear situation; even COD values for OLS are above the recommended upper limit (17% > 15%). The obtained results for the sales ratio (SR) were adequate for both applied methods for both the training and test data sets in accordance with the approved range of 0.9–1.1 [29].

Table 3. Prediction accuracy for ordinary least square (OLS) and RF training and test data sets.

	OLS		RF	
	Train	Test	Train	Test
SR	1.0447	1.0465	1.0191	1.0197
MAPE [%]	16.85	17.48	7.04	7.27
COD [%]	16.52	17.12	7.05	7.28
R^2	0.23		0.57	

The effects of predictions performed by two methods were also compared by detailed visual inspection of differences between the sales ratios (SR) of OLS and RF predictions at identical locations. Figure 5a. shows the kernel density [32] of the differences between the average sales ratio values of the OLS and RF models for the apartments in each building (SR(OLS)—SR (RF)). The spatial distribution of the kernel density of sales ratio differences is shown within seven classes, from −0.100 to 0.100 (from dark brown to azzuro blue, middle class is transparent). The locations representing positively signed differences between sales ratios of OLS and RF assessments, coloured azzuro blue, are predominantly situated at the north of the CBD (north, northeast and northwest), which are the main directions of business activity development. They are also located in smaller quantity towards the east (at the confluence of the river Ljubljanica) and southwest and are radially dispersed from the CBD along the regional connecting roads.

Most interesting is the distribution of negatively signed differences between the average sales ratios (RF sales ratios values are higher than OLS sales ratios). The locations of negative differences represent contemporary settlements of apartments, and they are marked by a red check mark symbol (Figure 5a).

In order to obtain more insight into how the prediction models behave over the case study area, the Hot Spot Analysis was performed by calculating Getis–Ord Gi statistics [33]. The best way to interpret the Getis–Ord Gi statistic is in the context of the standardized Z-score values. A positive Z-score of Gi statistics (red points, H-H, high clustering of high values) appears when the spatial clustering is formed by similar, but high, values (in our case average SR > 1). If the spatial clustering is formed by low values (in our case average SR < 1), the Z-score (blue points, L-L, high clustering of low values) tends to be negative. A Z-score of around 0 (transparent points, Insignificant clustering) indicates no apparent spatial association pattern.

The hot spot spatial clusters of average SR were mapped over the massive appraisal map obtained by kriging interpolation of the considered transactions (Figure 5b,c).

It is obvious that both models followed similar spatial patterns over the case study area. Both methods underestimated the higher prices of apartments (SR < 1, blue points over orange areas), and overestimated the lower prices of apartments (SR > 1, red points over light green areas).

By coupling the results of the Hot Spot Analysis results with the kernel density of the difference between average SRs for OLS and RF, it is evident that blue points where RF underestimated actual prices are coincided with dark brown areas (areas where SR(RF) > SR(OLS)). Therefore, it can be concluded that RF predictions are closer to actual prices than OLS predictions in those areas. Those particular areas are the CBD area as well as areas with contemporary locations, i.e., the areas with high apartment prices.

On the basis of the above facts, and considering the obtained performance metrics, it is suggested that RF predictions outperform OLS predictions. Namely, at the locations of higher differences in sales ratios (where the values are slightly higher), the RF model shows more sensitivity than the OLS model for capturing differences in values.

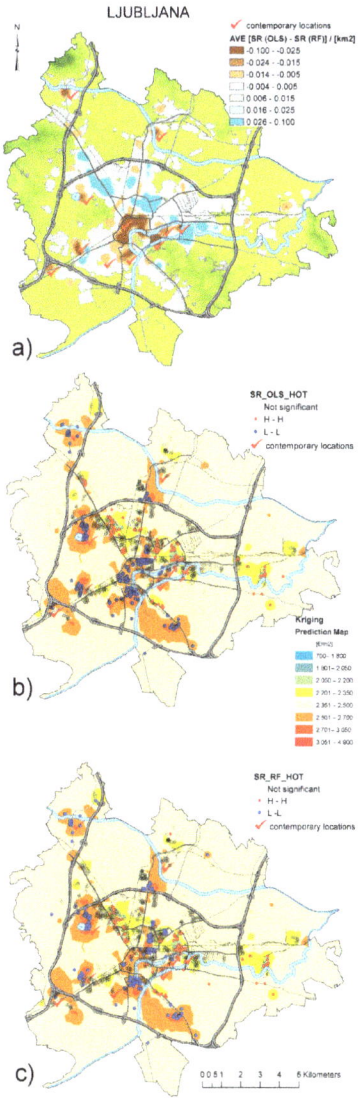

Figure 5. (**a**) Kernel density of the difference between sales ratios of OLS and RF; (**b**) Hot Spot Analysis of average sales ratio (SR)(OLS); (**c**) Hot Spot Analysis of average SR(RF).

5. Conclusions

The objective of this research was to empirically compare the predictive power of the OLS hedonic model with a random forest model for predicting apartment prices in Ljubljana, for the period between 2008 and 2013.

Before OLS modelling was performed, the initial set of 36 predicting variables was transformed into a Principal Components Analysis feature space in order to avoid immanent multicollinearity between variables. The 10 extracted PCAs were analysed by component loadings and clustering of initial explanatory variables in the component space in order to obtain an interpretation and semantic description in the original feature space.

Analogous to the OLS model, the random forest (RF) and out of the bag (OOB) permuting error estimate was adopted to select 10 of the most important predicting variables that were used for RF modelling.

We discovered a relatively high rate of equivalent semantic relationships (approximately 70%) between the set of interpretations of the top ten PCAs with the set of top ten ranked predictors selected by RF.

The commonly applied adjustment of prices over time for the sales data was purposely skipped in order to examine the sensitivity of the predictive models to the influence of time variability. Hence, the time period with the greatest change of prices in Slovenia, the six consecutive years between 2008 and 2013 that showed a 28% decline, was chosen for this research. The OLS model did not account for the time specific variable, "date of transaction", which represents the basic information for adjustment of prices over time. However, the "date of transaction" variable was considered strongly by RF and was determined to be the third most influential variable and is effectively used for time adjustment.

All performance measure—R^2 values (0.23 for OLS and 0.57 for RF), the sales ratios (1.04 for OLS and 1.02 for RF), the MAPE (17% for OLS and 7% for RF) and the COD (17% for OLS and 7% for RF)—revealed significantly better results with random forest. The low R^2 value for the OLS model indicated that non-linear modelling was required.

Visual inspection of the differences between the sales ratios (SR) of the OLS and RF predictions showed that the models perform similarly at identical locations. Both methods underestimated the higher prices of apartments (SR < 1) and overestimated the lower prices of apartments (SR > 1). However, we found that the RF predictions were closer to actual prices than the OLS predictions by combining results of kernel density for the differences of average of sales ratios between OLS and RF (SR (OLS)-SR (RF)) for the apartments in the buildings and the results of the Hot Spot Analysis. In addition, negative values of differences between the average SR (sales ratios of RF are larger than OLS sales ratios) were located at the spots where elite groups of condominium buildings are raised. Apartments in these specific locations would be under-valued using OLS predictions. In contrast, RF captures their differences due to amenities attributed to them.

Finally, the entire analysis of the spatial distribution of sales ratios for both methods has revealed that the random forest algorithm could provide better detection of the variability in apartment values and predicts them more effectively than multiple regression in complex urban forms like the city of Ljubljana, Slovenia.

Author Contributions: All authors worked on conceptualization, design and analysis of results. The first author collected and preprocessed input data, second and fourth author were involved in data processing, implementation and execution of the experiments and generation of results. All authors participated in the writing of the manuscript, but the first author took the lead, especially in the interpretation of the results.

Acknowledgments: This research is supported by the Slovenian-Serbian bilateral research project, No. 451-03-3095/2014-09/34.

Conflicts of Interest: The authors declare no conflict of interest.

References

1. Lake, I.R.; Lovett, A.A.; Bateman, I.J.; Day, B. Using GIS and large-scale digital data to implement hedonic pricing studies. *Int. J. Geogr. Inf. Sci.* **2000**, *14*, 521–541. [CrossRef]
2. Din, A.; Hoesli, M.; Bender, A. Environmental variables and real estate prices. *Urban. Stud.* **2001**, *38*, 1989–2000. [CrossRef]
3. Zhang, Y.; Dong, R. Impacts of Street-Visible Greenery on Housing Prices: Evidence from a Hedonic Price Model and a Massive Street View Image Dataset in Beijing. *ISPRS Int. J. Geo-Inf.* **2018**, *7*, 104. [CrossRef]
4. Schernthanner, H.; Asche, H.; Gonschorek, J.; Scheele, L. Spatial modeling and geovisualization of rental prices for real estate portals. In *Computational Science and Its Applications—ICCSA 2016*; Gervasi, O., Ed.; Springer: Cham, Switzerland, 2016; Volume 9788. [CrossRef]
5. Bajat, B.; Kilibarda, M.; Pejović, M.; Samardžić Petrović, M. Spatial Hedonic Modeling of Housing Prices Using Auxiliary Maps. In *Spatial Analysis and Location Modeling in Urban and Regional Systems*; Thill, J.C., Ed.; Springer: Berlin/Heidelberg, Germany, 2017; pp. 97–122.
6. Meen, G. Spatial housing economics: A survey. *Urban. Stud.* **2016**, *53*, 1987–2003. [CrossRef]
7. Tay, D.P.; Ho, D.K. Artificial intelligence and the mass appraisal of residential apartments. *J. Prop. Valuat. Invest.* **1992**, *10*, 525–540. [CrossRef]
8. Do, A.Q.; Grudnitski, G. A neural network approach to residential property appraisal. *Real Estate Appraiser* **1992**, *58*, 38–45.
9. Borst, R.A. Artificial neural networks in mass appraisal. *J. Prop. Tax Assess. Adm.* **1995**, *1*, 5–15.
10. Chiarazzo, V.; Caggiani, L.; Marinelli, M.; Ottomanelli, M. A Neural Network based model for real estate price estimation considering environmental quality of property location. *Transp. Res. Proc.* **2014**, *3*, 810–817. [CrossRef]
11. Yalpir, S.; Durduran, S.S.; Unel, F.B.; Yolcu, M. Creating a Valuation Map in GIS Through Artificial Neural Network Methodology: A Case Study. *Acta Montan. Slovaca* **2014**, *19*, 89–99.
12. Fan, G.Z.; Ong, S.E.; Koh, H.C. Determinants of house price: A decision tree approach. *Urban. Stud.* **2006**, *43*, 2301–2315. [CrossRef]
13. Vapnik, V. *The Nature of Statistical Learning Theory*; Springer: New York, NY, USA, 1995; p. 768.
14. Kontrimas, V.; Verikas, A. The mass appraisal of the real estate by computational intelligence. *Appl. Soft Comput.* **2011**, *11*, 443–448. [CrossRef]
15. Yu, D.; Wu, C. Incorporating Remote Sensing Information in Modeling House Values. *Photogramm. Eng. Remote Sens.* **2006**, *72*, 129–138. [CrossRef]
16. Breiman, L. Random forests. *Mach. Learn.* **2001**, *45*, 5–32. [CrossRef]
17. Antipov, E.A.; Pokryshevskaya, E.B. Mass appraisal of residential apartments: An application of Random forest for valuation and a CART-based approach for model diagnostics. *Expert Syst. Appl.* **2012**, *39*, 1772–1778. [CrossRef]
18. Yoo, S.; Im, J.; Wagner, J.E. Variable selection for hedonic model using machine learning approaches: A case study in Onondaga County, NY. *Landsc. Urban Plan.* **2012**, *107*, 293–306. [CrossRef]
19. Lake, I.R.; Lovett, A.A.; Bateman, I.J.; Langford, I.H. Modelling environmental influences on property prices in an urban environment. *Comput. Environ. Urban. Syst.* **1998**, *22*, 121–136. [CrossRef]
20. Lancaster, K.J. A new approach to consumer theory. *J. Polit. Econ.* **1966**, *74*, 132–157. [CrossRef]
21. Rosen, S. Hedonic Prices and Implicit Markets: Product Differentiation in Pure Competition. *J. Polit. Econ.* **1974**, *82*, 34–55. [CrossRef]
22. Se Can, A.; Megbolugbe, I. Spatial dependence and house price index construction. *J. Real Estate Financ. Econ.* **1997**, *14*, 203–222. [CrossRef]
23. Zuur, A.F.; Ieno, E.N.; Elphick, C.S. A protocol for data exploration to avoid common statistical problems. *Methods Ecol. Evol.* **2010**, *1*, 3–14. [CrossRef]
24. Kaiser, H.F. The application of electronic computers to factor analysis. *Educ. Psychol. Meas.* **1960**, *20*, 141–151. [CrossRef]
25. Breiman, L. Bagging predictors. *Mach. Learn.* **1996**, *24*, 123–140. [CrossRef]
26. Ho, T.K. The random subspace method for constructing decision forests. *IEEE Trans. Pattern Anal.* **1998**, *20*, 832–844. [CrossRef]
27. Liaw, A.; Wiener, M. Classification and regression by random Forest. *R News* **2002**, *2*, 18–22.

28. Moore, J.W. Performance comparison of automated valuation models. *J. Prop. Tax Assess. Adm.* **2006**, *3*, 43–59.
29. International Association of Assessing Officers. Guidance on International Mass Appraisal and Related Tax Policy. 2014. Available online: http://www.iaao.org/media/Standards/International_Guidance.pdf (accessed on 3 March 2018).
30. Kuhn, M. Caret package. *J. Stat. Softw.* **2008**, *28*, 1–16.
31. Orton, T.; Pringle, M.; Bishop, T. A one-step approach for modelling and mapping soil properties based on profile data sampled over varying depth intervals. *Geoderma* **2016**, *262*, 174–186. [CrossRef]
32. Silverman, B.W. *Density Estimation for Statistics and Data Analysis*; Chapman and Hall: New York, NY, USA, 1986; p. 175.
33. Getis, A.; Ord, J.K. The Analysis of Spatial Association by Use of Distance Statistics. *Geogr. Anal.* **1992**, *24*, 189–206. [CrossRef]

© 2018 by the authors. Licensee MDPI, Basel, Switzerland. This article is an open access article distributed under the terms and conditions of the Creative Commons Attribution (CC BY) license (http://creativecommons.org/licenses/by/4.0/).

Article

An Efficient Visualization Method for Polygonal Data with Dynamic Simplification

Mingguang Wu [1,2,3], Taisheng Chen [4,5,*], Kun Zhang [1,2], Zhimin Jing [1,2], Yangli Han [1,2], Menglin Chen [4,5], Hong Wang [1,2] and Guonian Lv [1,2,3]

[1] Key Laboratory of Virtual Geographic Environment of Ministry of Education, Nanjing Normal University, Nanjing 210023, China; wmg@njnu.edu.cn (M.W.); kunznnu@gmail.com (K.Z.); hbxsjzm@163.com (Z.J.); HanYangLi_1@163.com (Y.H.); maswanghong@126.com (H.W.); gnlunjnu@126.com (G.L.)
[2] College of Geographic Sciences, Nanjing Normal University, Nanjing 210023, China
[3] Jiangsu Center for Collaborative Innovation in Geographical Information Resource Development and Application, Nanjing 210023, China
[4] Department of Geographic Information Science, Chuzhou University, Chuzhou 239000, China; ml_chen@163.com
[5] Anhui Engineering Laboratory of Geo-Information Smart Sensing and Services, Chuzhou 239000, China
* Correspondence: taisheng.chen@163.com; Tel.: +86-550-3510030

Received: 12 February 2018; Accepted: 21 March 2018; Published: 2 April 2018

Abstract: Polygonal data often require rendering with symbolization and simplification in geovisualization. A common issue in existing methods is that simplification, symbolization and rendering are addressed separately, causing computational and data redundancies that reduce efficiency, especially when handling large complex polygonal data. Here, we present an efficient polygonal data visualization method by organizing the simplification, tessellation and rendering operations into a single mesh generalization process. First, based on the sweep line method, we propose a topology embedded trapezoidal mesh data structure to organize the tessellated polygons. Second, we introduce horizontal and vertical generalization operations to simplify the trapezoidal meshes. Finally, we define a heuristic testing algorithm to efficiently preserve the topological consistency. The method is tested using three OpenStreetMap datasets and compared with the Douglas Peucker algorithm and the Binary Line Generalization tree-based method. The results show that the proposed method improves the rendering efficiency by a factor of six. Efficiency-sensitive mapping applications such as emergency mapping could benefit from this method, which would significantly improve their visualization performances.

Keywords: vector polygon; level-of-detail rendering; cartographic simplification; tessellation; trapezoid

1. Introduction

Cartographic representation is an effective way to model real geographic space. As data acquisition techniques have developed, a large volume of geographic data has been collected, and more is being gathered continuously. These raw data are often symbolized for perception, cognition and communications [1]. Although geographic data are gathered at specific scales, they can be simplified based on zoom level, where each zoom level emphasizes a different level of detail (LoD) [2]. In this paper, rendering symbolization at a certain LoD is called LoD visualization. While LoD visualizations of vector geographic data benefit map legibility, their visualization efficiency is of critical concern in efficiency-sensitive mapping applications such as Human–Computer Interaction mapping, in which maps need to be rapidly responded. There is a critical need for an efficient LoD visualization algorithm not only in distributed mapping architectures but also in desktop mapping environments.

This paper focus on the efficiency of LoD visualization for polygonal data. Polygons are a major geometric type used to model geographic objects such as land cover and administrative boundaries [3,4]. LoD visualization for polygonal data involves three operations: symbolization, simplification and rendering. All three operations are both algorithmically complex [5] and time-consuming to perform; therefore, LoD visualization often suffers from low efficiency, especially when the number of polygons becomes massive. As a compromise, static LoD visualization methods such as the map tiles technique, in which maps are rendered offline for different zoom levels to promote rapid responses, are widely used in current mapping systems. Such static LoD visualization techniques are suitable for applications in which maps are used as background images. In contrast, dynamic LoD visualization methods perform symbolization and simplification on-the-fly, which provides more flexibility for perception and cognition. For example, using dynamic LoD visualization, users can specify the characteristics of symbols used to draw the polygonal data, such as colors or fill textures; users can also customize the geometric details for different zoom levels. However, improving the performance of dynamic LoD visualization is challenging [6].

The available dynamic LoD visualization methods for polygonal data can be classified into three groups: multiresolution meshes, simplification-based methods, and hardware-accelerated methods. In the first group, multiresolution meshes are data structures commonly used for dynamic LoD visualization in the computer graphics field [7]. Various multiresolution meshes have been proposed for geometric modeling and visualization [8]. As a typical example, Hoppe [9] presented a scheme called a "progressive mesh" to organize, transmit and render geometric models in multiple resolutions. By introducing an edge collapse transformation, progressive mesh representations allow efficient, continuous resolutions for arbitrary triangle meshes. Multiresolution mesh techniques, including the progressive mesh methods, are focused on highly detailed geometric models and adapt best to certain data types, such as terrain data [10]. However, because these techniques do not consider cartographic simplifications of polygons, they are limited in their ability to implement polygon LoD rendering [11].

In the second group, the simplification-based methods, many works have focused on polygon LoDs with cartographic simplifications [12,13]. Detailed discussions on polygon and polyline simplifications can be found in Li [14], Galanda [3], Shi et al. [15], Podolskaya et al. [16] and Haunert [17]. An exhaustive investigation of those algorithms is beyond the scope of this paper. Instead, we focus on solutions that use those methods to implement LoD visualization for polygonal data. A straightforward solution is to divide the polygon boundaries into segments and then apply polyline simplification algorithms. Based on the Douglas Peucker (DP) algorithm, Van Oosterom [18] presented a data structure called the Binary Line Generalization tree (BLG-tree), which recursively divides a polyline and organizes the polyline segments into a binary tree. To maintain topological consistency, Van Oosterom [19] proposed the GAP-tree (Generalized Area Partitioning) method, which organizes area partitioning hierarchically. Further, based on the R-tree, a storage structure called the reactive-tree was presented, which was capable of implementing area partitioning using a dynamic LoD. Several improvements on the GAP-tree have been presented, such as the tGAP, which is used to avoid redundant data storage and slivers [17,20], and the smooth tGAP, which is used for smooth zooms and 3D data [21]. In addition, because topological incorrectness (e.g., self-intersections) and shape dissimilarities (e.g., area or perimeter dissimilarities) may occur when simplifying polygons, various topological and shape-preserving techniques have been proposed [22,23], such as using Delaunay triangulation to detect topological errors and using a hierarchical topological data structure to maintain topological consistency between different LoD results [24,25].

Focusing on the LoD of polygonal geometry, the above-mentioned methods are definitely helpful for applications such as progressive data transmission over the Internet [21,26,27]. However, because these methods do not consider rendering operators such as filling, their ability to facilitate LoD visualization of polygonal data is limited. In fact, polygons, no matter how complex they are [28], may be tessellated into drawable primitives, such as triangles or trapezoids (e.g., *triangle-strip* or quad-strip in OpenGL) for cartographic filling [29]. The drawable primitives are then sent to a rendering engine for display [30,31].

Within this process, the tessellation operation is computationally expensive [4], and the rendering performance is also dependent on the efficiency with which drawable primitives can be sent [32]—i.e., the performance is rate sensitive. By applying existing LoD polygonal geometry techniques such as BLG-tree, the polygons can be efficiently simplified. However, the simplified polygons still need to be re-tessellated and re-sent, causing computational and data redundancies that reduce efficiency.

In the third group, hardware-accelerated methods, the speed of both cartographic simplifications and rendering are improved by using hardware-accelerated techniques such as chain-based tessellation [1], graphics processing unit (GPU)-based rendering [31,33,34], and parallel algorithms for simplification [35]. In recent years, hardware-accelerated vector tile rendering has been widely used. However, simplifications, symbolization and rendering are still addressed separately. For example, MapBox uses OpenGL as its native map rendering engine to improve the map-rendering performance. MapBox even provides a WebGL interface to support advanced map rendering in web clients, including polygon symbolization [36]. However, in MapBox, LoDs are achieved by specifying the zoom level of the underlying data rather than dynamically simplifying them. In addition, both cartographic simplifications and rendering are considered in the hybrid vector- and raster-based approach proposed by Mustafa and Krishnan [6], which employs hardware buffers to efficiently create a Voronoi diagram to help simplify polygon boundaries via pixel-color checking. Because Voronoi diagrams and pixel-color checking can be hardware accelerated, this method is efficient for stroking the boundaries of polygons. However, it does not consider polygon filling, which is critical for cartographic representations.

From the above discussion, the existing methods of LoD visualization are focused on geometric models rather than on polygonal data. While LoD techniques for polygonal geometry have been widely addressed, efforts focused on LoD visualization for polygonal data are limited. A common issue is that simplification, symbolization and rendering are addressed separately, yielding computational and data redundancies that reduce efficiency. To address this issue, this paper presents an efficient method to support polygon LoD visualization. The remainder of this paper is organized as follows. Section 2 provides an overview of the proposed method. Section 3 presents a detailed explanation of the method. The approach is then tested in Section 4 and discussed in Section 5. Finally, Section 6 highlights the contributions of this paper and suggests related future works.

2. Method Overview

Polygon LoD visualization involves three major operations: simplification, tessellation and rendering. As discussed in the previous section, this process is computationally expensive and rate sensitive. Notably, for a polygon, different versions of simplified instances are similar. The closer they are in zoom level, the more similar their geometries will be. For example, when a user zooms in on a map by scrolling a mouse wheel, the simplified instances at two consecutive zoom levels may differ only slightly. When a user uses drags a rectangle over an area of interest and then zooms out, the critical boundary points can be preserved to maintain similarity. Furthermore, because polygon instances are mutually similar, drawable primitives, which are the intermediate visualization result, are correspondingly mutually similar. Ignoring similarity, computational redundancy occurs when tessellating similar polygon instances, and data redundancy occurs when rendering similar polygon instances.

Recognizing the similarity, the basic idea of this paper is to use similarity to reduce the computational redundancy and mitigate rate sensitivity. Unlike existing methods, we organize simplification, tessellation and rendering operations into a single mesh generalization process to avoid having to completely re-execute tessellation operations and resend all the drawable primitives. First, based on the sweep line method proposed by Žalik et al. [37], we proposed a topology embedded trapezoidal mesh data structure to organize the tessellated polygons. Second, we use DP algorithms to weight the trapezoidal meshes and then introduce horizontal and vertical generalizations to simplify them. Finally, we define a heuristic testing algorithm to preserve the topological consistency efficiently. Beyond the application of supporting techniques such as the sweep line method and the DP algorithm, the primary contributions of this paper are the trapezoidal mesh data structure to encode tessellated polygons, the horizontal and vertical generalizations to simplify tessellated polygons, and the heuristic testing algorithm to preserve the topological consistency. These three contributions will be presented in more detail in the following sections.

3. Detailed Method

3.1. Trapezoidal Graph

Three forms of polygon are considered for LoD visualization. While polygons have only one exterior boundary, they may contain zero or more interior boundaries, called simple polygons and polygons with holes, respectively. The regions bounded by these interior boundaries may contain additional sets of interior boundaries; these cases are called polygons with islands. Polygons with cut lines, spikes or punctures are not considered in this paper. The considered types of polygons have three forms of topological relationships: islands may not intersect their surrounding boundaries; all boundaries may not self-intersect; and all boundaries must not mutually intersect. These three types of polygons are illustrated in Figure 1a–c, respectively.

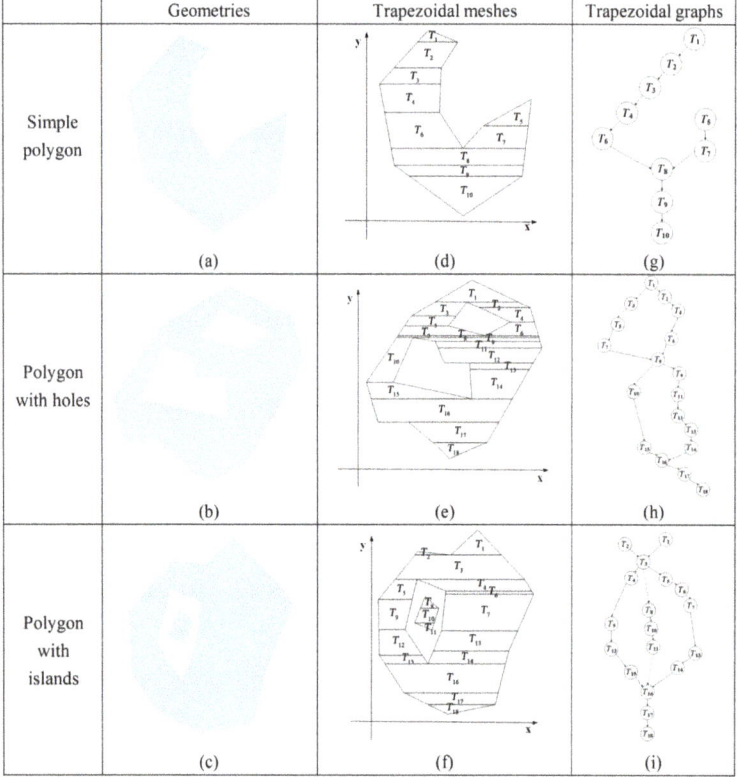

Figure 1. Three types of polygons, their trapezoidations and trapezoidal graphs. (**a**) is a geometry of a simple polygon, (**d**) is the tessellated result of (**a**), (**g**) is the trapezoidal graph of (**a**), (**b**) is a geometry of a polygon with holes, (**e**) is the tessellated result of (**d**), (**h**) is the trapezoidal graph of (**b**), (**c**) is a geometry of a polygon with islands, (**f**) is the tessellated result of (**c**), (**i**) is the trapezoidal graph of a simple polygon of (**d**).

Polygons are tessellated into trapezoidal meshes. For cartographic filling, polygons may need to be tessellated into triangles or trapezoids. To reduce the data rate and increase rendering efficiency, these triangles and trapezoids should be carefully ordered, such as via Hamiltonian triangulations or sequential triangulations in which consecutive triangles share an edge [32]. Trapezoidation is often performed as a first step of triangulation, and with modern hardware, consecutive trapezoids, i.e., those that share an edge, can achieve similar rendering efficiencies to those of sequential triangulations [38]. Trapezoidal meshes are chosen to perform polygon LoD visualization. Here, we simplify the trapezoidal meshes of polygons rather than the polygon boundaries (see Section 5.2 for a more detailed discussion of triangulation and trapezoidation).

Many solutions have been proposed for trapezoidation. One popular solution is the sweep-line algorithm, which can decompose a polygon into trapezoids in any direction [37]. In this paper, horizontal sweep lines are employed to sweep through each vertex of a polygon from top to bottom. All of the sweep lines are parallel, and they decompose a polygon into a series of vertical strips. A sweep line may cross one or more vertexes, decomposing each strip into one or more trapezoids. Generally, a trapezoid consists of four sides (left, right, bottom and top), of which the top and bottom sides are parallel. In practice, a trapezoid may degenerate into a triangle, as shown in T_1 in Figure 1d.

Then, the tessellated polygon is organized as a graph in which a trapezoid is modeled as a node and the relationships between two connected trapezoids are modeled as links; the product is called a trapezoidal graph. Various trapezoidal graphs can be created for different polygon instances [39]. When a node (trapezoid) is connected on one side, either its top or bottom, the node is called a suspended node, as shown by T_1, T_5 and T_{10} in Figure 1d. A convex polygon will be tessellated into a series of trapezoids that are consecutively connected via connecting links. Joined links occur in graphs tessellating a concave polygon, and a division relation occurs when tessellating a polygon with holes. For example, the polygon shown in Figure 1d is a concave instance that includes several concave points at its exterior boundary. In its corresponding trapezoidal graph, shown in Figure 1g, T_6 and T_7 join at T_8. The example shown in Figure 1e is a polygon with two holes. In its corresponding trapezoidal graph, shown in Figure 1h, T_1 will be divided into T_2 and T_3. If a subgraph starts from a suspended node and ends at a join node or starts from a division node and ends at a join node, then its nodes are consecutively chained, creating a trapezoidal chain. Because the relationships between two connected trapezoids are identical in a trapezoidal chain, trapezoidal chains are isomorphic in terms of their links. Therefore, trapezoids are consecutive, and trapezoidal chains are able to facilitate rendering. For example, when using OpenGL as the rendering engine, a trapezoidal chain can be directly translated into a quad-strip for fast rendering. In addition, because self-intersections and intersections are not allowed, triangles' (degenerated trapezoid) nodes exist only at the initial or end node of a trapezoidal chain.

Islands are also tessellated into trapezoidal meshes. The trapezoidal mesh of an island will certainly be disjoined from the other trapezoidal meshes. Nevertheless, the trapezoidal meshes of islands are surrounded by other trapezoidal meshes. Thus, pseudo-divided links and pseudo-joined links are derived from divided links and joined links, respectively, to organize these forms of topological relationships (delineated as dashed arrow lines in Figure 1). The trapezoidal mesh of an island is organized as a subgraph with a pseudo-divided link and a pseudo-joined link. For example, the polygon shown in Figure 1c is a polygon with an island. In its corresponding trapezoidal graph, shown in Figure 1i, T_8 and T_3 are connected via a pseudo-divided link, and T_{16} and T_{11} are connected with a pseudo-joined link.

Trapezoidal graphs encode spatial orders and topological relationships. Because a node corresponds to a trapezoid that specifies a concrete location, nodes are spatially ordered from top to bottom according to the y-coordinates of their top sides and from left to right according to the x-coordinates of their left sides. Specifically, in a trapezoidal graph, a connection link exists for two vertically neighboring trapezoids. A division link also connects two vertically neighboring trapezoids, but the bottom one has at least one sibling. Furthermore, all siblings are mutually separately and ordered via the increasing x-coordinates of their left sides. Similarly, a joined link connects two vertically neighboring trapezoids, but the top one has siblings. All siblings are ordered by their increasing x-coordinates.

The topmost and bottommost nodes are selected as the starting and ending nodes, respectively. If the topmost sweep line crosses more than one vertex, then several top nodes exist and the leftmost node one is chosen as the starting node. Similarly, the rightmost node is chosen as the ending node when several candidates exist. From the starting node, through the aforementioned three types of links (connection, division and joined, including pseudo-divisions and pseudo-joins), all nodes, including the nodes representing islands, can be tracked downward, upward, and to the left and right. From the starting node, trapezoidal chains can also be generated by tracking the connection links.

3.2. Trapezoidal Mesh Simplifications

Given the cartographic simplification rules, a trapezoidal mesh simplification method is introduced in this section. First, a vertex's weight for preserving the polygon shape is measured. Second, two types of generalization strategies are proposed to generalize the trapezoids. Third, a simplification method is presented that dynamically adapts the trapezoidal meshes according to the zoom level. These operations are discussed in detail below.

One commonly used cartographic simplification rule is to maintain critical points when simplifying polygons. Many methods have been proposed to determine these critical points [14,15], including the widely accepted DP algorithm, which uses a point-to-edge distance to a measure vertex's weight [3]. Here, the DP algorithm is chosen to calculate the vertex weights for polygon LoD rendering (see Section 5.2 for further discussion of the cartographic simplification rules). Similar to the DP-based BLG-tree, all the boundary vertexes are weighted by their point-to-edge distances through binary recursive partitioning. For example, in Figure 2, V_2, V_3, and V_4 are weighted as H_2, H_1 and H_3, respectively.

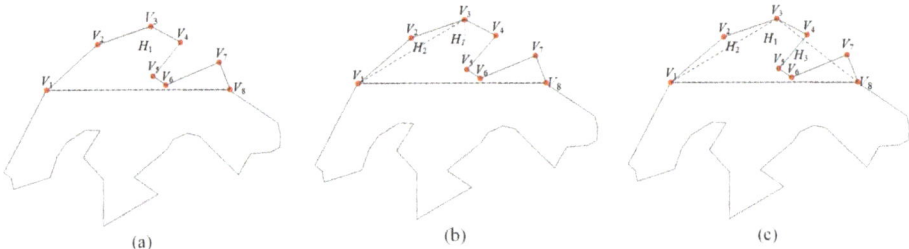

Figure 2. Using the Douglas Peucker (DP) algorithm to weight vertexes [18]. (a) V_3 is weighted according to H_1, (b) V_2 is weighted according to H_2, (c) V_4 is weighted according to H_3.

Trapezoidal generalizations are then introduced to simplify the trapezoidal meshes according to the vertex weights. Given a zoom level, a threshold value of the point-to-edge distance, denoted as ε, can be calculated. When a vertex's weight is less than the threshold value, then that vertex should be deleted; otherwise, it should be kept to preserve the polygon's shape [20]. Considering the diversity of polygonal geometries, various trapezoidal and spatial relationships may exist in concrete trapezoidal meshes. Each node may be singly connected with another node above or below itself (i.e., located at the beginning/ending node of a trapezoidal chain). Such nodes are referred to as one-sided connected nodes. Nodes may also be connected with two nodes, one on either side. These nodes are referred to as two-sided connected nodes. For a connection link, the vertically connected trapezoids should be generalized. For a division or a joined link, horizontally connected trapezoids should be generalized.

In a vertical generalization, removing a vertex may lead to trapezoid merging, degeneration, elimination or adjustment. When tessellating a polygon into trapezoids, one horizontal side of a trapezoid may cross at least one vertex (its weight is denoted as w_1), which is called a one-vertex horizontal side; it also may cross two vertices (whose weights are denoted as w_1 and w_2, respectively, such that $w_1 < w_2$), which is called a two-vertex horizontal side. Specifically, four cases exist for vertical merges, distinguishing whether the vertex which needs to be deleted is shared by two trapezoids and whether the horizontal side is a one-vertex horizontal side or a two-vertex horizontal side: (1) if the vertex is shared by two trapezoids and the horizontal side is a one-vertex side ($w_1 < \varepsilon$), then the two connected trapezoids will be merged into one. Let the symbol $\oplus$ denote the trapezoid merging operator such that $T_i \oplus T_j$ stands for the merged result of trapezoids T_i and T_j. As shown in Figure 3, assume that the weight value of V_{10} is relatively small. To remove V_{10}, T_2 and T_4 should be merged. Then, $T_2 \oplus T_4$ may be further merged with T_1 if V_9 needs to be removed, generating $(T_2 \oplus T_4) \oplus T_1$. (2) If the vertex is shared and the horizontal side is a two-vertex side, then two cases are possible. If the two vertexes that share the horizontal side both need to be deleted ($w_1 < \varepsilon$ and $w_2 < \varepsilon$), as shown in Figure 4b, then the two connected trapezoids will be merged; if the other vertex needs to be kept ($w_1 < \varepsilon$ and $w_2 > \varepsilon$), as shown in Figure 4e, then the two connected trapezoids will be adjusted. (3) If the vertex is not shared and it is a one-weight side ($w_1 < \varepsilon$), as shown in Figure 4a, then the trapezoid will be eliminated; (4) If the vertex is not shared and the side is a two-vertex side, as shown in Figures 4g and 4h, the trapezoid may collapse into a triangle at the vertex with the smaller weight ($w_1 < \varepsilon$ and $w_2 > \varepsilon$), or be removed ($w_1 <$ and $w_2 < \varepsilon$). In total, eight horizontal generalization prototypes are summarized, as shown in Figure 4.

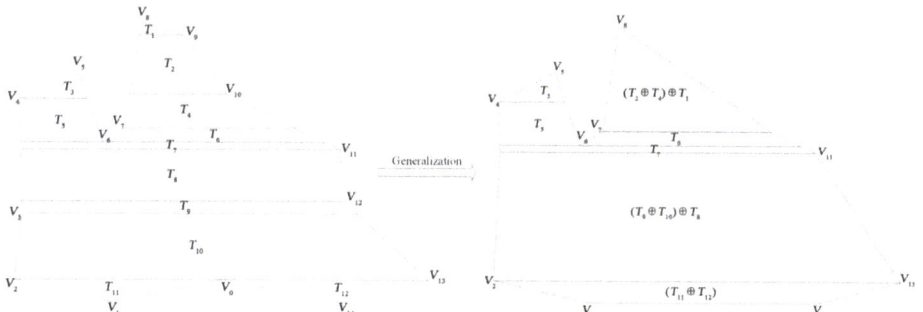

Figure 3. Simplifying a trapezoidal mesh via trapezoidal generalizations.

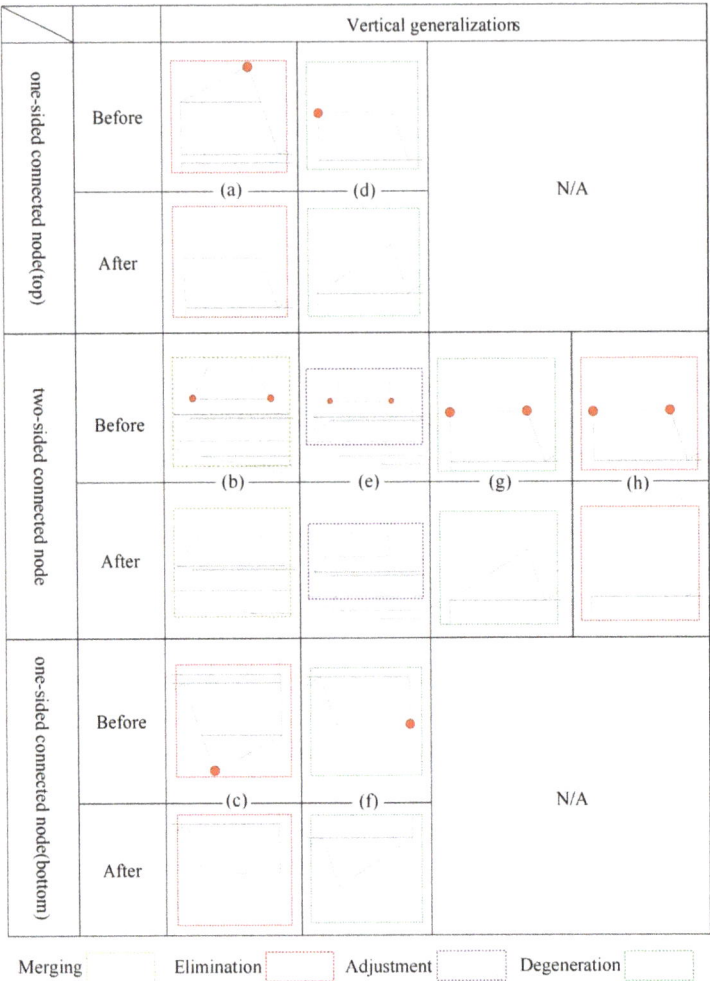

Figure 4. Vertical trapezoidal generalizations, comprising four trapezoidal operators: merging, degeneration, elimination and adjustment. (**a**) trapezoid elimination, (**b**) trapezoid merging, (**c**) is the same with (**a**), but the vertex is at the bottom, (**d**) trapezoid degeneration, (**f**) is the same with (**d**), but the vertex is at the bottom, (**g**) trapezoid degeneration, in which the vertex is a two-weight side and the other vertex needs to be kept, (**h**) trapezoid elimination, in which the vertex is a two-weight side and both need to be deleted, the trapezoid will be removed.

Similarly, trapezoid merging and adjustment also occur with horizontal generalization. Two horizontally neighboring trapezoids can be involved in horizontal merging, which occurs only at division or joining nodes. The two neighboring trapezoids may be merged into a new trapezoid (see Figure 5a) or may be adjusted (see Figure 5c). In total, four merging prototypes are summarized for horizontal generalization, as depicted in Figure 5.

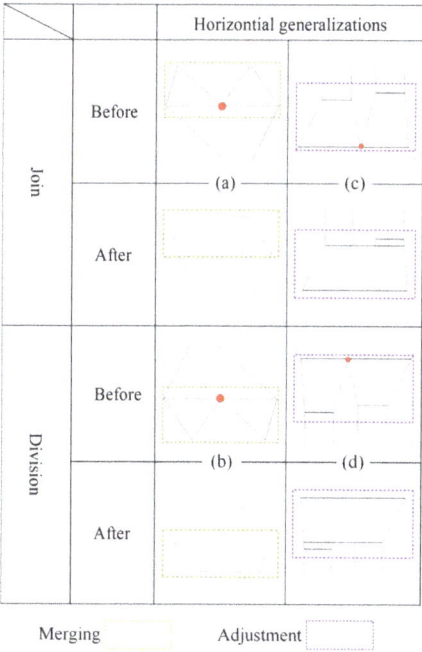

Figure 5. Horizontal trapezoidal generalizations, comprising two trapezoidal operators: merging and adjustment. (**a**) and (**b**) are two cases of merging, the two connected triangles will be merged into a trapezoid, (**c**) and (**d**) are two cases of adjustment, the two connected trapezoids will be adjusted.

Because only two trapezoids experience both horizontal and vertical generalization, their nodes and corresponding links can be updated locally without globally rebuilding the graph (the topological changes will be discussed in next section). For example, Figure 3 shows that merging T_2 and T_4 allows $T_2 \oplus T_4$ to replace T_2 and T_4, and $T_2 \oplus T_4$ will correspondingly inherit the connection relationships of T_2 and T_4. That is, $T_2 \oplus T_4$ are upwardly connected with T_1 and downwardly connected with T_6. Thus, a simplified graph will be generated. The simplified graph represents a simplified trapezoidal mesh and can be translated into consecutive trapezoids for fast rendering.

Based on the generalization prototypes, a trapezoidal mesh simplification method is presented that dynamically chains trapezoidal operators according to their zoom levels. First, a priority stack is introduced. Using binary recursive partitioning, the weighted value of a low level of the partition may be greater than that of a high-level one [18]. In this paper, the original weight values calculated using the DP algorithm are adjusted as follows to guarantee that the vertex with lower weight value has less importance for preserving the polygon shape:

$$H_i = H_i + level_j, \qquad (1)$$

where H_i is the weight value for V_i and is calculated at $level_j$ though binary recursive partitioning, and $level_j$ is the parameter for all vertexes that are weighted at $level_j$. Sorting the vertexes according to their weights in descending order generates a priority stack. Then, given a zoom level, a threshold weight value can be calculated. By searching the priority stack, those vertexes whose weights are below the threshold are popped from the priority stack. The related nodes and links of popped vertexes are searched, and the relevant trapezoid is then generalized according to the generalization prototypes. By storing the node and corresponding link statuses before and after each generalization operation, trapezoidal merging, degeneration, elimination and adjustment can be undone. After processing all the popped vertexes, the trapezoidal mesh is dynamically simplified. For a simplified trapezoidal mesh, moving to a larger zoom level may cause more vertexes to be popped, causing the trapezoidal mesh to be further simplified. Then, a final version of the tessellated polygons can be generated. If the weight of a popped vertex becomes greater than the threshold value, the vertex is pushed back into the priority stack and its status restored. In this manner, a trapezoidal mesh can be dynamically adapted to a zoom level, and the adapted trapezoidal mesh can be translated into consecutive trapezoids for fast rendering.

3.3. Preserving Topological Consistency

As discussed in Section 3.1, three forms of topological relationships are considered and should be kept consistent when performing LoD visualization: for an individual boundary, the boundaries should not self-intersect; no two boundaries, exterior or interior, should intersect; and islands should be preserved without intersections. Using the generalization operators discussed in the previous section, when two neighboring trapezoids are generalized, there is a risk of introducing intersections, which violates topological consistency. We simplify the trapezoidal meshes rather than the polygon boundaries. Using this method, topological errors such as self-intersections of a boundary and any intersections between boundaries, including those of islands, are embodied as intersections between trapezoids. Checking for topological correctness is therefore translated into a problem of testing whether the generalized trapezoids intersect with any other trapezoids.

Clearly, topologic errors can be avoided by exhaustively checking whether a generalized trapezoid intersects with any other trapezoid; however, such checks may be too computationally expensive. Therefore, we propose a heuristic testing algorithm to efficiently check for intersections. First, in a trapezoidal mesh, a trapezoid, T_i cannot intersect with a trapezoid whose projection on the y-axis does not overlap the y-span of T_i. For example, in Figure 6, assuming T_3 and T_8 will be merged, only trapezoids whose y-span intersects the y-span of $T_3 \oplus T_8$ need to be checked.

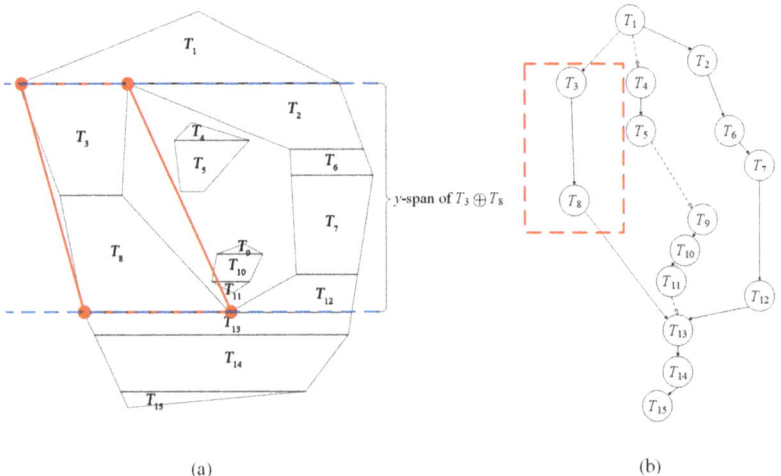

Figure 6. Trapezoid tracking to check for possible intersections. (**a**) is the tessellated result, (**b**) is the trapezoidal graph.

Furthermore, T_i may cover several strips of horizontal trapezoids. In each strip, the trapezoids are ordered by their increasing x coordinates. The trapezoid closest to T_i at its right side is denoted as T_{i+1}. If T_i does not intersect with T_{i+1}, then T_i will not intersect with T_j when $j > i + 1$ and the y-span of T_j is within the y-span of T_{i+1}. For example, in Figure 6, if T_3 does not intersect with T_5, then it will not intersect with T_6. By selecting the closest trapezoids of all the involved strips at both the right and left sides, a minimal surrounding trapezoid set can be found and denoted as S. S can be identified via trapezoid tracking. For example, in Figure 6, the upwardly tracking node of $T_3 \oplus T_8$ can be identified as the division node T_1. The closest sibling of $T_3 \oplus T_8$ to the right, T_4, can also be identified. For the downwardly tracking node T_4, the node whose y-span is within the y-span of $T_3 \oplus T_8$ belongs to the minimized surrounding trapezoid set. If the y-span of $T_3 \oplus T_8$ is not completely covered, then the downwardly tracking nearest sibling node of $T_3 \oplus T_8$ to the right (if any) is checked until the y-span of $T_3 \oplus T_8$ is either totally covered or all horizontal neighbors to the right side are analyzed. In this manner, S can be generated without performing a brute-force search of the entire trapezoidal mesh. When a trapezoid belonging to S is found, it is checked to determine whether it intersects with $T_3 \oplus T_8$. If the trapezoids intersect, testing ends because an intersection will certainly be introduced. Otherwise, the test continues to the next closest trapezoid. When all items in S have been visited and no intersection has been reported, $T_3 \oplus T_8$ is guaranteed to not intersect with any other trapezoid. In this case, the merging operation will not introduce topological inconsistencies.

More generally, a trapezoid may degenerate, be removed, be merged or be adjusted. In any case, the y-span of a generalized trapezoid can be determined, and the minimized surrounding trapezoid set can also be tracked via graph visiting. Benefiting from the structure of a graph in which both order and topology are embedded, heuristic testing of all generalization cases can be performed without a brute-force search. By rejecting generalization operations that introduce trapezoid intersections, topological consistency can be preserved efficiently without exhaustive checks.

4. Tests and Evaluation

4.1. Test Dataset and Compared Methods

We implemented the algorithm described in Section 3 in C++, using OpenGL 3.0 as the supporting rendering engine. We use the sweep line method proposed by Žalik et al. [37] to tessellate various polygons. While the GAP-tree and its improvements focus on hierarchically organizing an area partitioning, this paper focuses on LoD visualizations of individual polygons. In this sense, GAP-tree and the proposed method are not comparable. Two solutions to support LoD rendering are selected to evaluate the proposed method: in the first compared solution, the polygons are dynamically simplified using BLG-tree (also called the BLG-tree-based method). In the second solution, the polygons are dynamically simplified using the DP algorithm (also called the DP-based method). In both solutions, the simplified polygons are tessellated into trapezoidal meshes and then rendered. Three OpenStreetMap [40] polygon datasets (i.e., including buildings, nature, and land use) were selected as the test datasets. The covered area is located at Shenzhen (113°22′21″ E, 114°57′48″ E; 22°13′30″ N, 22°44′38″ N) in southeast Guangdong Province, China and contains a total of 42,334 polygons. These three datasets are organized as three map layers and are symbolized using solid-color fills. Zoom (in and out) and pan functions were implemented to control the zoom level and view. A volunteer was invited to operate the map to arbitrarily explore these datasets. All the tests were performed at a display resolution of 1600 × 1200 on a PC running Windows 7 with a 2.66 GHz Intel Core 2 Quad CPU, 8 GB of RAM and an ATI Radeon HD 5870 GPU (driver version 10.6).

4.2. Results

The performance efficiencies (in terms of drawing time, including the simplifying, tessellating and rendering times) of 72 consecutive views were recorded both with and without preserving the topological consistency. Five example views and their corresponding trapezoidal meshes are shown in Figure 7. We use the method suggested by Corcoran et al. [23] to preserve topological consistency in both the DP-based and the BLG-tree-based methods. Efficiency comparisons of all three algorithms are shown in Figure 8. For the DP-based method, simplification and trapezoidation were performed for every view. In the BLG-tree-based method, the simplification speed was improved by employing the BLG-tree; therefore, the BLG-tree-based method was significantly more efficient than the DP-based method. However, trapezoidation was still executed for every zoom level. Because the simplified polygons must be tessellated for every zoom level, the trapezoidal meshes must be sent to the rendering engine for every views when directly applying both the BLG-tree-based method and the DP-based method. In contrast, the proposed method requires the trapezoidal meshes to be generated only for the initial frame; thus, simplification and tessellation can be achieved concurrently though trapezoidal generalization. Using the generalization prototypes, the computational cost of the trapezoidal generalization is far less than when separate simplification and tessellation operations are used. In the proposed method, none of the generalization operators except adjustment introduce any additional vertexes. Therefore, the trapezoidal meshes need to be sent to the rendering engine only once. Only the index of the trapezoidal meshes must be sent for rendering and the trapezoidal meshes are updated only when they are adjusted. Thus, the data rate is dramatically reduced, and, consequently, the rendering efficiency increases. For the above reasons, as illustrated in Figure 8, the proposed method runs significantly faster, achieving speeds approximately six times faster than the other two methods.

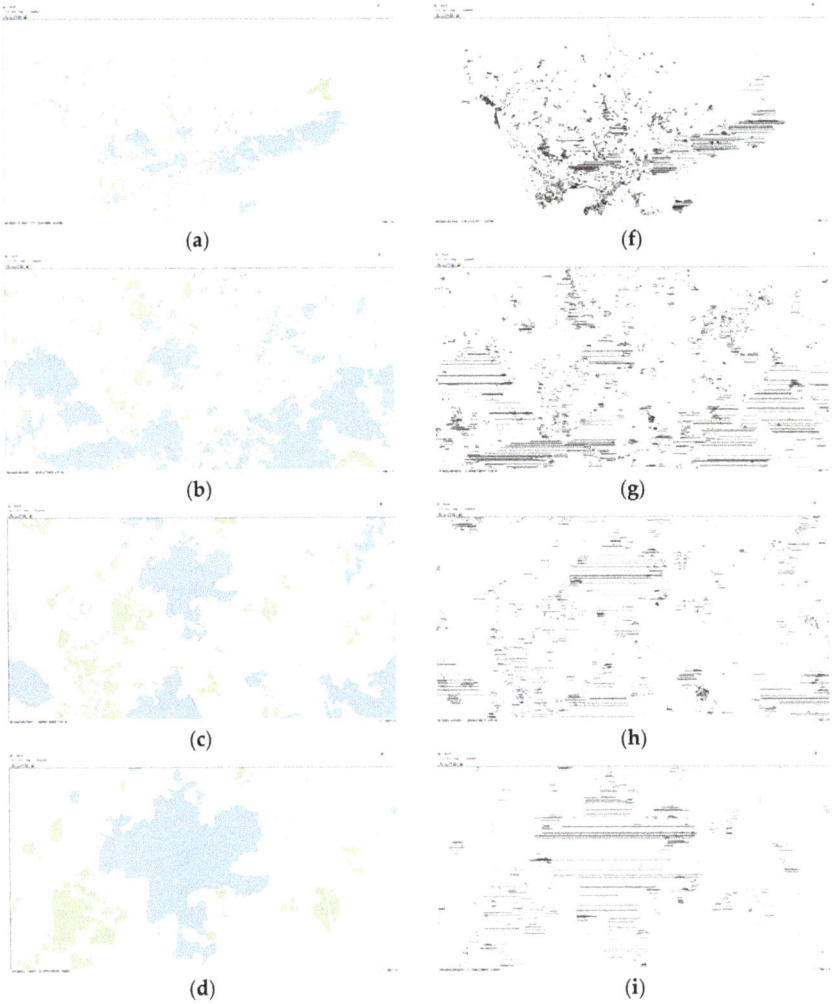

Figure 7. *Cont.*

(e)   (j)

Figure 7. Screenshots of polygon level of detail (LoD) rendering [2]. (a–e) are the rendered results of the test polygons at five zoom levels (1:250,000, 1:80,000, 1:50,000, 1:29,000, 1:3,000, respectively), while (f–j) are the corresponding adapted trapezoidal meshes.

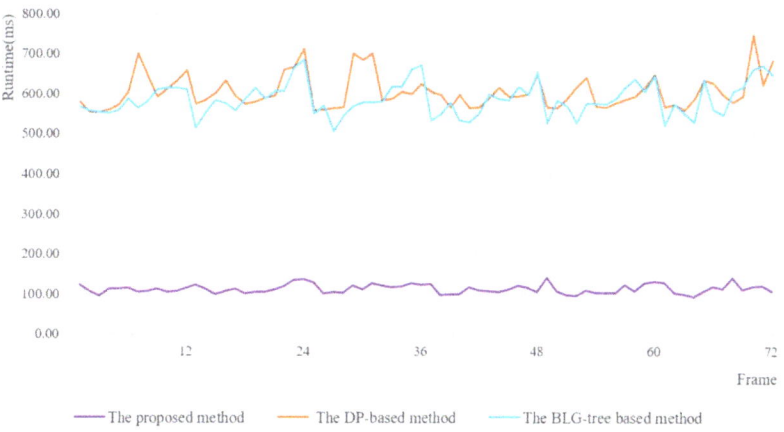

Figure 8. Rendering times for the test polygons using the three compared algorithms.

5. Discussion

5.1. Efficiency

Simplification, tessellation and rendering are the three major phases of polygon LoD visualization. The detailed time costs for simplification, tessellation and rendering steps were analyzed, and the results are shown in Figure 9. Generally, in this test, the average proportions of the time consumed by the simplification, tessellation and rendering stages of the DP-based method are approximately 24%, 9% and 67%, respectively. The BLG-tree-based method speeds up simplification by employing the BLG-tree; thus, the average proportions of its time consumed by the simplification, tessellation and rendering stages are approximately 17%, 8% and 74%, respectively. In the proposed method, the simplification and tessellation stages are achieved concurrently by performing trapezoidal generalizations. By defining the generalization prototypes, the trapezoidal generalizations can be efficiently implemented. As shown in Figure 9, the combined simplification and tessellation step of the proposed method costs significantly less time than do the separate steps in the DP-based and BLG-tree-based methods. Furthermore, because the proposed method also reduces the data rate, the rendering time is significantly less than that of the other two methods. These statistics will certainly vary for different polygons and different software and hardware environments, but they help explain why the proposed method performs significantly better than the other two methods.

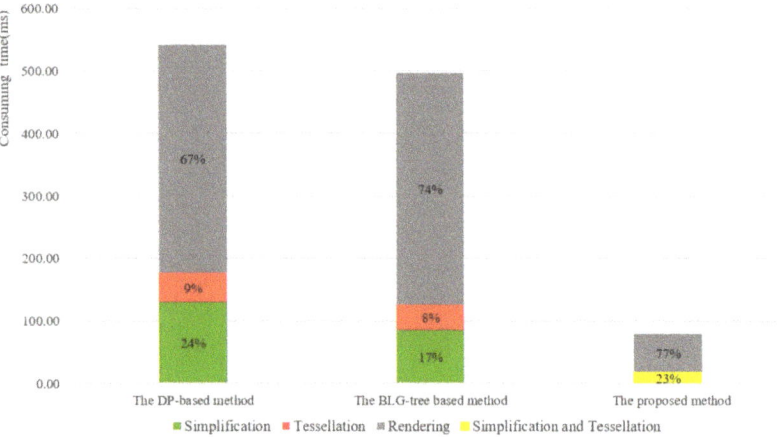

Figure 9. Detailed statistics of the time costs (in milliseconds) of the simplification, tessellation and rendering steps.

In this study, trapezoids are selected as the base unit to simplify and tessellate the polygons. A triangle is also a candidate base unit for polygon simplification, tessellation and rendering. When tessellating polygons into triangle meshes, a single vertex may be linked to many triangles, which can lead to algorithmic complexities when removing vertexes for LoD purposes. In contrast, when tessellating polygons into trapezoidal meshes, a vertex can be connected to only one or two trapezoids, which helps in straightforwardly and efficiently generalizing connected trapezoids for LoD. Certainly, new vertexes could be introduced in trapezoidation that would facilitate simplifying trapezoidal meshes; however, introducing new vertexes would also increase the required memory and the data rate at the rendering stage. In fact, these vertexes are not necessary for rendering. As discussed in Section 3.1, trapezoids in a chain are consecutive: connected trapezoids share an edge, and thus a trapezoidal chain can be translated into a quad-strip. Breaking a quad-strip at the introduced vertexes allows a trapezoidal chain to be translated as a series of triangle-strips without using the introduced vertexes. Then, the data rate can be further reduced, but this method can also result in a relatively large number of drawable primitives and negatively affect the rendering efficiency. The impact of the introduced vertexes is also dependent on the implemented rendering technique, such as whether GPU-accelerated rendering is used, which is an effect that requires further research. In addition, maintaining the graphs needs considerable memory, but it is also needed when tessellating the polygon in the DP-based and BLG-tree-based methods.

The computational complexity of the trapezoidation of simple polygons is $O(n)$, where n is the vertex count of the polygon [37]. Using this method, trapezoidation needs to be conducted only once. Furthermore, only two neighboring trapezoids are involved in the generalization operators discussed in Section 3.2. Tessellated polygons can therefore be simplified in linear time without topological check, and the computational complexity of generalization operations is $O(m)$, where m is the trapezoid count of the tessellated polygon. This approach also offers the possibility of parallelizing the horizontal and vertical generalization operations, which will be addressed in future work.

5.2. Quality

In this paper, vertexes are weighted using the DP algorithm. A variety of methods have been proposed to simply polygons, such as the B-spline snake model [41] and the energy minimization method [3]. Different methods may yield considerably different simplified polygons. Trapezoidal generalizations are based on weighted vertexes. Theoretically, these generalizations are compatible with different methods of calculating the weights. In future work, we will extend our method to support additional methods of cartographic simplification.

In this study, self-intersections and intersections are checked using the heuristic testing algorithm. Many other issues, such as size conflicts (wherein a simplified polygon may be too small) and proximity conflicts (wherein a simplified polygon may be too close to another simplified polygon), should also be examined in advanced polygon simplifications, or, more generally, in any polygon generalization [3]. Four types of trapezoidal generalization operators, including merging, degeneration, elimination and adjustment, are introduced in this paper; however, more sophisticated operators, such as displacement and exaggeration, can be developed to support other advanced polygon generalizations. For example, as shown in Figure 10a, when a simplified trapezoid mesh is too close to its neighbors after simplification, it should purposely be moved to the opposite side. Additionally, as shown in Figure 10b, if some trapezoids of a simplified trapezoidal mesh are too small, then those trapezoids should be purposefully enlarged while still preserving the connections at shared faces. Those sophisticated operators are also potentially suitable to generate point, and polyline objects because they also need to be tessellated into drawable primitives for symbolization. In this sense, this method can be extended for general maps consisting of point, polyline and polygon objects. Defining these sophisticated operators will require further research.

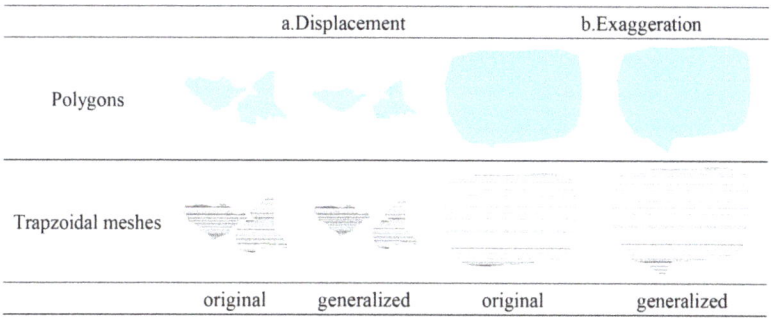

Figure 10. Additional possible sophisticated operators to support polygon displacement and exaggeration.

6. Conclusions

Polygon LoD visualization is functionally necessary in geo visualization but suffers from low efficiency, especially when visualizing complex polygonal data. Simplification, tessellation and rendering are three major successive phases that are treated as isolated processes in the existing methods, yielding computational and data redundancies that reduce efficiency. In this paper, an efficient method is proposed to facilitate polygon LoD visualization. The contributions of this method are summarized as follows.

Unlike the existing methods, we organize simplification, tessellation and rendering operations into a single mesh generalization process that avoids having to completely re-execute tessellation operations and resend all drawable primitives for rendering. Beyond the supporting techniques such as the sweep line method and the DP algorithm, to the best of our knowledge, this paper is the first to propose the trapezoidal mesh data structure to encode the spatial and topological elements of tessellated polygons, the horizontal and vertical generalizations for rapid trapezoidal mesh simplification, and the heuristic testing algorithm to efficiently preserve topological consistency. In our approach, the simplification and tessellation operations are systematically organized into a single process that avoids computational and data redundancies and helps to mitigate the rate sensitivity.

The tests conducted on real world datasets suggest that, compared with the DP-based and BLG-tree-based methods, the proposed method significantly improves the efficiency of polygon

LoD visualization. This method can benefit efficiency-sensitive vector mapping applications such as emergency mapping cases in which polygonal data need to be symbolized and simplified in a timely fashion. We implemented and test this algorithm in a desktop environment; however, it could be implemented in a client/server architecture or an embedded system to provide rapid vector mapping responses. Future work will include the consideration of additional criteria for polygon simplification, such as shape preservation, and additional operators to support more complex cartographic generalizations such as displacement and exaggeration. In addition, while trapezoids are generalized individually in this paper, batch generalization will also be addressed in future work. Extending this method to support polygonal maps and even general maps also requires future work.

Acknowledgments: This work was supported by the National Natural Science Foundation of China (No. 41571433, 41271446, 41571439, 41201485).

Author Contributions: Mingguang Wu wrote the paper; Mingguang Wu, Taisheng Chen and Guonian Lv conceived and designed the experiments; Kun Zhang and Zhimin Jing performed the experiments; Yangli Han and Menglin Chen analyzed the results. Hong Wang conducted the literature search and created the charts.

Conflicts of Interest: There is no conflict of interest.

References

1. Wu, M.; Zhu, A.; Zheng, P.; Cui, L.; Zhang, X. An improved map-symbol model to facilitate sharing of heterogeneous qualitative map symbols. *Cartogr. Geogr. Inf. Sci.* **2017**, *44*, 62–75. [CrossRef]
2. Zeiler, M. *Modeling Our World: The Esri Guide To Geodatabase Design*, 2nd ed.; ESRI Press: California, CA, USA, 1999; ISBN 978-1589482784.
3. Galanda, M. Automated Polygon Generalization in A Multi Agent System. Ph.D. Thesis, University of Zurich, Zurich, Switzerland, 2003.
4. Zhou, M.; Chen, J.; Gong, J. Rendering interior-filled polygonal vector data in a virtual globe. *Int. J. Geogr. Inf. Sci.* **2016**, *30*, 2208–2229. [CrossRef]
5. Wu, M.; Zheng, P.; Lu, G.; Zhu, A. Chain-based polyline tessellation algorithm for cartographic rendering. *Cartogr. Geogr. Inf. Sci.* **2017**, *44*, 491–506. [CrossRef]
6. Mustafa, N.; Krishnan, S.; Varadhan, G.; Venkatasubramanian, S. Dynamic simplification and visualization of large maps. *Int. J. Geogr. Inf. Sci.* **2006**, *20*, 273–302. [CrossRef]
7. Floriani, L.D.; Magillo, P. Multiresolution Meshes Representation: Models and Data Structures. In *Tutorials on Multiresolution in Geometric Modelling*; Iske, E., Quak, E., Floater, M.S., Eds.; Springer: Berlin, Germany, 2002; pp. 193–234. ISBN 978-3-662-04388-2.
8. Azuma, D.I.; Wood, D.N.; Curless, B.; Duchamp, T.; Salesin, D.H.; Stuetzle, W. View-dependent refinement of multiresolution meshes with subdivision connectivity. In Proceedings of the 2nd International Conference on Computer Graphics, Virtual Reality, Visualisation And Interaction in Africa, Cape Town, South Africa, 3–5 February 2003; pp. 69–78.
9. Hoppe, H. Progressive meshes. In Proceedings of the 23rd Annual Conference on Computer Graphics and Interactive Techniques, New York, NY, USA, 4–9 August 1996; pp. 99–108.
10. Hoppe, H. Smooth View-Dependent Level-of-Detail Control and Its Application to Terrain Rendering. In Proceedings of the Visualization'98, North Carolina, NC, USA, 18–23 October 1998; pp. 35–42.
11. Follin, J.M.; Bouju, A. An incremental strategy for fast transmission of multi-resolution data in a mobile system. In *Map-Based Mobile Services*; Springer: Berlin, Germany, 2008; pp. 57–97. ISBN 978-3-540-26982-3.
12. Putten, J.V.; Oosterom, P.V. New result with Generalized Area Partitionings. In Proceedings of the International Symposium on Spatial Data Handling, SDH'98, Vancouver, Canada, 12–15 July 1998; pp. 485–495.
13. Meijers, M.; Oosterom, P.V. The space-scale cube: An integrated model for 2D polygonal areas and scale. In Proceedings of the 28th Urban Data Management Symposium, International Archives of Photogrammetry, Remote Sensing and Spatial Information Sciences, Delft, The Netherlands, 28–30 September 2011; pp. 95–102.
14. Li, Z. An examination of algorithms for the detection of critical points on digital cartographic lines. *Cartogr. J.* **1995**, *32*, 121–125. [CrossRef]

15. Shi, W.; Cheung, C. Performance evaluation of line simplification algorithms for vector generalization. *Cartogr. J.* **2006**, *43*, 27–44. [CrossRef]
16. Podolskaya, E.S.; Anders, K.H.; Haunert, J.H.; Sester, M. Quality Assessment for Polygon Generalization. In *Quality Aspects in Spatial Data Mining*; Taylor & Francis: Oxford, UK, 2009; Volume 211. [CrossRef]
17. Haunert, J.H.; Dilo, A.; Oosterom, P.V. Constrained set-up of the tGAP structure for progressive vector data transfer. *Comput. Geosci.* **2009**, *35*, 2191–2203. [CrossRef]
18. Oosterom, P.V.; Bos, J.V.D. An Object-Oriented Approach to the Design of Geographic Information Systems. *Comput. Graph.* **1989**, *13*, 409–418. [CrossRef]
19. Oosterom, P.V. The GAP-tree, an approach to "On-the-Fly" Map Generalization of an Area Partitioning. In Proceedings of the GISDATA Specialist Meeting on Generalization, Compiègne, France, 15–19 December 1993.
20. Oosterom, P.V. Variable-scale topological data structures suitable for progressive data transfer: The GAP-face tree and GAP-edge forest. *Cartogr. Geogr. Inf. Sci.* **2005**, *32*, 331–346. [CrossRef]
21. Oosterom, P.V.; Meijers, M. Vario-scale data structures supporting smooth zoom and progressive transfer of 2D and 3D data. *Int. J. Geogr. Inf. Sci.* **2014**, *28*, 455–478. [CrossRef]
22. Zhou, S.; Jones, C.B. *Shape-Aware Line Generalisation with Weighted Effective Area*; Springer: Berlin, Germany, 2005; ISBN 978-3-540-22610-9.
23. Corcoran, P.; Mooney, P.; Winstanley, A. Planar and non-planar topologically consistent vector map simplification. *Int. J. Geogr. Inf. Sci.* **2011**, *25*, 1659–1680. [CrossRef]
24. Jones, C.B.; Kdner, D.B.; Luo, L.Q.; Bundy, G.L.; Ware, J.M. Database design for a multi-scale spatial information system. *Int. J. Geogr. Inf. Syst.* **1996**, *10*, 901–920. [CrossRef]
25. Han, Q.; Bertolotto, M. A multi-level data structure for vector maps. In Proceedings of the 12th Annual Acm International Workshop on Geographic Information Systems, Washington, DC, USA, 8–13 August 2004; pp. 214–221.
26. Ai, T.; Li, Z.; Liu, Y. Progressive transmission of vector data based on changes accumulation model. In Proceedings of the Developments in Spatial Data Handling: 11th International Symposium on Spatial Data Handling, Leicester, UK, 23–25 August 2004; pp. 85–96.
27. Yang, B.; Purves, R.; Weibel, R. Efficient transmission of vector data over the internet. *Int. J. Geogr. Inf. Sci.* **2007**, *21*, 215–237. [CrossRef]
28. Papadimitriou, F. The Algorithmic Complexity of Landscapes. *Landsc. Res.* **2012**, *37*, 591–611. [CrossRef]
29. Wood, J.; Kirschenbauer, S.; Döllner, J.; Lopes, L.; Bodum, L. Chapter 14—Using 3D in Visualization. In *Exploring Geovisualization*, 1st ed.; Elsevier: Amsterdam, The Netherlands, 2005; pp. 295–312. ISBN 9780080445311.
30. Zhang, J.; Zhu, Y. A Method Based on Graphic Entity for Visualizing Complex Map Symbols on the Web. *Cartogr. Geogr. Inf. Sci.* **2015**, *42*, 44–53. [CrossRef]
31. Yue, S.; Yang, J.; Chen, M.; Lu, G.; Zhu, A.; Wen, Y. A function-based linear map symbol building and rendering method using Shader language. *Int. J. Geogr. Inf. Sci.* **2016**, *30*, 143–167. [CrossRef]
32. Arkin, E.M.; Held, M.; Mitchell, J.S.B.; Skiena, S.S. Hamiltonian triangulations for fast rendering. *Vis. Comput.* **1996**, *12*, 429–444. [CrossRef]
33. Rueda, A.J.; Miras, J.R.; Feito, F.R. GPU Based Rendering of Curved Polygons Using Simplicial Coverings. *Comput. Graph.* **2008**, *32*, 581–588. [CrossRef]
34. Rougier, N.P. Shader-Based Antialiased Dashed Stroked Polylines. *J. Comput. Graph. Technol.* **2013**, *2*, 105–121.
35. Ma, J.; Xu, S.; Pu, Y.; Chen, G. A real-time parallel implementation of Douglas-Peucker polyline simplification algorithm on shared memory multi-core processor computers. In Proceedings of the International Conference on Computer Application and System Modeling (ICCASM), Taiyuan, China, 22–24 October 2010.
36. MapBox. Available online: https://www.mapbox.com/pricing (accessed on 31 January 2018).
37. Žalik, B.; Jezernik, A.; Žalik, K.R. Polygon trapezoidation by sets of open trapezoids. *Comput. Graph.* **2003**, *27*, 791–800. [CrossRef]
38. Lorenzetto, G.P.; Datta, A.; Thomas, R.C. A fast trapezoidation technique for planar polygons. *Comput. Graph.* **2002**, *26*, 281–289. [CrossRef]
39. Mąka, M. The recurrent algorithm for area discretization using the trapezoidal mesh method. *Zesz. Nauk. Akad. Morska w Szczec.* **2012**, *29*, 134–139.

40. OpenStreetMap. Available online: http://www.openstreetmap.org/ (accessed on 25 May 2018).
41. Guilbert, E.; Saux, E. Cartographic generalisation of lines based on a B-spline snake model. *Int. J. Geogr. Inf. Sci.* **2008**, *22*, 847–870. [CrossRef]

© 2018 by the authors. Licensee MDPI, Basel, Switzerland. This article is an open access article distributed under the terms and conditions of the Creative Commons Attribution (CC BY) license (http://creativecommons.org/licenses/by/4.0/).

Review

Progress and Challenges on Entity Alignment of Geographic Knowledge Bases

Kai Sun [1,2,3], Yunqiang Zhu [1,2,4] and Jia Song [1,2,4,*]

1. State Key Laboratory of Resources and Environmental Information System, Beijing 100101, China; sunk@lreis.ac.cn (K.S.); zhuyq@lreis.ac.cn (Y.Z.)
2. Institute of Geographic Sciences and Natural Resources Research, Chinese Academy of Sciences, Beijing 100101, China
3. University of Chinese Academy of Sciences, Beijing 100049, China
4. Jiangsu Center for Collaborative Innovation in Geographical Information Resource Development and Application, Nanjing 210023, China
* Correspondence: songj@igsnrr.ac.cn; Tel.: +86-010-6488-9906

Received: 23 November 2018; Accepted: 29 January 2019; Published: 6 February 2019

Abstract: Geographic knowledge bases (GKBs) with multiple sources and forms are of obvious heterogeneity, which hinders the integration of geographic knowledge. Entity alignment provides an effective way to find correspondences of entities by measuring the multidimensional similarity between entities from different GKBs, thereby overcoming the semantic gap. Thus, many efforts have been made in this field. This paper initially proposes basic definitions and a general framework for the entity alignment of GKBs. Specifically, the state-of-the-art of algorithms of entity alignment of GKBs is reviewed from the three aspects of similarity metrics, similarity combination, and alignment judgement; the evaluation procedure of alignment results is also summarized. On this basis, eight challenges for future studies are identified. There is a lack of methods to assess the qualities of GKBs. The alignment process should be improved by determining the best composition of heterogeneous features, optimizing alignment algorithms, and incorporating background knowledge. Furthermore, a unified infrastructure, techniques for aligning large-scale GKBs, and deep learning-based alignment techniques should be developed. Meanwhile, the generation of benchmark datasets for the entity alignment of GKBs and the applications of this field need to be investigated. The progress of this field will be accelerated by addressing these challenges.

Keywords: geographic knowledge bases; entity alignment; similarity metrics; similarity combination; knowledge conflation; knowledge integration

---

1. Introduction

Geographic knowledge bases (GKBs) are the formal and explicit representation of geographic entities and their mutual semantic relationships. The formalized and interconnected geographic knowledge provided by GKBs can help to achieve high-quality and intelligent geographic information services, such as semantic search and personalized recommendations of geographic information, and enhance human–machine interaction (e.g., intelligent question answering). GKBs are also important knowledge sources for constructing geographic knowledge graphs [1–4], which is an important infrastructure for the applications of artificial intelligence (AI) in GIScience.

GKBs have emerged with the continuous development of technologies such as the semantic web and linked data [5,6]. GKBs are mainly represented in three different forms, namely geographic semantic webs, geographic ontologies, and digital gazetteers. Geographic semantic webs (Table 1), which mainly include GeoNames (http://www.geonames.org/), LinkedGeoData (http://www.linkedgeodata.org/), the OpenStreetMap (OSM) semantic network (https://wiki.

openstreetmap.org/wiki/OSM_Semantic_Network), the Alexandria Digital Library gazetteer (ADL) (http://legacy.alexandria.ucsb.edu/), and GeoWordNet, represent and publish geographic knowledge in the format of a resource description framework (RDF). GeoNames is a commonly used database of global toponyms, and all toponyms are categorized into nine feature classes and further subcategorized into 645 feature codes. OpenSteetMap is represented with three basic elements, including nodes, ways, and relations, and all the features are categorized into 28 classes. LinkedGeoData and the OSM semantic network have the same data source as OpenStreetMap (http://www.openstreetmap.org/), and the difference between them is that the former performs RDF conversion on all the data of OpenStreetMap and the latter only contains concepts and properties. ADL provides normalized and standardized digital gazetteers and is divided into six feature classes. GeoWordNet is the result of a semantic fusion of GeoNames and WordNet (https://wordnet.princeton.edu/), which is currently inaccessible. Some general semantic webs also contain large quantities of toponymic data, such as DBpedia (http://wiki.dbpedia.org/).

Table 1. The numbers of concepts, properties, and instances in some geographic semantic webs (obtained on 18 January 2019).

Name	Number of Concepts	Number of Properties	Number of Instances	Formalized Format
GeoNames	654	28	11,809,910	OWL
LinkedGeoData	1222	137	3,000,000,000	NT
OSM Semantic Network	1222	137	Null	RDF
ADL	210	Null	8,000,000	RDF

Geographic ontologies [7,8], such as the semantic web for Earth and environmental terminology (SWEET) ontology, GeoNames ontology (http://www.geonames.org/ontology/documentation.html), and some other domain ontologies [9,10], also include substantial geographic knowledge. Digital gazetteers, such as the Getty thesaurus for geographic names (TGN) (http://www.getty.edu/research/tools/vocabularies/tgn/), the GEOnet names server (GNS) (http://geonames.nga.mil/gns/html/), and the geographic names information system (GNIS) (https://geonames.usgs.gov/domestic/), play an important role in the recognition and ambiguity resolution of geographic entities.

These GKBs with different sources and forms, however, are independent, resulting in a problem of locally well-organized but overall dispersed and independent "information islands" [11]. This problem is also termed semantic heterogeneity, which exists in the lexicon, structure, spatial position, category, shape, data-type of property, range of property, and property value of the entities from different GKBs. The semantic heterogeneity is a significant barrier for the integration of different GKBs [12]. GKBs integration is to form the resulting global GKBs by identifying mappings between local GKBs. The integrated global GKBs can solve overlapping and gap of knowledge, therefore providing more comprehensive and clear geographic knowledge to facilitate retrieval, integration, and exchange of geospatial information.

An effective way to deal with semantic heterogeneity is entity alignment (i.e., entity resolution [13,14], duplicate detection [15], record linkage [16], etc.). For two entities of the same type from different GKBs, entity alignment can judge the relationship between them and find correspondences by measuring the semantic correlation over multidimensional information, thereby eliminating the inconsistency, such as conflict and referent ambiguity of entities in the heterogeneous GKBs.

Entity alignment, a fundamental semantic technology, has become a research hotspot as knowledge bases provide an effective way to encode meaning of information [17,18]. In computer science, the last decades have witnessed extensive studies in this field [17], and many well-known alignment systems have been developed, such as the association rule ontology matching approach (AROMA) [19,20], AgreementMaker [21,22], as well as generic ontology matching and mapping management (GOMMA) [23]. In GIScience, there have also been a great number of studies on this subject. The topics of these previous studies can be roughly separated into three categories: Similarity metrics, alignment techniques, and processing frameworks. The first category focuses on the similarity measures based on the heterogeneous features of entities. The second category includes the methods of similarity combination, alignment judgement, and result evaluation. The third category centers on the effective employment of the similarity metrics and alignment techniques.

While numerous studies exist and have led to many achievements, there is a lack of a unified definition and framework on the general concept, and a systematic summarization. To fill this gap, we present a formal and explicit framework, which could provide readers, especially novices, an introduction to understand the entity alignment as a field of study [24]. Based on this coherent framework, we organize the insights from previous studies and provide a comprehensive review to help readers to understand the existing algorithms and techniques. We also explore the key challenges for future works to facilitate progress in this field. This paper makes the following contributions:

- A formal and explicit coherent framework for the entity alignment of GKBs;
- A systematic classification and summarization of previous studies in terms of the algorithms of similarity metrics, similarity combination, alignment judgement, and result evaluation;
- A set of challenges for future research.

The remainder of this paper is structured as follows. In Section 2, the definitions and framework for the entity alignment of GKBs are formally defined and presented. In Section 3, the algorithms from previous studies are systematically examined from the three aspects of similarity metrics, similarity combination, and alignment judgement. Section 4 shows the methods and benchmarks for evaluating the alignment result. Section 5 articulates the key challenges for future research. Finally, Section 6 summarizes this study.

2. Definitions and Framework for Entity Alignment of GKBs

2.1. Basic Definitions

2.1.1. Problem Statement

The process for the entity alignment of GKBs can be simplified as shown in Figure 1. Given two entities e_1 and e_2, from two GKBs, entity alignment is performed to determine whether they are matching pairs. Some optional parameters (e.g., the relevant weights or thresholds) and background knowledge (e.g., generally accepted knowledge bases or domain lexicons) can be used to facilitate this process.

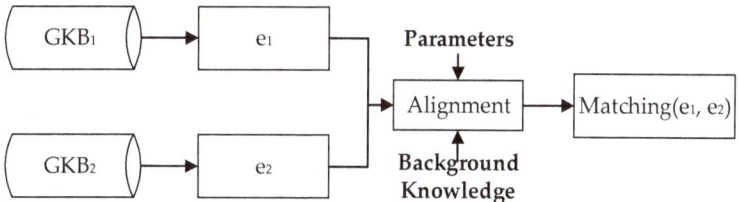

Figure 1. Schematic diagram for entity alignment of geographic knowledge bases (GKBs). (Note: GKB_1 and GKB_2 represent two geographic knowledge bases to be integrated, and e_1 and e_2 are two entities to be aligned from GKB_1 and GKB_2, respectively.).

The entity sets from GKBs can be defined as in Equation (1):

$$E(GKB) = \{(GC \cup GP \cup GI) | GC, GP, GI \in GKB\}, \qquad (1)$$

where $E(GKB)$ represents the entity set of a GKB and GC, GP, and GI represent the sets of geographic concepts, properties, and instances of the GKB, respectively.

The entity alignment of GKBs can be defined as in Equation (2):

$$Align(e_1, e_2) = \{Fun(Sim_1(e_1,e_2), Sim_2(e_1,e_2)\ldots)?Matching(e_1,e_2): \\ Null | e_1 \in E(GKB_1), e_2 \in E(GKB_2), Sim(e_1,e_2) \in [0,1]\}, \quad (2)$$

where $Sim(e_1, e_2)$ represents the normalized similarity scores computed over heterogeneous features of two entities: e_1 and e_2; $Fun(Sim_1(e_1,e_2), Sim_2(e_1,e_2)\ldots)$ represents the judging function for the relationship between them, leveraging their multidimensional similarity scores. $Matching(e_1, e_2)$ indicates that e_1 and e_2 are a matching pair, and $Null$ means that e_1 and e_2 are a nonmatching pair.

2.1.2. Explanation for Heterogeneities in Geographic Entities

The heterogeneities refer to the various differences that may arise between entities. Based on in-depth analysis of the connotations and extensions of the entities in GKBs, we identified eight types of heterogeneities: Heterogeneity in lexicon, structure, spatial position, category, shape, data-type of property, range of property, and property value. To provide a formal representation for them, we used the function $Diff(a,b)$ to represent the heterogeneities between a and b. Given two entities, $e_1 \in E(GKB_1)$ and $e_2 \in E(GKB_2)$, the eight types of heterogeneities can be defined as follows.

Heterogeneity in Lexicon (HL)

The lexical characteristics include the labels and comments of entities. HL can be defined as in Equation (3):

$$HL(e_1, e_2) = ((Diff(e_1.Label, e_2.Label)) \cup (Diff(e_1.Comment, e_2.Comment))), \quad (3)$$

where $e.Label$ and $e.Comment$ are the label and comment of entity e, respectively.

Heterogeneity in Structure (HS)

For a specific entity, structural characteristics refer to its linked entities, including hypernyms (Hypers), hyponyms (Hypos), and siblings (Siblings). HS can be defined as in Equation (4):

$$HS(e_1, e_2) = ((Diff(e_1.Hypers, e_2.Hypers)) \cup (Diff(e_1.Hypos, e_2.Hypos)) \cup (Diff(e_1.Siblings, e_2.Siblings))), \quad (4)$$

where $e.Hypers$, $e.Hypos$, and $e.Siblings$ are the hypernymic, hyponymic, and sibling nodes of entity e, respectively.

Heterogeneity in Spatial Position (HSp)

HSp refers to the difference in the spatial positions of entities and is defined as in Equation (5):

$$HSp(e_1, e_2) = Diff(e_1.Pos, e_2.Pos), \quad (5)$$

where $e.Pos$ is the spatial position of entity e.

Heterogeneity in Category (HC)

HC refers to the differences in the category to which the entities belong and is defined as in Equation (6):

$$HC(e_1, e_2) = Diff(e_1.Cat, e_2.Cat), \quad (6)$$

where $e.Cat$ is the category information of entity e.

Heterogeneity in Shape (HSh)

HSh refers to the difference in the shapes of entities and is defined as in Equation (7):

$$HSh(e_1, e_2) = Diff(e_1.Shape, e_2.Shape), \tag{7}$$

where $e.Shape$ is the shape of entity e. HSp is different than HSh. HSp is the difference in spatial distance between entities, which is usually computed over the spatial coordinates of entities. HSp exists in all types of geometry object, including point, polyline, and polygon objects. HSh just stands for the difference in geometric shapes, which has nothing to do with the spatial distance between entities. HSh exists only in two types of geometry object (i.e., polyline and polygon).

Heterogeneity in Data-Type of Property (HPdt)

There are two types of property: Data property and object property, and their data-types may be string, numerical value (for example int, float), entity, etc. HPdt refers to the heterogeneity of data-types of two properties and can be defined as in Equation (8):

$$HPdt(e_1, e_2) = Diff(Pro_1.dt, Pro_2.dt), \tag{8}$$

where $Pro.dt$ is the data-type of property Pro.

Heterogeneity in range of property (HPr)

The range of property refers to the range of values for a property. HPr represents the difference in the ranges of two properties and is defined as in Equation (9):

$$HPr(e_1, e_2) = Diff(Pro_1.range, Pro_2.range), \tag{9}$$

where $Pro.range$ is the range of property Pro.

Heterogeneity in Property Value (HPv)

HPv refers to that the values corresponding to the same property of two entities are different and is defined as in Equation (10):

$$HPv(e_1, e_2) = (Diff(e_1.Pro.Value, e_2.Pro.Value) \cap (e_1.Pro \equiv e_2.Pro), \tag{10}$$

where $e.Pro$ is the property of entity e, and $e.Pro.Value$ is the value corresponding to this property.

The heterogeneities involved in specific entity pairs are closely related to the type of entity (concept, properties, and instance). The heterogeneities in each type of entities are analyzed, as shown in Table 2. The differences in concepts are reflected in their lexicon and structure, and the possible heterogeneities in properties include heterogeneity in their lexicon, structure, data-type, and range, and the heterogeneities in instances are reflected in their lexicon, space, category, shape, and property value.

Table 2. Heterogeneities in each type of entities.

Entity Type	Heterogeneities							
	HL	HS	HSp	HC	HSh	HPdt	HPr	HPv
Concepts	✓	✓						
Properties	✓	✓				✓	✓	
Instances	✓		✓	✓	✓			✓

2.2. General Framework

2.2.1. Basic Ideas

Entity alignment can be divided into one-dimensional and multidimensional entity alignment according to the number of entity types for alignment. One-dimensional entity alignment is to align one type of entities from concept, property or instance. Most studies are on concept-level alignment [25], followed by those on instance-level alignment [26], and property-level alignment [27,28]. Multidimensional entity alignment is to simultaneously align two or all three types of entities, and there are few studies on this subject. Only Yu leveraged the similarity scores computed over multidimensional features and the approval voting strategy to construct an integrated framework, which could simultaneously align all three types of entities [29].

The basic ideas of entity alignment are tightly associated with the relationship among different types of entities. The three types of entities (concept, property, and instance) are not isolated from each other and show a relationship of comparatively strong cognitive logic. Properties are descriptions of the characteristics of things, which are the first level to cognize things. According to the similarities and differences in properties, things that have common properties belong to the same class, which is called the concept. Things of the same class can be repartitioned according to the differences in their properties, and then the hypernymic and hyponymic concepts can be defined. The hyponymic concept inherits all the properties of the hypernymic concept. An object, which conforms to all the properties of a certain class, is an instance belonging to this class, indicating that the instance inherits all the properties of concept to which it belongs. Thus, the relationship among the three types of entity can be summarized as follows: Properties are the definition of concept, concept is the abstraction of instances, and instances are the instantiation of the concept and properties.

According to the above relationship among the three types of entity, the basic ideas for entity alignment can be divided into schema-level and instance-level ideas. The former mainly aims at concept alignment and includes three types of approaches. The commonly employed type of approach is instance-based concept alignment. It is based on the cognitive logic that instances are the instantiation of concept, and it is assumed that if the instances belonging to two concepts are matched, these two concepts are matched. Thus, this approach discriminates matched concept pairs or nonmatched concept pairs by measuring the similarity between the instances belonging to the concept pairs to be matched [30]. The second type of approach is property-based concept alignment. It is based on the cognitive logic that properties are the definition of concept and is on the basis of the assumption that if the properties corresponding to two concepts are aligned, these two concepts are aligned. Li et al. used water body ontology as a case study and summarized 17 properties shared by all the concepts in the water body ontology. The similarity scores among these properties were computed over the shared members of the range domain of properties [28]. Then, the aligned concept pairs can be identified according to the similarity scores of properties. This method can actually perform alignment leveraging the semantic information of properties. The third type of approach directly performs concepts alignment based on their own information [29]. Instance-level alignment mainly relies on the information of instances to perform alignment.

Specific implementation techniques are consistent across different basic ideas and can be divided into three types: Element-based, structure-based, and hybrid techniques [31]. Element-based techniques consider entities in isolation, leveraging information about entity itself to perform alignment [32]. Structure-based techniques examine the structural information of entities, considering the linked entities of an entity in the structure of knowledge bases [33]. Hybrid techniques combine element-based and structure-based techniques.

In addition, performing entity alignment with background knowledge, which involves enough entities in common with entities to be aligned, can help to improve the result. For example, the near-synonyms, synonyms, and hypernymic–hyponymic relationships among the vocabularies provided by WordNet can support the calculation of the lexical similarity of entities [34–37]. Involving human experts can also optimize the alignment process [38]. Prior to performing entity alignment, preprocessing steps can be adopted to remove entity pairs that are impossible to be matched or select potential matching entity pairs, thereby avoiding performing calculations over all entity pairs and reducing computational complexity. This is especially important when the number of entity pairs to be matched is large. For example, a blocking algorithm is performed to group possible matching entities into one block according to the similarity of literal description of entities to reduce the computational requirement [39].

2.2.2. Standard Workflow

The standard workflow for the entity alignment of GKBs is consistent across different basic ideas and implementation techniques. It includes four steps, as shown in Figure 2:

Step 1. Similarity measurement. Determining suitable similarity metrics for each type of heterogeneities in entities.
Step 2. Similarity combination. Selecting an effective method to combine multidimensional similarity scores.
Step 3. Alignment judgement. Taking a decision for entity pairs to be matched based on a predefined threshold or leveraging an effective judging approach.
Step 4. Result evaluation. Using suitable benchmarks and evaluation metrics to assess result quality.

The next two sections detail the algorithms from previous studies about the four steps.

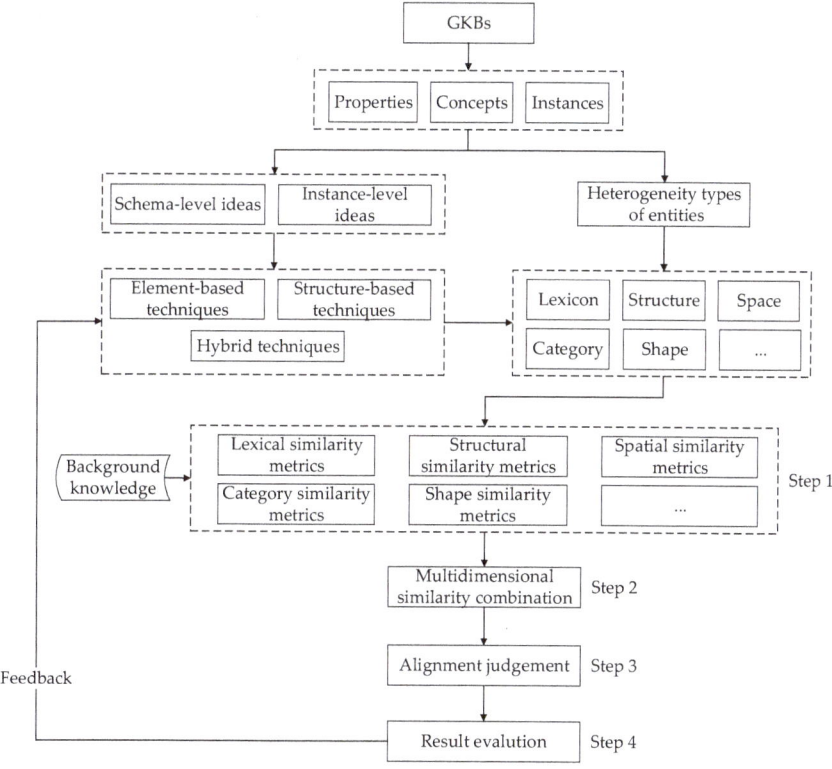

Figure 2. Standard workflow for entity alignment of GKBs.

3. Algorithms of Entity Alignment

This section analyzes and reviews the algorithms of entity alignment in detail from the three aspects of similarity metrics, similarity combination, and alignment judgement.

3.1. Similarity Metrics

Although there are eight types of heterogeneities in entities from different GKBs, the first five types are commonly used. Previous studies targeted the concepts and instances as the main entity types to align and ignored the alignment of properties. Moreover, it is difficult to define essential properties, which can actually represent the connotation of concepts and the range domain of properties. Thus, the latter three types, which focus on the differences in geographic properties, are extremely rarely used or have never been leveraged for the aligning entity of GKBs. Thus, we only conducted a review on the similarity metrics for lexicon, structure, spatial position, category, and shape.

3.1.1. Lexical Similarity Metrics

Lexical similarity metrics are the most useful metrics for entity alignment, although there are many other types of similarity metrics for different types of heterogeneities [40]. The lexical corpuses of geographic entities are composed of their labels and comments. Santos et al. and Recchia and Louwerse conducted comprehensive comparisons of various lexical similarity metrics. They pointed out that the differences in performance of the involved lexical similarity metrics were relatively small [40,41]. The lexical similarity metrics can be roughly grouped into three categories, namely character-based, token-based, and vector-based metrics. Character-based metrics calculate lexical similarity by measuring the difference of two original strings. Token-based metrics extract tokens from original strings, based on which the similarity between original strings is computed. Vector-based metrics compute similarity based on vector representations of original strings.

A basic character-based metric is edit distance (Levenshtein distance) [42]. Edit distance leverages the minimum number of editing operations required to transform a string a into another string b. Allowable editing operations include insertion, deletion, and substitution. This metric is commonly employed in lexical similarity computations for geographic entities [43–45]. However, due to the various variabilities of gazetteers, such as abbreviations and merges of strings, edit distance is not particularly suitable for measuring the similarity of feature names [46]. The Jaccard similarity coefficient is also a commonly used metric. It measures similarity by the ratio of the number of characters in common between two strings to the total number of characters. Sehgal et al. measured the similarity of location names by this metric [26]. However, this metric does not take the character transposition of strings into consideration.

The Jaro metric is a heuristic character-based metric. It computes similarity based on the number of characters that are present in both two strings and the number of character transpositions. Auer et al. used this metric to measure the similarity of labels of entities in LinkedGeoData and DBpedia [47]. A refined version of the Jaro metric is the Jaro–Winkler metric, which considers the weight assignment of characters based on their different positions in strings. This metric suggests that the strings, which begin with the same characters, should be given a higher similarity score. Therefore, the matched beginning part of the strings should be assigned greater weight. Stadler et al. used this metric to measure the similarity among the labels of entities from LinkedGeoData, DBpedia, and GeoNames [48]. Martins also employed this metric in the detection of duplicate gazetteer records [43]. There are also other character-based metrics employed in the alignment of geographic entities, such as the soft-term frequency-inverse document frequency (Soft-TFIDF) distance, Monge–Elkan distance, and Double Metaphone distance [29,43].

As for the token-based metrics, standard steps for extracting tokens from strings include tokenizing (extracting the recognizable substrings and marked symbols from strings), removing punctuations, stemming, removing words in a stop words list (stop words refer to words which are either insignificant or too common), and completing abbreviations. After this procedure is completed, the token set of strings can be obtained [49]. Given the token sets Token(S_1) for string S_1 and Token(S_2) for string S_2, there are many algorithms for calculating the similarity between them. A simple method is to compute the ratio of the shared tokens of the two sets to the total numbers of the two sets [50], but this method does not tolerate the spelling errors of token words. A more complex method is to calculate the edit distance between all token pairs of the two token sets [49]. This method has high accuracy, but when the number of token pairs is comparatively large, it will suffer from high computational complexity. To simplify this method, for all the token pairs, a match score of 1, 0.5, 0.25, and 0 is assigned for four types of situations corresponding to exact match, prefix or stemmed match, infix match (partial existing in anywhere within a string, except in its beginning), and complete mismatch, respectively [51].

Standard vector-based metrics compute cosine similarity between vector representations of strings. Wang et al. constructed virtual documents for entities by combining their labels and comments and represented the virtual documents with a vector. Every element of this vector was weight computed using the TF-IDF method [52], and the weight was assigned to the corresponding words of virtual documents [45]. Then, the lexical similarity between two entities was computed as the cosine value between the two vectors of their virtual documents. A more sophisticated method proposed by Ballatore et al. extracted the definitional terms (nouns, verbs, adjectives, etc.) for geographic entities from their comments to construct semantic vectors. A matrix was constructed, each cell of which contained a similarity between two terms from the vectors [53]. The similarity scores between term pairs were computed with WordNet. Then, the matrix would be used to compute the vector–vector similarity scores. When the comments of entities are rich, this method is able to attain higher accuracy. However, the accuracy will be greatly reduced with sparse text.

Word embedding, which is a research focus in the field of natural language processing (NLP), is a more advanced method to transform strings into vector representation. For a given document (word sequence), each different word in this document will be represented as a low-dimensional vector of real numbers by a mapping model. This method is based on the assumption that the representations in terms of the contexts of "similar words" are similar. Word2vector achieves the idea of word embedding and contains two model architectures: Continuous bag-of-words (CBOW) and Skip-Gram [54,55]. The currently commonly used toolkits: Word2vector (https://code.google.com/archive/p/word2vec/source/default/source) and gensim (https://pypi.org/project/gensim/) are the implementation of Word2vector model. In terms of entity alignment, word embedding-based methods initially transform original strings of entities into vector representations. Whether entity pairs are matching or nonmatching will be decided by comparing their vector representations. Instead of defining and extracting feature vectors for entities manually as in previous methods, this method can automatically generate vector representations for original strings of entities, thereby improving automation and reducing manual intervention. Santos et al. achieved a word embedding-based method using a deep neural network to generate representations for toponyms. These representations were processed by a feed forward network to judge entity alignment [56].

3.1.2. Structural Similarity Metrics

A knowledge base can be represented with a tree-like or graph-like structure. With the position of entity and the relationship with other entities in the tree-like or graph-like structure, the structural similarity between entity pairs can be measured. In the general alignment systems, structural similarity is an important metric. Due to the different perspectives and purposes for constructing different GKBs, there are great differences in their structures [39]. Therefore, it is inappropriate to assign greater weight to the structural factor in geographic entity alignment. Delgado and Finat used a string-based method, WordNet-based method, and general alignment system to perform the concept alignment of GKBs, including DBpedia, LinkedGeoData, and CityGML (http://schemas.opengis.net/citygml/).

Their results showed that the general alignment system, which put emphasis on structural factors, presented the worst precision and recall [57], thereby proving the aforementioned conclusion.

For GKBs with a tree-like structure, structural similarity is computed based on the relationship between sets of hypernymic nodes, hyponymic nodes, and sibling nodes of entities [58]. The descendant's similarity inheritance considered the explanatory roles of ancestors of entity for the identification of the specific entity [59]. The ancestor nodes include all the nodes on the path from root node to the closest hypernymic node of entity. Then, the structural similarity between entity pairs was computed over the weighted sum of similarities between all the ancestor node pairs of entity pairs. Weights were computed over the distance from each ancestor node to the entity [33].

Similarly, the algorithms based on similarities between hyponymic node pairs (e.g., ancestor's similarity contribution (ASC)) or sibling node pairs (e.g., sibling's similarity contribution (SSC)) also used the cumulative value of similarities among the corresponding nodes [22,59]. The metric based on the Jaccard coefficient was relatively simple, and it calculated structural similarity by the ratio of the number of shared nodes to the number of all nodes linked with the entity pairs [43].

Different than the GKB with a tree-like structure, the GKB with a graph-like structure just emphasizes the simple links between entities and lacks in clear ancestor–descendant and sibling relationship between entities. Thus, the structural similarity metrics for tree-like structures are not applicable to graph-like structures. A commonly used algorithm for calculating structural similarity in graph-like structures is the similarity flooding algorithm [60]. This algorithm transforms the native structures of two GKBs to be matched into two labeled directed graphs, which are then merged into one directed graph named a pairwise connectivity graph. Each node in this connectivity graph refers to a node pair from the two graphs before merging and is called a map pair. Each map pair is with an initial similarity score. Then, the connectivity graph will be transformed into the induced propagation graph when the initial similarity of map pair propagates through the graph over a number of iterative calculations according to the similarities of its adjacent map pairs. When the fixpoint, which means the similarities of all the map pairs remain unchanged, has been reached, the algorithm will converge to the final results. The final similarity of each map pair in the propagation graph is regarded as the structural similarity between two entities. Yu et al. and Kim et al. used the similarity flooding algorithm to measure structural similarity between entities in GKBs [29,61].

The penetrating rank (P-Rank) algorithm is also a recursive algorithm for graph matching [62]. For two entities to be matched, this algorithm is based on two assumptions: (1) If they are linked with similar entities, then they are similar; (2) if they link to similar entities, then they are similar. Algorithms like co-citation and coupling are the variants of P-Rank [63,64]. These algorithms can obtain excellent results when there are dense links among entities in GKBs. Ballatore et al. applied the co-citation algorithm to compute the structural similarity of entities in OpenStreetMap [53,65].

3.1.3. Spatial Similarity Metrics

The spatial characteristic is the unique characteristic of geographic entities and makes them distinguishable from other types of entities. Spatial similarity is, thus, an important matching factor for geographic entity alignment [66], but it is not sufficient on its own [49]. It must be used in concert with other metrics emphasized in the general alignment system, such as lexical and structural similarity metrics [67].

Standard methods for computing spatial similarity are based on the spatial relationships (metric, topological, and sequential relationships) between entities. The metric relationship includes the distance, height, length, and proportion relationships, and the most commonly used is the distance relationship. A simple method is to calculate the Euclidean distance between entities based on the plane coordinates of spatial objects. Sehgal et al. and Yu et al. respectively used Euclidean distance and the inverse of it to calculate spatial similarity between two entities [26,29]. Safra et al. proposed a location-based algorithm, which computed Euclidean distance between points to find the corresponding entities for integrating geospatial datasets [68].

In order to make the spatial similarity more accurate, the distance between entities could be measured based on the spherical coordinate using a more complex haversine formula to simulate the ellipsoid surface of the earth [48]. The Hausdorff algorithm further considered the size of spatial entities [69]. The length relationship could be used to calculate the similarity between line objects [30,70]. The proportion relationship was mainly employed in measuring the proportion of coincidence in the spatial coverage of entities [51,71].

Integrating the metric relationship with other types of spatial relationships can help to calculate spatial similarity [72]. Beard and Sharma checked the topological relationship between entities before measuring the metric relationship [73]. Larson and Frontiera adopted a regression model to integrate topological and metric relationships to measure spatial similarity [74]. Li and Frederico proposed a method which comprehensively used metric, topological, and sequential relationships [75].

3.1.4. Category Similarity Metrics

Category similarity is often applied in toponym matching and location parsing. The traditional metrics for category similarity can be separated into three classes: Structure-based, content-based, and context-based metrics. Structure-based metrics are based on the category hierarchy of the classification system of toponyms. Given the category information of two toponyms, C_A and C_B, they are mapped to the category hierarchy. If C_A and C_B are on the same classification system, their closest common parent category C_P will be found; otherwise, C_A and C_B must be uniformly converted to a predefined classification system before C_P is found in this classification system. Category similarity is computed over C_P [51,71,76]. According to the different details of methods for calculating the similarity between two C_P, there are two types of methods. One of them directly represents the category similarity with the number of levels from the root node to C_P in the category hierarchy. The other type is performed based on the numbers of edges from C_A to C_P, from C_B to C_P, and from C_P to the root node in the category hierarchy.

Content-based metrics are based on the semantic information of categories of entities. According to information theory, the similarity between two categories depends on the information shared by them. Thus, category similarity can be calculated by quantitatively evaluating the common information content of two categories [77]. Kavouras et al. computed category similarity based on the semantic information, including cause, purpose, location, etc., which were extracted from the category description [78]. The matching-distance similarity measure (MDSM) algorithm combined the distinguishing features of categories with the semantic relationship between them to calculate their semantic distance, over which the computation of category similarity was performed [79].

Some improvements to the MDSM algorithm have been proposed. The MDSM algorithm is actually based on the assumption that the properties of category are equally important. However, the importance of different properties is completely different under different contexts. Thus, different weights were assigned to different properties of categories in different scenarios to improve this algorithm [80]. The synonym sets of category could also be used to improve this algorithm [81].

Context-based metrics calculate category similarity by means of background knowledge. For example, the similarity between geographic terminologies of thesaurus can be measured with the aid of a lexical database, such as WordNet [82].

3.1.5. Shape Similarity Metrics

Different than spatial similarity metrics for spatial distance between entities, shape similarity is to measure the difference between geometric shapes of entities. Shape matching is widely studied and applied in fields such as computer vision and pattern recognition [83], while this matching factor is rarely used in the alignment of geographic entities. The basic idea of shape matching is to represent the shape of entity into a normalized form, over which shape matching is performed indirectly [49]. The commonly used method is to match the nodes, which represent the shapes of entities. Safra et al. used a node matching algorithm to calculate the shape similarity of line objects [84]. Goodchild and

Hunter, as well as Fairbairn and Albakri, proposed a simpler method. The buffer zones for linear entities were initially constructed, and shape similarity between entities was indirectly computed over their buffer zones [85,86]. Du et al. also matched spatial objects leveraging the buffers of their geometries [87].

In addition to the abovementioned similarity metrics for lexicon, structure, space, category, and shape, we notice that some previous studies creatively used other features of geographic entities to complete alignment. Zhu et al. thought that if the respective spatial distribution patterns of all instances belonging to two concepts were similar, these two concepts were similar [88]. Based on this idea, the similarity between concepts was measured according to the similarity of local or global spatial distribution of instances using some metrics (e.g., Moran's I and the kernel density estimation). For the geographic concepts, which are described by description logics (DL), Janowicz et al. measured the similarity between concepts based on the degree of coincidence of their DL descriptions [89]. Kokla and Kavouras provided a formalized representation for geographic concepts based on concept lattices and integrated geographic concepts based on formal concept analysis (FCA) [90,91].

3.2. Similarity Combination

After the similarity scores on multidimensional features of geographic entities are measured, they will be combined organically, leveraging a suitable similarity combination algorithm [92]. Similarity combination includes two processes: (1) Selecting similarity scores computed over features, which can effective improve the alignment results; (2) selecting a similarity combination model to combine the selected similarity scores.

The strategies for feature selection can be divided into three types. The first type is to select the similarities on all features directly. The second type adopts suitable selection principles or algorithms to select effective features, which can actually contribute to the alignment process. Effective feature must meet two principles: (1) This feature can effectively distinguish the matching entity pairs from the nonmatching entity pairs; (2) the number of matching entity pairs obtained using this single feature is close to the minimum number of entities in two knowledge bases to be matched [93]. The algorithms for feature selection include principal component analysis (PCA), analytic hierarchy process (AHP), expert scoring, etc. The third type, called the single factor judgement method, is to select the single feature with the greatest contribution and set the similarity threshold. When the similarity computed over this feature between two entities exceeds the threshold, they are matching pairs.

The models for combining similarities over multidimensional features include the feature vector model, geometric model, and mathematical model [94]. The feature vector model is to represent the multidimensional similarities into feature vectors, and the overall similarity is calculated over the cosine between the two vectors. In the geometric models, multidimensional similarities are represented as multidimensional coordinates, over which the aggregation of similarities is performed. The mathematical model aggregates multidimensional similarities leveraging methods of mathematical operation, which include: (1) The minimum or maximum value method, (2) average value method, (3) weighted sum method, (4) probabilistic method, (5) fuzzy aggregation method, and (6) rough sets method [95].

The most commonly used method for similarity combination is the weighted sum in the mathematical model [96]. This method assigns weight to each similarity metric and calculates the weighted sum of similarities. Thus, the multidimensional similarities are linearly combined with this method [97]. The key to this method is the weight assignment for each metrics.

The simplest method for weight assignment is the average value method, which assigns equal weight to each factor. The most direct method is to select the optimal weight assignment through multiple experiments [51,61]. Zhu et al. adopted the weight assignment method based on expert scoring. In this method, the judgement matrix was initially designed. Each element of this matrix was a relative importance score for each metric provided by the invited domain experts. The elements of the normalized eigenvector of this matrix were the weights for each metric [71]. Tran et al. proposed a clustering-based weight estimation method. It used the K-means algorithm to divide the similarity matrix for each metric into two classes: One class with a higher mean value and the other class with a lower mean value. Then, all the similarities that belonged to the second class would be filtered out. The weight was calculated by the ratio of the number of rows that had a value in the matrix to the number of values in the first class [93]. Mckenzie et al. ranked the respective results in terms of accuracy, which were computed over each single feature of name, category, position, and topic. The weight for each feature was assigned according to the ordinal ranking [98]. Li et al. proposed an entropy-based weight assignment method to determine the weights corresponding to each feature for merging multisource geo-ontologies. In this method, the information entropy for each feature was initially computed using axiomatic characterizations of information entropy. The weight for a single feature was computed by the ratio of its information entropy to the total information entropy of all single features [99].

3.3. Alignment Judgement

The standard method for alignment judgement is based on a threshold over the overall similarity, computed by combining the multidimensional similarities. If the overall similarity between two entities is beyond the predefined threshold, they are regarded as aligned correspondence. A threshold that is too high or too low will probably lead to alignment misjudgment for entity pairs, thereby making bad results. Thus, tuning the threshold is important for achieving optimal results.

In order to avoid tuning the threshold manually and to minimize human intervention, some previous studies focused on discriminating alignments automatically based on multiple similarity metrics. Supervised machine learning was commonly used for automatic geographic entity alignment [26,43,44,76]. With multiple similarity scores regarded as input, supervised machine learning models were trained by labeled entity pairs. The trained model could decide whether entity pairs to be matched are aligned based on their multiple similarity metrics. Santos et al. leveraged support vector machines (SVM), decision trees, and random forests to match toponyms, and their results showed that decision trees could achieve better results [40]. Martins also used machine learning techniques to detect duplicate gazetteers [43,44]. Li et al. and Chen et al. used an artificial neural network (ANN) model to match geographic concepts [28,100]. The supervised machine learning method actually performs a nonlinear combination for multiple similarity metrics [100]. Although it can learn an optimal scheme for similarity combination automatically, it requires large-scale training datasets, which are difficult to prepare, for a satisfactory trained model.

There are also some other algorithms which classify entity pairs as either matching or nonmatching automatically based on multiple similarity metrics. The voting-based method does not directly perform a numerical calculation on the similarity scores but generates respective matched results based on each metric. All the matched results are aggregated by voting, and the entity pairs with more affirmative votes are the final matched entity pairs [45]. Yu et al. aligned entities from OpenStreetMap and GeoNames by performing a voting-based method on multiple metrics, including spatial, lexical, and structural metrics [29]. Bock and Hettenhausen formulated entity alignment as an optimization problem, which was tackled with an iterative algorithm based on particle swarm optimization [101]. Each entity pair to be matched was represented as a particle in this algorithm, and the convergence of swarm was guided by proportional likelihood values assigned to each correspondence. Pareto ranking, which is a multiobjective evolutionary algorithm, was also used to find correspondences in heterogeneous geo-ontologies based on various similarity metrics [102].

These classical methods showed a good performance for entity alignment. However, they rely on multidimensional similarities computed over features of entity. Thus, they are actually a semi-automatic method. In order to avoid computing similarity and realize completely automatic entity alignment, Santos et al. adopted a deep neural network to align toponyms based on their original strings rather than similarity scores [56]. They initially generated representations from the sequences of bytes of original strings, leveraging gated recurrent units (GRUs), a type of recurrent neural network (RNN) architecture. The feed forward network processed these representations and made an alignment decision. However, this method only leveraged lexicon features, thereby ignoring other features of geographic entities.

4. Evaluation of Entity Alignment

Evaluating alignment approaches of geographic entities is necessary to discover their weaknesses and strengths and choose the most suitable approach in a predefined context [103]. This step is to assess the correctness and effectiveness of entity alignment results using a suitable evaluation method and the same gold standard. Thus, the evaluation method and gold standard are two key factors in this process.

The evaluation methods can be divided into two classes: Cognitive plausibility-oriented and task-oriented methods [34]. The cognitive plausibility-oriented method is used to evaluate the simulation ability of the alignment algorithm for cognitive and behavior systems of humans [104,105]. The investigating method for cognitive plausibility is usually to compare the alignment results, which are provided by human subjects, and the alignment algorithm, for the same entity pairs to be matched. Subjects can easily decide whether entity pairs correspond based on their own cognition ability for entities. Thus, the stronger the simulating ability of an alignment algorithm for judging the process of subjects is, the higher its cognitive plausibility is, and the better the result computed by this algorithm is. Given the alignment result generated by human subjects R_S, which is usually regarded as the ground truth, and the corresponding computational result R_C, the cognitive plausibility of the alignment algorithm can be measured by calculating Spearman's correlation coefficient $\rho(R_S, R_C)$ between R_S and R_C.

The task-oriented method applies the alignment algorithm in a specific task and assesses its performance from what the degree of satisfaction is about the status of task completion with the indicators of precision, recall, and F1-measure [106], which are frequently used in information retrieval. The precision (P) is the ratio of the number of correctly aligned pairs R_T to the total number of discovered corresponding pairs N_A; the recall (R) is the ratio of R_T to the number of desired aligned pairs N_T in the gold standard, and N_T is the true value; and F1-Measure is the harmonic mean of P and R. All the three metrics have been defined in Equations (13) and (15).

$$P = R_T/N_A \tag{11}$$

$$P = R_T/N_A \tag{12}$$

$$F1 = 2 \times P \times R/(P+R) \tag{13}$$

The well-defined and widely recognized gold standards, which are also known as benchmark datasets, are necessary to provide a common objective basis to make the results of different algorithms comparable [103]. In the Oxford Dictionary of English, the term 'gold standard' is explained as "A thing of superior quality which serves as a point of reference against which other things of its type may be compared" (https://en.oxforddictionaries.com/definition/gold_standard). In computer science, gold standard refers to human-generated datasets which consist of testing data and correct output results (i.e., ground truth) [107]. For a specific task, it can capture the behavior and cognitive patterns of humans, quantify the relevance between machine-generated and human-generated results, and thus be used as a benchmark to evaluate the performance of the computational method. An actually valid gold standard should be open, accessible, persistent, and unbiased for providing reliable and fair evaluation results, and it needs to meet certain requirements, such as coverage, quality, and precision [103,107].

In computer science, dozens of benchmark datasets have been created [108], such as XBenchmatch [109] and STBenchmark [110]. In addition, some projects on assessing entity alignment have been carried out. The Semantic Evaluation at Large Scale (SEALS) project (http://www.seals-project.eu/) provides a software infrastructure for evaluating semantic web tools, including tools for entity alignment. The Ontology Alignment Evaluation Initiative (OAEI) (http://oaei.

ontologymatching.org/) provides benchmark datasets annually for participants to evaluate different systems and algorithms for ontology alignment [111]. Each benchmark dataset is composed of reference ontology, target ontology, and reference alignment. The reference ontology contains 33 concepts, 24 object properties, 40 data properties, and 50 instances. The target ontology is composed of many kinds of alterations of reference ontology, including lexical changes, synonym substitution, compression of annotation, and flattening or expanding the hierarchical structure. Each type of alterations aims at a specific type of heterogeneity issues. The reference alignment is the desired result of entity alignment. All the participating alignment systems are employed to match the reference ontology and target ontology. The performance evaluation for these systems is implemented by comparing their results with the reference alignment. The OAEI can relatively comprehensively evaluate the performance, coverage, stability, and reusability of alignment systems.

Due to the spatial feature of geographic entities, the entity alignment algorithms for GKBs are different from the ones for general knowledge bases. Thus, the benchmarks for evaluating the alignment systems of computer science may not be applicable to GIScience. Meanwhile, there are very few benchmarks exclusively targeting geographic entity alignment. For example, PABench (POI Alignment Benchmark) contains 1580 entities and several test cases covering different situations of heterogeneities [112].

Some benchmark datasets, which were designed for evaluating the similarity metrics for geographic terms, can also be used to evaluate entity alignment algorithms. GeReSiD (https://github.com/ucd-spatial/Datasets) (geo relatedness and similarity dataset) contains 97 geographic terms from OpenStreetMap and 50 term pairs, for which the similarity ranking was provided by 203 human subjects [107]. The MDSM dataset created by Rodriguez and Egenhofer for assessing their MDSM algorithm is composed of 33 geographic terms, which cover natural and man-made features, and 108 term pairs. Seventy-two human subjects were asked to rank these pairs by their similarity scores [80].

5. Challenges and Future Research

As shown in the previous sections, massive outstanding achievements for the entity alignment of GKBs, in terms of similarity metrics, similarity combination, alignment judgement, and result evaluation, have been made. Meanwhile, this semantic technique has been widely used in the integration and conflation of geographic data or knowledge [113,114], toponym resolution [26,43,44,66], correlation and discovery of geographic information [58,71,115–118], web service chain composition [119,120], and personalized recommendations [121,122]. However, there are still some challenges, which need to be addressed in the future.

5.1. Quality Assessment of GKBs

The quality of GKBs has a major impact on the result of entity alignment. There are significant differences in the knowledge quality of multisource GKBs. Especially for GKBs generated from volunteered geographic information (VGI), this problem is more prominent [123]. Therefore, quality assessment for geographic knowledge in GKBs needs to be investigated. There have been some studies focused on quality assessment of geographic knowledge from GKBs [123–126]. The quality measures to describe the quality of GKBs include positional accuracy, thematic accuracy, topological accuracy, completeness, consistency, temporal accuracy, and semantic accuracy. Many methods have been developed to assess the positional accuracy, thematic accuracy, and topological consistency by comparing with a reference dataset. However, few methods exist to assess the rest of the quality measures. More methods to handle these quality measures should be developed in the future.

5.2. Feature Selection and Algorithms Optimization

The various heterogeneous types of entities in GKBs have been explained in the Section 2.1, and each of them focuses on different aspects of entities. Meanwhile, alignment tasks usually have different requirements and constraints in terms of accuracy, completeness, and efficiency, thereby making feature selection a multiple criteria decision-making problem. Thus, it is very critical and challenging to determine the best composition of features for a specific task. A similar problem also exists in metrics selection, because there are many different metrics for each type of heterogeneity. The methods of AHP, PCA, machine learning, and ad hoc rules have been used for feature or metrics selection [127–130]. In addition, features that are not still employed should be considered. The data-type and range of properties should be further considered to align properties, and the instance alignment process should take the property value into consideration. Temporality is an intrinsic feature of the geographic entities, and spatial coverage and property values of geographic entity may change over time [67]. However, previous studies rarely take the temporal feature of entities into consideration [131], thereby sometimes leading to incorrect results of entity alignment.

Taking both the accuracy and efficiency of algorithms into account, how to optimize algorithms of similarity metrics, similarity combination, alignment judgement, and result evaluation is another issue [132]. The methods for finding the most suitable parameters of similarity measurement have been discussed [133,134]. Developing new algorithms with the benefit of new techniques in computer science can also facilitate the progress of this field. The methods of pareto ranking and particle swarm optimization have been employed for entity alignment [101,102]. The word embedding method in the field of NLP should be continuously studied and used for entity alignment. In addition, the majority of existing algorithms only align one type of entities, including concepts, properties, and instances, so developing holistic algorithms, which can complete a one-shot alignment for all types of entities, is necessary.

5.3. Alignment Techniques Integrated with Background Knowledge

GKBs are usually developed in specific contexts, which include relevant background knowledge, but the knowledge is often not directly represented in the developed GKBs. Moreover, some GKBs lack enough specifications. These problems may cause ambiguity in entities, thereby leading to incorrect alignments. Thus, integrating background knowledge into alignment is particularly necessary to achieve better results. The background knowledge is represented as multiple forms, such as domain corpora, domain ontologies or upper-level ontologies, existing aligned entity pairs, and web pages. There are some previous studies which performed alignment by means of lexicon, such as WordNet [34–37], but other forms of background knowledge have rarely been used. Thus, techniques which combine with multisource background knowledge need to be investigated.

5.4. Unified Infrastructure for Entity Alignment of GKBs

Most of the previous studies are experimental or in the prototype stage and cannot be applied in realistic scenarios. Thus, establishing a stable and unified infrastructure for the entity alignment of GKBs, which integrates a variety of alignment algorithms and can complete, store, share, and reuse alignments, is an important research mission in the future. This infrastructure will greatly facilitate the practical application of this field. In computer science, some systems, which provide many alignment methods and libraries of alignments, and can be used at design time and run time, have been designed [135–137]. This is of important reference value for designing similar infrastructures in GIScience.

5.5. Entity Alignment of Large-Scale GKBs

Under the era of geographic big data, the scales of GKBs have become increasingly large, and their structures are more complex, thereby bringing enormous growth in the computational complexity for alignment algorithms. However, existing methods rarely consider resource consumption, thus posing a challenge to the efficiency of entity alignment. There are two perspectives to tackle this problem.

From the perspective of data sources, the computation load of entity alignment is directly proportional to the size of GKBs and the number of entity pairs to be matched. Thus, a straightforward solution is to partition GKBs into proper fragments, namely modularization of GKBs, and to reduce the number of entity pairs to be matched with some preprocessing steps [138,139]. Alignment algorithms are performed over split, smaller GKBs and preprocessed less entity pairs.

From the perspective of methods, the basic idea is to make alignment algorithms scalable and parallelized. In computer science, some previous studies parallelized original algorithms based on the parallel programming environment, such as the message passing interface (MPI) [18], or deployed alignment algorithms on distributed computing platforms, such as Hadoop, Spark et al. [140–142]. The parallel and distributed processing of alignment tasks for GKBs needs to be covered in the future.

5.6. Deep Learning-Based Entity Alignment of GKBs

Traditional methods abide by the standard workflow for aligning geographic entities. Therefore, the result of entity alignment is mainly determined by the selection of features and similarity metrics, and thus with varying influence of human intervention. Deep learning methods can complete end-to-end learning and learn intrinsic features of original data automatically, thereby reducing the influence caused by human intervention at a maximum level. Thus, in order to avoid the subjective factors of humans, we should try to develop novel methods based on deep learning to achieve automatic alignment. The key to this method is that it requires large-scale training datasets, which are difficult to prepare. This method is well worth investigating, because it can break through the standard workflow.

5.7. Benchmark Datasets for Entity Alignment of GKBs

Standardized large-scale benchmarks are important prerequisites for finding the cons and pros of entity alignment algorithms. Each benchmark usually consists of one initial knowledge base, one altered knowledge base, which is an alteration over the initial one, and a reference alignment, which is used to compare with the returned alignment [143]. The OAEI has provided many artificial benchmarks, but their scale and comprehensiveness remain inadequate for dealing with a variety of existing alignment matchers, and they lack variability. Moreover, artificial benchmarks are becoming infeasible for evaluating large-scale alignment tasks. Thus, some approaches focused on a semi-automatic generation of benchmark datasets have been proposed [144,145] (e.g., Swing [145], Spimbench [146], and Lance [147]). These generators take the seed knowledge base and parameters which describe the modification types to be applied as input and generate the modified knowledge base and the corresponding reference alignment [148].

The benchmarks provided by OAEI, however, are obviously inappropriate for evaluating the entity alignment of GKBs due to the spatial feature of geographic entities. Existing generators do not also cover the alterations over spatial feature. Thus, the construction of benchmarks for geographic entity alignment is still performed manually [80,107]. However, the scales of developed artificial datasets are too small and are not suitable for a large number of correspondences. Moreover, these datasets can only be used to assess concept-level alignment, so there is lack of benchmarks for evaluating instance-level alignment. Thus, benchmarks which cover multiple alterations over geographic entities and are applicable for evaluating all types of geographic entities alignment and benchmark generators which can produce large-scale test sets automatically need to be developed.

5.8. Applications of Entity Alignment of GKBs

The practical applications of this field remain slightly limited. Broadening the application fields of acquired alignments in real-life projects needs to be further improved. Entity alignment is actually an important prerequisite for many applications. With the development of deep learning, completely automatic entity alignment may be achieved, which can support the automatic construction of large-scale geographic knowledge graphs. The strong and deep knowledge reasoning ability of huge GKBs will facilitate the progress of some fields, including mining and analysis of geographic big data, geographic knowledge services, and applying AI in the field of GIScience. Applying the entity alignment of GKBs in the practical applications of these fields needs to be further developed.

6. Conclusions

In this article, we provided a systematic and comprehensive analysis for research progress on the entity alignment of GKBs. We introduced the basic definitions and the multiple heterogeneities in entities, including differences in lexicon, structure, spatial position, category, shape, data-type of property, range of property, and property value. A general framework, which involved the basic ideas and standard workflow of this field, was also presented in this paper.

We provided a survey on the alignment algorithms of similarity metrics, similarity combination, alignment judgement, and result evaluation. For similarity metrics, we organized the insights from previous studies systematically from five aspects of lexical, structural, spatial, category, and shape similarity metrics. In terms of similarity combination, we introduced three models, a feature vector model, geometric model, and mathematical model. We also introduced some algorithms of alignment judgement, which can help to avoid tuning the threshold manually, including supervised machine learning, a voting-based model, etc. The insights for results evaluation were organized into two parts: Evaluation methods, including cognitive plausibility-oriented and task-oriented methods, and benchmark datasets. This review provides readers, especially new researchers in this field, with a general idea, and help them to understand the basics of this field.

On the basis of a systematic review, we presented key challenges facing this field, including the quality assessment of GKBs, feature selection and algorithm optimization, alignment techniques integrated with background knowledge, unified infrastructure, entity alignment of large-scale GKBs, alignment techniques based on deep learning, benchmark datasets, and application promotion. These insights will be helpful for promoting the progress and orienting future research for this field.

Author Contributions: All authors gave substantial contributions to this work. Conceptualization was conducted by all listed authors. Formal analysis and investigation were conducted by K.S. Writing—original draft preparation was conducted by K.S.; writing—review and editing were conducted by all authors. Supervision, project administration and funding acquisition were conducted by Y.Z. and J.S.

Funding: This research was funded by the National Natural Science Foundation of China, grant number 41631177, grant number 41771430; National Special Program on Basic Works for Science and Technology of China, grant number 2013FY110900.

Conflicts of Interest: The authors declare no conflict of interest.

References

1. Bizer, C.; Lehmann, J.; Kobilarov, G.; Auer, S.; Becker, C.; Cyganiak, R.; Hellmann, S. Dbpedia—A crystallization point for the Web of Data. *Web Semant. Sci. Serv. Agents World Wide Web* **2009**, *7*, 154–165. [CrossRef]
2. Suchanek, F.M.; Kasneci, G.; Weikum, G. Yago—A Large Ontology from Wikipedia and WordNet. *Web Semant. Sci. Serv. Agents World Wide Web* **2008**, *6*, 203–217. [CrossRef]
3. Wikidata. Available online: https://www.wikidata.org/wiki/Wikidata:Main_Page (accessed on 20 March 2018).
4. Bollacker, K.; Cook, R.; Tufts, P. Freebase: A Shared Database of Structured General Human Knowledge. In Proceedings of the AAAI Conference on Artificial Intelligence, Vancouver, BC, Canada, 22–26 July 2007; pp. 1962–1963.
5. Berners, T. Publishing on the semantic web. *Nature* **2001**, *410*, 1023–1024. [CrossRef] [PubMed]
6. DesignIssues: LinkedData. Available online: https://www.w3.org/DesignIssues/LinkedData.html (accessed on 20 March 2018).
7. Li, L.; Liu, Y.; Zhu, H.; Ying, S.; Luo, Q.; Luo, H.; Xi, K.; Xia, H.; Shen, H. A bibliometric and visual analysis of global geo-ontology research. *Comput. Geosci.* **2017**, *99*, 1–8. [CrossRef]
8. Liu, Y.; Li, L.; Shen, H.; Yang, H.; Luo, F. A Co-Citation and Cluster Analysis of Scientometrics of Geographic Information Ontology. *ISPRS Int. J. Geo-Inf.* **2018**, *7*, 120. [CrossRef]

9. Couclelis, H. Ontologies of geographic information. *Int. J. Geogr. Inf. Sci.* **2010**, *24*, 1785–1809. [CrossRef]
10. Bittner, T.; Donnelly, M.; Smith, B. A spatio-temporal ontology for geographic information integration. *Int. J. Geogr. Inf. Sci.* **2009**, *23*, 765–798. [CrossRef]
11. Zong, N.; Nam, S.; Eom, J.H.; Ahn, J.; Joe, H.; Kim, H.G. Aligning ontologies with subsumption and equivalence relations in Linked Data. *Knowl.-Based Syst.* **2014**, *76*, 30–41. [CrossRef]
12. Euzenat, J.; Shvaiko, P. *Ontology Matching*, 1st ed.; Springer: Heidelberg, Germany, 2007.
13. Bhattacharya, I.; Getoor, L. Entity Resolution in Graphs. In *Mining Graph Data*, 1st ed.; John Wiley & Sons, Inc.: Hoboken, NJ, USA, 2005; pp. 311–344.
14. Whang, S.E.; Menestrina, D.; Koutrika, G.; Theobald, M.; Garcia-Molina, H. Entity resolution with iterative blocking. In Proceedings of the 2009 ACM SIGMOD International Conference on Management of Data, Providence, RI, USA, 29 June–2 July 2009; pp. 219–232.
15. Elmagarmid, A.K.; Ipeirotis, P.G.; Verykios, V.S. Duplicate Record Detection: A Survey. *IEEE Trans. Knowl. Data Eng.* **2006**, *19*, 1–16. [CrossRef]
16. Li, C.; Jin, L.; Mehrotra, S. Supporting Efficient Record Linkage for Large Data Sets Using Mapping Techniques. *World Wide Web* **2006**, *9*, 557–584. [CrossRef]
17. Otero-Cerdeira, L.; Rodríguez-Martínez, F.J.; Gómez-Rodríguez, A. Ontology matching: A literature review. *Expert Syst. Appl.* **2015**, *42*, 949–971. [CrossRef]
18. Shvaiko, P.; Euzenat, J. Ontology Matching: State of the Art and Future Challenges. *IEEE Trans. Knowl. Data Eng.* **2012**, *25*, 158–176. [CrossRef]
19. David, J. AROMA results for OAEI 2011. In Proceedings of the 6th International Conference on Ontology Matching, Bonn, Germany, 24 October 2011; pp. 122–125.
20. David, J.; Guillet, F.; Briand, H. Association Rule Ontology Matching Approach. *Int. J. Semant. Web Inf.* **2007**, *3*, 27–49. [CrossRef]
21. Cruz, I.F.; Antonelli, F.P.; Stroe, C. AgreementMaker: Efficient Matching for Large Real-World Schemas and Ontologies. *Proc. VLDB Endow.* **2009**, *2*, 1586–1589. [CrossRef]
22. Cruz, I.F.; Sunna, W.; Chaudhry, A. Semi-automatic Ontology Alignment for Geospatial Data Integration. In Proceedings of the Third International Conference on Geographic Information Science, Adelphi, MD, USA, 20–23 October 2004; pp. 51–66.
23. Hartung, M.; Kolb, L.; Groß, A.; Rahm, E. Optimizing Similarity Computations for Ontology Matching—Experiences from GOMMA. In Proceedings of the International Conference on Data Integration in the Life Sciences, Montreal, QC, Canada, 11–12 July 2013; pp. 81–89.
24. Kalfoglou, Y.; Schorlemmer, M. Ontology mapping: The state of the art. *Knowl. Eng. Rev.* **2005**, *18*, 1–31. [CrossRef]
25. Hess, G.N.; Iochpe, C.; Castano, S. An Algorithm and Implementation for GeoOntologies Integration. In Proceedings of the VIII Brazilian Symposium on Geoinformatics, Campos do Jordão, São Paulo, Brazil, 19–22 November 2006; pp. 109–120.
26. Sehgal, V.; Viechnicki, P.D.; Viechnicki, P.D. Entity resolution in geospatial data integration. In Proceedings of the 14th annual ACM international symposium on Advances in geographic information systems, Arlington, VA, USA, 10–11 November 2006; pp. 83–90.
27. Zhao, T. The framework of a geospatial semantic web-based spatial decision support system for Digital Earth. *Int. J. Digit. Earth* **2010**, *3*, 111–134. [CrossRef]
28. Li, W.; Raskin, R.; Goodchild, M. Semantic similarity measurement based on knowledge mining: An artificial neural net approach. *Int. J. Geogr. Inf. Sci.* **2012**, *26*, 1415–1435. [CrossRef]
29. Yu, L.; Qiu, P.; Liu, X.; Lu, F.; Wan, B. A holistic approach to aligning geospatial data with multidimensional similarity measuring. *Int. J. Digit. Earth* **2017**, *11*, 1–18. [CrossRef]
30. Volz, S. Data-driven matching of geospatial schemas. In Proceedings of the International Conference on Spatial Information Theory, Ellicottville, NY, USA, 14–18 September 2005; pp. 115–132.
31. Shvaiko, P.; Euzenat, J. *A Survey of Schema-based Matching Approaches*; Springer: Berlin, Germany, 2005; pp. 146–171.
32. Lin, F.; Sandkuhl, K. A Survey of Exploiting WordNet in Ontology Matching. In Proceedings of the Artificial Intelligence in Theory and Practice II, IFIP World Computer Congress, Milano, Italy, 7–10 September 2008; pp. 341–350.

33. Sunna, W.; Cruz, I.F. Structure-Based Methods to Enhance Geospatial Ontology Alignment. In Proceedings of the International Conference on Geospatial Semantics, Mexico City, Mexico, 29–30 November 2007; pp. 82–97.
34. Ballatore, A.; Wilson, D.C.; Bertolotto, M. Computing the semantic similarity of geographic terms using volunteered lexical definitions. *Int. J. Geogr. Inf. Sci.* **2013**, *27*, 2099–2118. [CrossRef]
35. Ballatore, A.; Bertolotto, M.; Wilson, D.C. Grounding Linked Open Data in WordNet: The Case of the OSM Semantic Network. In Proceedings of the International Symposium on Web and Wireless Geographical Information Systems, Banff, AB, Canada, 4–5 April 2013; pp. 1–15.
36. Ballatore, A.; Bertolotto, M.; Wilson, D.C. Linking geographic vocabularies through WordNet. *Ann. GIS* **2014**, *20*, 73–84. [CrossRef]
37. Giunchiglia, F.; Maltese, V.; Farazi, F.; Dutta, B. *GeoWordNet: A Resource for Geo-spatial Applications*; Springer: Berlin/Heidelberg, Germany, 2010; pp. 121–136.
38. Hu, Y. Geospatial Semantics. In *Comprehensive Geographic Information Systems*; Elsevier: Oxford, UK, 2017; pp. 80–94.
39. Zheng, J.G.; Fu, L.; Ma, X.; Fox, P. SEM+: Tool for discovering concept mapping in Earth science related domain. *Earth Sci. Inform.* **2015**, *8*, 95–102. [CrossRef]
40. Santos, R.; Murrieta-Flores, P.; Martins, B. Learning to combine multiple string similarity metrics for effective toponym matching. *Int. J. Digit. Earth* **2018**, *11*, 913–938. [CrossRef]
41. Recchia, G.; Louwerse, M.M. A Comparison of String Similarity Measures for Toponym Matching. In Proceedings of the ACM Sigspatial Comp'13, Orlando, FL, USA, 5–8 November 2013; pp. 54–61.
42. Levenshtein, V.I. Binary codes capable of correcting spurious insertions and deletions of ones. *Probl. Inf. Transm.* **1965**, *1*, 707–710.
43. Martins, B. A Supervised Machine Learning Approach for Duplicate Detection over Gazetteer Records. In Proceedings of the International Conference on Geospatial Semantics, Brest, France, 12–13 May 2011; pp. 34–51.
44. Martins, B.; Galhardas, H.; Goncalves, N. Using Random Forest classifiers to detect duplicate gazetteer records. In Proceedings of the 7th Iberian Conference on Information Systems and Technologies (CISTI 2012), Madrid, Spain, 20–23 June 2012; pp. 1–4.
45. Wang, Z.; Li, J.; Zhao, Y.; Setchi, R.; Tang, J. A unified approach to matching semantic data on the Web. *Knowl.-Based Syst.* **2013**, *39*, 173–184. [CrossRef]
46. Hastings, J.; Hill, L. Treatment of duplicates in the alexandria digital library gazetteer. In Proceedings of the GeoScience, Boulder, CO, USA, 25–28 September 2002.
47. Auer, S.; Lehmann, J.; Hellmann, S. LinkedGeoData: Adding a Spatial Dimension to the Web of Data. In Proceedings of the International Semantic Web Conference, Chantilly, VA, USA, 25–29 October 2009; pp. 731–746.
48. Stadler, C.; Lehmann, J.; Ffner, K.; Auer, S. LinkedGeoData: A core for a web of spatial open data. *Semant. Web* **2012**, *3*, 333–354. [CrossRef]
49. Samal, A.; Seth, S.; Cueto, K. A feature-based approach to conflation of geospatial sources. *Int. J. Geogr. Inf. Sci.* **2004**, *18*, 459–489. [CrossRef]
50. Aoe, J.I. *Computer Algorithms: String Pattern Matching Strategies*; John Wiley & Sons: Hoboken, NJ, USA, 1994.
51. Hastings, J. Automated conflation of digital gazetteer data. *Int. J. Geogr. Inf. Sci.* **2008**, *22*, 1109–1127. [CrossRef]
52. Salton, G.; Yang, C.S. The Specification of Term Values In Automatic Indexing. *J. Doc.* **1973**, *29*, 351–372. [CrossRef]
53. Ballatore, A.; Bertolotto, M.; Wilson, D. A Structural-Lexical Measure of Semantic Similarity for Geo-Knowledge Graphs. *ISPRS Int. J. Geo-Inf.* **2015**, *4*, 471–492. [CrossRef]
54. Mikolov, T.; Chen, K.; Corrado, G.; Dean, J. Efficient Estimation of Word Representations in Vector Space. *arXiv*, 2013; arXiv:1301.3781.
55. Mikolov, T.; Sutskever, I.; Chen, K.; Corrado, G.; Dean, J. Distributed representations of words and phrases and their compositionality. *Adv. Neural Inf. Process. Syst.* **2013**, *26*, 3111–3119.
56. Santos, R.; Murrieta-Flores, P.; Calado, P.; Martins, B. Toponym matching through deep neural networks. *Int. J. Geogr. Inf. Sci.* **2018**, *32*, 324–348. [CrossRef]
57. Delgado, F.; Finat, J. An evaluation of ontology matching techniques on geospatial ontologies. *Int. J. Geogr. Inf. Sci.* **2013**, *27*, 2279–2301. [CrossRef]

58. Reza, K.; Ali, A.; Majid, H. A mixed approach for automated spatial ontology alignment. *J. Spat. Sci.* **2010**, *55*, 237–255. [CrossRef]
59. Cruz, I.F.; Sunna, W. Structural Alignment Methods with Applications to Geospatial Ontologies. *Trans. GIS.* **2008**, *12*, 683–711. [CrossRef]
60. Melnik, S.; Garcia-Molina, H.; Rahm, E. Similarity flooding: A versatile graph matching algorithm and its application to schema matching. In Proceedings of the International Conference on Data Engineering, San Jose, CA, USA, 26 February–1 March 2002; pp. 117–128.
61. Kim, J.; Vasardani, M.; Winter, S. Similarity matching for integrating spatial information extracted from place descriptions. *Int. J. Geogr. Inf. Sci.* **2017**, *31*, 56–80. [CrossRef]
62. Zhao, P.; Han, J.; Sun, Y. P-Rank: A comprehensive structural similarity measure over information networks. In Proceedings of the ACM Conference on Information and Knowledge Management, Hong Kong, China, 2–6 November 2009; pp. 553–562.
63. Small, H. Co-citation in the scientific literature: A new measure of the relationship between two documents. *J. Assoc. Inf. Sci. Technol.* **1973**, *24*, 265–269. [CrossRef]
64. Kessler, M.M. Bibliographic coupling between scientific papers. *J. Assoc. Inf. Sci. Technol.* **1963**, *14*, 10–25. [CrossRef]
65. Ballatore, A.; Bertolotto, M.; Wilson, D.C. Geographic knowledge extraction and semantic similarity in OpenStreetMap. *Knowl. Inf. Syst.* **2013**, *37*, 61–81. [CrossRef]
66. Kang, H.; Sehgal, V.; Getoor, L. GeoDDupe: A Novel Interface for Interactive Entity Resolution in Geospatial Data. In Proceedings of the International Conference Information Visualization, Zurich, Switzerland, 4–6 July 2007; pp. 489–496.
67. Hess, G.N.; Iochpe, C.; Ferrara, A.; Castano, S. Towards Effective Geographic Ontology Matching. In Proceedings of the GeoSpatial Semantics, Second International Conference, Mexico City, Mexico, 29–30 November 2007; pp. 51–65.
68. Safra, E.; Kanza, Y.; Sagiv, Y.; Beeri, C.; Doytsher, Y. Location-based algorithms for finding sets of corresponding objects over several geo-spatial data sets. *Int. J. Geogr. Inf. Sci.* **2010**, *24*, 69–106. [CrossRef]
69. Janée, G.; Frew, J. Spatial search, ranking, and interoperability. In Proceedings of the 27th Annual International ACM SIGIR Conference, Sheffield, UK, 29 July 2004.
70. Walter, V.; Fritsch, D. Matching spatial data sets: A statistical approach. *Int. J. Geogr. Inf. Sci.* **1999**, *13*, 445–473. [CrossRef]
71. Zhu, Y.; Zhu, A.X.; Song, J.; Yang, J.; Feng, M.; Sun, K.; Zhang, J.; Hou, Z.; Zhao, H. Multidimensional and quantitative interlinking approach for Linked Geospatial Data. *Int. J. Digit. Earth* **2017**, *10*, 923–943. [CrossRef]
72. Bruns, H.T.; Egenhofer, M.J. Similarity of Spatial Scenes. In Proceedings of the Symposium on Spatial Data Handling, Delft, The Netherlands, 12–16 August 1996; pp. 31–42.
73. Beard, K.; Sharma, V. Multidimensional ranking for data in digital spatial libraries. *Int. J. Digit. Libr.* **1997**, *1*, 153–160. [CrossRef]
74. Larson, R.R.; Frontiera, P. Spatial Ranking Methods for Geographic Information Retrieval (GIR) in Digital Libraries. In Proceedings of the Research and Advanced Technology for Digital Libraries, European Conference, Bath, UK, 12–17 September 2004; pp. 45–56.
75. Li, B.; Frederico, F. TDD: A Comprehensive Model for Qualitative Spatial Similarity Assessment. *Spat. Cogn. Comput.* **2006**, *6*, 31–62. [CrossRef]
76. Zheng, Y.; Fen, X.; Xie, X.; Peng, S.; Fu, J. Detecting nearly duplicated records in location datasets. In Proceedings of the ACM Sigspatial International Symposium on Advances in Geographic Information Systems, San Jose, CA, USA, 3–5 November 2010; pp. 137–143.
77. Resnik, P. Using information content to evaluate semantic similarity in a taxonomy. In Proceedings of the 14th International Joint Conference on Artificial Intelligence, Montreal, QC, Canada, 20–25 August 1995; pp. 448–453.
78. Kavouras, M.; Kokla, M.; Tomai, E. Comparing categories among geographic ontologies. *Comput. Geosci.* **2005**, *31*, 145–154. [CrossRef]
79. Rodriguez, M.A.; Egenhofer, M.J.; Rugg, R.D. Assessing Semantic Similarities among Geospatial Feature Class Definitions. In *Interoperating Geographic Information Systems*; Springer: Berlin, Germany, 1999; pp. 189–202.

80. Rodriguez, M.A.; Egenhofer, M.J. Comparing geospatial entity classes: An asymmetric and context-dependent similarity measure. *Int. J. Geogr. Inf. Sci.* **2004**, *18*, 229–256. [CrossRef]
81. Rodriguez, M.A.; Egenhofer, M.J. Determining semantic similarity among entity classes from different ontologies. *IEEE Trans. Knowl. Data Eng.* **2003**, *15*, 442–456. [CrossRef]
82. Chen, Z.; Song, J.; Yang, Y. An Approach to Measuring Semantic Relatedness of Geographic Terminologies Using a Thesaurus and Lexical Database Sources. *ISPRS Int. J. Geo-Inf.* **2018**, *7*, 98. [CrossRef]
83. Veltkamp, R.C.; Hagedoorn, M. State of the Art in Shape Matching. In *Principles of Visual Information Retrieval*; Springer: London, UK, 2001; pp. 87–119.
84. Safra, E.; Kanza, Y.; Sagiv, Y.; Doytsher, Y. Ad hoc matching of vectorial road networks. *Int. J. Geogr. Inf. Sci.* **2013**, *27*, 114–153. [CrossRef]
85. Goodchild, M.F.; Hunter, G.J. A simple positional accuracy measure for linear features. *Int. J. Geogr. Inf. Sci.* **1997**, *11*, 299–306. [CrossRef]
86. Fairbairn, D.; Albakri, M. Using Geometric Properties to Evaluate Possible Integration of Authoritative and Volunteered Geographic Information. *ISPRS Int. J. Geo-Inf.* **2013**, *2*, 349–370. [CrossRef]
87. Du, H.; Alechina, N.; Jackson, M.; Hart, G. A Method for Matching Crowd-sourced and Authoritative Geospatial Data. *Trans. GIS* **2017**, *21*. [CrossRef]
88. Zhu, R.; Hu, Y.; Janowicz, K.; Mckenzie, G. Spatial signatures for geographic feature types: Examining gazetteer ontologies using spatial statistics. *Trans. GIS* **2016**, *20*, 333–355. [CrossRef]
89. Janowicz, K.; Schwarz, M.; Wilkes, M.; Panov, I.; Espeter, M. Algorithm, implementation and application of the SIM-DL similarity server. In Proceedings of the International Conference on Geospatial Semantics, Mexico City, Mexico, 29–30 November 2007; pp. 128–145.
90. Kokla, M.; Kavouras, M. Fusion of top-level and geographical domain ontologies based on context formation and complementarity. *Int. J. Geogr. Inf. Sci.* **2001**, *15*, 679–687. [CrossRef]
91. Kavouras, M.; Kokla, M. A method for the formalization and integration of geographical categorizations. *Int. J. Geogr. Inf. Sci.* **2002**, *16*, 439–453. [CrossRef]
92. Peukert, E.; Maßmann, S.; König, K. Comparing Similarity Combination Methods for Schema Matching. In Proceedings of the 40th Annual Conference of the German Computer Society (GI-Jahrestagung), Leipzig, Germany, 1 October 2010; pp. 692–701.
93. Tran, Q.V.; Ichise, R.; Ho, B.Q. Cluster-based similarity aggregation for ontology matching. In Proceedings of the International Conference on Ontology Matching, Bonn, Germany, 24 October 2011; pp. 142–147.
94. Schwering, A. Approaches to Semantic Similarity Measurement for Geo-Spatial Data: A Survey. *Trans. GIS* **2008**, *12*, 5–29. [CrossRef]
95. Jan, S.; Shah, I.; Khan, I.; Khan, F.; Usman, M. Similarity Measures and their Aggregation in Ontology Matching. *Int. J. Comput. Sci. Telecommun.* **2012**, *3*, 52–57.
96. Do, H.H.; Rahm, E. COMA: A system for flexible combination of schema matching approaches. In Proceedings of the VLDB Endowment, Hong Kong, China, 20–23 August 2002; pp. 610–621.
97. Hu, Y.H.; Ge, L. Learning Ranking Functions for Geographic Information Retrieval Using Genetic Programming. *J. Res. Pract. Inf. Technol.* **2009**, *41*, 39–52. [CrossRef]
98. Mckenzie, G.; Janowicz, K.; Adams, B. A weighted multi-attribute method for matching user-generated Points of Interest. *Cartogr. Geogr. Inf. Sci.* **2014**, *41*, 125–137. [CrossRef]
99. Li, J.; He, Z.; Zhu, Q. An entropy-based weighted concept lattice for merging multi-source geo-ontologies. *Entropy* **2013**, *15*, 2303–2318. [CrossRef]
100. Chen, Z.; Song, J.; Yang, Y. Similarity Measurement of Metadata of Geospatial Data: An Artificial Neural Network Approach. *ISPRS Int. J. Geo-Inf.* **2018**, *7*, 90. [CrossRef]
101. Bock, J.; Hettenhausen, J. Discrete particle swarm optimisation for ontology alignment. *Inf. Sci.* **2012**, *192*, 152–173. [CrossRef]
102. Bharambe, U.; Durbha, S.S. Adaptive Pareto-based approach for geo-ontology matching. *Comput. Geosci.* **2018**, *119*, 92–108. [CrossRef]
103. Daskalaki, E.; Flouris, G.; Fundulaki, I.; Saveta, T. Instance matching benchmarks in the era of Linked Data. *J. Web Semant.* **2016**, *39*, 1–14. [CrossRef]
104. Keßler, C. What is the difference? A cognitive dissimilarity measure for information retrieval result sets. *Knowl. Inf. Syst.* **2012**, *30*, 319–340. [CrossRef]

105. Janowicz, K.; Keßler, C.; Panov, I.; Wilkes, M.; Espeter, M.; Schwarz, M. A Study on the Cognitive Plausibility of SIM-DL Similarity Rankings for Geographic Feature Types. In Proceedings of the Agile, Washington, DC, USA, 4–8 August 2008; pp. 115–134.
106. Goutte, C.; Gaussier, E. A Probabilistic Interpretation of Precision, Recall and F-Score, with Implication for Evaluation. In Proceedings of the European Conference on Information Retrieval, Santiago de Compostela, Spain, 21–23 March 2005; pp. 345–359.
107. Ballatore, A.; Bertolotto, M.; Wilson, D.C. An evaluative baseline for geo-semantic relatedness and similarity. *GeoInformatica* **2014**, *18*, 747–767. [CrossRef]
108. Fundulaki, I.; Ngonga-Ngomo, A.C. Instance Matching Benchmark for Spatial Data: A Challenge Proposal to OAEI. In Proceedings of the International Semantic Web Conference, Kobe, Japan, 17–21 October 2016; pp. 233–234.
109. Duchateau, F.; Bellahsène, Z. Designing a Benchmark for the Assessment of XML Schema Matching Tools. *Open J. Datab.* **2014**, *1*, 3–25. [CrossRef]
110. Alexe, B.; Tan, W.C.; Velegrakis, Y. STBenchmark: Towards a benchmark for mapping systems. *VLDB Endow.* **2008**, *1*, 230–244. [CrossRef]
111. Euzenat, J.; Ferrara, A.; Hollink, L.; Isaac, A.; Joslyn, C.; Malaisé, V.; Meilicke, C.; Nikolov, A.; Pane, J.; Sabou, M.; et al. Results of the Ontology Alignment Evaluation Initiative 2009. In Proceedings of the 4th ISWC Workshop on Ontology Matching, Chantilly, VA, USA, 25 October 2009; pp. 73–95.
112. Berjawi, B.; Duchateau, F.; Favetta, F.; Miquel, M.; Laurini, R. PABench: Designing a Taxonomy and Implementing a Benchmark for Spatial Entity Matching. In Proceedings of the Seventh International Conference on Advanced Geographic Information Systems, Applications, and Services, Lisbon, Portugal, 22–27 Feburary 2015; pp. 7–16.
113. Janowicz, K.; Pehle, T.; Pehle, T.; Hart, G. Geospatial semantics and linked spatiotemporal data—Past, present, and future. *Semant. Web* **2012**, *3*, 321–332. [CrossRef]
114. Stock, K.; Cialone, C. An Approach to the Management of Multiple Aligned Multilingual Ontologies for a Geospatial Earth Observation System. In Proceedings of the International Conference on GeoSpatial Sematics, Brest, France, 12–13 May 2011; pp. 52–69.
115. Cruz, I.F.; Sunna, W.; Makar, N.; Bathala, S. A visual tool for ontology alignment to enable geospatial interoperability. *J. Visual Lang. Comput.* **2007**, *18*, 230–254. [CrossRef]
116. Mata, F. Geographic Information Retrieval by Topological, Geographical, and Conceptual Matching. In Proceedings of the Second International Conference on GeoSpatial Semantics, Mexico City, Mexico, 29–30 November 2007; pp. 98–113.
117. Vaccari, L.; Shvaiko, P.; Pane, J.; Besana, P.; Marchese, M. An evaluation of ontology matching in geo-service applications. *GeoInformatica* **2012**, *16*, 31–66. [CrossRef]
118. Duckham, M.; Worboys, M. Automated Geographical Information Fusion and Ontology Alignment. In *Spatial Data on the Web*; Springer: Berlin, Germany, 2007; pp. 109–132.
119. Lutz, M. Ontology-Based Descriptions for Semantic Discovery and Composition of Geoprocessing Services. *GeoInformatica* **2007**, *11*, 1–36. [CrossRef]
120. Vaccari, L.; Shvaiko, P.; Marchese, M. A geo-service semantic integration in spatial data infrastructures. *Int. J. Spat. Data Infrastruct. Res.* **2009**, *4*, 24–51.
121. Ding, R.; Chen, Z. RecNet: A deep neural network for personalized POI recommendation in location-based social networks. *Int. J. Geogr. Inf. Sci.* **2018**, *32*, 1–18. [CrossRef]
122. Zhu, Y.; Zhu, A.X.; Feng, M.; Song, J.; Zhao, H.; Yang, J.; Zhang, Q.; Sun, K.; Zhang, J.; Yao, L. A similarity-based automatic data recommendation approach for geographic models. *Int. J. Geogr. Inf. Sci.* **2017**, *31*, 1403–1424. [CrossRef]
123. Senaratne, H.; Mobasheri, A.; Ali, A.L.; Capineri, C.; Haklay, M. A review of volunteered geographic information quality assessment methods. *Int. J. Geogr. Inf. Sci.* **2017**, *31*, 139–167. [CrossRef]
124. Moreri, K.K.; Fairbairn, D.; James, P. Volunteered geographic information quality assessment using trust and reputation modelling in land administration systems in developing countries. *Int. J. Geogr. Inf. Sci.* **2018**, *32*, 1–29. [CrossRef]
125. Barron, C.; Neis, P.; Zipf, A. A Comprehensive Framework for Intrinsic OpenStreetMap Quality Analysis. *Trans. GIS* **2015**, *18*, 877–895. [CrossRef]

126. Bordogna, G.; Carrara, P.; Criscuolo, L.; Pepe, M.; Rampini, A. A linguistic decision making approach to assess the quality of volunteer geographic information for citizen science. *Inf. Sci.* **2014**, *258*, 312–327. [CrossRef]
127. Marie, A.; Gal, A. Boosting Schema Matchers. In Proceedings of the OTM Confederated International Conferences On the Move to Meaningful Internet Systems, Monterrey, Mexico, 9–14 November 2008; pp. 283–300.
128. Mochol, M.; Jentzsch, A.; Euzenat, J. Applying an Analytic Method for Matching Approach Selection. In Proceedings of the International Workshop on Ontology Matching, Athens, GA, USA, 5 November 2006; pp. 37–48.
129. Huza, M.; Harzallah, M.; Trichet, F. OntoMas: A Tutoring System dedicated to Ontology Matching. In *Enterprise Interoperability II*; Springer: London, UK, 2007; pp. 377–388.
130. Mochol, M.; Jentzsch, A. Towards a Rule-Based Matcher Selection. In Proceedings of the International Conference on Knowledge Engineering: Practice and Patterns, Acitrezza, Italy, 29 September–2 October 2008; pp. 109–119.
131. Parent, C.; Spaccapietra, S.; Zimányi, E. Conceptual Modeling for Traditional and Spatio-Temporal Applications. In *The MADS Approach*; Springer Science & Business Media: Berlin/Heidelberg, Germany, 2006; pp. 188–189.
132. Shvaiko, P.; Euzenat, J. Ten Challenges for Ontology Matching. In Proceedings of the OTM Confederated International Conferences on the Move to Meaningful Internet Systems, Monterrey, Mexico, 9–14 November 2008; pp. 1164–1182.
133. Lee, Y.; Sayyadian, M.; Doan, A.; Rosenthal, A.S.; Sayyadian, M.; Doan, A.; Rosenthal, A.S. eTuner: Tuning schema matching software using synthetic scenarios. *VLDB J.* **2008**, *16*, 97–122. [CrossRef]
134. Duchateau, F.; Bellahsene, Z.; Coletta, R. A Flexible Approach for Planning Schema Matching Algorithms. In Proceedings of the OTM Confederated International Conferences on the Move to Meaningful Internet Systems, Monterrey, Mexico, 9–14 November 2008; pp. 249–264.
135. Noy, N.F.; Musen, M.A. The PROMPT suite: Interactive tools for ontology merging and mapping. *Int. J. Hum.-Comput. Stud.* **2003**, *59*, 983–1024. [CrossRef]
136. Ghazvinian, A.; Noy, N.F.; Jonquet, C.; Shah, N.; Musen, M.A. What Four Million Mappings Can Tell You about Two Hundred Ontologies. In Proceedings of the International Semantic Web Conference, Chantilly, VA, USA, 25–29 October 2009; pp. 229–242.
137. Euzenat, J. Alignment infrastructure for ontology mediation and other applications. Proceedings of 1st ICSOC international workshop on Mediation in semantic web services, Amsterdam, Netherlands, 12 December 2005; pp. 81–95.
138. Do, H.H.; Rahm, E. Matching large schemas: Approaches and evaluation. *Inform. Syst.* **2007**, *32*, 857–885. [CrossRef]
139. Ehrig, M.; Staab, S. QOM—Quick Ontology Mapping. In Proceedings of the International Semantic Web Conference, Hiroshima, Japan, 7–11 November 2004; pp. 683–697.
140. Kirsten, T.; Kolb, L.; Hartung, M.; Groß, A.; Köpcke, H.; Rahm, E. Data Partitioning for Parallel Entity Matching. *Comput. Sci.* **2010**, *3*, 1–8. [CrossRef]
141. Bianco, G.D.; Galante, R.; Heuser, C.A. A fast approach for parallel deduplication on multicore processors. In Proceedings of the ACM Symposium on Applied Computing, TaiChung, Taiwan, 21–24 March 2011; pp. 1027–1032.
142. Hungsik, K.; Dongwon, L. Parallel linkage. In Proceedings of the ACM, Lisbon, Portugal, 6–10 November 2007; pp. 283–292.
143. Euzenat, J.; Meilicke, C.; Stuckenschmidt, H.; Shvaiko, P.; Trojahn, C. Ontology Alignment Evaluation Initiative: Six Years of Experience. In *Journal on Data Semantics XV*; Springer: Berlin/Heidelberg, Germany, 2011; pp. 158–192.
144. Giunchiglia, F.; Yatskevich, M.; Avesani, P.; Shivaiko, P. A Large Scale Dataset for the Evaluation of Ontology Matching Systems. *Knowl. Eng. Rev.* **2009**, *24*, 137–157. [CrossRef]
145. Ferrara, A.; Montanelli, S.; Noessner, J.; Stuckenschmidt, H. Benchmarking Matching Applications on the Semantic Web. In Proceedings of the Extended Semantic Web Conference on the Semanic Web: Research and Applications, Heraklion, Crete, Greece, 29 May–2 June 2011; pp. 108–122.

146. Saveta, T.; Daskalaki, E.; Flouris, G.; Fundulaki, I.; Herschel, M.; Ngonga Ngomo, A.C. Pushing the Limits of Instance Matching Systems: A Semantics-Aware Benchmark for Linked Data. In Proceedings of the International Conference on World Wide Web, Florence, Italy, 18–22 May 2015; pp. 105–106.
147. Saveta, T.; Daskalaki, E.; Flouris, G.; Fundulaki, I.; Herschel, M.; Ngomo, A.C.N. LANCE: Piercing to the Heart of Instance Matching Tools. In Proceedings of the International Semantic Web Conference, Bethlehem, PA, USA, 11–15 October 2015; pp. 375–391.
148. Euzenat, J.; Roşoiu, M.E.; Trojahn, C. Ontology matching benchmarks: Generation, stability, and discriminability. *J. Web Semant.* **2013**, *21*, 30–48. [CrossRef]

© 2019 by the authors. Licensee MDPI, Basel, Switzerland. This article is an open access article distributed under the terms and conditions of the Creative Commons Attribution (CC BY) license (http://creativecommons.org/licenses/by/4.0/).

MDPI
St. Alban-Anlage 66
4052 Basel
Switzerland
Tel. +41 61 683 77 34
Fax +41 61 302 89 18
www.mdpi.com

ISPRS International Journal of Geo-Information Editorial Office
E-mail: ijgi@mdpi.com
www.mdpi.com/journal/ijgi

www.ingramcontent.com/pod-product-compliance
Lightning Source LLC
LaVergne TN
LVHW071948080526
838202LV00064B/6703